Bonds *of* Affection

D1447041

RELIGION AND POLITICS SERIES
John C. Green, Ted G. Jelen, and Mark J. Rozell, series editors

RELIGION AND POLITICS EDITORIAL BOARD MEMBERS

Amy Black, *Wheaton College*
Clarke Cochran, *Texas Tech University*
Anthony Gill, *University of Washington*
Geoff Layman, *University of Maryland*
Laura Olson, *Clemson University*
Corwin Smidt, *Calvin College*
Mary Segers, *Rutgers University*
Chris Soper, *Pepperdine University*
Clyde Wilcox, *Georgetown University*

Bonds *of* Affection

CIVIC CHARITY *and the* MAKING *of* AMERICA—
WINTHROP, JEFFERSON, AND LINCOLN

Matthew S. Holland

CARRINI COLLEGE LIBRARY
610 KING OF PRUSSIA ROAD
RADNOR. PA 19087

GEORGETOWN UNIVERSITY PRESS
Washington, D.C.

#85019027

As of January 1, 2007, 13-digit ISBN numbers have replaced the 10-digit system.

13-digit
  Paperback: 978–1-58901–183–0
  Cloth:

10-digit
  Paperback: 1–58901–183-X
  Cloth:

Georgetown University Press, Washington, D.C. www.press.georgetown.edu

© 2007 by Georgetown University Press. All rights reserved. No part of this book may be reproduced or utilized in any form or by any means, electronic or mechanical, including photocopying and recording, or by any information storage and retrieval system, without permission in writing from the publisher.

Library of Congress Cataloging-in-Publication Data

Holland, Matthew Scott, 1966-
  Bonds of affection : civic charity and the making of America—Winthrop, Jefferson, and Lincoln / Matthew S. Holland.
     p.   cm.—(Religion and politics series)
  Includes bibliographical references and index.
  ISBN 978-1-58901-183-0 (alk. paper)
     1. Democracy—United States—History—Sources.   2. Democracy—Religious aspects—United States—Sources.   3. Charity—Political aspects—United States—Sources.   4. United States—Politics and government—Sources. I. Title.
  JK411.H65   2007
  320.973—dc22

                                                                    2007007358

♾ This book is printed on acid-free paper meeting the requirements of the American National Standard for Permanence in Paper for Printed Library Materials.

14 13 12 11 10 09 08 07   9 8 7 6 5 4 3 2
First printing

Printed in the United States of America

To Paige,

her "constant and easy" practice of charity
made the study of it possible

He used to emerge at eventide from the seclusion of his study, and sit down in the fire-light of their home, and in the light of her nuptial smile. He needed to bask himself in that smile, he said, in order that the chill of so many lonely hours among his books might be taken off the scholar's heart.

The Scarlet Letter

"Let all your things be done with charity."

—*1 Corinthians 16:14*

"The realistic wisdom of the statesman is reduced to foolishness if it is not under the influence of the foolishness of the moral seer."

—*Reinhold Niebuhr*

CONTENTS

vii

ACKNOWLEDGMENTS

I did not know it at the time, but this book really began in my late teens and early twenties. During these years I was fortunate to work closely with several remarkable leaders who, despite operating in very different fields and with very different styles, shared a common determination. Each was committed in some fashion to honoring the often competing demands of human agency, transcendent love, and effective rule. Their memorable struggles first opened my eyes to the nobility and difficulty of such a task.

As a concrete scholarly endeavor, this book began at Duke University in Sandy Kessler's graduate course on Early American Political Thought. Besides introducing me to a subfield of political science where I could satisfy my interests in philosophy, politics, and history (interests initially stoked by a set of outstanding undergraduate teachers, namely Don Sorenson, David Magleby, and Frank Fox), Professor Kessler provided an inspiring introduction to a number of the classic texts that serve as the grist for this study. I completed his course with two convictions. One was that notions of Christian love, or charity, had played a greater role in the development of American political thought and practice than the voluminous secondary literature suggested. The other was that not only had some of early America's most philosophically minded and influential statesmen considered the merits and challenges of trying to make Christian love the basis of a political virtue, their insights were sage enough to remain relevant to our day—a day as vexed as ever over the appropriate role of religion in our public life. Animated by these two thoughts, I began a dissertation under the thoughtful and efficient direction of Ruth Grant and a dissertation committee (Michael Gillespie, Stanley Hauerwas, Sandy Kessler, and Tom Spragens) that was different, demanding, and congenial enough to stretch me to my limits but not beyond.

Generous friends like Richard Rust, Kent Lehnhoff, Alan Kantrow, and David Palmer read significant portions of my dissertation in draft form and offered a number of erudite suggestions. I also had the good fortune to present a series of afternoon seminars on material related to my dissertation to a coterie of morally serious and intellectually curious executives at Monitor Group, a global professional services firm based in Cambridge, Massachusetts. Besides providing much-needed financial help, these sessions—solicited and organized by the firm's visionary chairman, Mark Fuller, and attended faithfully by six impossibly busy invitees, Joe Fuller, Henry Eyring, Ralph Judah, Bill Miracky, Bill McClements, and Bill Young—bristled with questions and comments as stimulating and substantive as those one would expect to find in a first-rate faculty research group. My limited but continuing association with this unique firm remains a great source of satisfaction and support.

As I moved to the task—so much larger than I ever anticipated—of turning a dissertation into a book, I benefited from a number of incisive exchanges with fellow political theorists around the country, most notably Patrick Deneen, Jean Elshtain, Peter Lawler, Dan Mahoney, and the dearly departed Carey McWilliams. Part of chapter 3 and much of chapter 4 of this book originally appeared as a stand-alone article in the *Review of Politics*, a piece much improved by the advice of Walter Nicgorski and the review process he ran. I thank both the *Review of Politics* and *Perspectives on Political Science* for allowing me to republish here significant portions of material that initially appeared in those journals (portions of my essay on John Winthrop and Nathaniel Hawthorne published in *Perspectives on Political Science* can be found throughout part 1 and the conclusion of this book).

I also owe great thanks to a number of my colleagues at Brigham Young University, both in my department (Richard Davis, Brent Gilchrist, and Dan Nielson) and out (Steven Tanner, Don Norton, Hal Gregerson, Paul Kerry, Frank Fox, and Gary Daynes), who all gave thoughtful suggestions on either my prospectus or a chapter or more of material. A special debt of gratitude goes to Ralph Hancock for commenting on numerous versions of numerous chapters of this book with sharp intelligence and a devotion that went well beyond the basic obligations of his role as my official faculty mentor.

A string of BYU's best and brightest undergraduates also served ably as my research assistants on this project: Alicia Allen, Sarah Riding, Sheri Tanaka, Travis Smith, Ben Hertzberg, Gary Peterson, Talia Strong, and Tara Westover. Ben Hertzberg's contribution to the introduction to part 3 nearly warrants coauthorship. At the administration level, deans Clayne Pope and David Magleby and associate dean Rulon Pope all provided timely counsel, encouragement, substantial research funds, and the unusual freedom to take a pretenure research leave to spend a year at Princeton University on the James Madison Program in American Ideals and Institutions. There the redoubtable Robby George has created, I believe, an unmatched milieu for studying the American Founding and its legacy. It is impossible to assess the full substantive impact of all the friendly and stimulating exchanges I had that year with Robby George, associate director Brad Wilson, and the other fellows, namely Alan Gibson, Carson Holloway, Cathy McCauliffe, Paul Moreno, and Brad Watson. As far as I could see, the sole flaw in their collective intelligence was considering me fit company for such a crowd.

Several Princeton folks beyond the Madison Program proper were also gracious enough to engage in extended and fruitful private discussions of my project, notably Eric Gregory (religion), Robert Wuthnow (sociology), and Barbara Oberg and Martha King (general and associate editors, respectively, of *The Papers of Thomas Jefferson*), who not only read and commented on my work but also supplied me with the galley sheets of the definitive, yet-to-be published copy of Jefferson's First Inaugural. And David Hall at Harvard's Divinity School, Peter Onuf at the University of Virginia's history department, and Bryon Andreason at the Abraham Lincoln Presidential Library and Museum all deserve some particular note of thanks for providing me with detailed suggestions on several chapters of material after I simply wandered into their lives while back on the East Coast.

Working with Richard Brown at the Georgetown University Press has been an absolute delight. Perhaps because his judgments so often comport with my own, it is hard not to consider him brilliant. This is to say nothing of his professionalism and disarming affability—traits shared widely by his staff.

However deep my professional and intellectual debts run to the cast of thousands just described—and here it should be noted that their contributions in no way make them responsible for the persistent shortcomings of the work before you—my deepest debts are familial. The support and influence of my parents, Jeff and Pat Holland, breathe on every page of this book in ways too enormous and personal to detail. An appropriate thanks to them is simply ineffable. David Holland, my younger brother but academic exemplar, repeatedly broke from his own research projects to discuss my work in a way that never failed to improve it and always provoked a healthy, mind-clearing guffaw. My in-laws, Dennis and Carryl Bateman, deserve a medal for not only watching but also facilitating (by providing at a key moment a heavily subsidized basement apartment) the horror of a daughter living life married to a graduate student turned junior faculty member. Surely they hoped for better for her—yet somehow they have never let slip even a whiff a disappointment. And to their daughter, my wife Paige, I am most indebted of all. She and my four children, Jacob, Mitzi, Grace, and Daniel, constitute the very marrow of my life. Their many years of cheering me on when spirits flagged and letting me work early, late, and often on "the book" have proven the very bonds of affection that make it impossible for me to be away from them too very long. Models of charity all, their lives—much more so than anything I will ever write—are paeans to the central ideals of this book.

"Bonds of Affection"—
Three Founding Moments

I

Like no other figure of founding importance for America, we remember his words but not his name. In the spring of 1630, John Winthrop, newly elected governor of the Massachusetts Bay Company, gave a lay sermon to those sailing with him on the *Arbella*, flagship of what would become a massive, decade-long exodus of English Puritans to this country. His audience listened intently, their reflexive reverence heightened by their anxiety over the perilous journey ahead. They were to live with each other, Winthrop insisted, "in the bond of brotherly affection." Among other things, he explained that this meant

> We must uphold a familiar commerce together in all meekness, gentleness, patience, and liberality. We must delight in each other, make each others' conditions our own, rejoice together, mourn together, labor and suffer together, always having before our eyes our commission and community in the work.

This was more than mere rhetoric. As Winthrop saw it, only by becoming "A Model of Christian Charity" (the common title of his remarks) could this company be sure to avoid the all too real possibilities of destruction at sea or extinction in the harsh wilderness of the New World. Moreover, by successfully grounding their personal character and communal practices on ideals of biblical love, they were destined to rise up a prosperous, powerful, and widely admired "City Upon a Hill."[1]

Today, prominent scholars across a range of disciplines praise Winthrop's address as the "most famous text in 17th century American history," the "Ur-text of American literature," and a distinctive and

I

sophisticated piece of political philosophy from someone who "stands at the beginning of our consciousness." In a 1999 special "millennial" issue of the *New York Times Magazine,* Peter Gomes of Harvard's Memorial Church called it the greatest sermon of the past thousand years, a stirring vision for America that "still lives." That major political leaders from John Adams to Bill Clinton—including almost every president and presidential aspirant since John Kennedy—have explicitly appropriated Winthrop's name and speech to chart national aspirations and identity only underscores the point.[2]

Despite such a contribution, the name John Winthrop rings familiar for relatively few Americans. This is perhaps best explained by the efforts of brilliant nineteenth- and early twentieth-century critics—from Nathaniel Hawthorne to H. L. Mencken and beyond—who accepted American Puritanism's lasting influence but emphasized, in differing degrees, how bad it was for the country. This prominent effort to repudiate the whole Puritan legacy and everything connected with it has broadly diminished Winthrop's prominence in the national pantheon, making him "America's Forgotten Founding Father."[3] But Winthrop's current fate may stem from more than just guilt by association with a rejected era. Lurking within his soaring rhetoric of empathetic care, democratic principle, and high public purpose—all found in the "Model" speech—rests theoretical support for a punishing intolerance, rigid exclusion, and self-righteous judgmentalism without sense of proportion. Of course, this too affirms Winthrop's significance for American politics. Arguably, he is at once a significant founding father of some of America's best and worst impulses.

II

In the predawn dark of March 4, 1801, John Adams petulantly rode out of Washington, D.C., for Quincy, Massachusetts. At noon that day, Thomas Jefferson would succeed him as president of the United States. The discourteousness of Adams's early departure was symptomatic of the times.

The presidential election of 1800 was possibly the most important and most brutally fought in American history. With the country divided like it never had been since the ratification debates of the Constitution, this was the first real test of whether democratic power could be transferred peacefully. To Jefferson's Republican followers, an Adams victory threatened nothing less than a return of English monarchism, sectarian tyranny, and a morally corrupting commercial excess. To Adams's Federalist followers, a Jefferson victory betokened a rush to French anarchy, radical secularity, economic weakness, and international vulnerability. In short, each side saw the other as certain to abolish the gains of the grand and unifying Revolution of 1776. With so much at stake, tactics were ruthless on all sides. Though certain cultural conventions and perhaps even the smoldering embers of the once bright friendship between Adams and Jefferson meant that neither executed, let alone directly approved, much campaign activity, neither stands guiltless of the atmosphere of slander and machination that prevailed.

Thus many of Jefferson's most implacable Federalist foes sat through his inaugural address fairly riveted by his message. "We are all republicans, we are all federalists," Jefferson famously exclaimed. More significantly, he declared that fostering "affection" between citizens of all parties was nearly as important as securing the safe exercise of natural, individual rights—the lifelong, bedrock aim of his political philosophy. Not only that, Jefferson, whose election prompted some New Englanders to hide their Bibles for fear of confiscation, made it clear that the wide practice of "benign religion," defined as a variety of theological persuasions all of which encouraged "the love of man" and an "adoring [of] an overruling Providence," was among America's greatest blessings.[4] Unbeknownst to virtually all his closest friends and family, and still overlooked by most scholars today, Jefferson's First Inaugural was uttered in the midst of an intense reconsideration of the New Testament—a text Jefferson had roundly rejected in his youth. While he remained steadfastly opposed to certain core elements of traditional Christianity and steadfastly committed to philosophical liberalism as the ground of his politics, he developed around this time a powerful appreciation for a rationalized version of Christ's teachings on love. Jefferson's First Inaugural—which along with his Declaration of Independence essentially brackets the era we consider the traditional founding of America—is the first and best glimpse of how he thought such teachings should be brought to bear on America's fledgling democracy.

III

Washington, D.C., was awash in mud from several days of rain, and the skies remained grimly overcast as dignitaries shuffled onto the dais in front of the U.S. Capitol. It was March 4, 1865, the start of Lincoln's tragically short-lived second administration. With storm clouds threatening to break open again at any moment on an already bedraggled audience, Lincoln stepped forward clutching a copy of his Second Inaugural Address. As he did so, a broad ray of sunlight punched through the cloud line. Chief Justice Chase saw it as "an auspicious omen of the dispersion of the clouds of war and the restoration of the clear sun light of prosperous peace."[5]

It was a day to celebrate. Lee and his forces were trapped near Richmond, Virginia, between Grant's dug-in troops and long-range guns just to the west and Sherman's unopposed march of destruction up from the south. The downfall of the Confederacy's capital city, largest army, and best general was imminent. Yet here, as triumph in America's bloodiest and bitterest conflict appeared certain, Lincoln—whose leadership had so often been publicly savaged (even by members of his own administration) and whose prospects for reelection got so dim that he prepared an executive memo on transferring power to his opponent—offered a most unusual address.

No soothing prediction of the end of military action. No cathartic attack on Southern secessionists. No cheering vindication of his long-embattled presidency. No promising plan for the future. With respect to the future, all that was offered was a single-sentence paragraph urging the North, among other things, to "finish the work" of the war—a war that began as an effort to save the Union, but that by Gettysburg had been transformed into an effort to give a "new birth" of democratic liberty to "all men." In this same sentence, as Lincoln rallied the North to press ahead in the waning moments of conflict with "firmness in the right," he simultaneously appealed for "malice toward none" and "charity for all." Even before the war ended, Lincoln was already at work to restore the "bonds of affection" between North and South that he so memorably extolled four years earlier in the peroration of his First Inaugural. It is also clear that the Second Inaugural's awe-inspiring sense of love for *all* "who shall have borne the battle" is connected in some way to the watchful eye and intervening hand of God, referred to in explicitly biblical terms more than a dozen times in an address of only 703 words—one of the shortest yet most celebrated inaugural addresses in American history.

Winthrop, Jefferson, and Lincoln were all uniquely philosophical statesmen who exercised an enduring influence at decisive junctures in the rise and establishment of American democracy. At the height of their influence, all three figures delivered a seminal speech appealing to certain communal "bonds of affection" which they argued were essential to a stable, flourishing polity. In attempting to draw out and sustain these bonds of affection, each leader consciously worked to channel some understanding of Christian love—what the New Testament calls "charity" (1 Cor. 13:13)—into a central *civic*, rather than strictly *religious*, virtue. In doing so, they helped establish a unique and important strain in the American political tradition, one more often appealed to by political leaders than studied by scholars.

Long gone—and rightly so—are the days of believing that nations are built on the words and deeds of great leaders alone. We have also come to recognize that America's early development was grounded on a rich mosaic of ideas and forces rather than any single historiographical category or intellectual, cultural tradition. However, these particular speeches, and a smattering of related political and literary classics, do reveal that broadly shared ideals of biblical love, artfully refashioned into a guiding public principle by these and other figures, played a distinct role in the genesis and trajectory of America's peculiar form of liberal democracy. By telling such a story, this book seeks to call greater attention to, and further fill, this modest gap in our historical consciousness.[6]

Moreover, this book seeks normative insight for our troubled times. The debate in this country over the appropriate role of religion in American public life is as old as the country itself—and as heated as ever. Arguably, Winthrop, Jefferson, and Lincoln did as much as any three to establish the general contours of this debate. Beyond the fact that all three wielded immense political power at foundational moments in American history, their continuing relevance to this debate is rooted in their sheer sophistication of thought on the matter—a sophistication leavened with careful attention to concrete reality and delivered with a poetry that reaches across the ages. Such gifts make their words almost as relevant to our day as their own. Thus, this project is part intellectual history (detailing the development and nature of several thematically related texts from the canon of American political thought) and part political philosophy (bringing these texts into conversation with one another as a way to ruminate on fundamental issues concerning wise and legitimate rule). As such, the book takes advantage of space recently pried open in both political science and history where a solid understanding of our past is considered not just useful but perhaps "necessary" to sound moral reflection and choice in the present.[7]

Precisely what we can learn about our past, and for our present, from the three episodes described above is embodied in a concept I call "civic charity," which finds its most compelling expression in the mature thought of Abraham Lincoln—his Second Inaugural especially. At a minimum, some such concept appears vital to past, and possibly present, attempts to forge the "bonds of affection" that Winthrop, Jefferson, and Lincoln considered an integral component of ongoing political health. However, before we can understand what is meant by civic charity, its meaningful role in helping to establish and sustain American self-rule, and the resources it still may offer our day, we must first consider its animating source and the deeply problematic relationship between that source and modern political life.

Charity and Modernity

Civic charity draws upon and is closely connected to (in Winthrop's case was virtually indistinguishable from) charity as a Christian virtue. But these days, the charity of New Testament texts has "acquired connotations that make it unsuitable for modern readers as the bearer of the biblical writers' meaning."[8] This challenge is compounded by the inherent difficulty of providing a clear sense of what is meant by Christian charity, a morally complex concept (like justice, freedom, forgiveness, etc.) that wholly resists full and indisputable definition. Numerous contemporary scholars have written long essays and long books in an effort simply to explain and define the concept.[9] Jesus himself, when asked for greater clarity concerning the love he was preaching, avoided elaborate definitional specificity in favor of broadly illustrative parables like that of the Good Samaritan in Luke 10. Nevertheless, a fairly concise statement by Jonathan Edwards—considered America's greatest theologian by many—and a quick gloss on a few key biblical passages might well suffice here.

In the first of a series of sermons delivered on the topic of charity in 1738 (sermons later published as a book, *Charity and its Fruits*), Edwards writes

What persons often mean by "charity," in their ordinary conversation, is a disposition to hope and think the best of others, and to put a good construction on their words and behavior; and sometimes the word is used for a disposition to give to the poor. But these things are only certain particular branches, or fruits of that great virtue of charity which is so much insisted on throughout the New Testament. The word properly signifies *love*, or *that disposition or affection whereby one is dear to another*; and the original (agape), which is here translated "charity," might better have been rendered "love," for that is the proper English of it: so that by charity in the New Testament, is meant the very same thing as Christian love; and though it be more frequently used for love to men, yet sometimes it is used to signify not only love to men, but love to God.[10]

What Edwards said in the eighteenth century concerning different usages of the term "charity" remains largely true today. More often than not, charity is currently employed to describe a spirit of good will (being charitable) or an act of material generosity (giving charity). But charity as Christian love, *agape* in New Testament Greek and *caritas* in the Vulgate, entails those things and more.[11] Here, we can profitably turn to the Bible.

In the book of Matthew (22:35–40), in response to a lawyer's question about which scriptural command is greatest, Jesus says

Thou shalt love the Lord thy God with all thy heart, and with all thy soul, and with all thy mind. This is the first and great commandment. And the second is like unto it, thou shalt love thy neighbor as thyself.

Charity, it has often been remarked, is the one-word summation of this demanding double commandment of love. Charity is a single principle with a dual dimension: a clear *vertical* axis—humans in loving relationship to God—and a clear *horizontal* axis—humans in loving relationship to other humans. As Edwards puts it, charity simultaneously embodies a deep "affection" or "love" for God and man, whereby both God and man are "dear" to oneself.[12] In postmodern parlance, charity centrally entails a "theocentric otherness" and a "social otherness."

With respect to the love of God, the account in Matthew 22 makes clear that this is not only the "first" of all scriptural commandments (the starting point of both Jewish and Christian religious life), but something to be done with all of one's heart, soul, and mind. Elsewhere in the New

Testament, John repeatedly establishes: "For this is the love of God, that we keep his commandments" (1 John 5:3; also see 2:5 and John 14:15, 21). Thus, the vertical axis of *agape* is understood by many to call for a devout, monotheistic piety—a constantly worshipful acknowledgement of, reverence for, and obedience to the "one Lord" (Deut. 6:4).

With respect to the love of others, the New Testament emphasizes that *agape* demands a deeply benevolent care and active compassion for our neighbors. This remains true even when our "neighbors" are total strangers, as Christ emphasized with the parable of the Good Samaritan (Luke 10), or still yet when our neighbors are outright enemies, as Christ emphasized in the Sermon on the Mount (Matt. 5:44). Together, the parable of the Good Samaritan and the Sermon on the Mount not only suggest the vast range of who might be considered a neighbor, but also the scope of how we are to love that neighbor. In the story of the Good Samaritan, charity attends to our stranger-neighbor's most pressing physical needs. In the Sermon on the Mount, charity's concern stretches beyond the merely physical, commanding us to "pray for them which despitefully use you, and persecute you" (Matt. 5:44). Christian eschatology dictates that charity's horizontal axis not be limited to care for another's corporeal comfort alone but must also include care for their spiritual standing before God, even when those others mean us harm.

At this point, it should be apparent why *agapic* love is typically distinguished from erotic love or romantic desire (*eros*) and fraternal love or friendship (*philia*). Unlike these other concepts, charity requires a devotion to God and care for other human beings whether or not those human beings reciprocate that care or provide some personal gratification. This leaves unaddressed for now what if any relationship may exist between charity and other forms of love, as well as other virtues, such as justice. These issues will be addressed in chapter 1, where Winthrop's treatment of charity as a primary and sweeping social ideal is examined in detail.

That such an understanding only begins to give us a faint outline of the concept is found in the fact that Jesus' response to the lawyer in the book of Matthew repeats, verbatim, critical Old Testament teachings.[13] Though New Testament *agape* clearly grows out of and retains distinct affinities with Old Testament *ahab*, Christian love is not a simple carbon copy of Jewish antecedents. A more detailed understanding of what *agape* might mean in practice, and how it might be acquired, will have to come in the chapters that follow. Because this study is not, strictly speaking, a theological account and ethical analysis of the concept of charity itself—in the long tradition of Christian ethics running from Augustine and Aquinas to Paul Tillich and Paul Ramsey—but rather a study of how such a concept has been variously understood by and influenced a discrete set of figures central to the genesis of the American republic, our remaining definitional work is best provided by these figures themselves.

That noted, if this brief discussion of charity in its older biblical sense partially closes a cognitive gap with respect to the meaning of the term, it likely only opens a larger one with respect to how charity relates to politics. Both the intellectual freight and tangible appeal of the modern world stack the deck against accepting *agape* as a concept of political merit and relevance. With the dawning of modernity, and all it has meant for individual freedom and the humane mastering of nature, has come a diminution of Christian ideals of love as pertinent to political reality. An increasingly potent theme in the last five centuries of Western civilization is that charity should remain largely removed from the logic of civic life. A handful of classic texts and paradigmatic thinkers emphasize different aspects of this larger point.

In *The Prince*, arguably the most famous book on politics ever written and ground zero of political modernity, Niccolò Machiavelli argues that it must be understood that a prince "cannot observe all those things for which men are held good, since he is often under a necessity, to maintain his state, of acting against faith, against *charity*, against *humanity*, against *religion*."[14] The problem with a leader determined to exercise Christian love and goodness "in all regards" is that such a figure (and the state he or she rules) is doomed to "come to ruin among so many who are not good." Thus, for Machiavelli, *the* defining characteristic of a successful modern leader is knowing "how to enter into evil, when forced by necessity."[15] This remains one of the earliest and most devastating arguments against the powerful medieval aspiration for a "reign of charity" on earth.[16]

A less ruthless, more democratic version of Machiavelli's position is found in Max Weber's classic lecture "Politics as Vocation." Weber argues that the "genius or demon of politics" stands in direct tension with the "ethic of the Sermon on the Mount," or what he calls elsewhere the "ethic of the gospel" or "acosmic ethic of love." For Weber, this tension stems from his observation that violence is central to all forms of political rule, whereas the "ethic of the gospel" demands that one must live like Jesus—being "saintly in everything"—and Jesus never "operated with the political means of violence."[17] This puts political leaders aspiring to the virtue of *agape* in a double bind. If even nonaggressive, modern democracies must—to establish internal order and external security—be led by those who are prepared to engage in acts of violence and perfidy, then saintly, uncompromising commitments to Christian love are bound to make one unfit to rule. Correlatively, enthusiastic endeavors in modern political rule are bound to make leaders seeking salvation unfit to inherit the Kingdom of God. In sum, the practice of charity may be as dangerous to the state as the practice of politics is to the soul.

Francis Bacon, instrumental in establishing the methodological principles of modern science, understood that his *scientific* aim embodied a significant *political* challenge—how to harness the immense new power of modern science for human good instead of human misery. In several of his works, he repeatedly claims that the answer to this challenge is the encouragement and practice of Christian charity. However, Bacon's *New Atlantis* fully repudiates the sincerity of such claims. In this novella, Bacon's vision of scientific utopia on the fictitious island of Bensalem, traditional Christian charity is replaced by a heterodox, even non-Christian concept of compassion, but one completely subordinate to scientific reasoning and political necessity.[18]

If early moderns like Machiavelli and Bacon seek to dramatically diminish charity's civic role in the name of executive strength and a materially comfortable citizenry, John Locke launches modern pluralism and secular liberal democracy in the name of charity itself. In "A Letter Concerning Toleration," Locke explains that far too often under the "Principle of Charity," humans express their love and concern for the salvation of others by confiscating their property, punishing their bodies, and even taking their lives. To render impotent this patently "unchristian Cruelty" masquerading as *agape*, Locke esteems it above all things necessary "to distinguish exactly the Business of Civil Government from that of Religion, and to settle the Bounds that lie between the one and the other." In the world of Lockean politics, the duty of the magistrate is limited to preserving the "civil interests" of its citizens—meaning the impartial execution of laws protecting citizens equally in their natural rights to life and liberty and legal possessions such as "money, lands, houses, furniture, and the like."[19] There are other passages in the *Letter on Toleration* and the *First Treatise of Government* that suggest Locke actually sees the situation as a bit more complicated than all this. But in general, Locke, like so many quarters of the liberal tradition that follow in his wake, strives to separate church and state and replace charity with justice as the "first virtue of social institutions," where justice is largely considered embodied in a set of secular decision procedures, political institutions, and economic arrangements predicated on inherent human freedom and equality.[20]

What Locke argued for government specifically, Sigmund Freud later argued for human psychology more broadly.[21] "Justice" is the "first requisite of civilization," he claimed in his most widely read book, *Civilization and Its Discontents*. For Freud, man's natural, instinctive, and happiest state is individualistic, erotic, and aggressive.[22] But the joy of wolfish acquisition and sexual activity will largely go unrealized for all but a few characters of exceptional strength and ability. Thus, man's best hope is to band together and try to impose a culture of justice that channels the human libido into long-term monogamy and nonsexual affection for loyal family, friends, and community members in return for some security and other physical and emotional goods.[23]

In light of this position, Freud finds the world-renowned standard of "thou shalt love thy neighbor as thyself" utterly incomprehensible—a *"Credo quia absurdum."*[24] The problem with *agape* is that its command to love everyone just like we love ourselves stipulates obligations no one could possibly ever keep and which would often be repaid by others with violent harm. Thus charity, more often than not, leaves people neurotic and vulnerable. It also makes them unjust. To treat all human beings, even enemies, with the same level of care we have for a spouse, child, or friend is to be, Freud holds, grossly unfair to those with whom we have special ties and obligations because of the good they do for us. And as for actually channeling man's aggressiveness against others, Freud paints historical Christianity as no more effective than the old Roman paganism or new German Nazism.[25]

Freud's attitudes toward the ideals of *caritas* are different from but were influenced in no small part by one of his near contemporaries, Nietzsche—modernity's first antimodern whose arguments forcefully attack all traditional claims of moral truth. As he notes in his early work *The Birth of Tragedy*, Nietzsche's philosophical project is "purely artistic" and explicitly "anti-Christian." Looking to reveal the truly free and admirable being—the creative "overman"—Nietzsche posits and defends a universal "will to power" over and against a Christian inspired "will to decline." Perhaps even more so than Machiavelli, Nietzsche sees *agape* making people too weak for the demands of individual liberation and cultural greatness found only through an aesthetic life of power ever seeking more power. We must move beyond the morality of love of God and others, Nietzsche argues, because the God who authored such commandments "is dead." A more sweeping claim even than God simply does not exist or has met some kind of divine demise, Nietzsche is announcing—as Martin Heidegger later observed—"the impotence not only of the Christian God but of every transcendent element under which men might want to shelter themselves."[26]

Machiavelli's political realism, Bacon's scientific materialism, Locke's philosophical liberalism, Freud's therapeutic justice, and Nietzsche's radical skepticism of any traditionally understood moral norms all remain exceptionally strong influences in our post-Christian present. Together they form—whatever their differences—a most imposing barrier for charity to play any meaningful part in the formation of an important civic ideal. But it is this very fact that makes the study at hand all the more necessary and interesting. Despite such powerful forces, various notions of *agape* remain both religiously central and politically salient throughout American life. In more recent times, the most obvious example of this is found in the hymnal rhetoric of Martin Luther King Jr.'s civil rights push. An even more recent if less sustained and less successful manifestation is found in George W. Bush's idiom of "compassionate conservatism" on particular display during his gubernatorial years and first presidential campaign.

Civic Charity

To begin to understand how *Christian* charity got so firmly implanted in the soil of the American political tradition, flowering into a *civic* charity of broad influence, and to adequately reflect on how well such a phenomenon comports with reasonable accounts of political necessity and justice, we must turn first to John Winthrop. The reasons for this have already been indicated. He is not only the first to introduce charity as an ideal of more than solely religious significance, but he does so in a way that is both memorable and alarming. It is in Winthrop and his Model of Christian Charity speech—examined in detail in part 1 of this book—that one most clearly sees both the sunlit uplands and the dark narrows that stand as possible outcomes for the polity anxious to be formally ruled by the imperatives of Christian love. For the reader still sure at this point that in Winthrop only negative lessons can be learned, part 1 begins by showing that Nathaniel Hawthorne, this most famous of all critics of the Puritans, seemed to recognize distinctly redeeming qualities in Winthrop and his charity-oriented leadership, namely a sense of genuine human compassion and noble purpose that made him the most attractive of his Puritan peers.

Part 2 of this book details a monumental shift in thinking about charity and politics by highlighting Jefferson's radical break with the ancient religious norms of *agape* so central to Winthrop. We do see here, however, that even Jefferson's devout commitment to a largely secular model of liberal democracy is suffused with an attention to securing a fraternal affection between citizens, an attention increasingly colored for him by New Testament teachings. We also see that the impact of Jefferson's position is modulated in its break from certain Winthropian positions by the influence of more traditionally religious figures of influence in the revolutionary-constitutional generation.

It is not until Lincoln, considered in part 3, that we see a full-bodied model of civic charity that harnesses many of the respective benefits of both Winthrop's and Jefferson's positions without eviscerating the essential claims of either. While it will take the rest of this book to explain adequately what is meant by civic charity, how it came into existence, and how it reaches its apotheosis in the thought and rhetoric of Lincoln, one might at this point anticipate its vague contours. Civic charity, like its theological parent Christian charity, has both a vertical (pious) and horizontal (compassionate) dimension which play off each other in dynamic interaction. Furthermore, both dimensions are simultaneously and acutely attuned to the traditions of liberal democracy and Judeo-Christianity. To be more specific, civic charity's vertical dimension calls for a public recognition of and gratitude for a God of judgment and providence even as it respects and helps establish a constitutionally robust pluralism, including a substantial degree of separation of church and state. As for the horizontal dimension, civic charity calls for a generous and forgiving affection among citizens at the same time that it recognizes and vigorously protects the individual as an inherently free being. And, while civic charity is explicitly grounded in claims of revelatory and self-evident truth, it strikes a very cautious stand in fathoming God's work and will in the world and in embracing normatively charged certitudes of political policy and consequence given its poignant awareness of inherent human weakness and limitation.

As previously noted, fusions of philosophical liberalism and Christian *agapism* still seem very much with us in American civic life, even if not perfectly faithful to the rudimentary formulation just described. Certainly the continuing influence of Winthrop, Jefferson, and Lincoln helps to explain the unique and enduring status of biblical notions of love at work in our national politics despite the strictures of so much modern and postmodern political theory. Yet it has been observed that we often only name a concept, like civic charity, when we recognize that it is something we have had had all around us for a long time but now sense we are losing. One cannot help but wonder if the constant drumbeat of various intellectual forces of the post-Christian West, forces which see themselves in purely secular terms and which have dominated scholarly debate and inquiry for decades, is not drowning out aspirations to blend important religious concepts of love with genuine commitments to human freedom—a blending that has long been a critical part of our political heritage. Civic charity, while by definition respectful and caring of all citizens as free beings, is not a principle that will, or needs to, speak to everyone. But given the continuing political and religious convictions of vast numbers of Americans today, it is a concept that may be well worth identifying and reviving. To do so—even to see if we should do so—we must first return to the past to elucidate the concept's origins and comprehend its most profound articulations.

Notes

1. The definitive edition of the speech is found in *Winthrop Papers*, Vol. II: 282–295. Selections here are taken from Appendix A of this book—my own transliteration of this speech into modern English (a move explained in chapter 1).

2. Dawson, "Rite of Passage," 219; Delbanco, *The Puritan Ordeal*, 72. For Winthrop as a sophisticated political philosopher whose influence is still felt, primarily through the "Model" speech, see Miller, *New England Mind,* 422; Miller, *Nature's Nation*, 6; McWilliams, *Fraternity in America*, 133; Schaar, "Liberty/Authority/Community," 493–518; and Baritz, *City on a Hill*, 13–14. Gomes, "Pilgrim's Progress," 102–3. Presidential uses of Winthrop detailed in Holland, *Remembering John Winthrop*.

3. In addition to Hawthorne's classic treatment of Puritanism in *The Scarlet Letter* (discussed at length in the introduction to part 1), see Brooks Adams, *The Emancipation of Massachusetts*; Charles F. Adams, *Three Episodes of Massachusetts*

History; Mencken, *A Mencken Chrestomathy*, 624; Brooks, *Van Wyck Brooks: The Early Years*, 194. The line "America's Forgotten Founding Father" is from the subtitle of Bremer, *John Winthrop: America's Forgotten Founding Father*. Also see Bremer's "Remembering—and Forgetting—John Winthrop and the Puritan Founders."

4. For a pithy description of events, see Ellis, *American Sphinx*, 182–83, with excellent larger treatments in Ferling, *Adams v. Jefferson*, and Weisberger, *America Afire*; discussion of Bible hiding in Dreisbach, *Wall of Separation*, 18.

5. Quoted in Donald, *Lincoln*, 566.

6. The topic of Christianity's general influence on the American founding has, of course, received considerable scholarly treatment. For notable recent contributions that together provide an excellent survey of the relevant scholarship, see Frank Lambert's *The Founding Fathers and the Place of Religion in America* (Princeton University Press, 2003) and the various essays in *Protestantism and the American Founding*, edited by Thomas S. Engemen and Michael Zuckert (Notre Dame Press, 2004). For an older and less historical but uniquely Catholic treatment, John Courtney Murray's *We Hold These Truths: Catholic Reflections on the American Proposition* (Sheed and Ward, 1960) remains a standard classic. Mark Noll's work *America's God* highlights the previously underappreciated fact that not only did American religion influence American politics, but American politics influenced American religion. None of these works, though, treat in any depth the specific issue of Christian charity as a civic virtue. There are few books by major historians and political scientists that touch directly on Christian charity and closely related themes as important to the early development of American political life. James A. Morone, in *Hellfire Nation: The Politics of Sin in American History*, acknowledges, as I do, that some understandings of *caritas*—especially those with Puritan connections—can separate the political world into manifestations of a self-righteous "us" versus a wicked "them." I nevertheless challenge his argument that only something like the nineteenth and twentieth century's "social gospel" movement is religion's most legitimate and useful American political legacy. In *The Lost Soul of American Politics*, Patrick Diggins comes to a positive appraisal of Lincoln's fusion of liberalism and Christian love. However, Diggins is less sanguine about the continuing political purchase of any virtuous ideal, Christian or otherwise. He leans instead toward a strong economic determinism and thus pays more attention to class interests whereas I focus on statesmanship. Though ostensibly a book on a separate topic, Wilson Carey McWilliams's *The Idea of Fraternity in America* stands as a highly related and vital, if now too often overlooked, gem. Given that fraternity is something of a conceptual cousin to, and in some cases (as I will argue) dependent upon the sustaining influence of, Christian love, the central topics of McWilliams's work and mine are complementary but not the same. There are also conscious differences in scope and method. My work probes fewer thinkers and texts but probes them more extensively. Not surprisingly then, it is the work of one of McWilliams's students, Patrick Deneen, which tracks closest to my own. Deneen closes his book *Democratic Faith* with a concept he calls "democratic charity." While there is considerable overlap here with what I am calling "civic charity," including a grounding of the concept in Lincoln's Second Inaugural with a nod to Winthrop's "Model of Christian Charity" speech, Patrick and I arrived independently at our most basic conclusions at roughly

the same time and hold some differences in our understanding and use of the concept. Much the same could be said of the work of theologian Timothy Jackson, whose *Priority of Love* advances a notion of "civic *agape*" (p. 67), though not as a canonical ideal in the American political tradition. To both Deneen and Jackson, I am very grateful for how their work helped define my own.

7. See the statement in David Hackett Fischer's seminal work on American cultural history, *Albion's Seed*, xi. For a more detailed exposition, see James T. Kloppenburg's chapter "Why History Matters to Political Theory" in *The Virtues of Liberalism*, 155–78. Kloppenburg's thesis is foreshadowed in the claim of political theorist Isaiah Berlin in *Four Essays*, 4, that "the historical approach is inescapable: the very sense of contrast and dissimilarity with which the past affects us provides the only relevant background against which the features peculiar to our own experience stand out in sufficient relief to be adequately discerned and described." A related though ultimately different kind of claim comes from those (political theorists, primarily) influenced by Leo Strauss. These scholars argue in different ways and often toward different conclusions that a continuing wisdom can be found in the words and deeds of America's most philosophical statesmen as such words and deeds, while necessarily reflective of the particular time and place in which they were offered, are also reflective of a deep engagement with the transpolitical ideals of right, good, and justice that are not contingent but true "everywhere and always." See the preface material in Jaffa, *Crisis of the House Divided*, iii–vi, and Frisch and Stevens, *American Political Thought*, vii–viii. For more recent discussions, one from an intellectual historian and the other from a political scientist, both of which blur the distinctions between a historicist and nonhistoricist point of view concerning the relevance of classic expressions of American political thought by political leaders, see Banning, *Jefferson and Madison*, xi, and Yarbrough, *American Virtues*, xvii.

8. Achtemeier, *Harper's Bible Dictionary*, 160.

9. For a sampling of some of the more recent notable treatments, see Nygren, *Agape and Eros*; Outka, *Agape: An Ethical Analysis*; Jackson, *Love Disconsoled*; Hallett, *Christian Neighbor Love*; Hauerwas, "The Politics of Charity."

10. Edwards, *Charity and Its Fruits*, 1–2; emphasis in original. Edwards's full treatment of charity is not controlling for this study, but this precise passage nicely lays out the common usages of the term that cloud its larger biblical meaning, and it highlights all the key aspects of the term that will be developed as Winthrop, Jefferson, and Lincoln are pursued in more detail.

11. Where some scholars, notably Nygren, make strict distinctions between *agape* and *caritas*, I follow Edwards, Jackson, and others who tend to use Christian love, charity, *agape*, and *caritas* interchangeably; see Jackson, *Love Disconsoled*, 11n25.

12. For the dual dimensions of charity, see Jackson, *Love Disconsoled*, 1–2. Also, the *Oxford English Dictionary*, 2nd edition, designates "charity" as "Christian love" and notes that it is often applied as "Man's love of God and his neighbor, commanded as the fulfilling of the law, Matt. xxii. 37, 39." Kierkegaard, *Works of Love*, 17.

13. In response to the question of what is the first commandment, Christ's answer followed Deut. 6:5 and 11:13—passages which figure prominently in the *Shema*, a

short collection of Old Testament verses that still serves as the first and most important Jewish declaration of faith and basic tenets. In the case of the second commandment, Christ was quoting verbatim Leviticus 19:18 and echoing—perhaps knowingly—the teachings of Hillel, the great first-century CE Jewish scholar who taught that all of Judaism could be summed up in the love commandment of Leviticus 19:18; see Grayzel, *A History of the Jews,* 123. The second verse of the Pirké Avot, one of the best-known and best-loved portions of the Talmud, reads, "Upon three things the world is based (literally, the world stands): upon the Torah, upon Temple Service, and upon the practice of charity." See Stern, *Pirké Avot,* vii; Schatz, *Ethics of the Fathers,* 36.

14. Niccolò Machiavelli, *The Prince,* vii, 70 (emphasis added). Nearly thirty years ago, Isaiah Berlin identified more than a "score of leading theories" and a "cloud of subsidiary views" related to how one ought to interpret Machiavelli (Berlin, *Proper Study of Mankind,* 269). Consciously avoiding this interpretive tar pit, all that is suggested here is that even with those interpreters inclined to see something humane lurking behind the dark conclusions of *The Prince* (like Clifford Orwin's "Machiavelli's Unchristian Charity"), it is generally agreed that the full demands of traditional Christian charity are directly at odds with the full demands of effective, lasting political rule.

15. Machiavelli, *The Prince,* 61, 70.

16. Augustine, *On Christian Doctrine,* 93.

17. Weber, *Essays in Sociology,* 119, 120, 126.

18. Bacon, *The New Organon,* 90; Innes, "Bacon's New Atlantis," 100; Bacon, *New Atlantis,* 32.

19. John Locke, *A Letter Concerning Toleration,* 24, 26.

20. For explicit civic overlap of the virtues of justice and charity, see Locke, *Two Treatises on Government,* 205–6; Rawls, *A Theory of Justice,* 3; Richardson, *Democratic Autonomy,* 37; Dworkin, *A Matter of Principle.*

21. Though much of Freud's original work has now been superseded if not widely repudiated by contemporary psychoanalysis, in the 1980s Ernest Wallwork plausibly posited that Freud's critique of the Christian neighbor-love commandment was "more familiar to educated persons" than any other ("The Freudian Critique," 264). Even more recently, Timothy Jackson convincingly argues the towering "shadow" of Freud's influence over modern attitudes toward *agape* (*Love Disconsoled,* 56).

22. Freud, *Civilization and Its Discontents,* 68–69.

23. Ibid., 32, 57, 73.

24. Ibid., 68.

25. Ibid., 73.

26. Nietzsche, *Basic Writings of Nietzsche,* 24, 23, 455, 171, 853. See Romand Cole's *Rethinking Generosity* for at least one very fine treatment of, and response to, the problems that postmodern critical theory raises for *caritas.*

PART ONE

Winthrop and America's Point of Departure

Your constant zeal for the things of God and man may truly entitle you to be the Father and first founder of this flourishing colony, and will have the happiness to leave behind you a lasting memory.

Francis Williams to John Winthrop, 1643

Hawthorne's Suggestion

I
t is now quaint to presume, as Tocqueville did in the 1830s, that there is "not one opinion, one habit, one law" in this country that does not tie back to our Puritan past. Still, few writers of our history question Puritan New England's decisive influence on American politics and culture. Even fewer dispute Cotton Mather's early claim that John Winthrop was the "Father of New England." For good reason, then, many distinguished observers of American politics continue to consider John Winthrop an admirable figure of founding importance, if not the "first great American."[1]

An attorney and respected man of means in Suffolk County, England, John Winthrop was elected governor of the Massachusetts Bay Company late in 1629. By the spring of 1630 he was aboard the *Arbella*, flagship of the "great migration" of eighty thousand English Puritans who sailed to America over the next decade. In 1649, he died in office, having presided over America's most important early colony for twelve of the colony's first nineteen years. During this time he settled Boston, skillfully established the rule of law and a number of remarkably democratic practices for wider Massachusetts, and held the colony's frontier communities together in the face of harsh winters, wild patterns of migration, violent conflicts with natives and foreign powers, and divisive theological disputes. In addition to all of this, he kept a journal that remains our single richest source of early New England history.[2]

Of course, no piece of writing—historical or fictional—has so captured and defined an American era the way *The Scarlet Letter* has our Puritan beginnings. The picture that many Americans have of this world comes almost entirely from a high school reading of this text. To know only this text is to know much, though. In addition to his obvious literary genius, Hawthorne devoured an array of secondary and primary sources on New England's Puritans. Arguably, he remains he who "knew them best." But this raises serious concerns about Winthrop's influence on America because Hawthorne, it seems, stands at the headwaters of an illustrious intellectual tradition that accepts Winthrop as a founding father of America but considers this mostly a tragedy.[3]

At a minimum, Hawthorne's most famous novel provides a withering critique of the Massachusetts Bay Colony's effort to become "A Model of Christian Charity"—the inaugural vision and founding aim of John Winthrop's leadership. In making this critique, Hawthorne is especially hard on Boston's rulers. Consider the striking contrast between the adulterous Hester Prynne and those who lead the colony. Eventually, there was

> none so ready as [Hester] to give of her little substance to every demand of poverty; even though the bitter-hearted pauper threw back a gibe in requital of the food brought. . . . Hester's nature showed itself warm and rich; a well-spring of human tenderness, unfailing to very real demand, and inexhaustible by the largest. Her breast, with its badge of shame, was but the softer pillow for the head that needed one. She was self-ordained a Sister of Mercy.[4]

Conversely,

> the rulers, and the wise and learned men of the community, were longer in acknowledging the influence of Hester's good qualities than the people. The prejudices which they shared in common with the latter were fortified in themselves by an iron framework of reasoning, that made it a far tougher labor to expel them. . . . Thus it was with the men of rank, on whom their eminent position imposed the guardianship of the public morals. Individuals in private life, meanwhile, had quite forgiven Hester Prynne for her frailty.[5]

While rank-and-file Puritans largely come to forgive Hester and recognize her patient and forgiving goodness, the text only holds out the slimmest hope that "in the due course of years" Boston's hardened leaders "might" develop "an expression of *almost* benevolence" toward Hester.[6] As the unsparing enforcers of the community's covenant with God, these leaders appear unable to appreciate classic expressions of Christian love in Hester or to embrace them themselves. Yet even as Hawthorne levels this accusation against the Puritan regime and its rulers, he seems to refrain from tarring Winthrop in the same way.

Our first clue is Winthrop's striking absence from the text. The novel opens with Governor Bellingham presiding over Hester's trial on the town scaffolding. Hester's next interaction with a political figure is roughly three years later and the leader is, again, Bellingham, who is no longer the governor but still holds an "honorable and influential place among the colonial magistracy." Ostensibly delivering a pair of gloves Bellingham ordered from her, Hester the seamstress had more pressing matters on her mind. Among those leaders known for "cherishing the more rigid order of principles in religion and government," there was supposedly a movement to deprive Hester custody of Pearl, the offspring of her illicit affair. Hester sought audience with the "grave old Puritan ruler" because among those promoting the design he was "the most busy."[7]

The first time the reader even encounters Winthrop's name is in chapter 12, "The Minister's Vigil," where it is noted that Hester and Pearl have just been "watching . . . at Governor Winthrop's death bed."[8] Now this comment is significant in that it offers the novel's one established date: Winthrop's death on March 26, 1649, has always been a matter of record. Thus it is only from this passage that we can determine the date of the novel's opening. Since we are told that later that night Hester and Pearl encounter Reverend Dimmesdale (Hester's illicit lover) making fake confession on the scaffolding where Hester stood in shame "seven long years" ago,[9] we know Hester's trial took place in June of 1642.[10] But this highlights several peculiarities.

First, Hawthorne makes Bellingham the governor for the novel's opening, when in fact Winthrop was. Bellingham was governor from 1641 to 1642, but Winthrop succeeded him that year after May elections. So, by June of 1642 Winthrop was the sitting governor.[11] Second, even though Winthrop dominated the actual stage of Boston politics during the time frame of the novel (Winthrop was governor when the novel opens in 1642 until 1644, then again from 1646 to 1649, the year that he died and the novel ends), Hawthorne makes Bellingham the focal political figure. Third, when Boston appears its very worst, its most "rigid" and tyrannical—meaning the year leaders threaten to take Pearl from Hester—is during the two-year gap when Winthrop was not governor. If Hester seeks out Bellingham three years after her trial, it would be 1645, when the colony was ruled by the notorious "Iron" John Endicott.

With respect to the first two points, most scholars agree that Hawthorne was too historically aware and meticulous to make such moves by mistake.[12] One compelling explanation is that Hawthorne intentionally commits these inaccuracies to highlight Puritan hypocrisy. Historical records known to Hawthorne suggest that Bellingham himself engaged in an illicit sexual relationship. With Bellingham at the forefront of Puritan politics, Hawthorne makes Hester's most powerful and punishing judge guilty of something approximating the crime she is forced to admit.[13]

This argument is persuasive, but if Hawthorne were *only* interested in establishing this irony, why not avoid the historical inaccuracy altogether and open the novel in April when Bellingham was in fact governor? This argument also fails to address other curiosities. To begin with, why would Hester and Pearl linger at the bedside of the dying Winthrop in the middle of the night? As seamstress of choice for the elite, Hester was there to take a measure for Winthrop's burial robe.[14] But why must she be there "watching" with her daughter? Hester might have been summoned to come and take measurements more quickly, or even just after Winthrop passed away, and in either case without her daughter following her into the chamber. Such scenarios seem more logical and appropriate than having the single most important man in the colony surrounded in his final moments, in the middle of the night, by a convicted adulteress and her very young daughter. Could not their lingering presence betoken some warm, appreciative relationship between the governor and these two figures of public scorn?

And what is the reader to make of all the heavenly imagery that surrounds Winthrop's death? Earlier in chapter 12, when Reverend Wilson passes by the scaffolding, he appears shrouded in a kind of "radiant halo." The light obviously came from the lantern he was carrying, but the imaginative suggestion is that it was "as if the departed Governor had left him an inheritance of his glory" as Winthrop triumphantly passed into "the distant shine of the celestial city."[15] Later in chapter 12, Dimmesdale thinks he sees a blazing "A" in the sky. Again an imaginative thought redounds in Winthrop's favor. The next day a sexton reports to Dimmesdale:

> But did your reverence hear of the portent that was seen last night? A great red letter in the sky—the letter A—which we interpret to stand for Angel. For as our good Governor Winthrop was made an angel this past night, it was doubtless held fit that there should be some notice thereof![16]

Certainly Hawthorne does not intend us to think of Winthrop—the central founder of Puritan New England—only in angelic light. Someone so vitally bound up with the establishment of the Puritan regime under attack could not entirely escape Hawthorne's indictment. Yet it now seems equally implausible that Hawthorne would have us believe that the "A" blazoned across the sky symbolizes Winthrop as a kind of "Antichrist," as some have suggested.[17] Hawthorne works too hard to put Winthrop out of sight when bad things are happening. And when Winthrop does appear, the purely heavenly imagery surrounding him contrasts sharply with uniformly negative pictures of other leaders. Finally, the perplexing presence of Hester and Pearl at his deathbed raises the distinct possibility that these semi-outcasts of Boston society felt some deep affection for him.

Together these things raise the strong suggestion that one of Puritan America's greatest observers and severest critics saw John Winthrop as a political ruler with some redeeming traits and insights. More evidence for this speculative claim can be found elsewhere in Hawthorne's literature. But those passages only really become convincing after a close examination of Winthrop's own writings and record.

Notes

1. For Francis Williams to John Winthrop (previous page), see *Winthrop Papers*, IV, 376. For Tocqueville's argument that Puritanism in general and Winthrop in particular provide a "point of departure" for all subsequent American social practice, see *Democracy in America*, 27–44, especially 29. The notion that this position has a point but clearly goes too far and thus rings "quaint" is argued by Andrew Delbanco, *The Real American Dream*, 15 and notes. For a broader sampling on the influence of New England Puritanism on American political culture and development, see Miller, *The Puritans*, 1; Foster, *The Long Argument*, 3–4; Fischer, *Albion's Seed*; Morone, *Hellfire Nation*. Michael Zuckert acknowledges Puritan New England as a founding moment and singles out Winthrop and his "Model" speech as central in *The Natural Rights Republic*, 133–47, though he does so even as he minimizes the continuity between Winthrop's America and that of the revolutionary and constitutional periods. For Winthrop as Father of New England, see Mather, *Magnalia Christi Americana*, 213; Moseley, *John Winthrop's World*, 126; Colacurcio, *The Province of Piety*, 234; and as a Founding Father of America, see, again, Tocqueville, *Democracy in America*, 42; Miller, *New England Mind*, 422; McWilliams, *Fraternity in America*, 133; Schaar, "Liberty/Authority/Community," 493; Cobb, *American Foundation Myth*, vii, 4–5; Morgan, *The Puritan Dilemma*, xii; Bercovitch, *Puritan Origins*, ix. For Winthrop as the "first great American," see Johnson, *American People*, 31; and Morgan, *The Genuine Article*, 5.

2. In addition to Winthrop's own journal, edited by Richard S. Dunn and Laetitia Yeandle, and Bremer's new biography titled *John Winthrop: America's Forgotten
Founding Father*, see biographies by James G. Moseley, *John Winthrop's World*;
Edmund S. Morgan, *The Puritan Dilemma*; Darrett Bruce Rutman, *Winthrop's Decision for America*; and Lee Schweninger, *John Winthrop*.

3. Hawthorne as he who "knew them best" is a line from "The Puritan" by noted
poet James L. Seay, *Open Field, Understory*, 47. As documented in the prologue,
the first scholarly assault on American Puritanism comes from the Adams brothers,
Charles Francis and Brooks, a fight later famously joined by early twentieth-century
public intellectuals like H. L. Mencken and Van Wyck Brooks and the Pulitzer
Prize–winning historian Vernon Parrington. More recently, prominent and specific
attacks on Winthrop are lodged in the literary works of Anya Seton, *The Winthrop
Woman*, 29–30, and Louis Auchincloss, *The Winthrop Covenant*, 7–10, 211, 244. Also,
see discussion in Morone, *Hellfire Nation*, 34.

4. Hawthorne, *Scarlet Letter*, 110.

5. Ibid., 111.

6. Ibid. (emphasis added).

7. Ibid., 69, 71.

8. Ibid., 105.

9. Ibid., 101.

10. In chapter 1, the narrator informs the reader that the opening scene takes
place "in this month of June" (ibid., 35).

11. A useful listing of the Massachusetts Bay Colony's governors and their terms
of office may be found in John Raimo's *American Colonial Governors*, 117.

12. Ryskamp, "New England Sources," 267.

13. Colacurcio, *Doctrine and the Difference*, 212.

14. Hawthorne, *Scarlet Letter*, 105.

15. Ibid., 103.

16. Ibid., 109.

17. See Auchincloss, *The Winthrop Covenant*, a collection of thematically related
short stories that moves through successive generations of fictionalized John Win-
throps, the last of whom is revealed "as a kind of Antichrist," an admitted "exaggeration" but one that is never repudiated, only toned down (211). An even more
pejorative portrayal of John Winthrop can be found in Anya Seton's *The Winthrop
Woman*.

CHAPTER 1

A Model of Christian Charity

In the spring of 1630, Christian love gave fertile seed to America's political heritage. The key moment came in a religious service for members of the Massachusetts Bay Company sailing to New England on board the *Arbella*. Addressing those gathered not as their minister but as their recently elected governor, John Winthrop delivered a rigorously argued and emotionally stirring vision of *agape* as the foundational ideal of the society these brave settlers were setting out to create.[1] His remarks stand as America's first great speech. No adequate reflection on charity as a national civic virtue can ignore this now classic text.

Between Old World and New

To gain a clear understanding of Winthrop's lay sermon, it is probably best to start with the tangled matter of its title, "A Model of Christian Charity." This title actually comes from a cover note that is written in neither Winthrop's hand nor that of whoever made the one existing contemporaneous transcription of the speech to which the cover note is attached.[2] According to the transcription, the title simply appears to be "Christian Charity," which is followed by two subheadings. The first subheading reads "A Model Hereof," which is immediately followed by the sermon's opening sentence, after which comes the second subheading, which reads "The Reason Hereof," after which follows the balance of the sermon. (See Appendix A for a visual picture of this.) To consider the title in this fashion is to suggest that Winthrop's concept of a community built on Christian love is captured in its essence by the very first line (the "model hereof"), a vision then justified by the rest of this very long sermon (the "reason hereof").

Placing such emphasis on the opening sentence is highly significant given what that sentence says, offered here in its entirety.

> God Almighty in his most holy and wise providence hath so disposed of the condition of mankind, as in all times some must be rich some poor, some high and eminent in power and dignity, others mean and in subjection. (¶ 1)[3]

To a contemporary audience weaned on that most sacrosanct verse in all of the American political canon, namely that "all men are created equal," Winthrop's opening line reads jarringly archaic—conservative in the oldest and coldest of ways. Certainly critics like Douglas Anderson see it as bald justification for nothing other than unequal privilege, wondering "where . . . is the charity in this?" Even a noted Winthrop admirer like Edmund Morgan suggests the message of subordination in Winthrop's first sentence is "*the* lesson, *the* 'model' which the rest of the sermon or essay was designed to uphold."[4] But is this really the case? Is it true that Winthrop's address—thus his vision for a society based on *agape*—can simply be reduced to the tory spirit of its first forty words?

Winthrop indeed saw the stratification of society as a divinely decreed fact of life—a widely shared view in early seventeenth-century England. The first few sentences of Winthrop's sermon run remarkably parallel in phrasing and logic to a passage from a well-accepted and regularly read Anglican homily of the period titled "An exhortation, concerning good order and obedience, to rulers and magistrates."[5] By explicitly arguing that the recognition of providential inequality at work in the world is a stiff reminder to the "poor" and "despised" that they should not try to "rise up against their superiors, and shake off their yoke," Winthrop does manifest a thick and theologically driven commitment to preserving the existing social order with its conspicuous class divisions (¶ 3).

It is also the case that whatever sincere religious doctrinal perspective buttresses Winthrop's opening line, a strong message of subordination played very much to his political needs at the moment. He was leading the largest fleet of emigrating Englishmen ever assembled up to that point over a treacherous sea to erect, de novo, a polity in a land he would later describe as a "wilderness, where are nothing but wild beasts and beastlike men." As Machiavelli has warned, there may be nothing "more difficult to handle, more doubtful of success, nor more dangerous to manage, than to put oneself at the head of introducing new orders."

Even if Winthrop was not fully cognizant of the inherent dangers of his impending political task, the latent perils of sea travel and already famous accounts of disease, starvation, and attacks by natives that beset existing American colonies (mortality rates in the first fifteen years of Virginia hovered around 80 percent), he surely understood that the threat of revolt and anarchy sat ever close to the surface for this community. As it was, of the roughly seven hundred people who left with him on a fleet of eleven ships, roughly two hundred died during the voyage, and another one hundred would return to England soon after arrival. It is neither surprising nor entirely unreasonable that a leader in this situation would be inclined to call for his fellow citizens to subject themselves freely and lovingly to their leaders. Indeed, from this point on, such a theme became central in Winthrop's public rhetoric, reaching its fullest and clearest expression in his famous "Little Speech" on liberty delivered in the twilight of his rule of Massachusetts.[6]

So a combination of theological, cultural, and practical considerations well explain why Winthrop opened his address by emphasizing and legitimating inequalities of wealth and power. Still, one must ask, pace Morgan, is this really *the* model, *the* lesson of Winthrop's discourse on love? Is it true that Winthrop's concept of *caritas* does little more than reflect and justify an "arch-conservative theory of social hierarchy"?[7] Placing ultimate importance on the transcription's division headings makes it hard to conclude otherwise. However, the speech's internal logic and rhetoric robustly challenge the confines of these headings and produce a different conclusion.

Upon even closer examination, Winthrop's remarks fall into four distinct sections (rather than two), with only marginal overlap between the sections. Paragraphs 1 through 6 constitute section one, the clear focus of which is to situate Winthrop's community in the larger context of a Christian cosmos answerable to a providential God and a "gospel" law of love, or charity. The next section, paragraphs 7 through 19, is a lengthy discussion of the concrete duties of "mercy" that arise out of this law of love—at one point Winthrop himself describes this part of the address as a discussion of the "outward exercise" of charity (see ¶ 20). The third and longest section, paragraphs 20 through 37, analyzes the "inward" exercise of charity, or the genuine "affections of love in the heart" from which the previously discussed outward works of charity "must arise" (¶ 20). In the fourth and final section, paragraphs 37 through 46, Winthrop explicitly takes the insights of the first three sections to "make some application" to the Massachusetts Bay Company, soon to become Colony (¶ 37). Read this way, the speech—contrary to the impression one gets from an overemphasis on the formally designated division headings of the transcription (which, again, may have been intended by Winthrop but are not recorded in his hand)—emerges as a political manifesto that in many respects is so ahead of its time that it still warmly lights America's modern political imagination despite its Old World shibboleths.

"Holy and Wise Providence"

While this first section (¶¶ 1–6) does assert a permanent social inequality as the condition of man, consider the three numbered reasons Winthrop offers for this. First, God prefers to dispense his gifts indirectly, "to man by man," the point being that those with abundance are to be partners with God in actively aiding the impoverished (¶ 2). Second, a hierarchical society better enables God to show the work of his "Spirit," which inspires a "moderating and restraining" influence on all. And while this does mean that the "poor" and "despised" must not "rise up against their superiors," it also means the "rich" and "mighty" must "not eat up the poor" (¶ 3). Third, and perhaps most significantly, God establishes these inequalities so that humans will come to understand that they "have need of [each] other" and in turn will be "knit more nearly together in the bond of brotherly affection" (¶ 4). (This is the first of roughly a dozen more specific references to establishing communal bonds of "affection" or "love"—the single most visible theme in all of Winthrop's discourse and an important if rarely recognized theme in a number of early America's most prominent political documents.)

Two points here are striking. First, if a permanent existence of social inequality is the lot of man, all three of these reasons adjure a caring and active response to such. This is no recipe for a callous, laissez-faire sociality, or even a tepid noblesse oblige. This is a call to affectionate action (or self-restraint as the case may warrant) deployed against excessive class differences. Furthermore, Winthrop's sense of ordained inequality reveals that the *haves* must actively help the *have-nots* because the *have-nots* do not necessarily deserve their condition any more than the *haves* deserve theirs. As one can draw out from Winthrop's arguments, the "regenerate" righteous are not always the rich and "great ones"; some may be of the "poor and inferior sort." In fact, he says that it "appears plainly" that no man is made more honorable than another or more wealthy etc., out of any particular and singular respect to himself but for the glory of his Creator and the Common good of the Creature, Man (¶ 4).

Through his particular strain of Calvinism, Winthrop holds that it is ultimately the unknowable will of God and not the righteous efforts of man that determines whether one is wealthy or impoverished. Divine purposes never fully apparent to the faithful may often lead God to afflict his saints or make sinners prosper. In any case, since the poor do not necessarily merit their own poverty, they remain an integral part of the community and have a certain moral claim upon the attentive assistance of the rich, whose wealth comes in similarly unmerited fashion.

This hardly makes Winthrop a modern egalitarian. John Winthrop is not John Rawls in high-crowned hat. However, critical aspects of Winthrop's position do come closer to Rawls's notion that "no one deserves his place in the distribution of natural assets any more than he deserves his initial starting place in society" than, say, William Graham Sumner's notion that there is no "class in society which lies under the duty and burden of fighting the battles of life for any other class."[8] No talk here of the deserving poor or the deserving rich. There is just the family of man in God's distributed order all needing one another for physical and spiritual blessings. In this respect, then, Winthrop's position better anticipates a view like that of Søren Kierkegaard:

> Christianity has not wanted to storm forth to abolish distinctions, neither the distinction of prominence nor that of insignificance . . . ; but it wills that differences shall hang loosely about the individual, loosely as the cloak the king casts off in order to show who he is, loosely as the ragged costume in which a supernatural being has disguised itself. When distinctions hang loosely in this way, then there steadily shines in every individual that essential other person, that which is common to all men, the eternal likeness, the equality.[9]

Undoubtedly in Winthrop's seventeenth-century view, the cloak of socioeconomic difference hangs tighter than it does in Kierkegaard's nineteenth-century view. Still, Winthrop's position, like Kierkegaard's, is that beneath the decreed socioeconomic differences that mark the human world lies a basic human sameness and a basic human equality before God. And it is this sameness, this equal dependence upon each other and upon God, which dictates an energetic effort to meet the needs of the poor even as recognition of a providential, earthly hierarchy restrains more radical attempts to establish political and economic parity.

Winthrop's fatalism regarding class differences remains anathema to many today. But those quick to dismiss Winthrop on these grounds must acknowledge that now, nearly four hundred years after he set sail for America—a period of human history shot through with attempts to achieve socioeconomic equality by various forms of liberalism, socialism, and communism—we are still faced with stark class distinctions in every country in the world. Though secular minds will understandably choke on Winthrop's theological reading of human existence, it is hard to deny that his basic sociological assumption—a belief in the insuperability of significant human inequalities—has proven far more accurate over the last four centuries than so many perfectionist hopes emanating from numerous ideologies anchored in modern rationalism.

Lastly, to see only the inherently conservative elements of Winthrop's position is to remain blind to the fact that other principles of his position left him highly impatient—incensed even—with what he felt was the heartless Tudor–Stuart caste of his day. England's general failure to care for its poor played prominently in his earliest political activity. And critical among his stated reasons for finally leaving England was that it had become a place where "children, neighbors and friends, *especially of the poor*, are counted the greatest burdens" instead of "the highest earthly blessings"—a clear sign things were not right (emphasis added). Defending this position to a friend, Winthrop exclaimed,

> Why meet we so many wandering ghosts in shape of men, so many spectacles of misery in all our streets, our houses full of victuals, and our entry-ways of hunger-starved Christians, our shops full of rich wares, and under our stalls lie our own flesh in nakedness?[10]

Thus, in the "Model" speech, Winthrop preaches with a passionate intensity that with respect to redressing the plight of the poor, among other things, "Whatsoever we did or ought to have done when we lived in England, the same must we do and more also where we go" (¶ 41).

Though this analysis lays the groundwork for a challenge to the view that the aristocratic orientation of Winthrop's concept of *caritas* eclipses any meaningful remedy of socioeconomic inequality, such analysis runs the risk of thinking about charity as most moderns do, as simple almsgiving or poor relief. But charity was something much more than this for Winthrop, a point he begins to explain in the second half of this first section of the address.

Charity as the Form of the Virtues

Paragraph 4 is one of a handful of paragraphs in Winthrop's speech that by virtually any modern standard of usage would be broken into smaller paragraphs. One natural breaking point comes halfway through the paragraph where Winthrop appears to finish giving the main point of his third reason for providential hierarchy and introduces the notion that all human relations are governed by "two rules," namely "justice and mercy." (This shift, by the way, further highlights the problem of holding too strictly to the transcription's two headings; doing so makes everything after paragraph 3 fall expressly under "Reason: Thirdly," which is obviously inaccurate). This is one of the more important but most opaque passages in the whole sermon.

Though justice is listed here ahead of mercy as the first of the two rules "whereby we are to walk one towards another," Winthrop never carefully defines nor extensively discusses the term. He does note in the next sentence that there are times when the poor may only be due "*mere* justice . . . in regard of some particular contract" (emphasis added). This suggests that, at a minimum, justice is closely connected to the keeping of commercial agreements, and the use of the qualifier "mere" indicates that justice entails obligations that are ethically less demanding than mercy but still ethically satisfying in certain situations. Winthrop discusses mercy in more detail, but not until the speech's second section. Thus, one immediately wonders here what basic relationship both mercy and justice have to charity.

The question gets amplified a line later where Winthrop speaks of a double law by which man is "likewise" to be "regulated" in his actions "one towards another." This only makes things more confusing because this double law is not a reference to the dual rules of justice and mercy per se, but a reference to charity—a point requiring explanation.

The double law is called such because, according to Winthrop, it is really one basic law that varies in name and nature according to the situation of mankind. One situation is before the fall of Adam, when man lived in a state of innocence; there the double law was known as the "moral law" or "law of nature." In another situation, namely man after the fall of Adam, the double law is known as the law of "the gospel" or the "law of grace." To this murky relationship between the "two rules" (of justice and mercy) and the two forms of the "double law," where both forms have two names, Winthrop adds more confusion by noting that the "ground" of the double law is God's commandment to man to "love his neighbor as himself." In other words, Winthrop is preaching that "all the precepts" of the double law rest upon *agape*. But, as noted in the prologue, *agape* is typically defined as the one-word summation of the double-commandment of love found in Matthew 22, where double in this case refers to the two objects of *agapic* love: God and neighbor.[11] Working through all this "double, double" with careful "toil and trouble," we can conclude the following: For Winthrop, charity takes two forms (one prelapsarian, the other postlapsarian), each form takes two names (prelapsarian = the "moral law" and "law of nature" and postlapsarian = the "law of grace" and "the gospel"), and each form aims at two ends (loving God and loving neighbor). Yet this still leaves unaddressed how the "two rules" of justice and mercy relate to the "double law" of love.

As noted, Winthrop initially pairs justice and mercy—two obviously different and seemingly competing moral categories—as the two basic rules for moral human interaction. In doing so, he sets justice and mercy, as a pair, apart from charity as the double law of love, which he goes on to argue is the ground of human morality. But in doing so, he indicates that while justice and mercy are distinctly different concepts from each other, they share one thing: they both operate subordinately to *agape*—the overarching law of ethical life.

Seeing a strong though subordinate connection between mercy and charity is relatively easy. Conventional usage has long lent itself to recognizing a clear connection between the two concepts. And in section three (¶ 20), Winthrop is explicit that the "practice of mercy" is set out "according the rule of God's law" of love. Yet it cannot be that mercy is perfectly synonymous with charity because charity also seems to encompass justice—a concept quite different from mercy. Seeing a strong though subordinate connection between justice and charity is more difficult. Conventional usage tends to obscure any robust association. Additionally, the moment charity as the double law of love is introduced, Winthrop specifically says that he will omit any further discussion of justice "as not properly belonging" to the purpose at hand. Yet this move must not overshadow the fact that Winthrop expressly admits in the same sentence—and will underscore repeatedly in section two—that with respect to the double law, justice may apply in "some particular cases." Therefore, it cannot be that justice is exclusively set off from charity.

What tortuously emerges in this section, then, is that Winthrop is following a long theological tradition that sees charity as a kind of "meta-value."[12] The classic articulation of this position is found in Aquinas, who argues that charity is the "form of the virtues," meaning that charity "directs the acts of all other virtues."[13] In this way, it could be said that *caritas* is larger than mercy and justice because it encompasses both, chartering their respective demands and negotiating the tradeoffs between them. Jonathan Edwards, quoted in the prologue, says much the same thing in *Charity and Its Fruits*:

> Love will show that it disposes men to all duties toward their neighbors. If men have a sincere love to neighbors, it will dispose them to all acts of *justice* toward those neighbors—for real love and friendship always dispose us to give those we love their due. . . . Love will dispose men to all acts of *mercy* toward their neighbors when they are under any affliction or calamity, for we are naturally disposed to pity those that we love when they are afflicted. It will dispose men to give to the poor, to bear one another's burdens, and to weep with those that weep, as well as to rejoice with those that do rejoice. It will dispose men to the duties they owe to one another in their several places and relations.[14]

To suggest that Winthrop, following Aquinas and anticipating Edwards, sees charity as the form of all the virtues is not to say that charity is the perfect essence of all other virtues perfectly combined—some sort of protean concept of virtue in its entirety. Rather it is to say that *agape* underpins and orders all the virtues one must live by and the duties that human beings owe each other and God. Underscoring all this later in the address, Winthrop argues that "this love is a divine spiritual nature, free, active, strong, courageous, permanent under valuing all things beneath its proper object, and of all the graces this makes us nearer to the virtues of our Heavenly Father" (¶ 35). Aquinas explains it this way: "Charity is included in the definition of every virtue, not as being essentially every virtue, but because every virtue depends on it in a way."[15]

Over the course of the speech, how such different virtues like justice and mercy can both draw their sustenance and shape from charity while retaining their own genuine essence will come into clearer focus. The main point here is that Winthrop simply establishes that while mercy and justice provide the rules of moral human interaction, these rules themselves arise out of *agape* as the double law of love.[16]

Charity and Difference

Winthrop concludes this first section of his address with a discussion of the distinctions between how charity plays out in Eden and the fallen world. In Eden, when man lived in a condition of innocence, God's law of love dictated that not only must "every man afford his help to another in every want or distress," but that such actions would be performed "out of the same affection which makes him careful of his own good" (¶ 4). Before the fall, this is not a tough stipulation because in that state it was "natural" to love in this manner. As Winthrop will explain in more detail in section three (¶¶ 30–31), love flows most naturally and easily between those things that are alike, and before the fall of Adam, all are "as the same flesh and image of God" (¶ 5). Thus, for prelapsarian man the law of God is called the "law of nature . . . or the moral law."

But the Massachusetts Bay Colony operated, as Winthrop saw it, in a fallen and sinful world, where all are not godly, innocent, and alike and therefore do not love one another naturally. Rather, the only natural love that exists is self-love and this in overabundance. To overcome the fundamental human selfishness triggered by Adam's fall, mortals require the power of God's grace and the light of his word (again see ¶¶ 30–31). Thus, for postlapsarian man, the double law is called the "law of grace or . . . law of the gospel" (¶ 5). And the law of grace/gospel makes several demands that are different from those of the moral/natural law.

In Eden, where humanity is basically alike "as the same flesh and Image of God" and the moral/natural law is operative, charity's requirements are universal: they apply to everyone and obligate everyone equally in all situations. But in the fallen world, where humans are corrupt and differentiated in a variety of ways and the law of grace/gospel is operative, charity's requirements are more particular: they produce special obligations to those similarly situated "in the estate of regeneracy" (those making their way back to God by grace). In something of a departure from original Calvinism here, Winthrop stresses that post-Edenic *agape* demands that saints feel for and respond to each other in a fashion greater than for those outside their community of faith (where Calvin himself stressed that "the whole human race, without exception, are to be embraced with one feeling of charity").[17] As Winthrop explains, after Adam was expelled from Eden, the law of love actually "teacheth us to put a difference between Christians and others." For scriptural support, Winthrop paraphrases Galatians 6:10, "do good to all, *especially* to the household of faith" (emphasis added). By this formulation, charity honors differences between the faithful same and profane other, even as it seeks to take the sting out of those differences.

To think of charity in this way is to follow, Winthrop indicates, in the path of the Puritans' great communal archetype, the children of Israel, who he explains were "to put a difference between the brethren of such as were strangers though not of the Canaanites." The comparison here is rich with significance. To begin with, the comparison is apt in the sense that the Israelites were also under an obligation to love God with all their heart (Deut. 6:5, 11:13) and love their neighbors as themselves (Lev. 19:18)—a reminder of how deep *agape*'s roots run in Christianity's preceding Hebraic tradition. Furthermore, it is while under just such obligations that the Israelites were instructed to treat strangers— typically defined as someone of non-Israelite birth living in the camp of Israel or the Promised Land—differently. Yet differently did not mean nastily. Because of their outsider status, strangers were under certain restrictions that did not apply to the covenant people, but strangers were to be treated with a distinct sense of friendship, fairness, and justice before the law (Exod. 12:43–49; Lev. 17:8–15). That strangers would be treated well, if not exactly the same as fellow Israelites, was true for all but those descendants of Canaan who were already inhabiting the Promised Land when God gave it to Israel. God commanded Israel to utterly destroy these (Exod. 23: 23–24, 29–30)—a point to which Winthrop's statement alludes. The record of how early Puritan Massachusetts treated its racial and religious others is, of course, mixed. But the record is perhaps better—especially in Winthrop's personal case—than is generally assumed.

With respect to the limited African American population, Winthrop and his fellow settlers accepted the institution of slavery, though there is no conclusive evidence Winthrop ever owned black slaves and there is evidence that early Massachusetts in general was better in its treatment

of this population than were other seventeenth-century English colonists to the south. They gave slaves the same protections as white servants, honored slave marriages before the law, afforded them rights to
trial by jury, forbade masters from inflicting arbitrary punishment on
them, and, most significantly, admitted them to local congregations on
the same basis as white applicants (though they were sometimes segre-
gated in worship afterwards). In his journal, Winthrop writes approvingly
of a "negro maid" who had shown "sound knowledge and true godliness,
[and] was received into the church and baptized."[18]

Despite their sense of affinity with the children of Israel, it could
hardly be said that these early Puritans saw local Indian populations as
akin to Canaanite squatters on their Promised Land, a people to be
utterly destroyed.[19] And the Puritans shared nothing like the cruel Spanish impulse to proselytize native heathens by manipulation and deadly
force—they found this abhorrent. Especially in the earliest years of the
Bay Colony, Puritan leaders, usually with Winthrop in the forefront, typically engaged Indians with a deferential spirit of friendship. Winthrop's
own journal records a number of generous and amicable encounters
with Indian leaders, including hosting them in his home, to dine at his
table and sleep overnight, with gifts exchanged in the process. Winthrop
and others were not free of prejudicially considering Indians their social
and moral inferiors, but rather than aggressively trying to subject native
populations to their control, they strove to form mutual alliances with
them and to treat them as basic equals in their political, legal, and economic relations. In general (with exceptions to be sure), contracts and
agreements were negotiated and honored, and colonists were policed to
treat Indians according to fundamental laws of the land. For example, a
colonist who made unwanted sexual advances on a squaw was whipped.
Another who stole some corn from a native was forced to pay back double. Yet another was executed for murdering an Indian—a crime tried
and punished by an entirely Puritan court.[20]

Such relatively warm and equitable relations with the Indians
changed in 1637. After a series of threatening and violent conflicts with
the Pequots—provocations coming from both sides, starting with the
Pequot murder of an unsavory English trader named Stone—
Massachusetts, along with Connecticut, Rhode Island, and several other
nervous Indian tribes in the area, declared war. Things came to an end
when a main Pequot village at Mystic was surrounded and set on fire.
Nearly all the six or seven hundred men, women, and children in the

village died in the fire or were killed when they tried to escape. This alarming and overpowering show of force not only annihilated the Pequots but cowed even Massachusetts's Indian allies into a greater state of subservience from which they never recovered.[21]

Winthrop was not governor during this episode nor did he play any direct role in the fighting. By all accounts, he was a man quick to forgive, one who took no delight in inflicting pain. For instance, early in the Atlantic voyage Winthrop stepped in and "with some difficulty" convinced the captain of the *Arbella* to remit a severe punishment issued against a crewman who had flagrantly mistreated a passenger (the crewman was to be tied up by his hands and have a heavy weight hung around his neck). But accounts also indicate that Winthrop supported the Pequot war, in general worked hard behind the scenes to ensure its successful outcome, and never denounced the colonials' final tactics. Whatever spirit of mercy and compassion he thought the model of charity demanded, Winthrop was clear from the very start that it did not demand pacifism or weak self-defense. Within days of departing for America, when ominous-looking ships were spied on the horizon, the gun deck that had been turned into sleeping quarters was restored to combat condition and, as Winthrop put it, "we all prepared to fight."[22] Thus, while it must be presumed that Winthrop tacitly accepted the brutal final assault and other aggressive tactics against the Pequots, Winthrop and others were not completely without justification in seeing this as an unwelcome last resort to deal with a particular group that appeared more aggressive (the very name Pequot meant "destroyer of men") and less trustworthy than other tribes in the area. Fears about and reaction to the Pequots were no doubt excessive, and shamefully so. But with the Virginia Massacre of 1622—where nearly a third of Jamestown was wiped out by a series of surprise attacks by the Pohawatans—vividly etched in the minds of Bay Colony magistrates and citizens alike, their concern that failure to deal forcefully with a threatening tribe could risk the very survival of their godly experiment in New England was far from unreasonable. It should also be recognized that nothing like the brutal events at Mystic ever happened again during Winthrop's lifetime or well after. Furthermore, having returned to the governor's seat shortly after the end of war, Winthrop quickly moved to use Massachusetts's influence with Connecticut to dissuade it from exacting a bloody retaliation on a tribe allied with the Pequots whose massacre of some Connecticut settlers in response to a real though modest miscarriage of justice did much to trigger the larger war. And finally, while Winthrop and other Massachusetts leaders were never again as accommodating to any Indian population, as shifting alliances between these tribes and other colonies seemed ever after a threat to Massachusetts's power to chart the course of its Puritan project, Indian-Massachusetts relations continued to be marked by a significant if imperfect attention to the rule of law and basic English notions of fairness.[23]

The treatment of religious dissenters was an even more complex matter. All who chose to emigrate to the Massachusetts Bay Colony knew that it was, by design and aim, a strict religious community. And even at that, the most threatening of dissenters were typically given ample warnings, engaged in dialogue, and patiently persuaded to abide by communal norms before major punishment was inflicted. If charity in the fallen world does "put a difference" between the orthodox household of faith and all others, Winthrop proved most seriously committed to his own reminder that with charity also comes a command to love and do good to one's enemies. Numerous are the observations of him striving diligently to maintain relations of peace and affection with those who opposed him personally and the orthodox views of the colony in general. The kind of virulent anti-Catholic statements so common at the time are noticeably absent from his writings. Until the day he died, Roger Williams, one of the most famous dissenters of Winthrop's Boston, spoke hardly anything but fondness and praise for Winthrop, who was actively involved in expelling Williams from Boston for his increasingly radical separatism.[24]

In addition to the differences charity recognizes in the treatment of different people when operating as the law of the gospel/grace in the fallen world, charity in this condition, according to Winthrop, recognizes that a "difference of seasons and occasions" may dictate different levels of selflessness for those following the commands of charity (¶ 6). In the most extreme situations—Winthrop mentions the apostolic beginnings of Christianity—there is a time and place to "sell all and give to the poor." In other less needful situations, there may not be call for saints to give their all, but still to give "beyond their ability." And a "community of perils" in particular may call for "extraordinary liberality." Undoubtedly this last notion was aimed right at Winthrop's listeners, who must have considered themselves in some degree of peril from the very moment they left the relatively safe and civilized shores of England.

With this thought, Winthrop segues into his second section (starting at ¶ 7), where he provides a detailed discussion of the outward duties of mercy required by *caritas* after Adam's fall.

"The Practice of Mercy According to the Rule of God's Law"

Winthrop teaches that the first obligation of mercy is "giving," which means that man is to give to the needy "out of his abundance" (¶¶ 8–9). Anticipating the counterargument that one's abundance should be stored up to provide a comfortable inheritance for one's family, or to prepare one to deal with uncertain future calamities, Winthrop acknowledges that laying aside for family and future is not only wise but is also expressly commanded of God when times "be ordinary." If, however, the time is extraordinary, one "must be ruled" by the "occasion," and accept that one "cannot likely do too much" to help the less fortunate, especially if one is able, at the same time, to provide comfortably for one's family. As Winthrop clarifies toward the end of section two, in a "community of peril," when one's immediate community is racked with want, the Christian must let his "own interest . . . stand aside" and act "with more enlargement towards others and less respect towards ourselves, and our own right" (¶¶ 18, 19). This is the first, and last, explicit mention of a personal right in the entire speech.

The second obligation associated with the rule of mercy is "lending" (¶ 14). Here Winthrop explains that before any economic transaction, if it appears that a person will not be able to repay, there is a duty to "*give* him according to his necessity*" as opposed to "*lend[ing]* him as he requires" (emphasis added). If the borrower's ability to repay looks only "probable" or "possible," then one is to go ahead and lend the needed sum even "though there be danger of losing it." However, if it is clear that the borrower "hath present means" to repay, Winthrop forbids the lender ("thou art not to") from treating the borrower as an "object of thy mercy." Rather lender and borrower are to enter into a commercial agreement and "walk by the rule of Justice."

This theme reemerges one more time in Winthrop's brief discussion of "forgiving," the third obligation he sees stemming from mercy. For Winthrop, the whole issue of forgiveness turns upon whether one gives money to someone "in mercy" or "by way of Commerce" (¶ 17). The latter dictates that the rule of justice should prevail. As Winthrop summarizes, if the borrower does not have the ability to repay his loans come payment time, those loans must be forgiven, "except in a case where thou hast a surety of a lawful pledge."

Again and again, Winthrop encourages his listeners to practice mercy—in all of its forms—more readily, even "cheerfully" (¶ 15). Yet at virtually every turn, he also firmly asserts that mercy cannot constantly be allowed to run roughshod over justice, which establishes a necessary degree of social order through commercial agreement and law. A community void of social order is neither a community nor a very humane place to live. Winthrop, like Plato's Cephalus in the *Republic*, seems to reduce justice to the repayment of debt. But even if justice is only that which Winthrop defines here so narrowly, it appears a critical component of any human community. A land of all mercy and no justice is a land of political and moral free-for-all, a situation that, in the end, is not likely to protect the most vulnerable members of a society. Thus justice retains a place—an important place even—alongside mercy in a community with *agapic* aspirations. Justice, though nearly the opposite of mercy in some conventional usages of the term, is, like mercy, often called for by charity—the form of the virtues.

With respect to the kind of mercy due a community in peril—the real focus of this section of the address—Winthrop's words proved more than pure rhetoric. A sizeable amount of historical scholarship now reveals that on Winthrop's watch considerable care was rendered to the poor. Of course, the New World's abundance of land made it so that virtually any able-bodied person could adequately sustain himself and his family. But it was largely an infertile wilderness, and for those who found themselves unable to support themselves, an impressive mix of public and private support was provided even when the entire colony was highly impoverished. As noted in a recent history of public housing in America, early Massachusetts, inspired in part by Winthrop's vision, found that when it came to poor relief, the "central question was not whether to accept the obligation, but to decide who should receive aid."[25]

Max Weber has explained, in one of the more influential sociological essays of the last century, that America's "spirit of capitalism" finds its roots even more in the religious zeitgeist of early Boston than the commercial zeitgeist of, say, Jamestown. True enough, the early New Englanders were spurred to industry by the hope that wealth earned would prove grace received, but again and again they spoke and acted against a completely unregulated pursuit of individual "pleasure, and profits" (¶ 45). At times, Winthrop's Massachusetts established wage and price controls to stem the kind of gouging that erupted during uneven patterns of migration and shipping. And all towns took local responsibility for rescuing and rehabilitating those who suffered from Indian attacks, disease, and death of the male breadwinner.[26]

Winthrop himself proved especially generous with his own energies and substance. In those first few years, despite his high station, of which he remained ever conscious, he was noted for wearing plain apparel and for working with his hands side by side with his servants and the rest of the colonists, setting an example such that there was in the eyes of one report "not an idle person to be found in the whole plantation." When a local minister died, he took the minister's son into his home as a foster child. After the colony's first harsh winter when roughly two hundred settlers died and promised funding from England vanished upon the news, Winthrop drew upon his own modest fortune to help sustain the colony. Cotton Mather reports that in February of that first winter, when Winthrop was "distributing the last handful of 'the meal in the barrel' unto a poor man distressed by the wolf at the door, at that instant they spied a ship arrived at the harbor's mouth laden with provisions for them all." It is for these and other acts that Mather dubbed Winthrop the "Joseph unto whom the whole body of the people repaired when their corn failed them."[27]

Mather's brief biographical sketch of Winthrop—which Sacvan Bercovitch shows is better history than is often granted, arguing that it is used by Mather with great effect to make Winthrop the archetypal "American saint"—reports that Winthrop's "cure" for a poor man seen pilfering wood one long, hard winter was to invite the man to take wood from Winthrop's pile when he needed it, so that the man was no longer stealing. And it was apparently Winthrop's "custom" to send a family member on a trumped-up errand to the house of a poor person around mealtime to see if they were in want and, if so, to send supplies. By 1641, Winthrop's constant generosity combined with the even more financially damaging effects of the gross mishandling of his estate by steward James Luxford transformed this once wealthy "Lord of the Manor" into a rather impoverished debtor, putting him in both political and legal jeopardy. This is to say nothing of the great personal loss his move to New England cost him—including the deaths of roughly a dozen people in his "household," three of them his own children.[28]

It may be that at several points in his life Winthrop took comfort from his own words that close out this second section of the speech, where he cites church history and scripture to argue that those who are "most bountiful to the poor" are "highly Commended to posterity" and blessed with the "sweetest promises." Their light shall "break forth as the morning," their health "shall grow speedily," and God will guide them "continually," making them like "a watered Garden" (¶ 19). Contrariwise, those who shut their ears from the "cry of the poor" fall under the "most heavy curses" and "shall cry and not be heard by God." Such themes appear again in the fourth and final section with an even more fevered pitch. The point here is that both Winthrop's imagery and his own practice were fixated on "the liberal and cheerful practice" of actively caring for those most in need.

"The Affection from Which This Exercise of Mercy Must Arise"

Winthrop begins this third section by indicating that the best way to draw men to works of mercy is "not by force of argument." (¶ 20) To make his point, Winthrop compares the operations of charity with those of a mechanical clock. One way to make a clock chime is to manually strike the hammer. But this is hardly useful—better to have a clock that can consistently chime on its own. To achieve this, one must properly set the "first mover of the main wheel." In terms of producing outward manifestations of charity, the problem with rational argument is that while it might temporarily produce works of mercy, like the hammer of a clock, it cannot create and sustain *feelings* of charity, a necessary precondition for making the "practice of mercy constant and easy" (¶ 29). The latter requires setting the main wheel of human action—meaning the "soul." If the soul is set right, then "affections of love in the heart" will be framed so as to "prompt upon all occasions" the requisite works of mercy.

C. S. Lewis, for one, went to some lengths to argue that "affection," which he considered the "humblest and most widely diffused" form of love, should not be confused with *agape*. Winthrop does not appear to be making the mistake of which Lewis would later warn, that is, taking a condition of love some people call affection—in Lewis's eyes a kind of common, natural, not-too-demanding "warm comfortableness" between decent people in shared communities—and conflating it with the "Divine Gift-love" of Christian understanding whereby man can and ought to love even the most different, distant, and wretchedly unlovable characters. Rather, Winthrop holds that deeply affectionate feelings—in the fraternal rather than romantic sense—for all other human beings is a by-product and obligation of one genuinely infused with charity. And neither C. S. Lewis, nor the apostle Paul for that matter, would dispute this (Rom. 12:9–10).[29]

Winthrop's particular formulation of Christian love as being defined by a profoundly caring "affection" for other human beings is something he may have just come up with from his own careful and thoughtful reading of the New Testament. More likely though, Winthrop's thinking was influenced by Thomas Wilson's *Christian Dictionary*, a bestselling book originally published in 1612 that was widely regarded in Protestant reform circles in England and America. Wilson's entry on "charity" reads: "that *affection* of love which moves us to hold our neighbors dear, and to desire and seek their good in everything which is dear unto them, and that for Christ and his sake, according to the will of God."[30] It is interesting how this particular phrasing not only closely mirrors Winthrop's 1630 discussion of the term, but also Jonathan Edwards's later eighteenth-century definition of *caritas*—discussed in the prologue—as "that disposition of affection whereby one is dear to another." It is also quite likely Winthrop was familiar with the writings of "Roaring John" Rogers, a popular Puritan divine from neighboring Essex County who in 1629 published a lengthy tract on *agape* called "A Treatise of Love," wherein he affirms Christians must love each other as "brethren" and that "to love as Brethren is this; to have brotherly affections each to other inwardly and to declare the same outwardly by brotherly actions."[31]

All of this noted, Winthrop suggests that to set the soul right so as to produce the right and regular kind of feelings of love, or affection, requires something more than rational argument. Exactly what is required is found in the heart of this section—the heart of the address really—where Winthrop discusses "how this love comes to be wrought" (¶ 30). Winthrop begins here with a view of Adam, who in Eden was the "perfect model" of all mankind, one in whom "this love was perfected." Winthrop explains, though, that by partaking of the forbidden fruit, Adam "[r]ent himself from his creator, [and] rent all his posterity also one from another." Consequently, Winthrop asserts, "every man is born with this principle in him, to love and seek himself only." Utterly selfish and isolated, fallen man stands in stark contradistinction to Edenic Adam, an anthropomorphic model of Christian charity. Charity is thus minimally distinguished as a principle opposite that of intense human selfishness. As Winthrop puts it, fallen man simply operates according to the principle of exclusive, overweening self-interest ("thus a man continueth") until "Christ comes and takes possession of the soul, and infuseth another principle." That other principle, Winthrop declares, is "love to God and our brother," or *caritas*. This is the speech's clearest, most succinct confirmation that Winthrop sees charity in the way it was basically defined in the prologue of this book: a single principle that firmly embraces both a love of other people and a love of God. But this part of the speech also emphasizes something concerning charity too much neglected in the discussion thus far, and that is that in man's fallen condition, while charity calls for man to love God and others, such love is only truly and fully possible by God's first loving man.

To put this in grammatical terms, the love of God in a subject-genitive sense (God's love of man) is foundational to the love of God in an object-genitive sense (man's love of God).[32] In Winthropian terms, it is not until Christ who "loves the creature" (¶ 31) comes and gets "predominancy in the soul" that the self-absorbed creature rent from God and man can expel his natural condition of complete selfishness for a new condition of "love to God and our brother" (¶ 30). For emphasis, Winthrop takes his listeners to 1 John 4, noting that "[l]ove cometh of God and everyone that loveth is born of God, so that this love is the fruit of the new birth, and none can have it but the new Creature." He might well have included verse 19, which reads, "We love him because he loved us first" (1 John 4:19, Geneva Bible, edition 1602).

By such reasoning, charity indeed stands as a "metavalue," for one appears incapable of even recognizing let alone addressing the mortal needs of others—whether those needs require acts of mercy, justice, friendship, or love—except as that person has first been changed by God's love. But this does not mean, even for Winthrop, that acts of love are the exclusive domain of God's manifestly elect. First, determining those that were or were not elect was always an uncertain thing for Puritans who, in good Calvinist fashion, saw God's will in such matters as above perfect human grasp. At best, the story of their lives carefully recorded in extensive journals (Winthrop's being one of the most extensive) or detailed accounts of a life "converted" (accounts eventually required for Church membership in New England) could only indicate the likelihood of their elect status before God. In fact, God could be working through any of them at any time without their knowledge. Winthrop did not make the point, although he could have, that when Christ was pressed to elaborate on the meaning of charity's command to love your neighbor as yourself, he showcased neither a Christian nor a Jew, but the actions of a Samaritan. Unwashed and unclean, so to speak, it was this figure that Jesus held up as reflecting a more genuinely charitable soul than so many of his day steeped in biblical tradition and law who gave the appearance of being "chosen."

Furthermore, Winthrop stresses that the process of spiritual regeneration is just that, a process, and often a slow one. As Winthrop says, it is typically by "little and little" that charity comes to replace man's natural state of selfishness (¶ 30). Besides strengthening the view that God's grace could well be at work among those of different faiths, or no faith at all, this notion also helps to reconcile what so far would appear a substantial contradiction in Winthrop delivering this sermon.

If Winthrop is right that rational argument is of limited value in producing charitable character, why does he expend such energy on an elaborately reasoned defense of Christian charity as the essential obligation of this community? (In the first four paragraphs, the word "reason" appears as many times.) Winthrop supplies the answer himself in the very last line of section three by indirectly acknowledging that while God's loving grace trumps reasoned argument for effecting godly conversion and steady ethical behavior, reasoned understanding often serves as an important instrument of God's grace. As Winthrop concludes section three, he admonishes his listeners that "the full and certain knowledge of these truths" concerning charity (here Winthrop explicitly calls attention to the famous Pauline discourse on charity in 1 Corinthians 13) must "work upon their hearts, by prayer, meditation, continual exercise . . . *till* Christ be formed in them and they in him, all in each other knit together by this bond of love" (emphasis added). Here again Winthrop suggests that the process of regeneration does not storm the soul all at once, but it is a more gradual process, and until Christ is fully formed in man and man in Christ, man must continue to ruminate, think, reflect—in short, man must reason—on the truths and knowledge God has given concerning *agape*.[33]

It is for this, and related purposes, that Winthrop himself takes a leading role in establishing a far-reaching program of public and private education even during the colony's earliest and most challenging years. In his journal, he records that a formal effort to establish a grammar school gets under way in Boston in 1635, proudly adding that "Indian children were to be taught freely." Other towns soon followed suit. This is also the same year the original town of Newtown was renamed "Cambridge," in honor of the fabled English university where a disproportionately large number of the early leaders of Boston had been educated, and in anticipation of its serving as home to a modest new college that would soon be called Harvard. Winthrop was one of the original eight overseers of that institution. By 1647, nearly the last year of Winthrop's life and rule of Massachusetts, the General Court—the colony's main legislative body—required that every town of fifty or more hire a reading and writing instructor, and towns with more than a hundred residents have a grammar school. Records are spotty enough that we do not know for sure, but most experts put Massachusetts's rates of reading literacy somewhere around 70 to 80 percent, which is significantly higher than English reading rates of the day, and not so far below Boston's 90 percent general literacy rate of today (writing literacy was quite a bit lower in early Boston).[34]

Section three ends almost word for word where it opened, with a vision of a "bond of perfection" made possible when "Christ comes and by his spirit and love knits all these parts to himself and each other" (¶ 21). When this is achieved, when the process of regeneration described here in section three is complete, a soul so infused with Christ and his principle of charity will see in others who are similarly infused "his own image and resemblance in another, and therefore cannot but love him as he loves himself" (¶ 31). In section one, Winthrop explains that bonds of affection will arise out of the fact that because of socioeconomic differences "every man might have need of other" (¶ 4). Again, nowhere does Winthrop lead us to believe that his vision anticipates a sweeping eradication of all social differences. Significant differences will remain, thus significant spiritual and physical needs will remain, drawing men toward one another for purposes of individual utility—earthly and heavenly. But here in section three, Winthrop argues more vigorously what was barely explicit in section one, that difference and utility alone are not enough to spark genuine love, concern, and communal unity. In fact, difference alone significantly undermines love. As Winthrop puts it, the "ground" of "disaffection" is a "dissimilitude . . . arising from the contrary or different nature of things," whereas the most powerful "ground of love is an apprehension of some resemblance" (¶ 31). And when that sense of human sameness is rooted in the very image of God, it would appear to create an incomparably "sweet" condition of community.

Consider several of the picturesque "patterns" Winthrop suggests the Massachusetts Bay Colony would emulate were it aflame with *agape*.

Christ himself, who "being knit with [his saints] in the bond of love, found such a native sensibleness of our infirmities and sorrows as he willingly yielded himself to the death to ease the infirmities of the rest of his body and so heal their sorrows" (¶ 29).

Numerous figures from Christian history, who demonstrated "sweet Sympathy of affections . . . one towards another, [and were renowned for] their cheerfulness in serving and suffering together, [and for] how liberal they were . . . without grudging and helpful without reproaching and all from hence they had fervent love amongst them" (¶ 29).

Eve, who upon recognition of her beloved (Adam), "desires nearness and familiarity with it. . . . She will not endure that it shall want any good which she can give it. . . . If she hear it groan she is with it presently. If she find it sad and disconsolate she sighs and mourns with it, she hath no joy, as to see her beloved merry and thriving, if she see it wronged, she cannot bear it without passion, she sets not bounds of her affections, nor hath any thought of reward" (¶ 31).

Today—just as in Winthrop's day—there are those who argue that the spirit of true Christian love requires utter self-abnegation, an absolute sacrificial forgetting of self for the good of others. Some of the passages just quoted seem to lean in that direction. But others stress that the famous *agape* commands of Matthew 22 involve loving three distinct parties: God, neighbor, and self (the instruction to love thy neighbor *as thyself* is echoed seven more times in the New Testament—often by Jesus himself). Winthrop sides with those who hold that while charity often involves a considerable denial of self, it does so without utterly extinguishing self-love and hoped-for personal reward.[35] Winthrop goes so far as to say that "it is not possible that love should be bred or upheld without help of requital" (¶ 31). How the selfless love of charity squares with a continuing love of self he never explains, in part because he finds this complex theological debate beside the point: "such is not our cause," he notes. This is because Winthrop is not just discussing *agape* in general, but *agape* broadly shared "among members of the same body," be that the body of the Church (the union of "all true Christians," ¶¶ 23–27), or a marriage (Adam and Eve), family (Ruth and Naomi), or friendship (Jonathan and David). And in such a condition, this "love and affection" are "always under reward," reciprocated between members of the body in "in a most equal and sweet kind of commerce." So sweet and so rewarding, Winthrop exclaims, that "to love and live beloved is the soul's paradise, both here and in heaven."

Even those for whom the distinctly Christian/other-worldly foundation of this unity is a nonstarter can and often do acknowledge that what is produced is an alluring vision of community.

> All the parts of this body being thus united are made so contiguous in a special relation as they must needs partake of each other's strength and infirmity, joy and sorrow, weal and woe. If one member suffers, all suffer with it, if one be in honor, all rejoice with it. . . . This sensibleness and sympathy of each other's conditions will necessarily infuse into each part a native desire and endeavor to strengthen, defend, preserve and comfort each other (¶¶ 26–27).

There are some distinct—perhaps finally crippling—challenges associated with Winthrop's position. But at this point, it is manifestly clear that whatever is going on in this speech, it cannot be understood as a purely and coldly hierarchical defense of the ordinary ways of English civil life.

The social vision—played out in early Massachusetts and especially in the life of John Winthrop himself—is in many respects inspiringly tender and humane. And though such compassion is checked by a pervasive sense of providential inequality and thus stops well short of a call for truly radical economic rearrangements, it utterly repudiates a selfish and inert stance with respect to the poor as well as a spiteful and antagonistic stance with respect to racial, religious, and political difference. Under the charitable bonds of affection that Winthrop urged on his fellow travelers, the general citizenry might be many things, but what it could not be was placidly indifferent to the needs, hopes, and desires of each other and those around them. Christian charity as brought into the civic realm by Winthrop is thus, at once, attentive to claims of mercy and justice. It eschews militarism and conquest without shrinking from a spirited defense of its own. It makes clear-eyed distinctions of when more and less is required of the individual to sustain suffering neighbors. It chastens utopian dreams of attacking all human difference even as it spurs on an active rescue of the poorest of the poor and an impulse for at least fraternity with those sitting outside the more tightly knit bond of charity of citizens similarly committed to the love of man and God.

However compelling such a picture may be, the full payoff for breaking with the English status quo and creating and sustaining such bonds of affection comes through in the fourth and final section of Winthrop's speech, complete with its closing image of Puritan New England as a "City Upon a Hill," one of America's most vivid and lasting metaphors. It is this same passage, though, where we see most clearly the greatest source of trouble for Winthrop's dream of a community of love and the reasons why, finally, America basically rejects Winthrop's model of Christian charity as the solution to the problem of how we ought to live together in civil society.

Notes

1. A note on the only existing contemporary copy of the speech indicates that the speech was given on board the *Arbella* while sailing on the Atlantic, but the accuracy of the note has been seriously called into question by Hugh Dawson, who argues that Winthrop gave the speech in England several weeks before embarking for America. See "Rite of Passage," 219–31, and "Colonial Discourse," 117–48. Bremer also believes that the speech was given on land sometime before departure but emphasizes that the historical evidence is too mixed to make any definitive claim about precisely when and where the speech was delivered, *John Winthrop*, 431–32n9. Edmund Morgan argues for the likelihood that the speech was part of a shipboard sacrament service ("John Winthrop's 'Model'").

2. The copy is currently held by the New-York Historical Society. Neither the cover note, written in one hand, nor the speech copy, written in another, match Winthrop's devilishly decipherable style—though the speech copy is generally accepted as a faithful transcription of Winthrop's remarks. See discussion in Dawson, "Rite of Passage," 220–23.

3. To smooth out the extensive reading of Winthrop's sermon that follows, I have taken the text as found in *Winthrop's Papers* (II: 282–95), modernized all archaic spellings, numbered each paragraph (treating all of Winthrop's stand-alone sentences as a paragraph), and included this as Appendix A. I have not adjusted or modernized Winthrop's punctuation. (In the future, where references to a particular passage in the text are not obvious, I will note the corresponding paragraph of Appendix A.) Here I reveal my agreement with Michael Walzer, who argues convincingly in *The Revolution of the Saints* that failure to modernize spellings leaves Puritan thought "hopelessly distant" and that the minor sacrifice in accuracy in doing so is a negligible price to pay for what is gained in "immediacy and understanding" (ix). Consequently, when I quote Winthrop (and his contemporaries) from any source, archaic spellings will be modernized. And when possible, quotations from *Winthrop's Journal* (a separate work from *Winthrop's Papers*) will be taken from the *abridged* version, where the editors Richard Dunn and Laetitia Yeandle have already modernized spellings, among other things (see discussion of their method on pages xxi–xxii).

4. A few lines later Winthrop's phrasing strikes an even closer and direct contrast with the Declaration when he asserts, "All men being thus (by divine providence) ranked into two sorts, rich and poor" (¶ 4). Anderson, *A House Undivided*, 10; Morgan, "John Winthrop's 'Model,'" 145, emphasis added.

5. Issued by the Church of England in 1562, the document was read regularly throughout the realm until the mid-1600s and says, in part, "some are in high degree, some in low, some kings, and princes, some inferiors and subjects, priests and laymen, masters and servants, fathers and children, husband and wives, rich and poor, and every one have need of other," as quoted in Rutman, *Winthrop's Decision for America*, 56.

6. "Wilderness" statement as quoted in Miller, *New England Mind*, 422. On the perils of introducing new orders, see Machiavelli, *The Prince*, 23; and Morgan, "John Winthrop's 'Model,'" 145–46. Virginia mortality rates and warnings of civil revolt are found in Bremer, *John Winthrop*, 155. For details on the fleet of 1630, see Banks, *Winthrop's Fleet*, 46–47.

7. Colacurcio, "The Woman's Own Choice," 134.

8. Rawls, *Theory of Justice*, 311; Sumner, *What Social Classes Owe*, 11, 144.

9. Kierkegaard, *Works of Love*, 96.

10. In 1624, long before thoughts of emigration, Winthrop coauthored a list of grievances intended to trigger the Parliament of James I into legislative reform. In "Grievance 10" Winthrop complained that the Church's system of assistance was being abused (because too far removed to make accurate assessment of need) and that this abuse had "cut the throat of charity amongst all men." People had stopped giving because their donations were being dished out to those who were not "fit to be relieved." See Winthrop, *Winthrop Papers*, 1: 302–3. For the "General Observations for the Plantation of New England," which Winthrop took the lead in authoring, see *Winthrop Papers*, II: 114–22, and related discussion in Rutman, *Winthrop's Decision for America*, 87–90.

11. Winthrop only speaks of the love-thy-neighbor component of *agape* here, making no mention of the love-thy-God component, because the passage is consciously focused on the aspects of *agape* "which concerns our dealings with men." He will go on to show, though, in section three of this speech that the "grounds" of "God's law" are inextricably tied up with man's love of God, as well as God's love of man (¶ 20).

12. In a much earlier draft of this passage, I originally wrote a "meta-ethical principle" but later discovered Timothy Jackson's more economical "meta-value," a term he adopts from the writings of Gerald Doppelt (see Jackson, *Love Disconsoled*, 20n34).

13. Aquinas, *Summa Theologica*, 2–2.Q23.A8, p. 1275.

14. Edwards, *Charity*, 10, 12, emphasis added.

15. Aquinas, *Summa Theologica*, 2–2.Q23.A4, p. 1272.

16. Also see discussion in Hauerwas, "The Politics of Charity," 261–62; and Jackson, *Love Disconsoled*, 142.

17. Foster indicates that this differed not only from "traditional Christian doctrine" in England but also the views of John Calvin, who "emphatically rejected any concept of charity that distinguished between Christians and other men" (Foster,

Their Solitary Way, 44). Foster quotes from Calvin's *The Institutes of the Christian Religion*: "But I say that the whole human race, without exception, are to be embraced with one feeling of charity: there is no distinction of Greek or Barbarian, worthy or unworthy, friend or foe, since all are to be viewed not in themselves, but in God" (see fn 9).

18. Bremer, *John Winthrop*, 312–15; Bremer, *Puritan Experiment*, 205–6; Winthrop, *Journal—Abridged*, 184. See Vaughan, *Roots of American Racism*, for discussion of slavery and racial views in early Virginia and the Caribbean.

19. To the contrary, Francis Bremer indicates that if anything, these early Puritans were initially given to the belief that these Indians were "descendents of the lost tribes of the Jews," as quoted in Bremer, *Puritan Experiment*, 199–201.

20. Proselytizing the Indians did figure prominently in the thinking of Winthrop and others in their decision for America, though there was a broad consensus that such should be done with great respect and "benevolence." As it was, Puritan congregationalism proved a poor support for a coordinated missionary program, so proselytizing activity remained minimal in New England. Winthrop, *Journal—Abridged*, 37–42; Moseley, *John Winthrop's World*, 52; Pulsipher, *Subjects*, 15–21.

21. "Destroyers of men" is noted in Vaughan, "Puritan Justice," 333. Jenny Pulsipher masterfully describes the complex change in Indian-English relations after the Pequot War. The Indians soon channeled their subservience toward the king to get leverage with the increasingly powerful Massachusetts Bay Colony, which still honored many practices of English law and fairness with the Indians, but not always, and when it did, it did so often with the assumption of sovereign authority over them—see her *Subjects*, chapter one.

22. Winthrop, *Journal—Abridged*, 22, 15–16.

23. For relevant accounts of the Pequot War, see Bremer, *John Winthrop*, 261–73; Alfred Cave, *The Pequot War*, esp. 69–97. After the war, Connecticut wanted to exact additional retribution on the Wongunks. This tribe greatly intensified the war by aligning with the Pequots for a ruthless massacre—two hundred Indians swooped down and killed nine colonists (six men and three women) working in a Connecticut meadow—as retaliation for their leader Sequin being forced out of an area to which he felt he had claim. Winthrop, now again governor, quickly assembled available Massachusetts leaders to consider the matter and in so doing forged a consensus that while Sequin's response mismatched the offense, he had indeed suffered a miscarriage of justice and had been offered no satisfactory recourse to address the matter, and thus Connecticut would do best to let the matter go. Though they were not obligated to, Connecticut followed the more peaceable inclinations of its Massachusetts neighbors now back under the rule of Winthrop. Alden Vaughan notes that this is an isolated instance but that if Winthrop and his fellow magistrates could decide in favor of an Indian who acted so ruthlessly, they must have had a real capacity for impartial justice. Vaughan also notes that in this case and in another famous incident around this time (the "Peach case"), Winthrop in particular prodded his fellow Puritans toward outcomes more favorable to the Indian position. Vaughan, *Puritan Justice*, 334–39, Vaughan, *Roots of American Racism*, 205–10.

24. Bremer, *John Winthrop*, 57; Morgan, *Puritan Dilemma*, 102–18. A significant source of Williams's devotion to Winthrop stems from the fact that Winthrop tipped

Williams off to the plan of Winthrop's fellow magistrates to forcibly return Williams to England—a punishment Winthrop found too extreme. After his escape, Williams regularly sent letters to Winthrop that are filled with an admiration that borders on adulation. For a nice sampling of Williams's letters to Winthrop, see Williams, *Old South Leaflets*, vol. III, no. 54.

25. Vale, *From the Puritans to the Projects*.

26. See Foster's chapter "Poverty: Affliction, Poor Relief, and Charity" as found in *Their Solitary Way*; Rutman's chapter "The Well Ordering of the Town" in *Winthrop's Boston* (esp. pages 217–20); all of Christine Leigh Heyrman's unpublished dissertation, "'A Model of Christian Charity': The Rich and the Poor in New England, 1630–1730," and Peter Richard Virgadamo's chapter "Charity in the New Jerusalem, 1630–1660" in his unpublished dissertation "Colonial Charity and the American Character: Boston, 1630–1775"; Vale, *From the Puritans to the Projects*, all of chapter one, see 22 for direct quote; Weber, *Protestant Ethic*; Bremer, *Puritan Experiment*, 93.

27. "Not an idle person" as quoted in Bremer, *John Winthrop*, 194; Mather, as found in Bercovitch, *Puritan Origins*, 192.

28. Bercovitch, *Puritan Origins*, 1–4, and "Life of John Winthrop" as found in 187–205; Bremer, *John Winthrop*, 187–95. Winthrop lost his sons Henry, who drowned just after arriving in New England a few days behind Winthrop but before getting a chance to greet his father, and Forth, who died in England, having stayed at home with Winthrop's pregnant wife who was coming later, and a daughter, Anne, whom his wife was carrying and delivered but died a week into the voyage.

29. Lewis, *Four Loves*, 31–56, 128.

30. Emphasis added. Wilson's dictionary is available at http://eebo.chadwyck .com/home. For the dictionary's general influence and popularity in Protestant circles, see Green, *Print and Protestantism*, 6, 25, 129–31, 671. Michael Paulick's online essay for the New England Historic Genealogical Society (http://www.newengland ancestors.org/publications/NEA//7-1_012_Mayflower.asp) shows that the book was known and used by Winthrop's Plymouth neighbors to the south, which with Green's analysis makes (1) Winthrop's familiarity with the work most likely, and (2) the work as an important if indirect influence on Winthrop a virtual certainty.

31. Rogers, *A Treatise of Love*. London, 1629. Available at http://eebo.chadwyck .com/home.

32. Jackson, *Love Disconsoled*, esp. 175.

33. For a thorough discussion of the Puritan view of how God uses sermons as "means" for converting his saints "by an influence of grace and yet also by a rational enlightenment" see Miller, *New England Mind*, 288.

34. Winthrop, *Journal—Unabridged*, 569. See discussion in Bremer, *John Winthrop*, 310–11, and chapter four of Amory and Hall, *Colonial Book*. Thomas Goddard Wright describes the level of education in early Massachusetts as "unique in the history of colonization," also pointing out that Massachusetts boasted far more university men than its Plymouth counterpart; see *Literary Culture*, 15–24. Also see Samuel Elliot Morison, *Intellectual Life*, 82–84—his thought that literacy rates were generally highest in seaports and earliest settled towns (Boston was both) gives reason to believe that reading literacy specifically in Winthrop's Boston, rather than

Massachusetts or New England in general, might even come closer to Boston rates of today. According to the Massachusetts Department of Education, 91 percent of adults over eighteen register above "limited English proficiency." See the Massachusetts Department of Education, "MFLC Community Profiles," *Boston*, 2002.

35. For the view that an extreme, even masochistic sense of self-abnegation is the potential fruit of Christian love, see Simone Weil, *Gravity and Grace*. Thanks to Timothy Jackson for the observation that the command to love neighbor as self occurs eight times in the New Testament, with Jesus himself "frequently endorsing the idea" (*Love Disconsoled*, 7). Jackson also offers a particularly thoughtful discussion of the self-love/self-abnegation challenge of charity (72–91), culminating in this statement worth noting here. "Christianity preaches patient self-abnegation, then, but this is paradoxically Good News for both individuals and groups. . . . Attention to others rather than assertion of self is the manifest rule of faith, yet precisely by so 'losing' the self, one 'finds' it. However painful or costly obedience to God and service to neighbor may be—and they will be both—there is no final contradiction between them and genuine love of self. 'Impersonal' virtue goes hand in hand with 'personal' fulfillment, though not necessarily with worldly prosperity or private happiness," 89–90.

Two Cities upon a Hill

Winthrop begins the last section of his "Model" speech by making "some application" of the previous material to present circumstances (¶ 37). He has four things in mind: a discussion of (1) the "persons" involved, (2) the "work" they are facing, (3) the "end" of that work, and (4) the "means" for accomplishing such. In this final section, the more attractive elements of Winthrop's model of *caritas* emerge with such rhetorical force that we still quote the speech today. At the same time, this section reveals the grounds for certain Puritan practices to which none of us would wish to return.

The "Persons"

Winthrop indicates that he and his listeners constitute "a Company professing ourselves fellow members of Christ" (¶ 38). Resounding here the dominant theme of the address, Winthrop concludes that therefore they "ought to account [themselves] knit together by this bond of love, and live in the exercise of it." Use of the term "company" is a reminder that Winthrop and his audience were part of the Massachusetts Bay Company, a trading enterprise as much as a means of refuge for Puritans escaping English corruption. But if some were making the move for reasons more financial than spiritual, Winthrop had good reason to believe that most of his listeners held some "comfort of our being in Christ."[1] Thus, for Winthrop, a communal condition of *caritas*, of living together in a "bond of love," was meant both as description and prescription. The company's effective religious unity at the moment of Winthrop's speech justified hopes that a substantial state of charity would be immediately visible. However, Winthrop's previously noted conviction that God's grace typically works "little by little" meant that charity's full and pure instantiation was still a future goal. Charity was thus to be practiced instantly and communally cultivated over time.[2]

The "Work" and "End"

Winthrop's thoughts on "the work we have in hand" come as a startling reminder at this point that his speech is the voice of a layman founding a body politic. The task before them, he says, is to "seek out a place of Cohabitation . . . under a due form of Government both civil and ecclesiastical" (¶ 39). Even a model of Christian charity requires a physical geography and something more than just church law and organization, or so Winthrop asserts. Given that everything Winthrop has said about charity thus far was said with the work of founding a new civil government in mind, and that this government he goes on to establish so profoundly influenced later American practices and institutions, a sketch of early Massachusetts government and Winthrop's leadership thereof is warranted.

A Theocratic Separation of Church and State

Winthrop's Massachusetts had no qualms about establishing religion, openly aiming in many cases to set civil and criminal law according to scriptural teachings. When studying Puritan public life, one seems to inhale, as Tocqueville suggests, a "biblical perfume" everywhere. Colonial voting was limited to male church members only, and by 1636 most congregations were requiring a formal and convincing account of true conversion in order to join. Furthermore, the only churches that could officially gather were those approved by the civil government. Nonmembers were required to attend church (though most went willingly anyway) and, when necessary, help financially support the ministry. Any citizen speaking with contempt against the ministry could be whipped.[3]

Much of this is explained by the "end" of the colony's "work." The end to which both the work of setting up church and human government must aim is, Winthrop states, to "improve our lives" (¶ 40). Winthrop specifies that this improvement means basically three things: engaging in "service to the Lord," rendering "comfort" to other members of the body of Christ, and "work[ing] out [their] salvation under the power and purity of [God's] Holy Ordinances." In short, the aim was to care about God and neighbor as they cared about their own souls. In a word, the aim was charity. The government, like the church and reasoned preaching, was to be a critical handmaiden of grace, creating conditions conducive to a constant walk of godly love.

To this extent, then, Winthrop's Massachusetts was a working theocracy—self-proclaimed as such by the likes of John Cotton and indicted as such by the likes of Roger Williams.[4] But a brief comparison with England showcases the limits of this stock historical label, for England, though less theocratic in some ways, suffered in other ways from a much tighter fusion of civil and ecclesiastical power. Not so widely bent on achieving the kind of religious utopia that was the aim of Massachusetts, England's monarch was nevertheless head of the country and of the church, Anglican bishops played an active and prominent role in parliamentary politics (when Parliament was allowed to be in session), and ecclesiastical courts infamously roamed beyond religious concerns in their adjudication of parish life, making things particularly difficult and dangerous for Puritan believers.

The memory and still looming threat of Anglican persecution, as well as their unique theology, drove the Puritans to reverse the English model. Where the Puritans would actively seek a much greater integration of religious principles and public policy, they would do so with a much more strict separation of the formal entities of church and state. Still deeply influenced by Calvin, they saw the world split into two kingdoms ordained to work together in the service of God but as separate entities. For the spiritual kingdom, God granted ecclesiastical authority to govern church affairs alone, and with very limited powers of coercion. For the temporal kingdom, God granted civil authority to govern state affairs alone, with more expansive powers of coercion. Such distinctions were fundamental.[5] In the Puritan view, the lack of separation in England had corrupted both the church and the state. In 1605 William Bradshaw summed up well the view taken to America:

> that no Ecclesiastical Minister ought to exercise or accept of any Civil public jurisdiction and authority, but ought to be wholly employed in spiritual Offices and duties to that Congregation over which he is set. And that those Civil Magistrates weaken their own Supremacy that shall suffer any Ecclesiastical Pastor to exercise any civil jurisdiction within their Realms."[6]

Of course, it was never as clear-cut as all that in Massachusetts. Ministers gave "election sermons" every year to inspire their parishioners to good and wise choices for magistrate and were often informally consulted on tough issues facing the colony. But for the most part, Winthrop and his counterparts held faithfully to this position. Church discipline could not impose corporeal or civil punishment. Not a single clergyman held office even though no actual law forbade the practice. Things that were managed by ecclesiastical courts in England like wills, divorces, and marriage ceremonies were managed in Massachusetts exclusively by the civil government (even at marriages ministers were at most allowed to offer some brief words of counsel). No ecclesiastical courts even existed in New England. Both sides (church and state) generally respected the autonomy of the other and each guarded its own spheres of responsibility tenaciously. Winthrop regularly pushed for—with some success—the position that civil leaders could not be punished by their respective congregations for action taken as a magistrate. The ministers vigorously and successfully opposed Winthrop when he became concerned that a proliferation of religious lectures meant that too many poor people were attending too many meetings to the neglect of their personal affairs and therefore moved for a law that would limit the length and number of non-Sunday sermons (a reminder here that Winthrop's model of charity would not be an excuse to indolence—welfare relief must ever be consistent with temporal diligence). Ministerial opposition was explicitly predicated on the basis that Winthrop's move "might enthrall them to the civil power," emphasizing that "liberty for the ordinances was the main end professed of [their] coming hither."[7]

With such practices and attitudes so centrally ingrained it must be recognized that this "theocracy" under the leadership of Winthrop embodied a strong and formal separation of church and state that did not exist in England, or anywhere else for that matter. It is also of note that it is Winthrop's Massachusetts that first attracts, then peacefully expels, Roger Williams, whose determination to establish in Rhode Island a "hedge or wall of separation between the garden of the church and the wilderness of the world" even more closely prefigured the church-state position of Jefferson a century and a half later.[8]

A Strong and Wise Executive

Winthrop's philosophy of rule was significantly influenced by his training in, practice of, and admiration for the English common law. While this tradition takes seriously the rule of law, it leaves considerable room for law to develop through the accumulated wisdom of precedent and appreciation of a particular situation, instead of demanding some kind of detailed, *a priori* codification of right and wrong for all possible situations. Devotion to common law ideals sometimes took a toll on Winthrop's popularity with other colonists who regularly pressured him to create more advanced transparency in, and to keep a stricter adherence to, established law. His political enemies (and he had them, indicating that even in his immediate circles Massachusetts never fully became the idyllic model of charity he envisioned) saw his failure to do these things as evidence of an improper authoritarianism on his part. In fact, Winthrop's famous "Little Speech" on liberty was given on the occasion of his impeachment trial in the General Court for allegedly overstepping the bounds of his office by intervening in a militia election dispute in Hingham without the express warrant of law to do so. Winthrop argued in his own defense that because the General Court, which had jurisdiction, was not in session and that peace and order were being threatened, it was necessary for him to act quickly and independently. Winthrop was cleared of the charges and, upon his request, was granted the privilege of addressing the gathered assembly. His statement, less than a thousand words, again affirms his acceptance of rigid distinctions between rulers and ruled, though—and this often goes less noticed—it also reveals an epistemological position not often associated with the character of Puritan America, one that significantly endeared him to many of his colonists.

The core of Winthrop's message begins with his assertion that the "great questions" of the day revolved around the nature of the magistrates' authority and the people's liberty. While the people have called the magistrates into office by colonial election, Winthrop claims "we have our authority from God" and notes that "contempt" for this authority invites "divine vengeance." Though working through a human electoral process, God invests elected civic leaders by decree, or "ordinance," with the wisdom and authority necessary to rule. As for liberty, the liberty of Massachusetts was not "natural" liberty to do whatever man sees is "good in [his] own eyes," which was nothing more than a freedom fallen man enjoyed "with beasts and other creatures." In Massachusetts, theirs was a "civil" (or "moral") liberty "to that only which, is good, just and honest." Where "natural" liberty was inimical to authority, "civil"

liberty absolutely depends upon authority. Thus, Winthrop tells his listeners, if they accepted these things they must "quietly and cheerfully
submit unto that authority which is set over [them] . . . for [their] good."
Nowhere in the New England canon can there be found such a grand
and succinct statement of Puritanism's political authoritarianism.[9]

That Winthrop was acquitted and was consistently reelected governor during the final years of his life is a testimonial that most did accept
the thrust of his argument, and also that his friends were greater than
his enemies. Part of the reason he had so many friends is that Winthrop's authoritarianism was tempered by a countervailing impulse that
can be observed in this episode. Though often decisive and strong in
areas where no specific legal ruling existed or the law was vague—and
wanting always to be free to do so—Winthrop was in general less sure
than were many of his contemporaries about how God's word should be
translated into hard political practice. He basically confesses such in
the Little Speech. As he explains to his listeners, magistrates are oath-
bound to "govern you and judge your causes by the rules of God's law
and our own, *according to our best skill*" (emphasis added). Not even the
stated rules of "God's law and our own" produce clear directions for
leaders to follow at all times. Consequently, rulers must be given leeway
to adapt general principles and accepted practices to new and ever-
changing circumstances. Moreover, citizens must be ever patient with
magistrates who will undoubtedly manifest "failings" and "infirmities"
in their public judgments, for no man has "sufficient skill" to be an
unerring magistrate.[10]

What Winthrop's famous defense of Puritan authority sometimes
masks is that despite his self-confidence and his fast and abiding faith in
the Bible and the Holy Spirit as moral and political compasses, Winthrop lacked a sweeping sense of certainty about what policies and punishments were appropriate for any given moment. His position would
seem to reflect a conscious Calvinistic appreciation for the limits of any
postlapsarian man's ability to fully fathom and execute the things of
God. It also reflects what is perhaps a less conscious but strong Aristote-
lian appreciation that the complexities of social life and moral truth
demand that wise and practically experienced statesmanship supply
what the simple enforcement of revealed scripture and human legal code
cannot: an imperfect but acceptable day-to-day reconciliation of competing moral claims at work in concrete situations.[11] While this degree
of politico-moral uncertainty left him reticent to codify things, which in

turn left him freer in the scope of his rule, it also left him more open to counsel and correction from others. Winthrop's "Little Speech" was given on the occasion of an impeachment trial which Winthrop not only freely submitted to but, to the great horror of his fellow assistants, for which he even stepped down from the magisterial bench to stand in the well of the accused during proceedings. Winthrop's sense of inherent mortal imperfection also made him less quick and punitive in his judgments against fellow colonials.

If anything, Winthrop was more often criticized by hard-liners for being too generous and lenient than he was criticized by the rank and file for being too tyrannical and authoritarian. And here too Winthrop shows a willingness to "learn" from his colleagues who saw things differently. In his journal he records the proceedings of a meeting where a fellow magistrate stood and

> spake of one or two passages wherein he conceived that Mr. Winthrop dealt too remissly in point of justice. To which Mr. Winthrop answered that it was his judgment that in the infancy of plantations justice should be administered with more lenity than in a settled state, because people were then more apt to transgress, partly of ignorance of new laws and order, partly through oppression of business and other straits. But if it might be made clear to him that it was an error, he would be ready to take up a stricter course. Then the ministers were desired to consider of the question by the next morning and to set down a rule in the case. The next morning they delivered their several reasons, which all sorted to this conclusion: that strict discipline both in criminal offences and in martial affairs was more needful in plantation than in a settled state, as tending to the honor and safety of the gospel. Whereupon, Mr. Winthrop acknowledged that he was convinced that he had failed in overmuch lenity and remissness, and would endeavor (by God's assistance) to take more strict course hereafter. Whereupon there was a renewal of love amongst them.[12]

A statement like this goes far in explaining why by the end of his life Winthrop was the most widely adored man of Puritan Boston, appreciated by sinners and saints alike. Winthrop was no pushover. He was strong, capable, and determined to protect and preserve Puritan religious rule—thus earning him the respect of tough-minded peers. But he was also pliable and instinctively kind and generous—thus earning him the trust of errant commoners as well as fellow leaders who might otherwise have felt threatened by his influence. Recall that it is just such a suggestion that Hawthorne seems to be making in *The Scarlet Letter*, when, among other things, he has Winthrop surrounded in his final moments by the adulterous Hester Prynne on one hand and the hardline Rev. Wilson on the other.[13] In other stories, Hawthorne is less suggestive and more explicit concerning the broad admiration that he sensed Winthrop's leadership seemed to engender among early Massachusetts colonists.

In "Main-street," where Hawthorne paints an ugly scene of cruelty carried out by his own progenitor, William Hathorne [*sic*], Winthrop is praised for having a "mild and venerable, though not aged presence,—a propriety, an equilibrium" that makes him attractive. In two other sketches, Hawthorne favorably compares Winthrop with John Endicott (governor during that stern year of 1645 when Hester thought she might lose Pearl). In "Endicott and the Red Cross," Endicott is forced to admit that the "worthy" Governor Winthrop is a "wise man—a wise man, and a meek and moderate" one. And, in "Mrs. Hutchinson," where Endicott is described as one "who would stand with his drawn sword at the gate of Heaven, and resist to the death all pilgrims thither, except they traveled his own path," Winthrop is described as "a man by whom the innocent and the guilty might alike desire to be judged, the first confiding in his integrity and wisdom, the latter hoping in his mildness."[14] Few were more wedded than Winthrop to the divinely ordained authority and repressive religious aim of Puritan political office, but perhaps no one was as benevolent, humble, and judicious in the exercise of such powers—virtues that sprang from his own commitment to Christian love and biblical recognition of every person's mortal imperfection before God.[15]

A Consensual and Constitutional Aristocracy

Even more influential than his leadership in marking off distinct boundaries between church and state, and his example of practical, charitable wisdom in rule—an example admired even by one of this country's most renowned Puritan critics—is Winthrop's contribution to America's culture of democracy.[16] One of his first major moves as governor in Massachusetts was to expand the franchise—something he was free to do because, unlike any other English colonizer, Winthrop had been able to transport the company's royal charter to the New World and run its governing meetings outside of London.[17] According to the royal charter, "freemen" members of the company were to meet four times a year in a "General Court" to pass laws for the company and colony. Once a year, the freemen were to gather and elect a governor, deputy governor, and eighteen "assistants" who together would served as the colony's magistrates and executive council ("Court of Assistants") to enforce the laws and manage affairs between sessions of the General Court. When Winthrop arrived in Massachusetts there were, besides himself, only eight other freemen, which included the deputy governor and seven assistants. Thus this group of nine constituted the Court of Assistants and General Court. Because the charter only specified that the governor, deputy governor, and six assistants must be present at any meeting of the General Court, this group of nine could have continued to exercise sole power over the colony indefinitely. They did not.[18]

In October of 1630, within months of arriving, Winthrop invited the entire colony to attend a meeting of the General Court, where it was decided by a "general vote of the people" to alter the charter so that freemen would choose all assistants, the assistants would then choose the governor and deputy governor (from among the assistants), and the assistants and governors would pass the laws. This effectively consolidated all legislative power into the Court of Assistants rather than the General Court—though, again, the two bodies were for the moment indistinguishable. That was until Winthrop's next move. Neither by requirement nor request, Winthrop next announced that any desiring adult male could apply to become a freeman. At the following General Court, in May of 1631, 116 colonists were admitted as freemen. Despite an added caveat at this meeting that freemen must be good standing members of a congregation, this appears to have included virtually every adult male in the colony, minus indentured servants.[19]

This move instantly gave the average male settler in Massachusetts a basic right to participate in the selection of all of his colonial legislative and executive leaders—a right well beyond anything recognized anywhere else in the world. And this from Winthrop and a group of assistants who were all decidedly aristocratic in outlook, personally ambitious, deeply imbued with a sense of divine mission, an ocean away from civilization and established authority, and holding legal documents that effectively granted them complete political control of the situation. It is hard to imagine a set of cultural ideals, human preferences, and physical circumstances more conducive to establishing a pure oligarchy. Instead, nascent democracy bloomed.

In 1632 Winthrop persuaded his fellow magistrates to go along with the freemen who were pressing to vote for the governor directly. Two years later Winthrop again acquiesced, after some strong initial resistance, to freemen requests that only the General Court be allowed to pass laws (as per the original clause in the royal charter, which the freemen had demanded to see), levy taxes, and admit new freemen. In this same session of the General Court, the freemen further flexed their muscle by failing to return Winthrop to the governor's seat (he had held the office continuously since leaving England)—part punishment for his early resistance to resting legislative power in the General Court and part worry that failure to rotate the highest office every so often might lead to the concentrated power and customary rule of one man. Of course, their ability to do so had been made possible in the first place by Winthrop, who accepted defeat gracefully.

A most striking development began in 1635, when, according to Winthrop's own journal, there was a desire of some to curb the arbitrary rule of magistrates by framing "a body of grounds of laws in resemblance to a Magna Carta . . . [to] be received for fundamental laws."[20] With his noted desire for magisterial flexibility, Winthrop naturally argued against such a move, and he stalled its progress. Eventually, though, it passed in 1641 as the Massachusetts Body of Liberties. And once passed, it became a document Winthrop faithfully enforced when sitting as governor. It lists roughly one hundred "liberties, immunities and privileges" specifically called for by "humanity, civility and Christianity." These include stipulations like punishment can only be inflicted for "published" law, the "same justice and law" applies to all "whether inhabitant or foreigner," military service can be conscripted for "defensive wars" only, and children may officially complain for redress if parents exercise "any unnatural severity towards them." Women were to be free of "bodily correction or stripes" inflicted by husbands. Any "tyranny or cruelty towards any brute creature which are usually kept for man's use" was forbidden. There were rights to leave the colony at any time provided there was no existing legal jeopardy, and to unpaid counsel if "unfit" to plead one's own cause before any court. And finally, consider the remarkable way that democratic voice was empowered in this clause:

> Every man, whether inhabitant or foreigner, free or not free, shall have liberty to come to any public Court, Council or town meeting, and

either by speech or by writing, move any lawful, seasonable and material question, or to present any necessary motion, complaint, petition,
Bill or information. . . .[21]

Throughout this same basic period, the freemen increasingly agitated
for more power against the magistrates, who both sat in the General
Court and controlled the Court of Assistants, which had a veto over any
decision made by the General Court. The freemen eventually turned the
General Court into a representative body ("deputies" were elected to
represent the freemen), which then sat as a body separate of the Court
of Assistants, and no act of either body could be ratified without the
approval of the other. Thus was created, largely on Winthrop's watch
and in no small part due to his original and unprecedented expansion of
the franchise, a ruling, bicameral, legislative body of rudimentary checks
and balances between a larger popular assembly of deputies and smaller
aristocratic assembly of assistants, anchored by a written body of fundamental liberties highly evocative of clauses that would come later in
America's Constitution and Bill of Rights. Also, hoping that a wider
involvement of all male citizens at the most local level would bring
greater legitimization and compliance to town ordinances, it is during
this same time frame that Massachusetts adopted the informal practice
of letting nonfreemen (i.e., non–Church members) vote in town meetings, effectively making it the most democratic entity in the world at the
time.[22]

That Winthrop opposed several of these institutional advances of
democracy says something, but hardly all. Winthrop was no egalitarian,
as the opening to his Model speech affirms. Nor were the freemen or
voting nonfreemen, really. As Stephen Foster puts it, during the seventeenth century the common citizen "entered every political struggle
under the handicap of implicitly accepting the idea of a ruling class."[23]
For years the broad Puritan franchise of this colony consistently elected
and supported a small caste of highly educated upperclass figures. And
these elected magistrates and their clerical counterparts tended to hold
decisive influence on most decisions. It was hardly government by the
people. It was an aristocracy. But when we speak of the Massachusetts
Bay being ruled by an aristocracy we must be careful about what we are
saying.

There was actually a firm consensus in Massachusetts against formally establishing anything like a hereditary political aristocracy based

on bloodlines and bank accounts. While Puritans did seek out men of merit who typically had wealth and came from notable families, their wealth and genealogy played second to concerns of whether these men were deemed righteous and capable. In any case, it was impossible to inherit or lay claim to any public office based on name and economic status alone. Thanks to Winthrop above all, every public office was chosen, directly or indirectly, by the freemen, whose one original qualification to vote was not property ownership but church membership, a qualification which early on covered most adult males and over time was dropped altogether. It is true that Winthrop is on record as condemning democracy as the "meanest and worst of all forms of government . . . always of least continuance and fullest of troubles." But in doing so, he is far from trying to eliminate democracy entirely in favor of an exclusive aristocracy. Rather, he is warning against "mere Democracy" where there is no sense or mechanism for recognizing that some people might be more qualified and wiser for rule than others.[24] Winthrop was convinced some were better fit to rule and therefore had to rule if the polity were to survive and flourish. Yet over and against this imperative was another embedded in Winthrop's thinking, and that was that rulers ruled by the choice and consent of the governed.

On this issue, Winthrop could not have spoken with more clarity—starting with the "Model" speech. In paragraph 39, Winthrop stresses that the work of setting up government is done "by a mutual consent through a special overruling providence." Though God is guiding them, setting up some to rule and others to follow, no power can compel any of them to join and fully sustain a community of love. Years later, Winthrop would again publicly and prominently hold that "consent" is "essential" to setting up commonwealth. "No common weale can be founded," he says at this time, "but by free consent." Furthermore, "no man hath lawful power over another, but by birth or consent." Winthrop's friend Thomas Hooker, an early Massachusetts settler turned founder of Connecticut, preached this notion even more directly, declaring in 1638 that "the foundation of authority is laid, firstly, in the free consent of the people."[25] For Winthrop and others, the state and even the church were ultimately answerable to the people, not vice versa.[26] Sentiments like these constitute just the start of why someone like Tocqueville would later say, "Puritanism was not only a religious doctrine; it also blended at several points with the most absolute democratic and republican theories."[27] Such a line, though, can be misleading, because Winthrop does not appear to rely on noted "democratic and republican theories" in any explicit way.

Even though Winthrop was speaking to a people in (or at least on their way to) a state of nature, who were freely coming together and consenting to accept a certain public authority with its various protections, blessings, and demands, he is not drawing upon familiar sources in philosophical liberalism even if what he says has a certain affinity with them. He is speaking roughly twenty years before Hobbes will publish the *Leviathan* and sixty years before Locke will publish his *Second Treatise*— generally considered the two foundational texts of modernity's natural rights politics of consent. While older Greek and Roman influences, mediated through England's developing republicanism are no doubt implicitly at work in Winthrop's thought here, he goes well beyond any of these traditions in his distinctly progressive commitment to consent. Such a position is thus better explained by the kind of basic human equality before God that Winthrop saw in Christianity in general (even if such equality was cloaked beneath the providential inequality of the mortal order), and the primacy of individual conscience and moral agency still reverberating for him and other reformers from Luther's stand at Worms and the teachings of John Calvin.

Furthermore, Winthrop's doctrine of consent does not lead to a social contract per se—the political end point of Hobbes and Locke. Where Hobbes and Locke presume a world of plain material interest and a dominating fear of violent death in a state of war against all (Hobbes) or of the dangerous and incommodious life in a state of nature (Locke), social contracts are struck between naturally free beings for the sake of individual survival and advantage which can be found only in consented surrender to a strong, central political power. Winthrop is on different metaphysical ground altogether. By presuming always a divine power at work, one that has power to bless and sets over man noble aims sometimes worthy of great individual sacrifice, Winthrop advocates covenants, or freely entered into promises between people and to God, in return for God's sustaining favor. And from Winthrop's particular perspective, it is possible that, given God's call for the noble practice of charity, once a covenant with God has been freely consented to, "the care of the public must oversway all private respects" (¶ 39).

Ironically, Winthrop's communal covenantal approach proved far less tyrannical than at least Hobbes's individual contractual approach in both theory and practice. Under Winthrop's model of charity, neither the people nor their rulers can ever emerge as absolutely sovereign, for they both operate under a set of moral constraints that they neither invented nor can dismiss, and should they fail to honor them, they jeopardize God's protecting care. Hobbes provides no such check and thus his model of proto-liberalism—again coming two decades *after* Winthrop—produces the "Leviathan," that vast and absolute earthly sovereign whose polity shares none of the many liberal, democratic practices that so characterized Puritan Massachusetts. And by the time Locke finally revised Hobbesian social contract thinking, purging it of its most tyrannical aspects, Puritan New England had already emerged from a state of nature with a flourishing civil society intact and had moved into its fourth generation of constitutional self-rule. The practical debt that America as a modern liberal democracy owes Winthropian covenantalism may be no less great than that owed to the great thinkers of natural rights.[28] Further analysis of the way Winthrop seeks to establish a covenant to become a model of Christian love emphasizes the point.

This notion of covenant is so central to Winthrop's framework that he "shut(s) up this discourse" on Christian charity not with the words of Christ but of Moses and his final farewell to the covenant children of Israel who were on the cusp of entering the Promised Land (Deut. 30:15–20) (¶ 45). Addressing his listeners as "Beloved," the first of several apt modifications of Moses's original, Winthrop concludes, "there is now set before us life, and good, and death and evil."[29] Like the children of Israel, Massachusetts is faced with two grand alternatives. The first alternative, which constitutes "goodness and life," is found in keeping the commandment to "love the Lord our God, and to love one another." (By inserting the charity commands that do not appear in the original farewell, Winthrop effectively merges the messages of Moses and Jesus.) By contrast, the second alternative, which constitutes "death and evil," is found in letting their "hearts . . . turn away" from and "not obey" God; it is found in serving "other Gods" and their own individual "pleasures, and profits" as opposed to the cares and concerns of each other.

As he crests into the penultimate line of the address, Winthrop intones, "Therefore let us choose life, that we, and our Seed may live." While Winthrop begins the "Model" address with an assertion of earthly hierarchy and godly providence, he most pronouncedly closes it on the note that charity is fundamentally a matter of human *choice*, one of two grand alternatives. Note the double emphasis on voluntary choice embedded in Winthrop's invitational imperative, "therefore let us choose," as compared with the command imperative in the Mosaic original, "therefore choose."

This closing, therefore, prompts a reconsideration of Winthrop's "Little Speech" on liberty. If, as Winthrop explains in that speech, Massachusetts government is based on a notion of "civil liberty," meaning the freedom to do "that only which is good," it appears that such a liberty is never entirely separated from a concept of and commitment to "natural liberty," or the freedom "to evil as well as to good." At the end of the "Model" speech, people remain free to choose good and evil, not just good. Even if, as Winthrop suggests later in this section, these folks have already "entered into" such a covenant simply by choosing to join the Company on its "errand into the wilderness," he still presents the covenant as a choice.[30] Any of them individually, or all of them collectively, could still reject or opt out of the general covenant he is describing. They were free to turn and head back to England at any practicable point— something many did immediately after arriving in New England. As has already been noted, Massachusetts will later enshrine a constitutional liberty to leave the colony at any time, short of impending criminal trial. It cannot be, then, that Winthrop's notion of "civil" liberty (the liberty only to be good) was in fact Puritan liberty purely. If so, why even bother with initial consent and a constitutional right to leave, among other things? It thus appears that for the Puritans, a condition of "civil" liberty arises with and in some respects monitors itself in light of a "natural" liberty respected in some significant degree.[31]

More committed to "natural liberty" than they were likely even aware, these theocratic Puritans under Winthrop's incomparable leadership and civic vision of *caritas* made a pivotal contribution to the institutions that now ground American self-rule and stand as bulwark against sectarian despotism. For this, Winthrop was a hero to at least one chief figure of the traditional founding period, namely John Adams, a man who once gushed of his Puritan ancestors

> Whatever imperfections may be justly ascribed to them . . . their judgment in framing their policy was founded in wise, humane, and benevolent principles. It was founded in revelation and reason too. It was consistent with the principles of the best and greatest and wisest legislators of antiquity. Tyranny in every form, shape, and appearance was their disdain and abhorrence.

At one point in the midst of his pre-Revolution fervor, Adams even adopts the alias of "Governor John Winthrop" for a series of essays designed to stir the masses to vigilance for liberty in the aftermath of the Stamp Act.[32]

To be clear, the Massachusetts that Winthrop established was most notably an aristocratic theocracy opposed to many of the critical assumptions that would soon produce a more secular liberal democracy in America. But it was, in Winthrop's own words, a "mixed aristocracy" that ruled by the support of and in conjunction with the voice of the people.[33] And, by the middle of the eighteenth century, as Jonathan Edwards battled a rearguard action against the agnostic, leveling forces of the Enlightenment, Puritanism's battle with modern democracy was largely over. In the felicitous phrasing of Ralph Barton Perry, "Puritanism could not resist an opposition with which it had so deep a kinship. A leaven working within itself conspired with external forces to bring about a gradual transition, rather than an abrupt reversal." What was that leaven? A deep and abiding commitment to "consent," something Winthrop regularly championed and actively institutionalized, even if he did so with the caution and imperialism of a virtuecrat.[34]

The "Means"

Winthrop's fourth point of application is a discussion of the "means" of pursuing the "work and end we aim at" (¶ 41). At first, Winthrop suggests that the means are, simply, "Conformity" to the stipulation that the effort of building a polity of *agape* is an "extraordinary" aim; thus "ordinary means" are unacceptable. As he proceeds with this point through the end of the address, he clarifies that the means are constituted by a most stringent keeping of the colony's unique national covenant of *agape*. At a minimum, this indicates that even a medium-grade commitment to love will not do. To make wholly good on this covenant, Winthrop's listeners must make the practice of charity "familiar and constant," must love one another "without dissimulation," "with a pure heart fervently," bearing "one another's burdens," looking not only on their own things "but also on the things of their brethren" (¶ 41). Later on he continues that

> we must be knit together in this work as one man, we must entertain each other in brotherly Affection, we must be willing to abridge ourselves of our superfluities, for the supply of other necessities, we must uphold a familiar Commerce together in all meekness, gentleness,

patience and liberality, we must delight in each other, make each others' Conditions our own rejoice together, mourn together, labor, and
suffer together, always having before our eyes our Commission and
Community in the work, our Community as members of the same
body, so shall we keep the unity of the spirit in the bond of peace.

Winthrop moves into his most moving, poetic best in this section as he
paints, yet again, a picturesque vision of the kind of community a genuine practice of *agape* would make real.

One sees here that Winthrop's bonds of love and affection are bonds
in at least two senses. At one level, such bonds stand as ligaments or
cords, holding and binding people together in a warm and unifying condition of love. At another level, though, such bonds stand as yokes or
reins, restricting individuals from their self-pursuits and obligating them
to other-regarding pursuits. Perhaps recognizing that the attraction of
the first meaning of bonds for his listeners may not be enough to make
it worth taking up bonds in the second sense (for you do not get the first
without accepting the second), Winthrop presses on with other blessings
sure to come should they establish a community of *caritas*:

> the Lord will be our God and delight to dwell among us, as his own
> people and will command a blessing upon us in all our ways, so that
> we shall see much more of his wisdom power goodness and truth than
> formerly we have been acquainted with, we shall find that the God of
> Israel is among us, when ten of us shall be able to resist a thousand of
> our enemies, when he shall make us a praise and glory, that men shall
> say of succeeding plantations: the Lord make it like that of New
> England: for we must consider that we shall be as a City Upon a Hill,
> the eyes of all people are upon us (¶ 45).

Inspiring in its day, Winthrop's beatific portrait—which draws from a
range of biblical images culminating in the renowned "city that is set on
a hill" iconography of Jesus's Sermon on the Mount (Matt. 5:14)—still
elicits frissons of national hope and pride nearly four hundred years
later. Promises of divine assistance in "all our ways," unmatched levels
of "wisdom" and "truth," David-like power against Goliath-like enemies,
and the chance to become a worldwide exemplar worthy of broad "praise
and glory" remain to this day very real aspirations in many American
quarters. Thus has Winthrop's speech become a staple source of material for modern American political rhetoric.

There is a danger here of overstating the nature and meaning of this passage, especially its most famous image. Winthrop's call to be a "City upon a Hill" has been alternatively praised but more often blamed as exhibit A of American exceptionalism, a tradition that proudly or arrogantly makes this country the "hub of the universe." Some scholars eager to distance Winthrop and this passage from such a tradition have challenged the whole notion of the Puritan "errand," the notion that Puritans moved to the wilderness from where they might strive to rescue, reform, and bless—in short purify—England, then the rest of the world. Rather, these scholars favor something more like a "desertion" thesis whereby the Puritans' move to the wilderness is primarily driven by the need to escape civilization before it crumbles. With this reading, Winthrop's City upon a Hill passage is reduced to a bit of commonplace scriptural hyperbole, an unimportant passing comment between meatier portions of the sermon.[35] But this goes too far.

Nothing Winthrop said or wrote before or after the Model speech comes close to suggesting that he thought Massachusetts, or even New England, was destined to be the one and only "City upon a Hill," the single shining example in mists of international darkness, the future sole source of the world's spiritual salvation. Textual evidence for any notion of a Puritan world mission, let alone a *unique* mission, is thinner than many might presume. Yet to deny that this speech embodies some kind of cosmopolitan charge, to suggest that it focuses solely on the parochial needs and aims of Winthrop's audience, simply contradicts what he actually said. Winthrop appears to be neither an exceptionalist nor a desertionist. As Winthrop acknowledges, the aim of this group was "extraordinary" (¶ 41), one that constituted a "special Commission" (¶ 44) akin to that of Moses and the children of Israel (¶ 45), something they must do for themselves and for their posterity, he says repeatedly (¶¶ 40, 44, 46). With the "eyes of all people" upon them, failure was destined to make them "a story and by-word through the world" (¶ 45). It may not have been their chief aim for coming to America, it may have become even less of a priority in the face of just slugging out survival in the New World, and it may not have been their errand alone, but clearly Winthrop's expectation was that this hardy band of Puritan-pilgrims would live such "exemplary lives" as to make them a highly admirable blessing to many well beyond the borders of their own distant land and beyond their own day.[36]

Whether we admire the Puritans today or not, we do appear to admire Winthrop's speech. But this has not always been the case. From the middle of the nineteenth century to the middle of the twentieth century, an effort steadily grew to sweep all things Puritan under the national carpet—treating the whole period as a historical embarrassment best forgotten. Much of this was fueled by public intellectuals like H. L. Mencken and Van Wyck Brooks, who were particularly adept at caricaturing the Puritans as cold spoilsports driven only by the desire for material possessions and the worry that "someone, somewhere, might be happy."[37] During this time, even in his own Massachusetts, busts and statues of Winthrop that once occupied prominent city spaces were literally relegated to side streets and alcoves. In contrast, images of hounded Puritan heretics like Mary Dyer and Anne Hutchinson began to take pride of place. Prominent references to Winthrop and his "Model" speech are virtually nonexistent during this period.

In 1961, however, John F. Kennedy pulled out and dusted off Winthrop's classic text, making the "City upon a Hill" passage the rhetorical centerpiece of his rapturous farewell address to the citizens of Massachusetts at the Beacon Hill statehouse.[38] By the end of his second term, Ronald Reagan had turned to Winthrop's "City upon a Hill" trope so much and so effectively that—in the estimation of word watcher William Safire—he made it "standard peroration" in American political life. Between Kennedy and Reagan, and since, numerous political luminaries across the spectrum (Lyndon Johnson, Mario Cuomo, Walter Mondale, Michael Dukakis, Bill Clinton, Trent Lott, Rudy Giuliani, George Bush, Arnold Schwarzenegger) have prominently turned to Winthrop and his words to give form and articulation to this country's most urgent moral obligations and most resounding civic aims.[39]

Each has used the same material differently, and often with a license that takes them well beyond or below the bounds of Winthrop's original substance. Nevertheless, whether these figures champion Winthrop's commitment to communal affection, poor relief, self-government, universal education, material prosperity, moral rectitude, spiritual blessedness, defensive strength, or the dream of America as an international beacon of civic goodness and right, each justly grounds their often exaggerated take on the rich canvas of this speech. This is not to suggest that the speech can simply be all things to all people. But it is to say that it brilliantly embodies a complex constellation of norms and self-understandings we might broadly categorize as American. Unfortunately, there is another side to this speech.

The Political Hazards of Winthrop's Charity

In many respects, Winthrop's charity made him a political figure far superior to any of his Puritan peers. His intense love of man and God made him genuinely attentive to the concerns of nearly all constituencies. It is revealing that the only contemporary comment we have on Winthrop in his capacity as an English officer of the law is that he maintained a kind and respectful disposition.[40] Similar testimony concerning his disposition as a Massachusetts magistrate abounds. It would seem that since his earliest adult days in Groton, England, where parishioners were formally precluded from celebrating communion for harboring feelings of "malice and hatred" toward a neighbor, Winthrop was determined to maintain feelings of charity for all in virtually every circumstance. He was not always successful. A perfect love for all was a goal he never fully achieved, though he strove for it his entire life and did so with enough success that his deep care for others remains the commonest recollection of his life and leadership.[41] Yet even as this is recognized, it must also be acknowledged that both the "Model" speech and his personal journal highlight a vexing tension between wise political rule in a fallen world and attempts to practice the "pure religion" of *caritas* (see James 1:27, 2:8).

Whether he realized it or not, Winthrop gave evidence for this in one of his examples of charity personified in the "Model" speech. Among his examples, Winthrop includes Jonathan of the Old Testament, whose heart was so knit to David that he "loved him as his own soul" and "strips himself" of his own robe to "adorn his beloved" friend (¶ 31). In doing so, he figuratively strips himself of his title to the crown, clearing the path for David's ascension; for as King Saul (Jonathan's father) angrily warned Jonathan, "as long as [David] liveth upon the ground, thou shalt not be established, nor thy kingdom" (I Samuel 20:31). But Jonathan's love was so great that he preferred to converse with David in the wilderness rather than with "the great Courtiers in his father's palace," for his "father's kingdom was not so precious to him as his beloved David." Though probably an unintended message, the point here is that charity may draw one so deeply to the love of others, or God, that interest and effectiveness in the bruising world of political achievement will significantly diminish. One thinks here of Max Weber's point that the decisive psychological quality of a successful political leader is an

> ability to let realities work upon him with inner concentration and calmness. Hence his *distance* to men and things. "Lack of distance" per se is one of the deadly sins of every politician.[42]

There do seem to be some poignant reminders of this notion in Winthrop's own life. Francis Bremer suggests that Winthrop's significant illness during his days of service in the notoriously corrupt Court of Wards was brought on by "agonies of conscience" from trying to maintain a devotion to God and honest walk with all men and still prosper in his new appointment. Also, in the last leaves of a journal he kept during the final five years of his life, Winthrop noted a series of historical examples where "wholesome" public actions had "ill success, even to public danger." Editors of Winthrop's journal guess that his primary motivation for making such a list was to justify his decision in 1643 to support Charles de La Tour over Charles Sieur d'Aulnay in their dispute over who controlled French Acadia just north of New England. Winthrop recorded in his journal that the chief reason for aiding La Tour was that the "royal law" of love dictated that "if our neighbor be in distress, we ought to help him." However, taking the Good Samaritan approach with La Tour proved to be one of Winthrop's more regrettable decisions. Not only did La Tour turn out to be weaker than D'Aulnay (eventually losing the struggle), but he also proved much more of a pirate. By the end of the summer, in a moment of unusually pointed self-criticism, Winthrop noted in his journal that he made several errors in handling the situation, berating himself for acting against wisdom and being "over sudden in his resolutions."[43] In this case, Winthrop's sense of charity was certainly not the only cause of his self-admitted and politically misguided impetuousness, but it clearly figured prominently in his determination to help where he probably should not have. To the degree that Winthrop's life is a lesson, charity aflame in the heart of an earthly ruler may intensify some political virtues even as it fosters imprudent impulses and tragically recognizes that some necessary political judgments are at odds with an individual quest for moral purity.

Winthrop's singular devotion to charity as he understands it creates other problems too. The first is connected to the considerable difference between the Massachusetts covenant he sees springing up out of *agape* collectively practiced and its Mosaic analogue, which Winthrop repeatedly references. With the children of Israel, God authors the covenant and then articulates it through his anointed prophet Moses. "These are the words of the covenant, which the *Lord commanded Moses* to make with the children of Israel in the land of Moab" (Deut. 29:1, emphasis added). Winthrop may have been a widely beloved governor, but he was never a widely accepted prophet—something neither he nor any Puritan ever claimed to be. Thus, Winthrop asserts, it is some undefined "We" who authors and articulates the covenant for Massachusetts (¶ 44). Winthrop tells his listeners that "the Lord hath given *us* leave to *draw our own articles*" (emphasis added). The pronouns and verbs that surround this statement emphasize the point further.

> *We are entered* into covenant with him for this work. *We have taken out* a Commission. . . . *We have professed* to enterprise these Actions upon these and these ends, *we have hereupon besought* him of favor and blessing.

This triggers a theocratic dilemma that Winthrop never fully resolves and one on which the colony ultimately founders. Who exactly is the "We" that will enumerate, broadcast, and police the articles of the covenant? Winthrop actually offered a clear answer to this question: duly elected, aristocratic magistrates. But such an answer became increasingly anathema even to freemen generally sympathetic to colonial orthodoxy. How could it not with the powerful leaven of "consent" constantly at work in the system? How, and by whom, the precise terms of the civic covenant would be made was a regular source of friction. As long as Winthrop was alive and influential, he adroitly steered the colony through the resulting clash of popular demands, clerical pronouncements, and residual English traditions—aristocratic, legal, and political. But it was the colony's inability after Winthrop to agree on the covenant-setting "We" that left them without cohesive strength to resist the forces of mother England, who resumed more active control of the colony partly to bring more and more order between competing factions.

In the end, Winthrop's concept of biblical charity as a political principle stands inseparable from epistemic claims of truth, but Winthrop could neither convincingly identify nor adequately establish a social framework critical to developing and facilitating such claims. As a result, the "truths" necessary to support the community's practices of charity were bereft of a stable footing and sure guide, especially after his death. As a result, Massachusetts proved unable to contain forever in Puritan wrapping the competing walks of life that step up out of its foundational reverence for consent. Ultimately, the hoped-for model of charity moved closer to Hutchinson's antinomianism than Winthrop's authoritarianism.

The final and most troubling indictment against Winthrop's model of charity surfaces at the close of the speech where he emphasizes that the weighty, communal mission he sees springing out of *agape* means that Massachusetts cannot afford to think that "the Lord will bear with such failings at our hands as he doth from those among whom we have lived" (¶ 41). While being fastened to God and to each other by the caring ligaments of *agapic* love is destined to produce a magnificent array of rewards, such a special coupling also involves monumental obligations. This idea is most colorfully illustrated by Winthrop's indication that, yoked by charity, the relationship between God and the Massachusetts Bay Colony would be a form of the strongest union available to earthly love: "the more near bond of marriage" (¶ 42). This was not the first nor the last time Winthrop would turn to images of marital union and even conjugal love to characterize godly relationships. Winthrop himself married four times—he lost two wives early on to childbirth and a third to illness—and each relationship was noted, in varying degrees, for its tenderness, mutual respect, and hale sexuality. Within the bonds of marriage, Winthrop found *eros* a God-sanctioned expression of *agape,* and more than once he described experiencing God's transforming love in passionate terms.

> I was so ravished with his love towards me, far exceeding the affection of the kindest husband, that being awakened it had made so deep [an] impression in my heart, as I was forced to unmeasurable weeping for great while, and had a more lively feeling of the love of Christ than ever before.[44]

Steered by the conviction that just as one comes to expect more loyalty and sacred devotion from a spouse than from any other person, Winthrop reasons that Massachusetts's national covenant of *agape* makes

God particularly "Jealous of the [colony's] love and obedience" (¶ 42). Where others may trifle with God's teachings and go unpunished, the colony must abide by God's word or face the retribution of a betrayed lover who is both enraged and omnipotent. This explains the repeated theme of strictness in the speech's final passages: they are to keep their covenant with God "after a strict and peculiar manner" (¶ 42), seeing that it is "strictly observed in every Article" (¶ 44), for God will "expect a strict performance."

Here the speech takes on a most ominous tone. The "price of the breach of such a covenant," he promises soberly, is that God will "break out in wrath against" them. For this group sailing across the Atlantic in seventeenth-century wooden vessels, how disturbing must have been his next statement that "the only way to avoid this shipwreck" is to follow all of *agape*'s obligations to man and God (¶ 45), a warning that swept from the rhetorical to the real. And the speech's very last line indicates that if they do not die by shipwreck, they will certainly "perish out of the good Land" of their destination should they stumble in their commitments of *caritas* (¶¶ 45–46)—a near-perfect echo of two lines previous where he says they will be "consumed out of the good land." That choosing charity is a matter of "life, and good" or "death and evil" is cast more as literal threat than literary hyperbole—thus the deafening drumbeat of imperatives throughout this section:

> we *must* not content ourselves with usual ordinary means whatsoever
> we did or ought to have done when we lived in England, the same *must*
> we do and more also where we go. . . . we *must* bring into familiar and
> constant practice, as in the duty of love we *must* love brotherly without
> dissimulation, we *must* love one another with a pure heart fervently,
> we *must* bear one another's burdens, we *must* not look only on our own
> things, but also on the things of our brethren, neither *must* we think
> that the Lord will bear with such failings at our hands as he doth from
> those among whom we have lived (¶ 41) . . . . we *must* be knit together
> in this work as one man, we *must* entertain each other in brotherly
> Affection, we *must* be willing to abridge ourselves of our superfluities,
> for the supply of other necessities, we *must* uphold a familiar Com-
> merce together in all meekness, gentleness, patience and liberality, we
> *must* delight in each other, make each others' Conditions our own
> (¶ 45, emphases added).

The problem with this formulation is that it wars fiercely with the very benevolence for which the passage just quoted—and the whole speech—

cries. It explains why even Winthrop, one of the most kind-hearted and
lenient of all early New England magistrates, could himself sometimes
fall prey to that Hawthornian horror of an "iron framework of reasoning"
that prompted Puritan leaders to impose a callous and severe "guardian-
ship of the public morals." Because the strict keeping of all their state
and church covenants was made an urgent and absolute matter of community survival, the leaders of the Massachusetts Bay Colony could not
afford to treat covenant breaking with indulgence. Said another way, the
tight community of *agape* Winthrop envisioned required such a stringent
and far-reaching communal obedience to, or love of, God—charity's vertical dimension—that it could considerably attenuate charity's horizontal dimension, or love of man. Nowhere was this more apparent in
Winthrop's life than in his dealings with Anne Hutchinson, for whom he
appears to have developed a rare sense of malice that never quite abated.

By stressing that direct, personal revelation is superior to ministerial
teaching or communal agreement, therefore radically marginalizing the
significance of the law, Hutchinson's teachings, Winthrop feared, would
have shattered Massachusetts's stable, single covenant of "We" into
anarchic, multiple covenants of "I." For a community whose very survival depended on establishing a seamless fabric of love to each other
and obedience to God, Hutchinson's charismatic antinomianism struck
at the core of Winthrop's vision like nothing else and therefore elicited
some of his nastiest behavior on record. Though not as vituperative
during her trial as Boston's senior minister, John Wilson, Winthrop was
certainly guilty of the arrogance he claimed to be combating in Hutchinson.[45] Even with the trial over, the controversy mostly out of breath, and
Hutchinson safely banished to Rhode Island, Winthrop was unable to
fully let go of his animus toward her. Hearing that she had midwifed for
a woman who gave birth to a stillborn "monster," Winthrop caused the
"monster be taken up" from the grave and a description of its hideous
deformities be recorded and attributed to Hutchinson's "deformed
beliefs."[46] When Hutchinson later produced her own "monsterous
birth," Winthrop solicited the details from her doctor, carefully noted
them in his journal, and then passed them along to John Cotton to use
in two sermons announcing the awful ramifications of her heresies.

While mostly a testimony to his compassion for others, Winthrop's
own journal indicates that the kind of harshness he displayed in the
Hutchinson affair was not a single aberration. In one entry he records
with little remorse that a couple caught in an act of adultery "proved very

penitent" but were executed nevertheless. In the last paragraph of his
last entry, Winthrop describes in unfeeling terms the death of a five-
year-old girl who, in the dark of night, stumbled into a cellar well and
drowned, placidly chalking this up to God's providence for a sin committed by the girl's father, who, in repairing the local mill dam, allowed his
Saturday toils to continue one hour into the Sabbath.[47]

The point here is not to imply that there is an inherent tension
between charity and any form of moral judgment and punishment.
Again, claims of *agape* cannot be separated from claims of truth. For
Christians, to love God is to love truth, for God is "the way, *the truth,*
and the life" (John 14:6, emphasis added). This is why for Winthrop and
his fellow travelers, and numerous other groups of Christian believers,
there is such concern over things like what God has to say about sin
and sacraments. Passionate feelings for God by definition translate into
passionate feelings about what God is understood to have taught
humanity concerning doctrinal matters, commandments, and forms of
worship—the ways of truth tied to happiness and salvation. From this
perspective, the most charitable thing one can do for someone who
stands outside the community of truth is to help bring them into it. And
the most charitable thing one can do for an erring brother or sister who
stands inside the community of truth is to discipline them in some fashion. The latter not only demonstrates love for the sinner, better enabling
him or her to see and adopt the ways of truth, it demonstrates concern
and love for the rest of the members of the community of truth, protecting them from influences that could jeopardize their own salvational
bond with God. As far as how harsh such disciplining may be, much
depends on the harshness of the God that sets out the ways of truth.

Having established that judgment and punishment are not inherently
in tension with *caritas,* it can now be stated with more precision that by
insisting that the immediate physical survival of the Massachusetts Bay
Colony is staked upon an exact adherence to the articles of a sprawling
covenant sprung from the love between God and his saints, Winthrop
woefully circumscribes the operation of Christian virtues like mercy and
forgiveness, which also constitute vital elements of New Testament
agape. Because a meticulous keeping of a most demanding and wide-
ranging social covenant is not just a matter of love but a matter of survival on a dangerous errand into the wilderness, the leaders of the Massachusetts Bay Colony cannot treat deviations from the covenant too
kindly. Should such deviations flourish, destruction would surely follow.

Consequently, the community response to heresy and transgression needed to be swift and in many cases severe—in other words, it needed to be fairly unmerciful.

These insights call for a re-examination of Winthrop's previously analyzed thoughts on mercy and justice. In chapter one, Winthrop's view of mercy was shown to be richer and more thoroughly developed than his concept of justice. Now, however, it is possible to see that though vibrant and compelling in some respects, in other respects Winthrop's concept of mercy remains quite narrow. Just consider his thoughts on mercy as "forgiveness" (¶¶ 16, 17). Typically, forgiveness is considered one of Christianity's warmest and most generous theological concepts. However, in this sermon, Winthrop explains forgiveness in exclusively economic terms, reducing it to the willingness to pardon financial debt in certain circumstances. This is still quite a lot—something more than a few Christians might shrink from today. But such a concept hardly compares to the one found in the New Testament, where, among other things, a penitent adulteress is spared a stoning (John 8:3–7), a dying but fair-minded thief is promised a place in Paradise (Luke 23:39–43), and crucifiers unwitting of their deeds are forgiven even without their asking (Luke 23:33–34). Certainly, then, one reason Winthrop's discussion of mercy focuses exclusively on monetary issues must be that the world of economic activity is the one realm where members of the Massachusetts Bay Colony could be generous and forgiving with each other and still not endanger their own lives and the success of their sacred social experiment. But to generously forgive or patiently accommodate those who expound theological heresy, commit adultery, fail to honor the Sabbath, or irreverently make merry at the maypole was, for early Massachusetts at least, a very different matter.[48] Too much moral latitudarianism was understood to jeopardize everything. Winthrop's paradigm of covenanted charity, presided over by an extremely jealous and demanding God, makes extending mercy in spheres of life other than the economic a mortally hazardous activity. Alternatively, financial welfare assistance becomes the one activity where showing love for man most neatly and harmoniously intersects with showing love for God in the Puritan schema.

Thus we see that the occasional severity of Winthrop, and the more regular severity of early Massachusetts in general, came not in spite of Winthrop's call for a community of charity, but because of it. It was the Puritan's love of God, and understanding of the nature of that God, that drove them to impose upon their community an uncompromising array of God's commandments, large and small. All of this could sometimes prompt in Winthrop, and regularly prompted in many of his peers, a hyperjudgmentalism and retributive excess counter to the spirit of empathy and affection that Winthrop so powerfully preached and generally practiced. This is not so much evidence of hypocrisy, schizophrenia, or even human shortcoming in Winthrop as it is additional evidence of a faithful man trying desperately to care for his neighbor, all of his neighbors, in the context of adoring his God as he understands that God. If at times Winthrop could be harsh in his human relationships, it was primarily because he perceived a God who could be harsh. As Winthrop explains in the "Model" speech, theirs was a God who revoked Saul's kingdom for failing "in one of the least" of the articles of his commission, which included a command to "destroy Amalek" (¶ 44).

As previously argued, there is a sense in which Winthrop's model of charity finally explodes, where its radically democratic impulses gave rise to burgeoning visions of the good life that could not ultimately be managed by the likes of anything approaching a Puritan orthodoxy. Here, though, we see that there is a sense in which the model implodes, where it simply buckles under the weight of its own understanding of what *caritas* demands from its citizenry. The insistence of hard and far-reaching requirements for the success of the Puritan experiment, coupled with the colony's inability to provide a unified institutional oracle for establishing those requirements, proved Puritanism's demise over time. While Winthrop and his sermon powerfully established and continue to stand for a national mythos that human beings are social beings and depend upon each other not just to survive but to flourish, the full workings of his definition of a cohesive and charitable community made such a community unsustainable. It appears that his famous sermon planted seeds of ruin for the very bonds of affection he yearned for personally, cultivated among his fellow settlers, and held out as an inspirational aim for all succeeding generations.

This all hints at something that appears to be as true of Winthrop as it is of the state he, more than any other, helped create. Both Winthrop and early Massachusetts demonstrated a kind of dual character, but one emanating significantly from a central vision of *agape*. In the end, Winthrop's model of Christian charity appears to have provided the blueprints for two cities upon one hill. There is a side of early Massachusetts to be rightly celebrated today for its power to draw forth a genuine care for the poor, broad democratic engagement, an often warm union of fellow citizens, optimism and industriousness in the face of great obstacles, and a stirring sense of human mission beyond one's own time and place. Much of this was directly born of the Puritans' heartfelt love for God and man bound up with their preliberal Protestant commitments to individual conscience and consent. There is also, though, the more infamous side of Massachusetts, a side often overdrawn and overemphasized but all too real, where a certain public paranoia—neighbors watching neighbors not watching God—fosters punishments without sense of proportion, a significant suppression of individual belief and preference, and a much restricted sense of mercy for those who act at odds with the colony's expansive covenant.[49] This too is an expression of the Puritans' sense of charity, bound up with their perceptions of a harsh and punishing God and the responsibilities to other human beings that flow therefrom.

Winthrop appears to have had his own feet in both cities, though they were planted in the first far more solidly than in the second. Surely this helps explain and affirm Hawthorne's complex sketch of Winthrop and his Puritan state discussed in the introduction of this section. Winthrop's understanding of and commitment to a genuine sense of Christian love very much makes him a plausible object of admiration and affection for Hester and Pearl, and for many Americans today. But his love and leadership cannot finally and fully redeem the excessively repressive and harsh civil structure of the Massachusetts Bay Colony, primarily because that structure was an expression of that love. Perhaps in the end, then, the wisest contemporary reaction to Winthrop in particular can be summed up by what appears to be Hawthorne's reaction to Puritanism in general:

> Let us thank God for having given us such ancestors; and let each successive generation thank him, not less fervently, for being one step further from them in the march of ages.[50]

Notes

1. Nearly every adult male (minus indentured servants) who traveled over in 1630 officially joined a New England congregation, yet for some the religious dimension of their journey was more significant than for others. See Bremer, *John Winthrop*, 164–65, 209. Hugh Dawson makes much of the line in this same passage "though we

were absent from each other many miles," arguing that this, among other passages, suggests that Winthrop's model of charity included the saintly members of the Massachusetts Bay Company remaining behind in England, which it probably did. See "Rite of Passage" and "Colonial Discourse." But this does not diminish that most of Winthrop's rhetorical energies appear spent not on England and those remaining behind, but on those departing and life "where we go" (¶ 41).

2. That grace works gradually and leaves room for outside teaching, correction, and incentive was not idiosyncratic to Winthrop; it was most prominently preached by William Perkins, who died in 1602. See Miller, *Errand*, 59–60. Also see Bremer, *Puritan Experiment*, 90.

3. Tocqueville, *Democracy in America*, 33. This and the next few paragraphs borrow liberally from Edmund Morgan's chapter on church-state relations in early Massachusetts (62–85) in *Roger Williams* and Bremer, *Puritan Experiment*, 89–94, 102.

4. Morgan, *Roger Williams*, 63. Cotton's statement in particular is worth reading in full. "It is better that the commonwealth be fashioned to the setting forth of God's house, which is his church: than to accommodate the church frame to the civil state. Democracy, I do not conceive that ever God did ordain as a fit government either for church or commonwealth. If the people be governors, who shall be governed? As for monarchy, and aristocracy, they are both of them clearly approved, and directed in scripture, yet so as referreth the sovereignty to himself, and setteth up *theocracy* in both, as the best form of government in the commonwealth, as well as in the church" (letter to Lord Say, 1636, as found in Hall, *Puritans*, 172, emphasis added).

5. Hall, *Faithful Shepherd*, 122. See all of chapter six for an extended discussion of the Puritan state.

6. As quoted in Morgan, *Roger Williams*, 66.

7. Winthrop, *Journal—Abridged*, 170.

8. Morgan, *Roger Williams*, 63; Dreisbach, "Sowing Useful Truths," 71, 76–79.

9. Winthrop, *Journal—Abridged*, 280–84.

10. For the "Little Speech," see Winthrop, *Journal—Abridged*, 281–82. For an excellent extended treatment of this point, see Schaar, "Liberty/Authority/Community," 495–505, a position endorsed by Bremer, *John Winthrop*, 305–6.

11. Aristotle holds that in any attempt to base society on moral truth, or the good, the best one can hope for is an imprecise, general outline of the good at which to take aim (*Ethics* I.2). This is best done and then implemented by those with "practical wisdom" (VI).

12. Winthrop, *Journal—Abridged*, 89.

13. For a lengthier explanation and defense of the role of Winthrop in the *Scarlet Letter,* particularly his death scene with Hester and Pearl, see Holland, *Remembering John Winthrop*. While this essay diverges in several respects from Lauren Berlant, *Anatomy of National Fantasy*, Berlant also treats the scenes and imagery of Winthrop's death as likely betokening Winthrop's "majestic virtue" as well as the sickening "stress" his authoritative regime fostered (see her chapter two in particular).

14. Hawthorne, *Tales and Sketches*, 1033 ("Mainstreet"), 546 ("Endicott and the Red Cross"), and 22 ("Mrs. Hutchinson").

15. This also appears to be largely the assessment of Michael Winship in his very detailed treatment of the Anne Hutchinson affair and related events, *Making Heretics*, 138, 237. It is certainly the opinion of Winthrop's two most thoughtful biographers, Edmund Morgan and Francis Bremer.

16. For a highly democratic reading of Winthrop's state, see Miller, *Rise and Fall of Democracy*, 21–49, to be contrasted with the more authoritarian reading by Foster, *Their Solitary Way*, 67–98. My argument draws on both of these and other material, falling somewhere in between.

17. The royal charter was secured just one week before Charles dissolved his last parliament. Perhaps because of the haste by which it was secured, the charter did not specify where the Company had to hold its governing stockholders' meetings. This fortuitous—some felt miraculous—turn of events meant that unlike any other colonial enterprise, the Massachusetts Bay Company was not locked into running its operations out of London under the watchful eyes of the Crown. The prospect of having the security of the royal grant (they were to enjoy "all liberties and immunities" of British subjects), but with an unusual amount of autonomy (they were only forbidden from passing laws repugnant to those of England), was key to convincing a still hesitant Winthrop that the enterprise was worth it. Now fully and officially committed to emigration, Winthrop vigorously pressed for the enterprise to be run not as a company out of England but as a colony out of New England. See Morgan, *Puritan Dilemma*, 31, 40, 75.

18. The ensuing discussion draws liberally from Morgan, *Puritan Dilemma*, 75–82; Bremer, *John Winthrop*, 196, 209, 214–15, 218, 241; and Foster, *Their Solitary Way*, 67–98.

19. Bremer, *John Winthrop*, 209.

20. Winthrop, *Journal—Abridged*, 81.

21. *The Colonial Laws of Massachusetts*, 29–68.

22. Brown, "Freemanship." See David Hall's essay "Experience of Authority" for a particularly recent treatment of how radical (in a liberal, democratic direction) Winthrop's early community was.

23. Foster, *Their Solitary Way*, 83.

24. Winthrop, *Winthrop Papers*, IV: 383; Brown, "Puritan Concept of Aristocracy."

25. Winthrop, *Papers*, III: 422–23. Michael Zuckert, *Natural Rights Republic*, 267, dismisses the significance of these statements by suggesting they are not tied to a larger "natural rights" doctrine like that of the traditional American founding. Furthermore, he notes that Winthrop is marshalling these statements in order to prevent immigrants from joining the community. It is true that Winthrop does not embrace the natural rights school of thought in some nakedly Jeffersonian or Lockean way. I will myself argue in part 2 that Jefferson offers a decisive break with Winthropian thinking. Yet it is hard to see how a statement like "no man hath lawful power over another, but by . . . consent" is anything other than a statement that trends very close to a statement of natural equality. If, finally, Winthrop's position is not a natural rights position (and I am arguing that it isn't), it is because core notions of consent are attached to other competing concepts that are missing, or are different, from most natural rights doctrines; nevertheless, core notions of consent remain

core—thus a certain affinity here with natural rights thinking seems most plausible. Also, the fact that this group of freely consenting citizens, having formed a community, wants to effectively control its borders is hardly indicative of an unliberal community. Even as modern America is learning, just because you and the rest of your fellow citizens have consented, by natural right, to be ruled by a particular commonwealth, it does not follow that that commonwealth must then admit anyone who applies. Thomas Hooker, "Two Sermons," I:20.

26. The famous "New England Way" was that each congregation was perfectly equal with any other congregation and reported to no higher ecclesiastical authority. Each congregation claimed to hold the "power of the keys"—meaning all members collectively held the authority to make decisions on all aspects of church government. By male-member vote, and with ministerial guidance, individual congregations decided for themselves who could be admitted, who could be expelled, and the finer points of contested theology. And while the minister and elders were generally looked to with much reverence and respect, it was finally the vote of the congregation that could hire and dismiss all sacerdotal officers. See Hall, *Puritans*, 5–6; Bremer, *Puritan Experiment*, 97–105.

27. Tocqueville, *Democracy in America*, 32.

28. For more on the covenantal precursors to America's social contractualism, see Niebuhr, "Covenant and American Democracy," 126–35; Elazar, *Covenant and Constitutionalism*, 17–45; Lutz, "Covenant to Constitution," 101–33.

29. For comparison, see Deuteronomy 30 in the Geneva Bible (standard Bible of use for early Puritan America).

30. This national covenant was one that Winthrop felt all believers effectively entered by their self-chosen decision to emigrate, knowing well the formal aim of the enterprise. Other covenants would follow—most notably a church covenant by formal application to membership in a particular congregation, and a second civil covenant, often referred to as a social covenant made, in the case of Massachusetts, upon application to freemanship. In addition to agreeing to the general laws of God and aims of the national covenant, each settler would have a chance to determine his or her additional acceptance of obligations and strictures associated with congregational and colonial government. See Morgan, *Puritan Dilemma*, 78–84; Bremer, *Puritan Experiment*, 21–22; Miller, *Errand*, 28. The "errand" phrase comes from Perry Miller's famous appropriation of the title of an election sermon by Samuel Danforth in 1670. See Miller, *Errand*, 1.

31. Winthrop, *Journal—Abridged*, 280–84.

32. Adams, *Revolutionary Writings*, 24, 59–60, 61–71.

33. Winthrop, *Winthrop Papers*, IV, 383.

34. Perry, *Puritanism and Democracy*, 191–92.

35. The phrase "hub of the universe" comes from Baritz, *City on a Hill*, 17. The desertion thesis is found in Delbanco, *Puritan Ordeal*, and Bozeman, *Ancient Lives*, who shows many pedestrian uses of "city on a hill" imagery by others at the time.

36. Bremer, "To Live Exemplary Lives," 27–39, offers an excellent survey of the historical debate on this issue. My reading here was significantly influenced by his argument for a real, if not so very unique, sense of Puritan mission among Winthrop's generation.

37. Mencken, *A Little Book*, 624; Brooks, *Early Years*, 194.

38. For a more detailed treatment of why Winthrop and his speech were forgotten and then were reclaimed in a sweeping, bipartisan embrace, see Holland, "Remembering John Winthrop"; Kennedy, *Let the Word*, 57. Kennedy's speech is duplicated in its entirety in *Mortal Friends*, James Carroll's 1978 novel which made the *New York Times* bestseller list. In Carroll's fictional recreation of the moment, Kennedy's short speech has an absolutely electrifying effect on the audience: "The roof of the place was listening to him . . . the legislators . . . were men who had heard such words before, but never so simply, so starkly. It was the simplicity of Kennedy's rhetoric that had held them. . . . They were weathered pols who knew better, yet the great image of the man's innocence struck root in their hearts," 497–98.

39. For Reagan, Kennedy, and Johnson, see U.S. President, *Public Papers of the Presidents of the United States*; for an account of "standard peroration," see Safire, "Rack up That City on a Hill"; Cuomo, "A Tale of Two Cities"; Taylor, "Mondale Rises to Peak Form"; Dukakis, "The Democrats in Atlanta"; Clinton, "Commencement Address at Portland State University"; Clinton, "Commencement Address at United States Coast Guard Academy"; Lott, *Response to President's Radio Address*; UN General Assembly, *Mayor Rudolf W. Giuliani, Opening Remarks*; Bush, "Excerpts from President Bush's Thanksgiving Day Proclamation"; Kasindorf, "Governor Schwarzenegger Takes Office."

40. Bremer, *John Winthrop*, 208.

41. In 1864 Robert Winthrop, a direct descendant of John, published for the first time large sections of original writings from Winthrop's journal and personal papers, titled *Life and Letters of John Winthrop*. In the preface, Robert Winthrop explains that "not a few of us had doubted how far these old Fathers of Massachusetts were men of charity. Not a few of us had feared that this greatest of the three pre-eminent Christian graces, upon which the richest treasures of apostolic eloquence were poured forth and almost exhausted, had found but a feeble recognition in some of their hearts. They have been associated, certainly with an austerity of disposition, a sternness of character, and a severity of conduct, which have often subjected them to the reproach of history, and which have sometimes rendered them repulsive even to their own posterity. We are glad to believe that the *Life and Letters of Winthrop*, as thus far given, have done something to mitigate, if not to dispel, this prejudice. They have served to exhibit at least one of the foremost of the Massachusetts Fathers as abounding in tenderness and love. . . . We have seen him severe indeed, but towards no one except himself. We have seen him dealing unsparingly with his own shortcomings, with his own 'sins, negligences and ignorances;' but overflowing with kindness and affection towards all around him." See Winthrop, *Life and Letters*, 2–3 of vol. II. The statement is certainly colored by a filiopietism, but its echo is clearly heard in Bremer's recent, not uncritical, and expansive survey of Winthrop's life, where Bremer concludes that the "enduring message" of Winthrop's words and actions is that we must "love one another with a pure heart, fervently" (Bremer, *John Winthrop*, 385).

42. Weber, *Essays in Sociology*, 15. Recognizable American variations of this theme have been sounded as long ago as George Washington and as recently as George Stephanopoulos. In his famous Farewell Address, Washington warned

America that while "just and amicable" relationships with other countries ought to be cultivated, "passionate attachments for others should be excluded" (Washington, *Collection*, 523). In his memoir about life as a senior advisor to President Clinton, Stephanopoulos acknowledges that one of the most important lessons he learned in the White House was that political judgment is clouded from "caring too much" (*All Too Human*, 221).

43. For Winthrop's "agonies," see Bremer, *John Winthrop*, 145. On actions of "ill success, even to public danger," see Winthrop, *Journal—Unabridged*, 772–74. In a letter he wrote to several magistrates who openly opposed him on this issue, he contended that help for La Tour rested "first in point of duty, in that our distressed neighbor calls to us for help" and that God's providence and "good opinion of our charitableness brought him to us" to be helped; see *Winthrop Papers* IV: 405. As to why Winthrop perceived La Tour to be more of a neighbor than D'Aulnay, it can only be noted that D'Aulnay had from time to time engaged in skirmishes with Puritan settlers in the north, and of the two, La Tour was the most active in courting Winthrop's support. See Winthrop, *Journal—Abridged*, 228. For "over sudden in his resolutions," see ibid., 236.

44. For information regarding John and Margaret's relationship, see Rutman, "My Beloved." Quotation as found in Bremer, *John Winthrop*, 97, also see 98, 320–21, 373. These characteristics of tenderness, respect, and sexuality were especially true of his third and longest marriage to Margaret Tyndall, who was much John's spiritual and intellectual equal. They were less true of his first marriage to Mary Forth, whose lack of spiritual and intellectual rigor was often a source of frustration to John. But even in this case, these differences were accepted and a stable relationship emerged. As quoted in *Winthrop Papers* I: 166.

45. An anonymous church report of Hutchinson's trial records Wilson screaming, "I command you in the name of Christ Jesus and of the Church as a leper to withdraw yourself out of this congregation." Hall, *Antinomian History*, 338.

46. Winthrop, *Journal—Abridged*, 142; Moseley, *John Winthrop's World*, 86.

47. Winthrop, *Journal—Abridged*, 247, 345.

48. It is also clear in this section of the "Model" speech that Winthrop's other two forms of mercy—giving and lending—take on an almost exclusively economic cast. Scott Michaelsen argues that the obsessive economic interest of these passages on mercy may be explained by the fact that the Massachusetts Bay Company was, ultimately, a financial enterprise in the form of a joint stock operation (Michaelsen, "John Winthrop's 'Model'"). Certainly Michaelsen is right to condemn what he calls the "radical communitarian readings" of this sermon for getting so caught up in the passages on "pure love and mutuality" that they fail to confront this "quite confusing first section" on economic mercy and justice (91). However, if the kinds of scholars Michaelsen criticizes are guilty of seeing too much love and community at the expense of acknowledging Winthrop's commitment to the realities of business, Michaelsen and Anderson (*A House Divided*) are guilty of seeing too much of the "Company Way" in Winthrop's thought. What the Michaelsen camp and the more communitarian readers both miss (for different reasons) is that the "quite confusing first section" on mercy is solidly linked to and explained by (at least in part) the latter passages on love.

49. For many, the paranoia of Puritan New England is simply captured in the infamous Salem witch trials—as if this were a characteristic snapshot of seventeenth-century Puritan New England. What needs to be kept in mind here is that the Salem witch trials were an isolated incident, coming forty years after Winthrop was dead, and never reaching anything the likes of which was seen in several places across Europe. For a discussion of witchcraft, see Macfarlane, *Witchcraft*; Levack, *Witch-Hunt*.

50. Hawthorne, *Tales and Sketches*, 1039.

PART TWO

Jefferson and the Founding

The principles of Jefferson are the definitions and axioms of free society. . . . All honor to Jefferson.

Abraham Lincoln, April 6, 1859

In extracting the pure principles which [Jesus] taught . . . we must reduce our volume to the simple evangelists, select, even from them, the very words only of Jesus . . . [and] there will be found remaining the most sublime and benevolent code of morals which has ever been offered to man.

Jefferson to John Adams, October 12, 1813

1776—The Other Declaration

I n May of 1776, George Mason drafted the Virginia Declaration of Rights, which the Virginia Convention of Delegates adopted unanimously the very next month with only a few changes. The impact of this document was immediate and widespread. Thomas Jefferson was almost certainly guided by a draft of it as he sat in Philadelphia composing the Declaration of Independence. Nine other colonies followed Virginia's lead and affixed similar statements to their new constitutions or passed comparable statutes. A few more years down the road, when drafting the Bill of Rights for the U.S. Constitution, James Madison would look to this text more than any other. And Condorcet felt that George Mason deserved nothing less than the "eternal gratitude of mankind" given the way the Virginia Declaration of Rights shaped France's Declaration of the Rights of Man.[1]

Rightly appreciated for its vast influence as the Revolution's prototypical assertion of fundamental natural rights tied to commensurate demands for popular sovereignty, separation of powers, and some basic civil liberties, this significant document is less recognized for its revealing commentary on the political status of Christian charity at the dawn of American independence. The last line of the last article of the Virginia Declaration of Rights asserts not a right, but a duty, specifically a "mutual duty of all to practice Christian forbearance, love, and charity, towards each other." To show that this line was more than just rhetorical window dressing, it is useful to consider how the whole of the final article that contains the line both changed and did not change through the drafting process.

Mason's original draft of the declaration passed out of committee with little modification. By the time of final passage, however, several small but significant edits were made. Here is the final article as amended (deleted committee draft language is shown with a line through the text, and new language is shown in italics).

That Religion, or the duty which we owe to our Creator, and the manner of discharging it, can be directed only by reason and conviction, not by force or violence; and, therefore, ~~that all men should enjoy the fullest toleration in the exercise of religion~~ *all men are equally entitled to the free exercise of religion*, according to the dictates of conscience; ~~unpunished and unrestrained by the magistrate, unless, under colour of religion, any man disturb the peace, the happiness, or safety of society.~~ and that it is the mutual duty of all to practice Christian forbearance, love, and charity, towards each other.[2]

Perhaps as important as what changes were made to the passage is who made them. Despite his junior status (he was only twenty-five at the time) and otherwise negligible contributions to the proceedings, James Madison engineered these highly significant alterations. Worried that the phrase "all men should enjoy the fullest toleration in the exercise of religion" would not go far enough to protect what he considered a more fundamental liberty, Madison, in the face of self-described "powerful forces that surged around this explosive issue," succeeded in replacing the worrisome committee draft language with the phrase "*all men are equally entitled to the free exercise of religion.*" In doing so, he transformed the freedom of religious worship from a gifted privilege conferred by conventional authority into an inherent, universal right. In the eyes of the celebrated historian George Bancroft, this was "the first achievement of the wisest civilian in Virginia."[3]

No known record indicates what Madison thought of the article's last line formally acknowledging the "mutual duty of all to practice Christian forbearance, love, and charity."[4] It may be that Madison did not care for such a line but felt he had already expended enough political capital on changing the preceding clause, which mattered to him more. Perhaps he endorsed it himself. In any case, it is noteworthy that even after Madison and the full Virginia assembly carefully scrutinized and edited the final article, they did so without disturbing George Mason's very last line. Minimally, this suggests that the notion of some kind of public duty to Christian love was more than just an idiosyncratic aspiration of a single thinker, but approached a basic political prescription prominently broadcast by one of the most notable electoral assemblies of the early republic.

Of course, it must be recognized that whatever is going on here is something considerably different from what is going on in the Model of

Christian Charity speech. Winthrop's notion of charity culminated in a strict covenant of religiously mandated behavior and orthodox belief. For Mason, on the other hand, whatever else charity entails, it entails a broad religious "toleration," and for Madison it either entails or must coexist with a legally protected right of religious "free exercise." This not only leaves open the possibility of worshipping God in unorthodox and highly personal ways, but of not worshipping, i.e., not loving, God at all. Yet still, Mason's text as revised by Madison indicates that nearly a century and a half after Winthrop's shipboard sermon, some concept of Christian charity as public "duty" is punctuating influential moments in American politics. That this will come as news to some and sound utterly anachronistic to others says less about the meaning and significance of the Virginia Declaration of Rights than it does about the long-term and incomparable influence of that other even more famous declaration of 1776.

Notes

1. For epigraphs on previous page, see Lincoln, *Collected Works*, 3: 375–76, and Jefferson, *Jefferson's Extracts*, 352. The influence of the Virginia Declaration of Rights on the Declaration of Independence will be discussed in more detail in chapter three. For other states borrowing from the Virginia Declaration, see Rutland, *George Mason*, 66–67. For the influence of the Virginia Declaration on the Bill of Rights and the Declaration of the Rights of Man, see Banning, *Jefferson and Madison*, 104. Condorcet as quoted in Mason, *Papers*, 276
2. Mason, *Papers*, 289.
3. Mason, *Papers*, 290. As quoted in Ketcham, *James Madison*, 73.
4. Mason, *Papers*, 285.

CHAPTER 3

A Model of Natural Liberty

Very late in life, Thomas Jefferson claimed that the Declaration of Independence was not "copied from any particular and previous writing." However, a side-by-side comparison of Jefferson's "original Rough draught" and George Mason's Virginia Declaration of Rights reveals a conspicuous likeness in the language and logic of these two texts.[1]

Just after Jefferson arrived in Philadelphia to attend the Continental Congress, the "Committee Draft" of Mason's text was printed in three different local papers just as Jefferson was tasked to draft the Declaration, and Mason, well-reputed "dean of the intellectual rebels" of revolutionary Virginia, was a key mentor to both Thomas Jefferson and James Madison in matters of political theory. All these things convincingly suggest that Jefferson read and in some fashion relied on Mason's text while composing his "original Rough draught" of the Declaration.[2] That so, it would appear that Jefferson decidedly left out from his text anything like Mason's final article concerning a duty to practice Christian love.

A most reasonable response to this is that Jefferson's Declaration was a formal break from England, and thus a call to war—hardly the place, it would seem, to make a case for a public commitment to *caritas*. Yet Mason's document, though not an explicit severing of ties with Great Britain and declaration of war, was tantamount to such and very much an expression of the revolutionary fervor of the day. And several years into the war, when faced with English threats to ravage and burn any city they could occupy, the Continental Congress issued its own warning that it would "take such exemplary vengeance as shall deter others from like conduct" to protect the "rights of humanity," but explicitly did so *not* in "anger and revenge" but in great anguish and regret because "the congress consider[ed] themselves bound to love their enemies, as children of that being who is equally the father of all."[3] The point here is

TABLE 3.1
Similar Phrasing in Virginia Declaration of Rights and "Original Rough Draught" of the Declaration of Independence

Virginia Dec. of Rights ("Committee Draft")	*Dec. of Independence* ("Original Rough Draught")
1. That *all men are born equally free and independent,* and have certain **inherent natural rights,** of which they cannot, by any compact, deprive or divest their posterity; among which are, the ENJOYMENT OF LIFE AND LIBERTY, with the means of acquiring and possessing property, and *pursuing and obtaining happiness* and safety.	We hold these truths to be self-evident; that *all men are created equal and independent;* that from that equal creation they derive **rights inherent and inalienable,** among which are the PRESERVATION OF LIFE AND LIBERTY, and the *pursuit of happiness;*
2. That **all power is** vested in, and consequetly **derived from, the People;** that magistrates are their trustees and servants, and at all times amenable to them.	that to secure these ends, governments are instituted among men, **deriving their just powers from the consent of the governed;**
3. That Government is, or ought to be, instituted for the common benefit, protection, and security of the people. nation, or community, of all the various modes and forms of government that is best which is capable of PRODUCING THE GREATEST DEGREE OF HAPPINESS AND SAFETY. . . . and that whenever *any government shall be found inadequate or contrary to these purposes,* a majority of the community hath an indubitable, **unalienable, indefeasible right, to reform, alter, or abolish it . . .**	that whenever any form of *government becomes destructive of these ends,* it is the **right of the people to alter or to abolish it,** and to institute new government, laying its foundation on such principles, and organizing its powers in such form, as to them shall seem most likely to EFFECT THEIR SAFETY AND HAPPINESS.

simply that Jefferson might well have fixed in the Declaration a principle of Christian love as some similarly situated revolutionary councils did. He did not. The reasons for this go beyond the martial aims prevailing in the summer of 1776, and the significance of all this is hard to overestimate.

The Declaration was instantly recognized by several key leaders as containing something even larger and more noteworthy than a compelling, lyrical, and official break with the crown. In forwarding a copy to

General George Washington, already engaged in the revolutionary conflict, John Hancock called it "the ground and foundation of government." Though the Declaration itself (as opposed to the act of declaring
independence) languished in relative obscurity for the next fifteen or
twenty years, the view announced by Hancock eventually spread more
broadly among the citizenry. By the time of the fiftieth anniversary of the
Declaration on July 4, 1826—a day marked by the astounding, simultaneous deaths of Jefferson and Adams—the document was well on its way
to becoming regarded as "American Scripture," a supernal statement of
national essence and aim, a luminous standard by which to assess the
justice and legitimacy of government at every level.[4] Consequently, by
not incorporating anything even like Mason's final article, Jefferson's
Declaration establishes for America a set of pre-eminent political norms
that depart considerably from an aspiration to be "A Model of Christian
Charity."

The extent to which Jefferson would steer America in 1776 away from
caritas as an explicit public ideal can be seen in even greater fashion by
comparing his "original Rough draught" of the Declaration with Winthrop's "Model" speech, as well as with later versions of the Declaration
itself as edited and approved by, respectively, the drafting committee and
the full Continental Congress. Zeroing in on Jefferson's early draft helps
avoid the common interpretive mistake of making the officially adopted
version the Declaration an unalloyed expression of Jefferson's thought.
While sanguine about the minor adjustments to his original prose by the
drafting committee (a number of those changes being his own), Jefferson was visibly depressed by the final changes made by the whole
assembly.[5]

Jefferson's Declaration and the Love of God

Jefferson begins his "original Rough draught" of the Declaration by basically recasting the world in which politics takes place for someone like
Winthrop. His very first clause points toward the conclusion that an earnest love of God—so central for Winthrop—is to be effectively emptied,
at least from the public sphere of American democracy. Where Winthrop's first line situates his constituents' departure from England in an
environment where God's providence is operating everywhere and at "all
times," Jefferson's memorable first seven words, "when in the course of
human events," suggest that even earth-shattering political movements

like the American Revolution seem more like acts in an unscripted, mortal drama rather than anything divinely directed. Where Winthrop asserts that "God Almighty" places people in different stations according to his will, Jefferson claims only that it is "necessary for a *people* to advance from that subordination in which *they* have hitherto remained." It is the people themselves who must see that they "assume among the powers of the earth" the political condition they deserve. Where Winthrop endeavors to satisfy fully the demands of a jealous, intervening God, Jefferson aims only to accommodate "a decent respect to the opinions of mankind." Repeatedly in this very first sentence, Jefferson delimits politics to the human realm.

God is not entirely missing, though, from the political cosmology of Jefferson's opening. In this same sentence Jefferson asserts that it is the "laws of nature and of nature's god" that "entitle" a people to throw off their subordinate status and acquire an "equal and independent station" in the world of nations. To be *entitled* to something presupposes the existence of a standard by which one might ascertain whether one is or is not entitled to that something. For Jefferson, such a standard exists in and through "nature's god." This puts Jefferson somewhere in the broad expanse between a Winthropian worldview where the providential God of traditional Christianity establishes a governing morality and orchestrates the operation of political life in light thereof and, say, a Machiavellian worldview where there is no apparent transcendent source or governing concern of right or wrong, only the raw demands and mortal rewards of getting and keeping power.[6] Jefferson's god of nature is an omnipresent force in the world, ever issuing a universal law by which basic political arrangements may be evaluated at all times and in all places. Yet "nature's god" appears to stand quite outside the world, allowing politics to take what "course" humans dictate and decide. Unseen and inactive—sustaining a foundational morality by which to judge politics, but neither punishing those who offend such a morality nor blessing those who follow it—this god provides no reason for Jefferson or anyone else to promote a reverent, public love of it.[7]

Among other things, all this reflects the fact that Jefferson, born and raised an Anglican, experienced something of a "religious crisis" in his early teens, and by the time he drafted the Declaration he had developed a "vaguely defined natural religion" based on reason (even though he continued to attend Anglican services throughout his life). Given a fire that destroyed Jefferson's childhood home and memorabilia and his reticence to publicly discuss his religious views—"say nothing of my religion," he once admonished a biographer, "it is known to my god and myself alone"—the best available portrait of Jefferson's early religious beliefs is found in his *Literary Commonplace Book* (hereafter *LCB*). This work consists of passages he painstakingly copied from noted poets, dramatists, and philosophers—a project he started in his teens, largely finished by the age of thirty, and referred to throughout his life.[8]

One of the earliest and longest selections in the *LCB* comes from Lord Bolingbroke, who provides "a veritable *summa* of rationalistic criticisms of revealed religion." As Eugene Sheridan has demonstrated, it is "almost certain" that these views reflect Jefferson's own.[9] In the passage copied, Bolingbroke attacks the miracles of Christ as evidence of his divinity because they were "equivocal at best" and are only found convincing where "ignorance or superstition abound," and, more importantly, because Jesus was not divine.[10] Bolingbroke further asserts that the fundamental Christian doctrines of the "fall of man" and Christ's redemptive sacrifice for sin are "absolutely irreconcilable to every idea . . . of wisdom, justice and goodness."[11] In like fashion, he rejects the whole concept of "inspiration" in favor of hard evidence "no reasonable man can refuse to admit,"[12] thereby repudiating the Bible as the word of God, which Bolingbroke claims is filled with "gross defects, and palpable falsehoods" on almost every page.[13]

Of course, many of Jefferson's editors—meaning the drafting committee and the full Continental Congress—maintained a more traditional Christian worldview and as a result did infuse the Declaration with just such a theological cast. In his "original Rough draught," Jefferson makes only two overtly religious references. One is the previously mentioned reference to "nature's god"—a noncapitalized deity quite different from that found in either the Old or New Testament. The other is Jefferson's sneering reference to King George as "the *Christian* king of Great Britain" (emphasis is Jefferson's), who, Jefferson alleges, "waged cruel war against human nature itself" by forcing upon the colonies a slave trade they did not want.

Alternatively, the drafting committee takes a key phrase from Jefferson's original second sentence, "that all men are created equal and independent, that from that equal creation they derive rights," and changes it to "that all men are created equal, that they are endowed by their *creator* with inherent and inalienable rights" (ultimately, the full Congress changes the second half of the phrase to read "with certain unalienable rights"). This adds a deity reference and one that sounds more like the traditional, creator God of the Bible. It also makes this creator God, rather than the fact of equal creation, the source of natural rights. Furthermore, by excising the entire passage about the slave trade, the full Congress eliminates Jefferson's sole and sarcastic use of the term *"Christian."* They also entirely rewrote his original ending, inserting two more traditional-sounding references to God in the process. Borrowing liberally from language offered by Jefferson's fellow Virginian Richard Henry Lee (who on June 7, 1776, moved the resolution to declare independence), Congress added an appeal "to the supreme judge of the world" and acknowledged "a firm reliance on the protection of divine Providence." It would seem that Harry Jaffa's observation that "the Declaration has reference to natural, not to revealed theology" is truer of Jefferson's original draft than the final version edited by his fellow delegates.[14] In any case, Jefferson appears different from his congressional colleagues, and quite a bit different from a John Winthrop, in wanting to replace the active, providential God of the Judeo-Christian tradition with a disinterested, nonrewarding god of nature as the deific power of American public life. And such a move clearly obviates the political significance of *agape*'s vertical dimension, or the love of God. Jefferson's core doctrine of natural rights, succinctly stated in his long second sentence, the best-known line in all of American political thought, works to much the same effect.[15]

"Self-evident Truths"

Jefferson begins the original version of his famous second sentence with "We hold these truths to be sacred and undeniable." Such language does have something of a religious air. It was likely that Jefferson himself, though, later changed "sacred and undeniable" to "self-evident" in the Committee Draft (Franklin is a competing candidate for the source of this change).[16] Some argue that the move to "self-evident" truths clearly situates the epistemology of the Declaration on the ground of reason alone, where others have defended the view that such truths are confirmed through an innate "moral sense" as described in the key texts of the Scottish Enlightenment, which Jefferson knew well and admired.[17] Given the strength of argument on both sides and how Jefferson's own writings have been effectively marshaled to support each side of this debate, it would seem most plausible that Jefferson takes the truth of such sentiments to be confirmable, in some degree, by both reason and feeling. Years after writing the Declaration, while serving as Washington's secretary of state, Jefferson would write to Washington concerning some disputes over French treaties, saying that all specific "questions of natural right" as concrete expression of natural law are

> triable by their conformity with the moral sense and reason of man. Those who write treatises of natural law, can only declare what their own moral sense and reason dictate in the several cases they state. Such of them as happen to have feeling and a reason coincident with those of the wise and honest part of mankind, are respected and quoted as witnesses of what is morally right or wrong in particular cases. Grotius, Puffendorf, Worlf, and Vattel are of this number. Where they agree their authority is strong: but where they differ, and they often differ, we must appeal to our own feelings and reason to decide between them.[18]

Whether Jefferson would have actually preferred "sacred and undeniable" to "self-evident," or however the reason/moral sense debate actually cashed out in his mind (we will probably never know precisely), the fact remains that Jefferson considered the basic truth claims of the Declaration as so manifestly true as to need no further justification. In particular what was not needed was the voice of God as found in biblical revelation or the whisperings of the Holy Spirit—epistemological cornerstones of Winthrop's model of charity—to confirm their truth; if anything, Jefferson thought those forms of moral knowledge got in the way of recognizing the truths of the Declaration. We can also see that in the content of the truths themselves comes a significant departure from Winthrop's model. Beyond recasting God as a being who neither actively loves his subjects nor expects obedient love in return, and beyond dismissing heavenly revelation as a source of earthly political truth, Jefferson articulates a set of truth claims that raises a significant barrier between the activities of government and devotion to God.

The first truth Jefferson tenders is that "all men are created equal." Years ago, Garry Wills argued that what Jefferson means by this is that all men are roughly equal in their mental and moral faculties, enough to make decisions of right or wrong on their own. Others, starting with a movement in the 1820s, have come to believe that Jefferson's statement indicates that all humans ought to enjoy roughly equal amounts of wealth and opportunity.[19] But Jefferson's statement is, strictly speaking, neither an empirical observation, a recognition of man's mental or material condition, nor a normative aspiration, a dream of social egalitarianism for all mankind. In more precise terms, it is a normative observation, an acceptance of a universal moral fact about humanity.

According to Jefferson, one may indeed possess superior physical, intellectual, or spiritual talents—one may be a member of what he will later dub a "natural aristocracy . . . of virtue and talents"—but one is not, ipso facto, entitled to rule over another.[20] The point is nicely emphasized in his "original Rough draught" where, as previously noted, he says that "all men are created equal *and independent*" (emphasis added). Interpreters must be wary of trying to prove points about one thinker by quoting passages from another—an all too common practice in Jeffersonian scholarship in particular. Nevertheless, it seems appropriate here to mention that in Locke's *Second Treatise,* which heavily influenced Jefferson, Locke uses the exact same phrase, "equal and independent," to characterize those in a "state of nature," which he argues is a "state of perfect freedom" where man is naturally free from the "will of any other man."[21] The notion that natural equality is tantamount to natural liberty is emphasized yet again in the "original Rough draught" where Jefferson argues that it is precisely "from that equal creation [human beings] derive rights inherent and inalienable," namely the rights of "life, liberty, and the pursuit of happiness."[22] And these rights, most agree, are simply equivalent to freedom from the rule of another.

Some argue that the last of this famous triad of rights actually denotes a governmental duty to provide happiness. But this is to confuse the Declaration's stated right to the *pursuit* of happiness with some unstated right to happiness itself. As Jefferson himself explained later in life, the same god who put it "in the nature of man to pursue happiness" also left man "free in the choice of place as well as mode" of that happiness. Certainly this helps explain why Jefferson did not bother to define happiness in the Declaration, and it suggests a kind of pointlessness to sober academic arguments over whether the pursuit of happiness language is really just Jefferson's euphemistic cover for Lockean antecedents of rights to property or a life of reason.[23] The meaning of happiness is purposely vague in the Declaration, and Jefferson's own thoughts about happiness are largely irrelevant. Ronald Hamowy has summed this up nicely:

When Jefferson spoke of an inalienable right to the pursuit of happiness, he meant that men may act as they choose in their search for ease, comfort, felicity, and grace, either by owning property or not, by accumulating wealth or distributing it, by opting for material success or asceticism, in a word, by determining the path to their own earthly and heavenly salvation as they alone see fit.[24]

In his "Little Speech" on liberty, Winthrop argues forcefully that Massachusetts is a polity predicated on establishing a "moral" or "civil" liberty to do only that which is good, not a "natural liberty" to choose good or evil as one wishes. But in Jefferson, it is precisely the securing of this more fundamental natural liberty that is the one and only justifying aim of government. Inherent rights of life, liberty, and even the pursuit of happiness leave the broadest possible swath of self-choice and direction, including the choice of many things that some people might think evil. (Jefferson's concept of natural liberty is not an utter moral free-for-all—which may have been what Winthrop actually had in mind—but it is certainly a freedom to pick and choose and ignore a wide range of religious and ethical principles as one is so inclined, which Winthrop most certainly would not have accepted and would have considered something approaching "natural liberty.") And, as Jefferson explains in his next truth, to "secure these rights, Governments are instituted among men."[25] Actually Jefferson's original language drives the point home even more emphatically. There, rather than saying "to secure these rights" he says to "secure these *ends*, governments are instituted among men" (emphasis added). As Jefferson sees it, the end of government, government's very raison d'être, is to secure the safe exercise of basic natural rights so that individuals can define and pursue happiness, as much as possible, as they alone see it.

The implications here for religion are significant. In short, as fundamental political principles, the self-evident truths of the Declaration dictate that religious aims and practices should basically stand apart from government activity and control. Because people are perfectly free, by right, to seek their own individual happiness as they individually are inclined, government, when it comes to religion, is restricted to establishing an environment that lets Christians be Christians, Hindus be Hindus, and atheists be atheists, in a peaceful and ordered environment. Jefferson puts it most memorably in his only published book, *Notes on the State of Virginia*,

> The legitimate powers of government extend to such acts only as are injurious to others. But it does me no injury for my neighbor to say there are twenty gods, or no God. It neither picks my pocket nor breaks my leg.[26]

While this last statement reveals much of Jefferson's own dismissal of anything like the Puritan's God of providence (no threat here of a national shipwreck caused by a jealous God blasting his slothful and profane followers), it should be stressed that the core liberal paradigm of Jefferson's natural rights doctrine is not necessarily anti-Christian, much less antireligious. At the time, plenty of religious Americans in and out of the Continental Congress were more than delighted with a foundational political doctrine that basically got government out of the business of making people good according to some sectarian outlook. For Jefferson, citizens as private individuals could worship and love God as they please. That was much of the point and a reason many religious Americans so eagerly embraced the Declaration. In any case, driven partly by his own grave doubts about the veracity of any traditional religion, and even more so by his firm conviction of the core truths of the Declaration and their implications, Jefferson devoted a significant amount of his political career to "building a wall of separation between church and State." The crowning achievement of this effort was the disestablishment of Virginia's state church, an effort Jefferson began just months after passage of the Declaration and something he considered, along with the drafting of the Declaration and his founding of the University of Virginia, to be one of the three most important accomplishments in his life.[27]

In his last extant letter written just days before passing away, Jefferson cordially declined Roger Weightman's request to come to Washington, D.C., for a gala celebrating the fiftieth anniversary of the signing of the Declaration. In doing so, he indicated that he saw the Declaration becoming an ensign to "all" the "world," and praised it for "arousing men to burst the chains under which monkish ignorance and superstition had persuaded them to bind themselves" to authoritarian rule. He continues,

> All eyes are opened, or opening, to the rights of man. The general spread of the light of science has already laid open to every view the palpable truth, that the mass of mankind has not been born with saddles on their backs, nor a favored few booted and spurred, ready to ride them legitimately, by the grace of God.[28]

For Jefferson, reason (the "light of science") working in tandem with a universal moral sense ("palpable truth," meaning truths felt) were steadily repudiating the ignorant and superstitious traditions of revealed religion that had long made it difficult to see clearly that "all men are created equal." Now "all eyes" can see, or will soon see, what America—thanks to the Declaration—stands for at its core, namely that no natural political authority exists and therefore people are naturally free to govern themselves.

By the time of his death, Jefferson had turned Winthrop's model of Christian charity—which Winthrop said attracted "the eyes of all people"[29]—inside out. By July 4, 1826, Winthropianism, with its basis in scripture and the Holy Spirit, providential human inequality, and the ever-present demand to worship God and actively care for our neighbor, is substantially eclipsed in public discourse by Jeffersonianism, with its basis in reason and a secular moral sense, natural human equality, and the preeminent need to respect the individual as free human agent. With this change, it is America as a model of natural liberty that now aspires to be a City upon a Hill shining to the rest of the world. While there is no evidence the Virginia founders were familiar with the story of John Winthrop, John Adams no doubt was and surely had Winthrop's famed speech in mind when, in 1780, he wrote fellow New Englander and vaunted Revolutionary War general Nathanael Greene that "America is the City, set upon a Hill," something he noted to stress how intensely the whole world was watching America to see what was to become of its bold move for republican independence.[30]

Given the Declaration's overwhelming influence on America's larger moral and political psyche, it is little wonder that the end of George Mason's Declaration now reads anachronistically. Mason's final passage on charity jars the modern reader long weaned on the ideals of the Declaration, which by its very logic takes statutory documents out of the business of making—to say nothing of enforcing—religious pronouncements. While this may constitute Jefferson's most obvious and fundamental break with the assumptions and aims of Winthrop's model of Christian charity, other important differences with Winthrop in particular and Christianity more generally must not go unnoticed, especially with respect to *agape*'s command to love thy neighbor as thyself.

Jefferson's Declaration and the Love of Others

It has already been noted that nowhere do we see in the Declaration Christian love as the kind of mild civic postscript Jefferson's mentor

George Mason wanted to make it, let alone the grand, overarching public aim John Winthrop wanted to make it. Jefferson's original text indeed lacks any mention of "charity" or Christian love. One might say it even suffers, in places, from an overwrought malice. Nevertheless, the document—at least Jefferson's original—does embrace some concept of human "affection" as a relevant civic ideal.

Mention was made earlier of Jefferson's pejorative reference to King George. John Adams was quick to criticize this section as "too passionate, and too much like scolding." Years later, Daniel Webster, in his famous eulogy of Jefferson and Adams, felt the need to contextualize what many still considered the unfair "asperity and anger" of this section. It is now generally acknowledged that in this section Jefferson grossly exaggerates the importance and atrocity of some peripheral events and sometimes attributes actions to King George that were actually carried out by Parliament or local colonial authorities often acting independently of the crown.[31]

In addition to excoriating King George, Jefferson also turns his pen against America's "British brethren." While acknowledging that the colonies diligently attempted to lay "a foundation for perpetual league and amity with them," Jefferson declaims that the British were too often "deaf to the voice of justice and consanguinity" and too often responsible for disturbing "our harmony," consequently rendering "the last stab to agonizing *affection*" (emphasis added). Therefore, Jefferson continues in rhetorical crescendo, Americans must "renounce forever these unfeeling brethren. We must endeavor to forget our former love for them." With that, Jefferson proposes an "everlasting Adieu" to Great Britain.

This all proved too much for Jefferson's fellow delegates, who neutralized Jefferson's acid edge by toning down his attack on King George. They struck more than two-thirds of the paragraph aimed at a spiteful break with England, basically reducing it to a single phrase from the original otherwise lost in Jefferson's surrounding invective. England would be regarded as "the rest of mankind, enemies in war, in peace friends!"

Surely some of the difference here is simply explained by age. Jefferson, one of the youngest delegates, needed to be restrained by men not more genuinely charitable but older, wiser, and calmer in the ways of the world. Joseph Ellis sees Jefferson's misstatements about the king ("historical and intellectual nonsense") and far more hostile rhetoric of renouncement as a verbal strategy calculated to inspire Americans to fight against Britain. But he also sees it as evidence of Jefferson's own deep "reservoir of hatred" against all things English.[32]

To the degree Jefferson held a basic malice toward the English, it can be explained in part by Jefferson's tendency to see the world in dichotomous terms. On one side were those who embraced the ideals of the Declaration and a practical implementation of such, and on the other were those who did not. In encountering those who would not realize well enough the ideals of natural liberty (British peers, Christian sectarians, and High Federalists), or those who would impractically push the ideals too far (radical anti-Federalists and abolitionists), Jefferson's patience quickly wore thin and his personal indignation raged even if he rarely exposed such feelings publicly.[33]

But Jefferson's original draft suggests that his pique specifically at the British was also rooted in something else. What comes through in the original is that England had earned Jefferson's profound animus because of its "agonizing" stab to American "affection." At least at this early stage of his life, the English were hardly foreigners evoking a xenophobic distaste, nor were they exclusively tyrants in the wrong. Their tyranny, in the relative sweep of things, was not nearly as oppressive as that of many other empires, including numerous examples that would have been familiar to Jefferson, great student of history as he was. What made their lighter though still real oppression so galling to Jefferson was that the English were their "brethren," a people with whom America had a relationship of "love." But that love could no more be remembered or reciprocated because a "long train" of active antagonisms and passive injustices had finally revealed the English as "unfeeling," therefore unworthy of the affection now drained from the American heart. Jefferson's great hope, laid out in his Summary View of the Rights of British America (Jefferson's most famous and important pre-Declaration writing composed in 1774), that instead of conflict, "fraternal love and harmony" would ultimately prevail between England and the American colonies, had finally proven unattainable. And like a betrayed brother, his anger was more than that typically directed at a foe with whom no prior relationship existed.[34]

The young Thomas Jefferson, spirited advocate of a new order of individual liberty that he was, was also a fervent sentimentalist, meaning, among other things, he was a devotee of the Scottish moral sense school, with all its doctrines of a natural love, care, and affection for other human beings.[35] If what seems to prevail in the Declaration is the opposite of that, a spirit of hate and malice toward the English, it surely had something to do with the fact that the English were, for Jefferson, striking at the fundamental twin roots of ethical decency. Not only were they at odds with his cherished doctrine of natural rights, but they were actively violating bonds of affection that in his eyes once prevailed and should still be prevailing given that they are ever a mark of a moral people.

While explicit ideals of love and affection were a vital component of the young Jefferson's moral outlook, it is important to recognize how little these ideals were consciously connected to any Christian teaching.[36] Among the other attacks of Lord Bolingbroke on traditional religion that Jefferson records in his *Literary Commonplace Book* is the following:

> It is not true that Christ revealed an entire body of ethics, proved to be the law of nature from principles of reason, and reaching all the duties of life. If mankind wanted such a code, to which recourse might be had on every occasion, as to an unerring rule in every part of the moral duties, such a code is still wanting; for the gospel is not such a code.[37]

Other evidence in the *LCB* indicates that at least before the end of 1762 and possibly as early as 1758, when Jefferson was still in his middle teens studying with the classical scholar James Maury, he developed a strong attachment to Epicureanism and Stoicism, the ideals of which he remained devoted to throughout life in some fashion. Jefferson believed that a "system of ethics" as found in the "ancient heathen moralists" of these two traditions "would be more full, more entire, more coherent, and more clearly deduced from unquestionable principles of knowledge" than anything offered in the New Testament.[38]

By 1771, however, a letter to a young in-law, Robert Skipwith, reveals that Jefferson's ethical outlook had grown to encompass something more than the rational individualism of these ancient Greco-Roman moralities he adopted during his earliest intellectual stirrings. In this piece of correspondence on recommended reading, Jefferson extols "the entertainments of fiction" specifically for how they help "fix us in the principles and practice of virtue." He continues,

> When any original act of *charity* or of gratitude, for instance, is presented either to our sight or imagination, we are deeply impressed with

its beauty and feel a strong desire in ourselves of doing *charitable* and grateful acts also.[39]

It is significant that as Jefferson writes here of principles of virtue, his very first *for instance* is "charity." It would be a gross mistake, though, to assume that this conception of charity stems from some favorable reconsideration of Christian teaching. To start, the letter clearly situates Jefferson's understanding of charity in the language of moral sense philosophy. Charity is described as something that can be presented to "our sight or imagination," by which we are "deeply impressed" and "feel led" to follow. Jefferson goes on to explain that witnessing an act of charity produces within us a positive emotion, which "is an exercise of our virtuous dispositions, and dispositions of the mind, like limbs of the body acquire strength by exercise." This is classic Scottish Enlightenment thinking, something Jefferson was well-grounded in by 1771, and something far from the standard Christian theology of his day.[40]

Furthermore, Jefferson encloses an extensive recommended reading list in which the Bible is proffered only as a useful text in "History. Ancient." Under the heading of "Religion," the closest thing to a standard Christian text mentioned is the collected sermons of England's unorthodox clergyman turned novelist, Laurence Sterne. Sterne's influence on Jefferson's early view of charity appears significant, but it is his fiction, even less orthodox than his sermons, that most affects Jefferson. Sixteen years later almost to the day, Jefferson will write to his favorite nephew, Peter Carr, that "the writings of Sterne particularly form the best course of morality that ever was written," the same letter wherein he admonishes Carr never to lose an occasion to exercise his dispositions "to be generous, to be charitable, to be humane." Here, in the 1771 letter to Skipwith, Jefferson specifically notes that a passage from Sterne's quasi-autobiographical novel *A Sentimental Journey* greatly exercised his own impulses of charity. Such a report would have gratified Sterne himself, given that Sterne's self-stated aim in writing the book was to "teach us to love the world and our fellow creatures better than we do."[41]

In this particular passage, a poor monk begging for his convent approaches the fictional Sterne, who has just arrived in Calais, France. Before the monk even speaks, Sterne describes buttoning up his purse and determining "not to give him a single sous." Then, after hearing the monk's appeal, Sterne launches into a speech that begins quite empathetically—"heaven must be their resource who have no other but the *charity* of the world"—but shortly turns caustic:

we distinguish, my good Father! Betwixt those who wish only to eat the bread of their own labour—and those who eat the bread of other people's, and have no other plan in life, but to get through it in sloth and ignorance, for the love of god (emphasis added).[42]

As the monk graciously departs, Sterne confesses, "My heart smote me the moment he shut the door." But several hours of rationalization keep him from running after the monk to apologize, and his resolve to "learn better manners" is delayed. Shortly thereafter, he encounters the monk a second time and promptly apologizes for his cutting comments and gives the monk his expensive snuffbox as a "peace offering."[43]

This fictional exchange made an indelible impression on Jefferson and is thus worth considering in some detail.[44] First, the story plainly comports with moral sense philosophy. Feeling, more than reason, triumphs as Sterne's ethical guide. It is his "heart" rather than head that smites him into charitable behavior, and it is his head that keeps him from giving anything to the monk in the first place and from making immediate amends. Sterne's model is also manifestly secular. While his heart is changed, that change is not wrought by some regenerative experience of divine grace. And Sterne's initial aversion to treating the monk charitably was partly because the monk's "love of god" led to a kind of "sloth and ignorance" in temporal affairs. While Sterne appears to regret the comment, it is not clear he ever sees much good in anything like ascetic devotion to God. Notwithstanding, Sterne opens his purse. The lesson that another's particular "love of god" should neither favor nor disfavor one's charitable inclinations was a moral imperative Jefferson tried to follow throughout his life. Jefferson's own financial generosity to religious organizations whose tenets he clearly did not support is a well-documented fact.[45]

While generous almsgiving appears to be a main component of Sterne's concept of charity here, it is not just the financial stinginess of Sterne at which Sterne's and Jefferson's moral sense recoils. Jefferson is also "sorrowful" over Sterne's initial "unkindly" rebuke and "secretly resolve(s)" to never behave that way himself.[46] So important is this to Jefferson over the years that he found most verbal political debate unsavory and rarely uttered a disagreeable word with anyone publicly—which some now denigrate as evidence of a dishonest and calculating disposition, which it may be to some degree, though it is just as easily evidence of a strong man with strong opinions determined since his youth to be polite in public. Jefferson is furthermore "pleased" by Sterne's effort at "atonement," meaning for Jefferson a candid acknowledgment of fault and an effort to make "just reparation." Thus, Sterne and Jefferson appear to share a view of charity that also encompasses notions of human sympathy, social civility, and, when necessary, humble reconciliation.

What all this indicates is that at the time of drafting the Declaration, Jefferson quite clearly did *not* share George Mason's commitment to a specifically Christian duty of charity in the public realm. However, some more worldly concept of *caritas,* perhaps with distant Christian roots but significantly shaped by the fiction of Sterne and the philosophy of the Scots, was a vital thread in the fabric of Jefferson's political and personal morality. Thus, whatever the reason, the excessive malice of Jefferson's "original Rough draught" comes not because of his conscious rejection of charity as a virtue of merit, but in spite of the charity very much a part of his social ethics. Youthful passion probably played a role. If it is a case of hypocrisy, it would not be Jefferson's first or most glaring. And, as noted, hatred was always the other side of the coin of Jefferson's moral universe—the British were to be detested because their repeated rejection of extended fraternal feeling made them detestable. But chief among the reasons that Jefferson smothers even his non-Christian sense of *caritas* in favor of a more malevolent position in the Declaration was that charity's "better manners" were subordinate to the aim of securing the natural rights of liberty, through bellicose rhetoric and martial means if necessary. His commitment to charity was important, but not primary. What was primary for Jefferson was establishing a republic on the ground of natural rights—a model of natural liberty.

From "Apple of Gold" to "Picture of Silver"

In the Declaration, Jefferson is remarkably vague about the particular form of government a model of natural liberty requires.[47] The one thing he does insist on, following the unfolding logic of his previously stated truths in his famous second sentence, is that government must derive its "just powers from the consent of the governed." In a world of natural equality, for "any form" of government to be legitimate, it must operate by consent whereby natural equals mutually agree on a form of government "most likely" to establish the "safety" necessary to pursue happiness as they individually see fit. In conditions of natural liberty, where everyone is equally endowed with the freedom to pursue his or her own view of happiness, conflicting claims of right are likely to emerge. Jefferson was ever conscious of this fact, once quoting late in life an unidentified author that "rightful liberty is the unobstructed action according to our will, within the limits drawn around us by the equal rights of others."[48] Thus, a model of natural liberty must see that the practical exercise of everyone's basic, inherent rights be limited to some degree in order to make them consistent with each other and realizable.

This does not signal in any way even a partial surrender of those rights, which are "unalienable." It only signals that natural equals have, of their own accord, agreed to a conventional form of authority to identify and enforce conventional limits to their rights so as to be able to exercise those rights in a condition of safety and order. It is precisely because natural equals can never surrender, or alienate, their rights to life, liberty, and the pursuit of happiness that citizens always have the additional right to "alter or abolish" that government that has become "destructive" of the exercise of such rights and establish one that protects them.[49] And this was exactly what was happening as Jefferson sat writing in the second-floor parlor of a home on the corner of Market and Seventh Streets in Philadelphia and as Washington readied to engage British troops arriving on a hundred-ship fleet headed for New York.

John Winthrop drew his city on a hill image from the Sermon on the Mount. In this classic text Jesus abandons the Mosaic principle of "eye for an eye" in favor of the ethical command to "resist not evil: but whosoever shall smite thee on the right cheek, turn to him the other also . . . and whosoever shall compel thee to go a mile, go with him twain" (Matt. 5:38–41). Winthrop, as he sailed out of the English Channel, was prepared to lead a violent force against what appeared to be the Massachusetts Bay Company's seagoing attackers. This suggests just how natural and human it is, even in the teeth of deep and genuine commitments to *agape*, to physically defend one's own and one's own way of life.

A key difference, though, between the Model speech and the Declaration is that where Winthrop is left to square his violence of self-defense against his own Christian rhetoric that draws in another direction, Jefferson offers an entirely different rhetoric. Where Jesus would apparently encourage humanity to "resist not" in the face of force and compulsion, Jefferson declares both humanity's "right" and "*duty*" to "throw off" governments of "arbitrary power" (emphasis added).[50] Where Jesus lauds a "meek" spirit (Matt. 5:5), Jefferson lauds a "manly spirit."[51] Where Jesus extols peacemaking (Matt. 5:9), Jefferson extols "opposing [tyranny] with manly firmness." It might be suggested that there is something of a "turn the other cheek" ethic in Jefferson's view that armed rebellion for liberty is justified only *after* a "long train of abuses." But this patient "suffer[ing] of evils" is called for, Jefferson indicates, by way of "prudence" rather than charity. Secular history may, like God, preach restraint, but for reasons more practical than moral.

The last remark to be made here about Jefferson's famous second sentence is that it specifically argues that governments are instituted "to secure" the natural rights of liberty. To speak of needing to secure rights that are inherent or inalienable may sound contradictory only if one fails to distinguish between the *possessing* of rights and the *exercising* of rights. Jefferson does not claim that governments are instituted to secure the possession of rights; quite clearly he asserts that rights are inherently possessed. Rather, he declares that governments are instituted to secure liberty, or the free exercise of those rights inherently possessed. The very fact that he must argue that governments must secure these rights implies a powerful standing threat to the free exercise of those rights, a threat so powerful that government alone is seen as the one antidote to fully "secure" rights. Except for the fact that the Declaration is a document of reason, written to persuade reasonable people of the justness of the American cause—suggesting that rational argument might, in some modest but important way, help secure natural rights—Jefferson does not even hint that something else might suffice. In the Declaration, Jefferson turns to neither religious principle, classical virtue, civic education, nor society's mediating institutions as central solutions to the standing threat against the exercise of rights (though he saw great value in most of these things).

In terms of what the particular source of that threat may be, we know from Jefferson's opening that he does not see a real threat from "nature's god" who stands over but outside politics. As he put it in the Summary View, "the god who gave us life, gave us liberty at the same time: the hand of force may destroy, but cannot disjoin them."[52] Nowhere, especially in Jefferson's original, is the reader led to believe that nature's god would be the force to destroy life or liberty, or having coupled life and liberty from the beginning would ever disjoin them. (Another far cry from Winthrop's model, where God's threatening punishments of death and refusal to countenance the broad practice of natural liberty loomed over all that Massachusetts did and said.) The only other real candidate, then, for such a "force" must be located somewhere in humanity itself.

It may be that the most threatening culprits of tyranny are human beings with tyrannical instincts and abilities. In the Declaration, Jefferson hurls almost all his invective at one single individual. By Jefferson's lights, the main provocation for America's Declaration came from King George's "establishment of an absolute tyranny," the fact that his character was "marked by every act which may define a tyrant," and that for twelve years he had committed "acts of tyranny without a mask," thus making him "unfit to be the ruler of a people who would be free." But in his Summary View, Jefferson is explicit that the threat of tyranny is larger than that emanating from the grasping clutches of a monarch. "History," he says, "has informed us that bodies of men as well as individuals are susceptible of the spirit of tyranny." An impulse to tyranny is not limited to the domain of the aggressive and talented despot but rather is an impulse common to man. This is, by the way, a different claim than to say, as some modern liberal theorists do, that humans are inherently and primarily selfish. Tyranny, or the will to dominate, may often be driven by the selfish desire for more power or wealth. But tyranny may also well up from selfless sources as well. To borrow a line from Chesterton, sometimes the "sin and sorrow of despotism is not that it does not love men, but that it loves them too much and trusts them too little." Indeed, much of the tyranny of Winthrop's Massachusetts was carried out in the name, if not true spirit, of concern for the salvation and welfare of others.[53]

Between Jefferson's Summary View and the Declaration, then, it is possible to see the most basic and competing concepts that the Framers of the Constitution would strive to bring together in a workable whole while toiling through the summer of 1787 as Jefferson served in Paris. By revealing natural equality as humanity's fundamental normative fact, the Declaration makes securing human liberty society's essential practical aim. This was, as Lincoln would later put it in 1861, America's animating goal—the theoretical "apple of gold" around which the practical Constitution sat as a "picture of silver," the latter being made for the former, not vice versa.[54] To secure the safe practice of human liberty requires government in some form, based on the consent of the governed. Free beings still require rulers to coordinate conflicting claims of right. But if Jefferson's position in the Summary View is right, the spirit of man is such that groups and individuals can easily become tyrannical for a variety reasons—both noble and base. Thus government faces a double duty, a duty most neatly summarized in Madison's couplet from Federalist 51 that "essential to the preservation of liberty" is the principle that "you must first enable the government to control the governed; and in the next place oblige it to control itself."[55]

If Madison put things more succinctly in the 1790s it is because by then the Founders saw the limits of their first attempt to institute a rights-protecting government. The Articles of Confederation, resting heavily on the willingness of each of the states to actively "perpetuate mutual friendship" among the people of the various states, proved too weak to address conflicting claims of right between the states. Bonds of affection alone between the states were clearly not enough to hold the colonies together in a peaceful, free whole. The national government had to be stronger. Yet it still had to be kept from becoming tyrannical. The specific primary and auxiliary mechanisms the Framers adopt in the Constitution to create a limited government of consent (strong enough to preserve liberty but kept in check enough to not encroach upon that liberty) need not be rehearsed here. It might be useful, though, to rehearse some of the key assumptions they made in developing a large, representative republic, with a sturdy national government and an elaborate system of checks and balances as the form of government best suited to institutionalize consent and protect individual liberties for the former American colonies.

Federalist 10 is as rich a resource for this discussion as perhaps any other text. There, Madison explains that somehow trying to resolve all conflicting claims of right by giving everyone the "same opinions, the same passions, and the same interests" is chimerical indeed. Many are the forces that have "divided mankind into parties," rendering humanity far more likely to engage in conflict and oppression than cooperation for the common good. "So strong is this propensity" Madison continues, that even "the most frivolous and fanciful distinctions have been sufficient to kindle their unfriendly passions, and excite their most violent conflict." Chief among these faction-causing forces are the powerful combination of man's "fallible" reason and natural "self-love," "unequal faculties of acquiring property," and a "zeal for different opinions concerning religions," all of which appear to be sown in the "nature of man."[56]

So much for any hope of achieving a utopia of Christian love where all are perfectly knit together in a selfless union of warm affection and high spiritual purpose. The practical statesmen will simply accept, Madison reasons, that the "spirit of party and faction" are "necessary and ordinary operations of Government." Unable to remove these causes of faction sown so deeply into human nature, the best that can be hoped for is to control their effects. Again, the controls *not* chosen are as illuminating as the ones chosen. Governmental attempts to forcefully redistribute wealth and property or to penalize the "faculties" for acquiring such are deemed both impractical and illiberal. Madison also asserts that it is "well know[n]" that "moral and religious motives can not be relied on as an adequate control." And he concludes that it is "vain to say, that enlightened statesmen will be able to adjust these clashing interests and render them all subservient to the public good" because even if such a complicated adjustment could be made—a dubious proposition at best—there is no promise that such a capable and trustworthy statesman will always "be at the helm."[57]

Jefferson's initial reaction to the Constitution was mixed—feeling alarmed in particular over a lack of a bill of rights and the failure to rotate the office of president. But he soon came to see its genius, in no small part due to his reading of the *Federalist Papers,* which he described in 1788 as "the best commentary on the principles of government, which was ever written," especially those letters written by Madison. Late in life, he mandated that it become a mainstay text in the political education of any student attending his beloved University of Virginia.[58] In light of this, it is possible to say that Jefferson accepted the Constitution and the assumptions behind it as generally appropriate to his model of natural liberty—though later fights with Federalist interpretations of the Constitution would test this acceptance.

In any case, he, like others who accepted and supported the Constitution, recognized that it was consciously designed to produce a large, fairly cacophonous republic, widely liberated in its moral practices and pursuits of pecuniary interests, consequently riddled with faction and a spirit of party interests, with no formal mandate for religious ideals or inspired leadership to act as restraints on that spirit. It does all this because the Framers took Jefferson's apple of gold—liberty to all—and framed it with what many agreed was the slightly lesser but necessary metal of protections—the silver frame of the Constitution—demanded by proven human tendencies. In structuring things this way, it would seem that Jefferson's model of natural liberty could hardly look more different from Winthrop's model of Christian charity. It was different, fundamentally different. Although, just as the Puritans' model of charity was perhaps more committed to aspects of natural liberty than someone like Winthrop would have cared to admit, it appears that some *agapic*-like ideals dappled the Founding in ways that defy a strictly secular, individualist understanding of natural rights liberalism.

One of the few clauses from the heavily edited ending of Jefferson's "original Rough draught" that made it into the final draft unscathed is the very last: "we mutually pledge to each other our lives, our fortunes, & our sacred honor." This commitment, offered up in "support of this Declaration," was anything but idle banter. Each signatory was, by signing, committing an official act of treason, for which they could be hanged. Faced off against the world's most powerful military force, the chance that the war for independence could prove unsuccessful and they would each meet such a fate was extraordinarily high. While serving as governor of Virginia during the war, Jefferson escaped capture by just minutes from British forces marching on Monticello. In that instance, both Jefferson and Monticello avoided destruction. Other signers proved less fortunate, losing homes, families, and even their own lives.

The rhetoric of sacrifice in the final clause of the Declaration sounds more classical than Christian. Undoubtedly, this final clause is a reflection of older Roman influences revived in colonial America through eighteenth-century English opposition thought.[59] But surely there is also something of the *agapic* in this rhetoric. The Book of John records that on the night of his Last Supper, Jesus meets with his apostles and discourses on many things, including a vital emendation to his previous teachings on charity. That night he gives his disciples a "new commandment" revising the old commandment to love your neighbor as yourself. Now, he says, the principle is "love one another; as I have loved you" (John 13:34). This was said in anticipation of his crucifixion and atoning sacrifice, which were only hours away. To love someone as you love yourself was, and remains, an astonishingly high moral bar. But Jesus would take his followers one step beyond, to the level of his love, where even thoughts of self—a right to life, if you will—become subordinate to higher aims and the needs of others. Later that same evening, Jesus will reiterate, "This is my commandment, That ye love one another, as I have loved you." He then immediately adds this detail: "Greater love hath no man than this, that a man lay down his life for his friends" (John 15:12–13).

There was an immense amount of laying down of life for others during the Revolution. It is estimated that the War for Independence cost the lives of a full 1 percent of all Americans living at the time—next to the Civil War, this remains the second highest casualty rate in American history. This is a level of sacrifice and devotion to others that a natural rights liberalism which begins and ends with a commitment to rights of individual expression, pursuit, and preservation cannot adequately explain. Motives for military service were then—as always—never purely, maybe not even predominantly, explained by a selfless devotion to others. Yet it is nearly impossible to explain this level of sacrifice in terms of bald self-interest. What can be said, then, of this obvious irony, that roughly twenty-five thousand Americans gave up their lives in the defense of an individual right to life, liberty, and the pursuit of happiness? Did they do it primarily for themselves, thinking only about their own immediate desires, needs, families, and futures? For some this was probably true. For others it was not. We might consider just one moment when bonds of affection and self-denying concern for others—whatever their source—seemed to make a difference at a critical point in the war.

It was the last day of that now fabled year 1776. Historians agree that Washington's successful surprise attack on Trenton on December 26, 1776, just a few days before, was a key turning point in the war. Immediately following that victory, Washington, in an unusually expressive moment, formally thanked his soldiers with, it was reported, "utmost sincerity and affection" for their daring and heroic efforts begun in the middle of the night on Christmas. But the work was not finished. The turning point had only begun. Now, just a few days after the battle at Trenton, he faced the daunting task of persuading many of these same soldiers, so vital to the looming battle of Princeton and other conflicts, to stay on even though their enlistments were to expire at the end of the day, and they were all, to a man, worn out with gnawing hunger and cold fatigue. Again it was noted by someone present that Washington addressed his troops "in the most affectionate manner." He explained the situation and asked them, en masse, to reenlist. No one spoke or moved. Acknowledging their immense physical travails and his own inability to know how to spare them such in the future, Washington sensibly made no passionate speech about individual rights, though even in this desperate hour he still honored those rights by only asking that they "*consent* to stay one month longer" (emphasis added) rather than con-scripting them to future service out of necessity. Without authorization from Congress, he did promise them an additional financial bounty to stay on and fight. But even with this second pitch, still no one stepped forward to re-enlist. In the end, it was the third of Washington's several affectionate appeals to them, where he spoke of their country and fami-lies and all that they held dear being at stake, that they began to step forward one by one and re-up for at least another month of fighting which would effect a decisive turn in the war. In the words of Nathanael Greene, on this third appeal, "God almighty inclined their hearts to lis-ten to the proposal and they engaged anew."[60]

History by anecdote can be misleading; thus no general claim is made here about how other-oriented the heart of the average revolutionary was—including those Washington addressed directly that last day of 1776. But just this one moment alone, with its affectionate appeals responded to by self-chosen deprivation and life-giving devotion, indi-cates that the Declaration called for, and many Americans offered, tremendous sacrifice—even the ultimate sacrifice of life which charac-terizes the "greatest" manifestation of charity's love of neighbor. This can hardly be the mark of an exclusively venal and egoistic America given over wholly to a spirit of party and faction.

In Jefferson's eyes, the Revolutionary War was fought to establish a model of natural liberty wherein a natural right to the individual pursuit of happiness looms large as a central tenet. Yet by the end of the war, this model's greatest warrior, George Washington, was quite clear that that tenet alone was insufficient for a broad happiness throughout the nation. Washington had no unrealistic view of human nature. He had witnessed plenty of human depravity on both sides of the Revolutionary War. Yet he ended his matchless military service to America with a letter to all the states announcing his retirement, concluding with the "earnest prayer" that

God . . . would incline the hearts of the Citizens to . . . entertain a brotherly affection and love for one another, for their fellow Citizens of the United States at large, and particularly for their brethren who have served in the Field, and finally, that we would most graciously be pleased to dispose us all . . . to demean ourselves with that Charity, humility, and pacific temper of mind, which were the characteristics of the Divine Author of our blessed Religion, and without an humble imitation of whose example in these things, we can never hope to be a happy Nation.[61]

Even Madison, just one week after publishing the famous *Federalist* 10 with its clear-eyed view of universal human selfishness, published the lesser noted *"Federalist* 14," wherein he pleaded,

Hearken not to the unnatural voice which tells you that the people of America, knit together as they are by so many cords of affection, can no longer live together as members of the same family.[62]

To whatever extent bonds of affection tied the American Revolution's soldiers, citizens, and commanding officer to each other—thus providing a historic chance for a model of natural liberty to develop—it is clear that after the war, America settled back more in the direction of the low view of human nature generally presumed by the Constitution. But even here, a real degree of affection between and amongst citizens was called for by key leaders, and it appeared important to forging the constitutional union that would form the key governmental framework necessary for Jefferson's natural rights republic. As time marched on, Jefferson himself stepped up to say how necessary national bonds of affection are to sustain liberal American democracy. At one point, he even turned to Christianity in some form to try to refashion a national character apparently so lacking in mutual affection as to threaten his cherished aim of a model of natural liberty.

Notes

1. Jefferson, *Writings*, 1500–1656. The definitive copy of Jefferson's "original Rough draught" is found in *The Papers of Thomas Jefferson*, 1:423–28. This document is not Jefferson's first full draft but a clean text submitted to the drafting committee, *after* several revisions had been made by Jefferson as well as by Adams and Franklin, who had been consulted independently prior to the formal submission of a draft to the full committee (Boyd and Gawalt, *Declaration of Independence*, 25–27). Nevertheless, scholars continue to refer to this version as the "original Rough draught," and it remains the one existing version that most closely approximates what Jefferson wrote prior to anyone else's emendations.

2. For information regarding the Committee Draft, see Maier, *American Scripture*, 126; Mason, *Papers*, 1:276–86; on Mason as a mentor, see Rutland, *George Mason*, xii; Ketcham, *James Madison*, 71. For two thorough, though slightly different,

treatments of Mason's influence on Jefferson's "original Rough draught," and Jefferson's claims about not copying, see Maier, *American Scripture,* 124–26, 268; and Boyd and Gawalt, *Declaration of Independence,* 21–22.

3. Niles, *Principles,* 404.

4. See Maier's chapter, "American Scripture," in *American Scripture,* especially 154–55, Hancock as quoted therein. Also, Zuckert, *Natural Rights Republic,* 14.

5. For all three texts ("original Rough draught," Committee Draft, and final draft) see Jefferson, *Papers of Thomas Jefferson,* 1:315–19, 423–32. Note that the version which captures the changes made by the drafting committee is the one from Jefferson's notes of the proceedings in the Continental Congress, later incorporated into his autobiography. The final draft is the one officially adopted by Congress on July 4, 1776. Jefferson himself would repeat more than once the story of Benjamin Franklin's being so aware of Jefferson's obvious misery over what the full assembly was doing to his handiwork that he leaned over and told Jefferson of the hat maker who thought of a sign for his shop which would read "John Thompson, Hatter, makes and sells hats for ready money" alongside the picture of a hat. After his friends got through criticizing the envisioned sign, all that was left was "John Thompson" and the picture of a hat.

6. For a pithy discussion of Machiavelli's amorality, see Mansfield's introduction to his translation of *The Prince,* vii.

7. As is often the case with Jefferson, he is on record with statements that appear at odds with this position. The most famous example comes from "Query 18" in his *Notes on the State of Virginia* where, in reference to slavery, he raises the possibility of "supernatural interference" in American politics and claims, "I tremble for my country when I reflect that God is just; that his justice cannot sleep forever. . . . The Almighty has no attribute which can take side with us in such a contest" (Jefferson, *Writings,* 289). Of course, if Jefferson was being sincere here about a god of justice, he appears to be of the mind that this god's sense of justice was at that time asleep. Furthermore, Jefferson did not take this statement seriously enough to get rid of his own slaves. He may have had—certainly did have—a genuine conviction that slavery was wrong, but he never appeared to feel any personal and immediate threat of divine retribution for owning slaves. Lastly, and most significantly, if Jefferson genuinely believed in such a god, this is not the god that appears in the Declaration. And it is the Declaration, not the *Notes on the State of Virginia,* that has had such a profound impact on American politics.

8. For a discussion on the role of religion in Jefferson's early years, see Eugene R. Sheridan's introduction to *Jefferson's Extracts from the Gospels,* 5. The quotation about Jefferson's early views on religion is found in a letter to Joseph Delaplaine, December 25, 1816, in Jefferson, *Extracts from the Gospels,* 382.

9. Sheridan, introduction to *Jefferson's Extracts from the Gospels,* 6.

10. Jefferson, *Literary Commonplace Book,* 33.

11. Ibid., 42.

12. Ibid., 24–25.

13. Ibid., 55.

14. Jaffa, *American Revolution,* 35.

15. Actually the phrase "natural rights" appears nowhere in the Declaration. However, the prior reference to the "laws of nature and nature's god" as the source of equality between different peoples—or nations—of the earth, coupled with Jefferson's lifelong association of the term "natural rights" with issues of individual self-government (see Jefferson, *Selected Writings of Jefferson*, 38, 50, 112, 219, 271, 288, 291, 293, 307, 449, 486, 576–77), and his statement in an oft-neglected letter to John Manners in 1817 where Jefferson explicitly links the rights of life, liberty, and pursuit of happiness with a "natural right" of expatriation (see Jefferson, *The Writings of Thomas Jefferson*, 15:124) confirm that Jefferson considers the rights mentioned in this sentence to be "natural rights."

16. Carl Becker is of the opinion that Franklin is the source of this change (Becker, *Declaration of Independence*, 142), whereas Julian Boyd and Allen Jayne strongly suspect Jefferson himself made the change (see Boyd and Gawalt, *Declaration of Independence*, 27–28; Jayne, *Jefferson's Declaration*, 118).

17. Morton White and Michael Zuckert both argue for a Lockean reading of Jefferson's commitment to a self-evidence of reason, though each reads Locke quite differently. See White, *Philosophy of the American Revolution*; and Zuckert, *Natural Rights Republic*, 45–69. See Allen Jayne's fine review of the various debates on this issue and persuasive argument for the "moral sense" position in *Jefferson's Declaration*, 109–138.

18. Jefferson, *Papers of Thomas Jefferson*, April 28, 1793, 25:613.

19. Wills, *Inventing America*, 210–13; Maier, *American Scripture*, 191, 214–15.

20. Jefferson, *Writings*, 1305.

21. Locke, *Second Treatise of Government*, 8, 9. According to Wills, "there is no indication that Jefferson read the *Second Treatise* carefully or with profit. Indeed, there is no direct proof he ever read it at all" (Wills, *Inventing America*, 174). For a thoroughly convincing refutation of this claim, see Ronald Hamowy's "Jefferson and the Scottish," 503–23.

22. As noted, in the final version these rights are not "derived" but are "endowed" by the "Creator." This is not necessarily a view Jefferson entirely rejects. In his Summary View, which Jefferson claimed was "penned in the language of truth," he mentions "those rights which god and the laws have given equally and independently to all" (Jefferson, *Papers of Thomas Jefferson*, 1:121). Jefferson's god is just not a biblical Creator God.

23. For arguments about governmental duty to provide happiness, see Schlesinger, "Lost Meaning," 325–28; and Wills, *Inventing America*, 251. For fuller treatment of the separation between *pursuit* of happiness and happiness itself, see Zuckert, *Natural Rights Republic*, 31–40; Hamowy, "Declaration of Independence," 457–58; and Maier, *American Scripture*, 136. For Jefferson's own interpretation of the *pursuit* of happiness, see Jefferson, *The Writings of Thomas Jefferson*, 15:124. For arguments regarding Lockean rights, see Boorstin, *Lost World*, 53; and Diggins, *Lost Soul*, 37. And for information about Locke and a life of reason, see Koch, "Power and Morals," 478.

24. Hamowy, "Jefferson and the Scottish," 519. Also see Lucas, "Justifying America," 85. Jean Yarbrough mounts the most plausible objection to this interpretation by showing that while Jefferson's own thoughts on happiness do not circumscribe the right to the pursuit of happiness, perhaps a larger "American"

understanding of happiness does. Yet in the end, even she admits that "nothing in the Declaration denies us the right to pursue happiness as we [today] understand it" (*American Virtues*, 14). Similarly, Richard Matthews, who sees a strong, nonliberal, public happiness component embedded in Jefferson's larger political thought, also agrees that Jefferson's rhetoric in the Declaration decidedly makes use of a more vaguely understood "universal" sense of happiness to be defined in the "private realm" (Matthews, *Radical Politics*, 88–89).

25. Jefferson originally writes "secure these ends," but since the antecedent of "ends" is the triumvirate of rights, the language of the final version offers a cleaner but still consistent representation of Jefferson's original.

26. Jefferson, *Writings*, 285.

27. Famous line about separation of church and state found in a letter to the Danbury Baptist Association, January 1, 1802; see Jefferson, *Writings*, 510. For the disestablishment of Virginia's state church, see Jefferson, *Papers of Thomas Jefferson*, 1:525–58.

28. Jefferson, *Writings*, 1516–17.

29. Winthrop, "A Model of Christian Charity," ¶ 45.

30. Adams, *Papers of John Adams*, I:192, II:382–83, IX:62

31. As quoted in Maier, *American Scripture*, 122; see also Webster, *Papers of Daniel Webster*, 1:251; Maier, *American Scripture*, 105–22.

32. Ellis, *American Sphinx*, 125.

33. Ellis, *Founding Brothers*, 231. See Helo and Onuf, "Jefferson, Morality," for a persuasive explanation of Jefferson's commitment to natural rights, but only feeling beholden to historically conditioned and practicable realities of implementing such ideals—a critical explanation for the way Jefferson excuses his and others' practice of slavery so otherwise at odds with the doctrines of the Declaration.

34. Jefferson, *Papers of Thomas Jefferson*, I:135.

35. Burstein, *Inner Jefferson*, intimately details this sentimentalist side of Jefferson's character and the influences that fostered it.

36. Note here that Jefferson, like Winthrop, uses terms like *love* and *affection* somewhat interchangeably. This is consistent with those terms as defined in Webster's 1828 dictionary published just after Jefferson's death where the lead definition of *affectionate* is to have "great love" and the lead definition of *love* is "to regard with affection." As will be shown, though, these concepts rest on very different grounds. See Noah Webster's *American Dictionary of the English Language*, 1828 vol. 1, s.v. "affectionate," "love."

37. Jefferson, *Literary Commonplace Book*, 35.

38. See Jefferson, *Literary Commonplace Book*, 5–8, 267–68. Adrienne Koch, in her too often neglected classic *The Philosophy of Thomas Jefferson*, notes that the *Literary Commonplace Book* has an almost perfectly even amount of Epicurean maxims on happiness and Stoic injunctions to discipline the will (2–3). Though Jefferson was not a literal disciple of either sect, and despite the familiar opposition between these two doctrines—which Koch points out is "more insuperable in theory than in practice"—Jefferson was "deeply sensible of the moral advantages inherent in each program" (2, 4). For Jefferson, Stoicism and Epicureanism were not mutually exclusive ethical categories, but equally essential, if sometimes competing components of

a life lived well. Epicureanism, with its focus on materialism, creature comforts, and personal happiness (perhaps best symbolized by Jefferson's lifelong, debt-ridden devotion to the aesthetic, culinary, and physical comforts of Monticello) greatly colored Jefferson's view about the good life. On the other hand, Stoicism provided, at least to Jefferson's mind, the discipline necessary to realize this good life (perhaps best symbolized by Jefferson's famous claim "whether I retire to bed early or late, I rise with the sun . . . [and have had] the habit of bathing my feet in cold water every morning, for sixty years past" (Jefferson, *Writings*, 1417)). For information about "a system of ethics," see Jefferson, *Literary Commonplace Book*, 35.

39. Jefferson, *Literary Commonplace Book*, 332–33, emphasis added.

40. As quoted in Jefferson, *Literary Commonplace Book*, 330. Jefferson's college tutors at William and Mary, especially Aberdeen-trained William Small, immersed him in the writings of, among others, Francis Hutcheson, Lord Kames, Adam Smith, and David Hume—leading figures of the Scottish Enlightenment and its moral sentimentalism (Wills, *Inventing America*, 175–80; Jayne, *Jefferson's Declaration*, 66–67). Garry Wills was the first to call attention to these influences. But his particular thesis—that Jefferson was influenced by Scottish moral sense thinkers to the virtual exclusion of John Locke—has been roundly refuted, see note 21. For more effective treatments of how this school of thought may have influenced Jefferson, see White, *The Philosophy of the American Revolution;* Yarbrough, *American Virtues;* Jayne, *Jefferson's Declaration;* and Frank Balog's "The Scottish Enlightenment and the Liberal Political Tradition," as found in *Confronting the Constitution* (edited by Allan Bloom and Steven Kautz). To any who study Jefferson today, it should be clear by now that Jefferson's inclination to adopt portions (rather than entire paradigms) of thinking from a variety of authors, then combine those portions into a unique whole, suggests a certain futility in proving that any one figure is the ultimate source of a particular Jeffersonian idea.

41. For information regarding Jefferson's recommended reading list, see Jefferson, *Papers of Thomas Jefferson*, 1:78–81. For Jefferson's letter to his nephew, see Jefferson, *Writings*, 902; Sterne, *A Sentimental Journey*, vi. Also see Burstein, *Inner Jefferson*, especially chapter two, "Sensitivity and Sterne."

42. Sterne, *A Sentimental Journey*, 5, 8–9.

43. Ibid., 34.

44. The profound effect of this story on Jefferson is confirmed fifteen years later when Jefferson himself, while serving as minister to France, passes through Calais and records in his Memorandum Book: "gave the successor of Sterne's monk at Calais, if, 4" (Jefferson, *Literary Commonplace Book*, 183). The editors of the *Literary Commonplace Book* note this among other pieces of evidence that Jefferson is at this time rereading the literature and sermons of Sterne that he had so enjoyed in his youth. Just one year later, Jefferson will make his earlier noted recommendation of these readings to Peter Carr. The editors also caution that his superlative claim about Sterne's writings constituting the "best course of morality" (Jefferson, *Writings*, 902) must be taken in the context of Jefferson recommending writings to younger readers something they would "remember and relish" as he did.

45. Gaustad, *Altar of God*, 5.

46. Sterne, *A Sentimental Journey*, 77.

47. In reference to King George, he says, "A prince whose character is thus marked by every act which may define a tyrant, is unfit to be the ruler of a people who mean to be free." King George's lack of fitness for rule stems from his character, not his office, suggesting that a prince of a different character might legitimately rule a people that would be a free people. At least in the Declaration, it is not monarchy per se that Jefferson rails against so much as it is tyranny—in whatever form it is found.

48. As quoted in Jayne, *Jefferson's Declaration,* 126.

49. Jefferson is quite clear that "prudence indeed will dictate that governments long established should not be changed for light and transient causes." In fact, America's right to revolt only comes *after* a "long train of abuses" of their fundamental rights.

50. The point has previously been made by Jayne, *Jefferson's Declaration*, 126–28.

51. Language in original rough draught.

52. Jayne, *Jefferson's Declaration,* 126–28.

53. Ibid., 124; Chesterton, *Wisdom of Father Brown*, 99.

54. Lincoln, *Collected Works*, 4:169.

55. Hamilton, Jay, and Madison, *The Federalist Papers* 289–90.

56. Ibid., 45–47.

57. Ibid., 47–49.

58. For a discussion on Jefferson's concerns regarding the Constitution, see letter to Madison in Jefferson, *Writings*, 914–18; for Jefferson's description of the *Federalist Papers*, see letter to Madison in Jefferson, *Selected Writings of Jefferson*, 418; for demands that students study the *Federalist Papers,* see Jefferson, *Writings*, 479.

59. Banning, *Jeffersonian Persuasion*, 70–83.

60. McCullough, *1776*, 113, 282, 285–86, 289.

61. Washington, *Collection*, 249.

62. Hamilton, *The Federalist Papers*, 71.

CHAPTER 4

"To Close the Circle of Our Felicities"

Throughout his career Thomas Jefferson consistently held up the Declaration of Independence as the preeminent guide of American politics.[1] Conversely, his regard for the public and personal relevance of the New Testament, Christianity's paramount guide, changed significantly over time. This change and its subsequent shaping of Jefferson's most important and influential political speech, his First Inaugural, plays a critical role in leading Jefferson to make a light but formal emendation to the model of natural liberty that emerges from the Declaration of Independence. Without dramatic departure from his general commitment to a rights-based, democratic government of limited proportions, Jefferson's first presidential address shows that he came to see a substantially rationalized version of Christian charity as necessary to the stability and happiness of the American republic.

Jefferson's Resignation and Washington's Farewell Address

In December of 1789, Jefferson reluctantly accepted George Washington's request to serve as secretary of state and returned home from France. Though cabinet relations during Jefferson's first few months were cordial, consistent with the great pains Washington had taken to establish a harmonious administration, it was not long before Jefferson locked horns with Washington's influential secretary of the treasury, Alexander Hamilton. Jefferson became certain that he saw in Hamilton's actions and counsel—which consistently favored a strong, centralized government over state and local control, big cities and manufacturing concerns over the agrarian interests of rural America, regal pomp and pageantry over democratic simplicity, and royal England over republican France—courtly intentions designed to turn America from its demo-cratic-republican moorings for which Jefferson had labored almost all his entire adult life. As it turned out, these early skirmishes were the initial foment of a decade-long political battle that would give rise to the world's first modern, democratic political parties—the Federalist party of Hamilton and John Adams and the Republican party of Jefferson and James Madison—and go down in history as one of the most acrimonious periods of American politics.[2]

While it may be argued that Jefferson's reactionary opposition to Hamilton is in some sense the initial cause of the ensuing party strife, it is Hamilton's Federalist followers and clerical allies who first employed organized, vicious, and personal attacks in the battle between the two camps. In 1792, without even an election at hand, Federalist forces pub-lished a pamphlet that smeared Jefferson as a dangerous philosophical dreamer with dictatorial ambitions, a man who was directly responsible for the violent excesses of the French Revolution, and one who pos-sessed "no Conscience, no Religion, no *Charity*" (emphasis added). Wounded by such public attacks, especially those on his moral charac-ter, and utterly frustrated over Washington's growing tendency to follow Hamilton's counsel over his own, Jefferson resigned from his cabinet post in 1793.[3]

Even with Jefferson situated in Monticello, quietly disengaged from national politics, George Washington saw party strife as an ever-increasing problem for the safe and sound functioning of the republic, so much so that he spoke firmly and at length against the "baneful effects of the Spirit of Party, generally" in his famous Farewell Address (actually an open letter to the nation), in which he announced he would not seek a third term despite significant pressure to do so. According to Washing-ton, the spirit of party is the "worst enemy" popular government has. The alternating "domination of one faction over another" cannot help but be accompanied by a "spirit of revenge," which together lead people to "seek security and repose in the absolute power of an Individual," result-ing in a "frightful despotism."[4] Washington was desperately trying to forestall what would prove an eventuality, the development of formal-ized, mass political parties.

Again, Washington's position here betrays no rose-colored view of human nature. Very much like Madison, he acknowledges that the spirit of party is "inseparable from our nature" and therefore something that "exists under different shapes in all Governments."[5] He also maintains a "just estimate of that love of power, and proneness to abuse it, which predominates in the human heart," and that such a tendency makes the spirit of party that much more dangerous.[6] A partisan spirit in general, then, is something he concludes cannot be eradicated. But for that very reason, he is convinced that it must "become the interest and the duty of a wise People to discourage and restrain it."[7] His recommendations for how to do so are of note.

Having acknowledged earlier in the speech the advantages of union over "so large a sphere,"[8] he continues here in even more Madisonian terms, touting the virtues of the Constitution's system of "reciprocal checks" with its "dividing and distributing" of power to keep raging self-interest and a factious party spirit channeled.[9] So successful is this arrangement that he strongly admonishes that citizens "resist with care the spirit of innovation" upon the basic principles of the Constitution.[10] In fact, so important to "liberty" and the "collective and individual happiness" of Americans everywhere is the preservation of this large, constitutional republic of checks and balances that Washington concludes that the Union as it stands ought to be loved like liberty itself, something on which the people must concentrate their *"affections"* (emphasis added). And those who would "weaken its bands" or its "sacred ties" should be called anything but a patriot.[11] Washington, it would seem, is pleading that America as model of natural liberty meld the insights of Federalist 10 and 14. That is, he pleads that America's individual liberty-loving, large-republic democracy of constitutional checks on selfish and partisan tyrannies sown in the nature of man be held together by "cords" (Madison) or "bands" (Washington) of some degree of affection between all citizens and for the Union as a whole. But if man is naturally so selfish, so universally given to exercising individual or partisan dominion over others, from where does this supervening affection come that helps to hold it all together? Washington does not make the point explicitly, in part because he does not form the question explicitly (this was, after all, a broad-ranging political letter to a nation, not a perfectly parsed tract of political theory). Nevertheless, the question looms and an implicit answer is not too difficult to tease out.

In the Farewell Address, Washington considers the "unity of government which constitutes you one people" the "main pillar" of America's model of natural liberty ("the edifice of your real independence, the support of your tranquility at home; your peace abroad; of your safety; of your prosperity, of that very liberty which you so highly prize"[12]). Yet he goes on to declare that "of all the dispositions and habits which lead to political prosperity, Religion and morality are indispensable supports." For Washington, morality is a different category from religion—the former essentially dependent on the latter—and together they stand as "pillars of Human happiness," a multifaceted source of "private and public felicity," and thus they remain things to be cherished by the "pious man" as well as the "mere Politician."[13] Reiterating the basic point later in the speech, he asks rhetorically, "Can it be, that Providence has not connected the permanent felicity of a Nation with its virtue?"[14] Here in the Farewell Address, Washington acknowledges that a full "volume could not trace all the connections" between a national felicity and a broadly religious morality, so he ventures not to make a single clear connection himself at this point. But he did do just that in the closing paragraph of his Circular to the States at the end of the war (discussed in chapter three) where he urges that without a "brotherly affection and love for another," without robust practices of "charity" and other characteristics of the "Divine Author of our blessed religion," America can "never hope to be a happy nation."

According to Washington, then, if American union is the "main pillar" of America's model of natural liberty, then religion and morality, bulwarks of human happiness in general, stand as an "indispensable support" to that "main pillar." Among other things, religion and morality will spawn that degree of "brotherly affection" without which man's more base, natural, and thus inescapably selfish partisan impulses overwhelm the system designed to accommodate just such impulses, thus sundering it. The model of natural liberty accepts and even facilitates the natural fact and right of man's instinct to live for himself first, according to his own interests, aspirations, and ideals, however little or great those ideals call forth a concern for others. But this can be true only up to a point, or so Washington holds. For him, as for some of his other noted revolutionary Virginians like Mason and Madison, at some point, charitable cords of affection must bring and hold America's natural rights republic together in a way that a constitutionally structured self-interest alone cannot.

A fourth revolutionary Virginian, Thomas Jefferson, came to the same conclusion. What is interesting and quite unexpected, though, given his early hostility to religion in general and Christianity in particular, is the degree to which Jefferson came to see New Testament teachings of love as supportive of these needed national bonds of affection and as genuinely compelling moral insights in their own right. Ironically, his move in this direction began right around the time Washington penned his Farewell Address. At that moment, Jefferson was in the initial throes of a lengthy process of reconsidering the Christian beliefs he rejected in his youth. This process would culminate in a transformation of his own personal views that stopped short of embracing a robustly traditional Christianity but nevertheless absorbed distinct New Testament ideals of love that significantly shaped the single most important speech of his political career.

Jefferson's "Embrace" of Christianity

In the previous chapter it was noted that early in life Jefferson became enamored with Epicureanism and Stoicism. His lifelong commitment to these two pre-Christian philosophies is manifest in an 1819 letter he sent to William Short—who had earlier written to Jefferson that Epicurus was the "wisest of the ancient philosophers" and the ultimate source of instruction for "the attainment of happiness in this poor world."[15] In response, Jefferson flatly asserts, "I too am an Epicurean. I consider the genuine (not the imputed) doctrines of Epicurus as containing every thing rational in moral philosophy which Greece and Rome have left us." And he adds, "Epictetus indeed has given us what was good of the Stoics." However, a few lines later, Jefferson concludes,

> But the greatest of all the Reformers . . . was Jesus of Nazareth. . . . [From him], we have the outlines of a system of the most sublime morality which has ever fallen from the lips of man. . . . Epictetus and Epicurus give us laws for governing ourselves, Jesus a supplement of the duties and *charities* we owe to others."[16]

Completely inverting the Bolingbroke claim that Jefferson had enthusiastically copied in his youth, Jefferson here (just seven years before his death) holds that Epicureanism and Stoicism are fine as far as they go, but ultimately *they* fail to reach "all the duties of life" because they hinge on an egoism that cannot instruct us in our moral obligations to others.[17] For such instruction, Jefferson now avers, we must turn to the charity of Christianity. The protracted philosophical and theological journey that ends with Jefferson finding singular moral merit in a concept of charity grounded in Christianity as he understands and accepts it is a neatly documented, if not often told, story.[18] During the decade before Jefferson's ascension to the presidency, a series of experiences unquestionably altered Jefferson's view of the role Christianity in general, and Christian charity in particular, should play in the public morality of the country over which he was shortly destined to preside.

We do not know for sure when, but sometime after Jefferson left Washington's cabinet, he read *An History of the Corruptions of Christianity* by Joseph Priestley, English chemist turned rationalist theologian. As he later said, "I have read [Priestley's] Corruptions of Christianity, and Early opinions of Jesus, over and over again; and I rest on them . . . as the basis of my own faith."[19] Priestley argues that the early apostles and Church leaders corrupted Christ's original teachings with cryptic doctrines like the Trinity, original sin, and the atonement. In doing so, Priestley eliminated much of what Jefferson had long found unacceptably mysterious and irrational in Christianity.

The other figure of undisputed influence in reshaping Jefferson's religious thoughts was Dr. Benjamin Rush. In 1798, while serving as a marginalized vice president under Adams, Jefferson began visiting regularly with Rush, who was prayerfully determined to bring Jefferson to believe in the divinity of Christ, see the success of the American experiment as part of a larger divine design to bring forward the kingdom of God on earth, and appreciate the morally essential and politically palliative nature of Christianity's doctrine of love. Though Jefferson never came to accept Rush's soteriology or his millennial view of America, these conversations, combined with his readings of Priestley, considerably transformed his attitude concerning the validity and significance of certain Christian ideals. Not long after these Philadelphia sessions, Jefferson wrote to Rush,

> To the corruptions of Christianity, I am indeed opposed; but not the genuine precepts of Jesus himself. I am a Christian, in the only sense in which he wished any one to be; sincerely attached to his doctrines, in preference to all others.[20]

What were those precepts? Jefferson spells these out in an attachment entitled "Syllabus of an Estimate of the merit of the doctrines of Jesus, compared with those of others," which he includes with his April 21, 1803, letter to Rush. Both the "Syllabus" and related correspondence

make it clear that Jefferson still did not accept Christ's divinity, the doctrines of the Fall and Christ's atonement, or the Trinitarian view of
God—though he does now appear to hold a Unitarian view of God, a
deity more robust and interactive with human life than, say, the utterly
distant and disinterested force of nature from the original draft of his
Declaration. Jefferson's "Syllabus" also follows Priestley in asserting that
parts of the Bible were made ruinously unintelligible by Christ's apostolic followers and the early Church fathers. However, what Jefferson
now admits is that he finds many New Testament passages—especially
those where Jesus is preaching messages of love—as constituting moral
teachings "more pure and perfect, than those of the most correct of the
philosophers."[21] For Jefferson, these teachings greatly surpassed all
other moral–ethical systems in

> inculcating universal philanthropy, not only to kindred and friends, to
> neighbors and countrymen, but to all mankind, gathering all into one
> family, under the bonds of love, charity, peace, common wants, and
> common aids.[22]

Underscoring the strength of Jefferson's blossoming interest in New
Testament teachings, about one year after sending Rush the "Syllabus,"
Jefferson spent several evenings while serving as president and "overwhelmed with other business" cutting out the verses he approved of from
multiple copies of the New Testament, which he then pasted onto blank
paper, had bound, and titled the "Philosophy of Jesus of Nazareth." Jefferson later said of this book, "A more beautiful or precious morsel of
ethics I have never seen. It is a document in proof that *I* am a *real
Christian*."[23]

Unsurprisingly, Jefferson's "Philosophy of Jesus" only includes passages from the four Gospels, with very little from the esoteric book of
John, and entirely excises the synoptic accounts of Christ's mysterious
conception and birth, the miracles of his ministry, and, most notably,
the atoning and sacrificial nature of his death. Prominent, though, are
excerpts from the Sermon on the Mount and the compassionate parables
of Luke ("Lost Sheep," "Prodigal Son," "Good Samaritan"), which, in
the table of contents, Jefferson labels as "true benevolence." Jefferson
also includes the passages from Matthew 22 concerning the "two great
commandments" of Christianity—"thou shalt love the Lord thy God

with all thy heart" and "thou shalt love the neighbor as thyself"—which Jefferson labels Jesus's "general moral precepts."[24]

Jefferson never came close to adopting anything like a Winthropian view of charity as *the* pre-eminent ideal of public life. It might be said, though, that he did come closer to a position like that of George Mason or George Washington, whose formal statements reveal biblical teachings of *caritas* as morally binding and politically important even if subordinate in important public respects to the assumptions and aims of liberal democracy. But even here, it must be stressed that Jefferson never fully embraced any *traditional* version of charity. Virtually all traditional biblical interpretations of *caritas* emphasize that man's love of God and neighbor is only made possible, and becomes obligatory, by God's first loving man—the apotheosis of which is Christ's redemptive sacrifice for sin.[25] Since Jefferson never accepted the divinity of Christ or the doctrine of atonement, God's graceful and obliging love is explicitly absent from his ideal of *caritas*. And, as he explains in an 1814 letter to Thomas Law, man's "love of god" is not the "foundation of morality," as many Christians would claim, rather it is merely but a "branch of our moral duties."[26] What this means, exactly, Jefferson never says.

Jefferson does explain, in the letter to Law, that the good we do for others we do because "the creator" has simply "implanted in our breasts a love of others." According to Jefferson, God has given us a "nature," or "moral instinct" or "moral sense," which "prompts us to feel and to succor [the] distress" of others.[27] In other words, Jefferson's concept of *caritas* expressly builds on the Scottish moral sense thinking he embraced so enthusiastically at William and Mary and from his reading of Laurence Sterne. These thinkers, who preached benevolence and love of others from a philosophic perspective, undoubtedly exerted a strong influence on Jefferson well before his reconsideration of Christianity. But Jefferson's engagement with the Gospels provided a new idiom and authority through which to express these old convictions, giving Jefferson's sense of charity a distinctly religious cast and greater political relevance than it had for him when he was younger. In the letter to Law, Jefferson explains that even if one accepts a moral sense foundation for charity, the "want or imperfection" of it will often require a "preacher" to encourage such love.[28] It is clear that as early as 1800 Jefferson saw Jesus, not Sterne or one of the famous Scots, as the preeminent moralist of this ideal—a position from which he never retreated. Just a few years before he died, Jefferson wrote to Benjamin Waterhouse that

The doctrines of Jesus are simple, and tend all to the happiness of man. 1. that there is one God, and he all-perfect: 2. that there is a future state of rewards and punishments: 3. that to love God with all thy heart, and thy neighbor as thyself, is the sum of religion.[29]

If Jefferson comes to consider a rationalized, moral sense reformulation of Christian charity as the *sine qua non* of religious morality and a key to human happiness, it raises the question of how, if at all, this alters his commitment to the liberal paradigm of the Declaration. No single document is as useful to answering this question as is Jefferson's First Inaugural.

Jefferson's First Inaugural—Its Importance and Context

Jefferson's First Inaugural was delivered in March of 1801 during the midst of Jefferson's intense Christian ruminations. As Fred Luebke has pointed out, during the fifteen years immediately preceding his election as president, religious topics are virtually absent from Jefferson's public and private writings; however, "from January, 1800, to August, 1801, Jefferson wrote more letters with religious content than during his entire life prior to that time." In correspondence with both Rush and Priestley, Jefferson is explicit that just prior to and during the early years of his administration, he "often" reflected on his "view of the Christian system."[30]

It is also significant that Jefferson's First Inaugural is arguably his most developed and revealing public statement concerning the foundational ideals of American politics. Jefferson made only two speeches as president—his two inaugural addresses. Of these, Jefferson himself acknowledged that the first stayed at a more fundamental and theoretical level than the second. And unlike when drafting the Declaration—while a thirty-three-year-old political neophyte, writing for a diverse, representative assembly—Jefferson composed his First Inaugural as a politically seasoned fifty-eight-year-old, speaking entirely for himself. His First Inaugural is Jefferson pure and mature. While widely recognized by scholars as the best speech of Jefferson's life and a "seminal statement in American history" and praised for its "panoramic wisdom" and "enduring appeal," exegetical work on it in the secondary literature has been surprisingly scant with a few recent exceptions.[31]

It should also be noted that Jefferson's First Inaugural follows the presidential campaign of 1800—one of the most critical, and therefore ugliest, in America history. Ever since his days as secretary of state in the Washington administration, but especially by the election of 1800, Jefferson saw Federalist assaults on democratic manners, local autonomy, and closer ties to republican France, America's great revolutionary ally, as virtual death knells for what he considered the practical imperatives of his most cherished political credo, the Declaration of Independence. This prompted Jefferson, despite his fabled opposition to parties ("If I could not go to heaven but with a party, I would not go there at all"), to become the leader of the first modern political party in America, one that proved nearly as aggressive and adept at the kind of mudslinging the Federalists began earlier in the decade and were practicing with vigor throughout the campaign of 1800. Again, conventions of the day were such that neither Jefferson nor Adams did much direct organizing or campaigning. And however virulent things got between Jefferson's camp and Adams's, no one wounded Adams politically more than his jealous Federalist colleague, Alexander Hamilton, whose fifty-four-page open letter to the country vilified Adams at every turn. But it appears Jefferson did little to lift the plane of discourse and approach of his supporters, and we do know that Jefferson supported in some fashion the hack journalist James Callender in his vicious and often unfounded attacks on John Adams's fitness for the presidency—an act Abigail Adams in particular regarded as unforgivable for many years afterwards.[32]

Federalist attacks on Jefferson were most vituperative and repeated when it came to his reputed religious infidelity; these run intermittently through the 1790s and come to a rolling boil in 1800.[33] So successful were these attacks that it was reported that upon hearing of his eventual election, some New England housewives buried Bibles for fear of confiscation. For Jefferson's part, the often acid and unjust quality of these accusations helps explain that while he came to enthusiastically embrace components of Christian morality, he never lost a deep antipathy toward zealously sectarian forms of Christianity. It was not just that he thought orthodox clerics were wrong intellectually or theologically; many had hurt him personally and profoundly. In a June 25, 1819, letter to Ezra Stile, Jefferson recognizes the discrepancy between the Christian morality he came to espouse and his hard feelings toward many in the clergy, confessing, "I am sometimes more angry with [certain

Christian ministers] than is authorized by the blessed charities [Jesus] preached."[34]

It is just this deeply partisan conflict that inspires Rush's efforts to convince Jefferson of Christian charity's vital role in stabilizing the union. And Federalist accusations factored heavily in Jefferson's own efforts to come more precisely to grips with what he really believed about Christianity.[35] This may prompt some to assume that Jefferson's "embrace" of Christianity during this period was mostly a political ploy. The problem with such a view is that Jefferson never tried to capitalize publicly on his religious reorientation during the campaigns of 1796 and 1800. His only statements concerning his changed views are found in private correspondence. If his purposes were purely for electoral advantage, this supremely talented politician did a poor job of capitalizing on his new views.

By the time of his inauguration early in March 1801, the increasingly brutal fight between Federalists and Republicans—which utterly ruptured his long and close friendship with John Adams—gave Jefferson pause to consider a different threat to the verities of 1776 than those he saw in Federalist policy. Now undermining successful self-rule was what Jefferson considered a dangerous lack of love among American citizens. In a letter written just weeks after his First Inaugural, Jefferson writes to Elbridge Gerry, "It will be a great blessing to our country if we can once more restore harmony and *social love* among its citizens. I confess, as to myself, it is almost the first object of my heart, and one to which I would sacrifice everything but principle."[36]

This statement illustrates the competing political values at play in Jefferson's outlook during this period. His careful qualifications ("*almost* the first object" and "sacrifice *everything but* principle") indicate that promoting what he calls here "social love" was solidly subordinate to protecting his understanding of the principles of the Declaration, which remained the "first object" of his heart and uncompromising ground of his politics. This "first object" explains Jefferson the rabid partisan in the election of 1800, defending with tactics high and low the liberty he perceived was under attack by Federalist rule. But what the letter says about the critical, if secondary, political importance of "social love"—a sense of love now richly colored by Synoptic teachings—explains Jefferson the statesman in the First Inaugural.

The First Inaugural—Alpha and Omega

Jefferson begins the First Inaugural with a statement of personal humility, confessing "a sincere consciousness" that the task ahead of him is "above [his] talents." He then contrasts his own human limitations with the superhuman—approaching otherworldly—responsibilities of his office. He is to preside over a nation "advancing rapidly to destinies beyond the reach of mortal eye," whose purposes and activities are "transcendent objects."[37] Often such juxtaposition in American political rhetoric leads to a prominent petition for God's blessing. Yet strikingly, there is no mention here of God. Jefferson specifically "humble[s him]self before the magnitude of the undertaking," not God. And it is "in the other high authorities provided by our constitution," not God, that he promises to seek the "resources of wisdom, of virtue, and of zeal, on which to rely under all difficulties." If the love of God remains an element of the *caritas* Jefferson has recently come to embrace, such a love almost entirely fails to produce politically standard expressions of divine adoration and dependence.

To say "*almost* entirely" here is crucial. The speech ends with the prayer, "And may that Infinite Power which rules the destinies of the universe, lead our councils to what is best, and give them a favorable issue for your peace and prosperity." Perhaps this can just be written off as a disingenuous rhetorical flourish proffered for an electorate generally more faithful about such matters than Jefferson was. As Joseph Ellis argues, Jefferson virtually "created a particular style of leadership" required for success in electoral democracies—a style that "rests comfortably with contradictions" and uses "language in ways that permit different constituencies to hear what they are listening for." Recall, however, that no such flourish exists in Jefferson's original draft of the Declaration, written when he was younger and even more politically ambitious. Also, Jefferson's final line reads much like the rhetoric of presidential proclamations issued on official days of fasting, prayer, and thanksgiving held by both Washington and Adams but which Jefferson refused to hold—at some political cost—because he saw them as a violation of a constitutional separation between church and state.[38] If Jefferson were really committed to some absolutely impermeable separation of the religious and the political, and he could resist the pressure to use religious rhetoric in these other public settings or documents, why would he, just elected to the nation's highest office, buckle here?

Perhaps a more reasonable conclusion is that while Jefferson's political theology—even after the influence of Priestley and Rush—does not make the Judeo-Christian God a figure to be praised, thanked, and importuned by national leaders in the most notable of ways, Jefferson's famous wall of separation is slightly more porous than is often supposed. Clearly, official religious proclamations and days of prayer do not pass constitutional muster for Jefferson. He does, however, appear willing to employ, while acting as an officer of the government, some very modest public rhetoric that directs his constituents' minds toward an acknowledgment and appreciation of a divine influence.

United for the Common Good

After the introductory paragraph, Jefferson's first move is to extend a charitable olive leaf to his former Federalist enemies. Jefferson begins his second paragraph with the phrase "during this contest of opinion through which we have passed." As Dumas Malone explains, this is "putting the most polite and magnanimous interpretation" on the awful electoral conflict through which the country had just passed.[39] Compared with the Jefferson of 1776, who was roundly criticized for drafting the Declaration with the *least* polite and *least* magnanimous interpretation of the difficulties with Great Britain, this is a striking contrast.

In addition to casting a warm blanket of harmonious rhetoric over the frigid battles of 1800, Jefferson also, in this second paragraph, simply assumes that "all will, *of course*, arrange themselves under the will of the law, and unite in common efforts for the common good" (emphasis added). And by assuming this, Jefferson helped to make it so. To their credit, the defeated Federalists peacefully deferred to the will of the electorate, though not without some ostentatious shows of bitterness.[40] Jefferson, in turn, not only avoids even a hint of recrimination for the electoral practices and public policies of the Federalists, he placates many of their worst fears—reassuring them that while "the will of the majority is in all cases to prevail" in a republic, "that will, to be rightful, must be reasonable [for] the minority possess their equal rights, which equal laws must protect." Toward the very end of the address, speaking directly to those who did not vote for him, Jefferson commits to "conciliate" them by "doing them all the good in [his] power." At a minimum this meant that Jefferson would not turn the Alien and Sedition Acts, notoriously used against Republicans, back on the Federalists.

Most famously, Jefferson says in the second paragraph, "But every difference of opinion is not a difference of principle. We have called by different names brethren of the same principle. We are all republicans: we are all federalists." Ellis among others downplays the conciliatory significance of this statement by stressing that Jefferson puts "republican" and "federalists" in lower case. They suggest that Jefferson is not making a grand and gracious statement about the "overlapping goals" or "common ground" shared by the two parties—Federalist and Republican. Rather, he was stating that all Americans, regardless of party affiliation, at root favor a "republican form" of democratic government and a "federal bond" among the states.[41]

At one level this must certainly be true. The next paragraph directly equates "our own federal and republican principles" with, respectively, "union and representative government." And certainly Jefferson was not now naively ignoring the dramatic policy differences between Federalists and Republicans, suggesting that someone could at once be allegiant to the ideals of both parties. Yet Ellis's point too much mutes the unifying power of this portion of Jefferson's message. It fails to appreciate that Jefferson undoubtedly knew his *listeners* that morning (which obviously included all the country's most influential political figures) would not hear nuances of capitalization more apparent to general *readers* seeing the published text later. Given the ordeal of the campaign, Jefferson must have known listeners would hear "all Federalists" and "all Republicans" rather than "all federalists" and "all republicans."

More than a mere platitude, Jefferson's phrasing conveys that there really is more uniting the two parties than dividing them—making them indeed "brethren of the same principle." Even Ellis shows that Jefferson's "pure republicanism" did not mean a radical removal of every Federalist aim and officer, which is what some Federalists feared, and acknowledges that two of Jefferson's most ardent Federalist foes, Hamilton and Marshall, were amazed at the apparent message of moderation.[42] Benjamin Rush, Jefferson's long-time evangelizing friend and ardent champion of the political virtues of Christian charity, was positively delighted to discover that in response to the publication of the address in Philadelphia, old friends who had long been divided over partisan differences were reunited.[43]

The time would come in Jefferson's administration when partisan differences would again overpower much of the charitable and reconciling spirit achieved via his First Inaugural. But this speech and its impact cannot be simply brushed off as some thin, flash-in-the-pan spasm of political harmony. Jefferson's address was the culmination of a historical turning point for America's great experiment with self-rule. It marked the peaceful and civil transfer of political power between democratic parties previously hostile toward each other. In the election of 1796, Adams's peaceful succession of George Washington appeared inevitable and acceptable to all, including Adams's main opponent, Thomas Jefferson. But leading up to March 4, 1801, no such placidness about succession was warranted. This was the first real test of whether American national power could be transferred without violent resistance beforehand or bitter retribution afterwards. That America successfully passed this test was due to many people and forces beyond Jefferson and his speech.[44] Yet Jefferson's speech deserves considerable credit for successfully modeling how political enemies could civilly and even charitably succeed their opponents in the face of malice rendered and received—setting a remarkable precedent for all future transfers of party in office in this country.[45]

The Declaration Revised

The contribution of Jefferson's First Inaugural to the making of American democracy extends beyond its practical showcase of political harmony in times of divisiveness and uncertainty. It also establishes a delicate revision to the liberal core of the Declaration, which for many remains the sacred starting point of American politics.

In the First Inaugural's opening paragraph, Jefferson refers to "the happiness . . . of this beloved country," the first of seven references to happiness (or related concepts) that pepper the speech. From beginning to end, national happiness rings as the First Inaugural's leitmotif. Despite this fact, this address has inexplicably been passed over by scholars as a source of insight into Jefferson's understanding of happiness and its connection to government.[46] And what this speech shows is that Jefferson weds happiness in America to a widely shared and practiced sense of *caritas*.

In his second paragraph, Jefferson pleads,

Let us, then, fellow citizens, unite with one heart and one mind. Let us restore to social intercourse that harmony and affection without which liberty, and even life itself, are but dreary things. And let us reflect that having banished from our land that religious intolerance under which mankind so long bled and suffered, we have yet gained little if we countenance a political intolerance as despotic, as wicked, and capable of as bitter and bloody persecutions.

The full-throated power of this passage is that it rhetorically underscores its substantive message of national unity and accommodation. By beginning each line with the phrase "let us," this anaphora conveys a tone of gentle persuasion, demonstrating respect, or care, for the will of all listening. But this passage is more than just a deferential and poetic plea that partisan citizens be kinder and more respectful toward each other. It contains within it a startling and important addendum to the Declaration's "pursuit of happiness" clause. In the second line, Jefferson explains that without "*affection* . . . liberty, and even life itself, are but dreary things" (emphasis added). By taking two prominent components of the Declaration's famous triad of rights (life and liberty) and linking them to a dreariness (a clear antonym of happiness) brought about by an absence of affection (a clear form of love), Jefferson is quite clear: The pursuit of human happiness will largely be abortive in a society—even a liberal republic—where love is lacking.[47] (It is of note that in 2000, Yale University published a large empirical study arguing just this same point.[48])

At one level, such a view simply draws upon the mainly secular, moral sense notions of affection that were at play in Jefferson's moral and political outlook dating back to the time he made his original draft of the Declaration, in which British brethren were maligned for their "agonizing" stabs to the "affection" that once prevailed between the two peoples. Yet there is evidence in this speech that Jefferson's view of, and attention to, affection here in this passage is also now tied to a plainly religious, and most presumably Christian, sense of *caritas*. In the very next paragraph, in fact, Jefferson explicitly avers that a widely practiced *caritas* in a more biblical vein is—just as he has argued for "affection"— essential to a happy republic of liberty.

In the next paragraph, Jefferson asks and answers the question "what more is necessary to make us a *happy* and prosperous people?" (emphasis added). Just before uttering the question, Jefferson designates several "blessings" he deems essential to that happiness. One of these is that America is enlightened by a benign religion, professed indeed and practiced in various forms, yet all of them inculcating honesty, truth, temperance, gratitude, *and the love of man; acknowledging and adoring an overruling Providence*, which by all its dispensations proves that it delights in the *happiness* of man here, and his greater *happiness* hereafter (emphasis added).

Given Jefferson's youthful avowals on the subject of religion, this statement is astonishing. Jefferson now openly congratulates America for its widespread religiosity, especially for the way it promotes happiness by fostering the "love of man" and an "adoring" of God—central elements of any concept of Christian charity. Again, Jefferson himself retains some highly unorthodox views concerning these elements. And, keeping consistent with his firm belief that government should not endorse or promote specific faiths, Jefferson is careful to praise "religion" in general, rather than Christianity. He makes a more pluralistic reference to "Providence," which then becomes an impersonal "it," rather than a more traditional, anthropological sounding reference to "God" or "Heavenly Father" as the stated object of religious devotion. However, given the content and timing of Jefferson's communications with Rush, Priestley, and others immediately surrounding this address, it seems certain his contemporaneous reconsideration of Christianity is driving much of this statement.

As Jefferson wraps up this paragraph, he mentions one other blessing "necessary to close the circle of our felicities." This line is significant because it again emphasizes that the specifically religiously oriented love he has just mentioned is constitutive of American happiness. By going on to discuss what is necessary to *close* the circle of felicity, Jefferson plainly insinuates that the love of man and the Providence he just extolled are critical arcs on that circle of civic bliss.[49] It is also significant because understanding this one additional blessing further distills Jefferson's thoughts on the role of *caritas* in American politics. This last blessing is

> a wise and frugal government, which shall restrain men from injuring one another, which shall leave them otherwise free to regulate their own pursuits of industry and improvement, and shall not take from the mouth of labor the bread it has earned.

For Jefferson, "this is the sum of good government." It also distinctly echoes another blessing Jefferson mentions earlier in the paragraph, which is a prevailing "due sense of our equal right to the use of our own faculties, to the acquisitions of our industry." And together, these two blessings reassert the core liberalism of the Declaration, where government is most fundamentally dedicated to leaving citizens "free to regulate their own pursuits" of happiness, industry, improvement, or whatever, so long as they do not injure or infringe on the rights of others.

Thought critical to national happiness, the demands of Christian love—at least Jefferson's understanding of it—do not dictate a government designed to significantly redistribute wealth or otherwise regulate man's efforts at self-improvement. Charity's still peripheral status with respect to the actual workings of government is ratified yet further in the next paragraph where Jefferson articulates in more detail "the essential principles of our government, and consequently those which ought to shape its administration."

The first principle Jefferson mentions is an "equal and exact justice to all men." An exacting justice, understood as the equal protection of basic, natural rights for all citizens, is the foundational ideal of government activity. Nowhere in this paragraph does Jefferson even seem to hint that charity, or traditionally component virtues (e.g., compassion, generosity, mercy, and piety), should play a part in government. He does laud "peace, commerce, and honest friendship with all nations," but then stipulates "entangling alliances with none" (a phrase often wrongly imputed to Washington). If, as Jefferson's "Syllabus" asserts, charity encompasses obligations to all members of the human family, this apparently does not translate into weighty national commitments to citizens of other countries—at least not at this point in America's history. Apparently a commonsense appreciation of the hard realities of international politics (that most nations "feel power and forget right," as Jefferson says at the start of the address) dictates vigorous defense and preferential treatment of one's own. As Wilson Carey McWilliams puts it, despite the distinctly universal cast to Jefferson's charity, "different obligations [remained] suitable for different categories of persons."[50]

As an aside—but an important one—it is in this vein, sadly, that Jefferson's newfound commitments to ideals of Christian love apparently do no more than his older commitments to natural rights liberalism did to prompt a more aggressive attempt to end the practice of black slavery in America, including on his own plantation. While the fault remains deplorable and difficult to comprehend, Jefferson's hypocrisies on this front do not appear absolute. The constellation of his ethical principles did make him, by all accounts, a more humane and beloved master than many of the era, and as early as the "original Rough draught" of his Declaration, he was a rhetorically impassioned opponent of the institution of slavery willing to initiate some public moves toward its demise. Of this latter tendency, Sean Wilentz has provocatively asked, who

> finally, is more admirable: a political leader [like Jefferson] who was against slavery early in his career, consistently expressed egalitarian ideals, but then fell short of those ideals by trimming his sails over the issue in politics and failing to free his slaves; or a political leader [like Washington] who never professed egalitarian ideals, kept his new antislavery opinions confined to his private correspondence, and then finally, but only at his death, arranged to free his slaves?"[51]

Jefferson's courage—such as it was—in speaking out against the principles of slavery with such vehemence and force at various times was not of much immediate help to his own slaves, but in the long run it probably proved a more powerful tool against slavery than the example of Washington's courage—such as it was—to quietly free his own slaves.

The remaining principles of good government that Jefferson discusses in this section constitute a kind of a Nozikian "night-watchman state," limited to ensuring peace, safety, social coordination, the rule of law, and fundamental liberties. These principles, Jefferson concludes, "should be the creed of our political faith."[52] It would thus appear that *caritas*, as understood by Jefferson, plays a modest part at best in the development of his public policy. The inherent right of individuals to live as they wish and keep what they earn continues to place significant restrictions on government's activity. A little more than a year after the First Inaugural, in a letter to Thomas Cooper, Jefferson explained that when it comes to government,

> A noiseless course, not meddling with the affairs of others, unattractive of notice, is a mark that society is going on in *happiness*. If we can prevent the government from wasting the labors of the people, under the pretence of taking care of them, they must become *happy*.[53]

So when Jefferson leads into his peroration of his address with a firm pledge "to be instrumental to the happiness and freedom of all," we must conclude that despite Jefferson's conclusion that a sense of national *caritas* is critical to forming national happiness, this recognition does not justify using the machinery of government to develop a comprehensive welfare state or to shape citizens into beings of heavenly sensitivities. In short, the classically liberal core of the Declaration has been amended, but only slightly here in the First Inaugural.

It must be kept in mind here, though, that this defense of the night watchman state was significantly influenced by Jefferson's sense of federalism, which held that most government should be carried on at the state and local level. The First Inaugural speaks primarily if not exclusively to the activities of the federal government. Jefferson did, for instance, see some role for local governments to play in actively caring for the needy.[54] He led the effort to pass a bill updating a 1775 Virginia statute designed to render aid and give care to the "poor, lame, impotent, blind, and other inhabitants of the county as are not able to maintain themselves."[55] The major difference between the old and new statute is that, in keeping with Jefferson's desire for a stronger separation of church and state, the care for the poor gets transferred from Anglican vestrymen to aldermen of the county. Also, in a 1785 letter from France to James Madison, Jefferson ruminates on the "wretchedness" he observed in Europe from the grossly unequal division of property and concludes that in such situations "legislators cannot invent too many devices for subdividing property." He emphatically clarifies that this does not mean he would advocate a forced equalization of property. His aims were far more modest and situated in the times. For instance, he would start by abolishing the laws of primogeniture, letting property be bequeathed to "all" children rather than the oldest, which would spread property more widely and follow the "natural affections of the human mind." He also thought that exempting all from taxation below a certain point and taxing others in geometric progression as their portions of property ownership rise would be "another means of *silently lessening* the inequality of property" (emphasis added).[56]

Nevertheless, Jefferson's theoretical point in the First Inaugural remains clear and applicable to government at all levels: The demands of Christian love do not radically alter an overall commitment to first ground government on broad principles of liberal individualism. In fact, in a letter to Moses Robinson written less than three weeks after the First Inaugural, Jefferson asserts that "the Christian religion when divested of the rags in which they have enveloped it, and brought to the original purity and simplicity of its benevolent institutor, is a religion of all others most friendly to liberty." That Jefferson sees a religious benevolence inseparably connected with giving ordinal priority to respecting the rights and freedoms of another is again found in a letter Jefferson writes to Miles King in 1814, where he notes that "god" has

> formed us as moral agents, . . . that we may promote the *happiness* of those with whom he has placed us in society, by acting honestly towards all, benevolently to those who fall within our way, respecting sacredly their rights bodily and mental, and cherishing especially their freedom of conscience, as we value our own.[57]

This last statement neatly brings together a number of strands of Jefferson's thought under discussion. According to Jefferson in his later years, "god" desires man's happiness on earth and has therefore made him a moral agent, specifically so that active *man* can promote the "happiness" of "all." How does one act morally so as to promote human happiness? One is to act *benevolently*, which is inextricably tied to "sacredly" respecting man's inherent rights—cutting wide swaths of freedom for others to think and act for themselves.

At this point, though, one begins to wonder how Jefferson's First Inaugural is theoretically distinguishable from the Declaration. To say that the differences are negligible would be understandable but finally incorrect. Some subtle and not insignificant differences exist between these two stages of Jefferson's thought.

Jefferson's Other Metaphor

By the start of his administration, and in a departure from his early career, Jefferson is arguing both privately and publicly that a rationally revised New Testament understanding of the love of man and god is a fundamental component of human morality and a healthy republic. Since Jefferson repudiates so much of traditional Christianity, his embrace of *caritas* requires little if anything in terms of orthodox belief or practice. It does, however, accommodate some public recognition and appreciation of a divine power at work in American affairs—an accommodation rarely made in Jefferson's earlier, official writings. More significantly, for Jefferson, it also invites an inspirational form of affection for other human beings, a concept of love capable of transcending bitter political divisions that risk potentially pulling a republic apart or permanently rupturing once-dear friendships. (Others have already pointed out that it is just this kind of love that ultimately heals the rift between Adams and Jefferson. Benjamin Rush, ceaseless in advocating the importance of Christian charity for American politics, patiently goads both men—at one point warning Adams that he and Jefferson will soon die and stand before a "Judge with whom the forgiveness and love of enemies is the condition of acceptance"—toward a heartfelt reconciliation.[58]) Furthermore, Jefferson's later concept of *caritas* brought a religious supplement to his arguments for an individual rights–based government that was previously grounded in a largely secular philosophical liberalism.

Earlier it was argued that Jefferson's personal views on happiness were largely irrelevant to the meaning of the Declaration and its famous triad of rights. This remains true. Jefferson's First Inaugural unmistakably reaffirms the liberalism of the Declaration. But this speech also indicates that Jefferson's practical experience convinced him that the wide and free exercise of the Declaration's core rights alone, unless coupled with a national character of *caritas*, would constitute a dismal republic indeed. So, while Jefferson's fundamental liberalism still prevents deploying the coercive workings of government to shore up some ideal of Christian charity, his First Inaugural both justifies and exemplifies a noncoercive, nonlegislative but nonetheless political and ceremonial use of office he thought could rightly and effectively advance important elements of this virtue made judiciously more pluralistic. For Jefferson, government was always a decidedly more secular enterprise than not. But the newfound political importance he gave to *caritas* tempered his secularism—however faintly—with the religiously tinged rhetoric of a statesman anxious to persuade citizens to recognize important connections between the general contours of public happiness and widely shared elements of biblical love.

Perhaps nothing captures the essence of Jefferson's mature thought on these matters better than a greatly underappreciated image found in his First Inaugural. The most famous Jeffersonian image concerning religion and politics is the "wall of separation between Church and State," a trope Jefferson did not invent but more than anyone else made prominent and permanent in our shared political lexicon. But this was not his only metaphor on the subject. In his First Inaugural, Jefferson speaks of a national "circle of felicities" and is explicit that at least one of the arcs on this circle is a national religious morality that inspires a love of others and appreciation of the divine.

Of course, the First Inaugural's circle of felicities cannot be taken to nullify or eclipse a wall of separation. Jefferson employed the latter figure of speech in a letter to the Danbury Baptist Association roughly ten months *after* the First Inaugural. And, as has been pointed out repeatedly here, the First Inaugural explicitly affirms Jefferson's Declaration liberalism, the foundation of his separationist philosophy. Further, recall that the last arc on Jefferson's circle is a government that leaves individuals free to regulate their own moral improvement, so long as they are not injuring others.

However, it must not be missed that the "wall of separation" phrase is found only once in all of Jefferson's writings—and that in a piece of private correspondence—whereas the image of a "circle of felicities" is put forward in Jefferson's single most important and visible political speech. If Jefferson's metaphor of a wall between the concrete entities of church and state is allowed to stand alone (and it gets invoked far more often than his circle of felicity image), it masks a certain reality concerning his ripened views on the interstitial space between religion and politics. Thus, Jefferson's metaphor of a circle of national happiness should be seen as gently complementing or correcting that of a wall of separation, giving fuller expression to the rich tapestry of his all too often caricatured thoughts on the nature of the relationship between Judeo-Christian ideals and Enlightenment-style liberalism.

Until the end of his life, Jefferson remained highly critical of many forms of Christianity, loathed rabid sectarianism, and looked to modern, secular "reason" as the final "umpire of truth"—a formulation not always typical of one with deep religious convictions.[59] Yet the context, language, and imagery of his First Inaugural establish that Jefferson did come to believe that some kind of religiously grounded love was far from irrelevant to America's political health and well-being. Jefferson's real hope was that a combination of liberal democracy and rationalized Christianity would, together, greatly bless America and finally supersede all types of Christianity that recognized a more prominent role for divine revelation, orthodox doctrines, and an active God of providence.

Jefferson worked harder and longer toward this end than most appreciate. His was nothing less than a twenty-year effort at a Baconian instauration—a revision and refounding—of Christianity itself.[60] Believing that his original redaction of the New Testament "was too hastily done" while serving as president, he developed a second version fifteen years later, repeatedly claiming—with a hubris shocking even by his own standards of supreme self-confidence—that separating out Jesus's pure and original teachings from the garbled contributions of his followers was as easy as identifying "diamonds in a dunghill."[61] Also, while serving as president, he quietly commissioned Joseph Priestley to produce an extended version of some of his previous work of rationalized Christianity. Because Priestley's work disappointed Jefferson and Priestley died shortly afterward, Jefferson was forced for a time to let the project cool. His hopes for progress revived in 1816 when he discovered a Dutch scholar named Adrian Van der Kemp with interest in producing what Priestley could not. Unfortunately for Jefferson, Van der Kemp proved even less reliable than Priestley.[62]

In contrast with Jefferson's not so successful attempt to popularize a radically refashioned version of New Testament teachings, the kind of liberal democracy Jefferson did so much to establish provided a fertile ground for the proliferation of just the types of Christianity Jefferson hoped would fade away.[63] America remains today home to the world's most varied and vibrant practices of fideistic Christianity and religion in general.

This at least makes one wonder about Jefferson's post-1800 position. If a stable and happy liberal republic requires the shaping and sustaining influence of *caritas*, will only a rationalized version do?

Jefferson's turn to a demystified *caritas* as a significant political resource appears to warm a colder understanding of America's constitutional liberalism, which does much to avoid the harsh and imprudent judgmentalism coming out of Winthrop's model of Christian charity. However, Jefferson's enterprise is based on a concept of charity that does great violence to charity's traditional roots, stripping it of those things that would allow biblical charity to do what perhaps it alone can do for democratic politics. This point is made most forcefully and eloquently by Lincoln—who begins his career in philosophical proximity to where Jefferson ended his.

Notes

1. As founding rector of the University of Virginia, an aging Thomas Jefferson insisted that students be "inculcated" in the Declaration of Independence, which he designated the first of four "best guides" to the "distinctive principles" on which

American government rests. See the "Minutes of the Board of Visitors," March 4, 1825 in Jefferson, *Writings*, 479. Jefferson's very last discernible words ("Is it the Fourth?"), uttered while slipping into a coma on July 3, 1826, before dying the next day, the fiftieth anniversary of the Declaration, melodramatically underscore his consuming desire to have his life, and even his death, inextricably connected with the Declaration and what it represented.

2. For Jefferson and Hamilton's relationship, see Peterson, *Thomas Jefferson*, 396; for the animus of the times, see Aldrich, *Why Parties*, 68–69; Lerche, "Jefferson and the Election," 467–68.

3. For more information about Hamilton's political attacks, see Lerche, "Jefferson and the Election," 468–70; for Jefferson's resignation, see Peterson, *Thomas Jefferson*, 516.

4. "Farewell Address," in Washington, *Collection*, 519–20.

5. Ibid., 519.

6. Ibid., 521.

7. Ibid., 520.

8. Ibid., 517.

9. Ibid., 521.

10. Ibid., 519.

11. Ibid., 515–17.

12. Ibid., 515.

13. Ibid., 521.

14. Ibid., 522.

15. Jefferson, *Extracts from the Gospel*, 390.

16. Ibid., 388, emphasis added.

17. Previously quoted in chapter one: "It is not true that Christ revealed an entire body of ethics proved to be the law of nature from principles of reason, and reaching all the duties of life. If mankind wanted such a code, to which recourse might be had on every occasion, as to an unerring rule in every part of the moral duties, such a code is still wanting; for the gospel is not such a code" (Jefferson, *Literary Commonplace Book*, 35).

18. For the historical analysis of Jefferson's reconsideration of Christianity during this period, I draw heavily, though not entirely, from Eugene Sheridan's impressive introductory essay found in the front of *Jefferson's Extracts from the Gospels*—a one-volume collection of Jefferson's biblical extracts (discussed later in this chapter) and related correspondence, published in 1983 by the Princeton University Press as part of a topical "second series" to complement the definitive, multivolume, yet-to-be-completed, chronological series of *The Papers of Thomas Jefferson*.

19. Jefferson, *Extracts from the Gospel*, 348 (letter to John Adams, August 22, 1813).

20. For information on Rush, see Wilson, introduction to Jefferson's *Literary Commonplace Book*, 16–17. Also see Donald J. D'Elia, "Limits of Philosophical Friendship," 336–37. In his autobiography, Rush notes that the accusation that Jefferson was "unfriendly to Christianity" when he drafted the Declaration "may be true. His notes contain some expressions which favor this opinion." But it was

Rush's sense that during their later Philadelphia conversations the "objects of [Jefferson's] benevolence were as extensive as those of his knowledge. He was not only the friend of his country, but of all nations and religions" (Rush, *Autobiography*, 152, 151). For Jefferson's letter to Rush, see Letter of April 21, 1803, in Jefferson, *Extracts from the Gospels*, 331.

21. Jefferson, *Extracts From the Gospels*, 334.

22. Ibid.

23. "The Philosophy of Jesus," lost shortly after Jefferson's death, has been ingeniously reconstructed by Dickson Adams. See "The Reconstruction of 'The Philosophy of Jesus'" in Jefferson, *Extracts from the Gospels*, 45–53. So important was this book to Jefferson that late in retirement Jefferson redid it (titling it "The Life and Morals of Jesus"), feeling that the first one was "too hastily done" (Jefferson, *Extracts from the Gospels*, 37–38, 369, 352). For the *"real Christian"* quote, see letter to Charles Thomson, January 9, 1816, 365 (emphasis in original).

24. Jefferson, *Extracts from the Gospels*, 57–59.

25. In the First Epistle of John (4:10–21)—a book entirely excluded from Jefferson's New Testament—one reads, "Herein is love, not that we loved God, but that he loved us, and sent his Son to be the propitiation for our sins. Beloved, if God so loved us, we ought also to love one another. . . . We love him because he first loved us. . . . And this commandment have we from him, That he who loveth God love his brother also."

26. Jefferson, *Extracts from the Gospels*, 355.

27. Ibid., 356–57.

28. Ibid., 357.

29. Ibid., 405 (letter of June 26, 1822).

30. Luebke, "Jefferson's Anti-Clericalism," 344, 352; Jefferson, *Extracts from the Gospels*, 327 (letter to Joseph Priestley, April 9, 1803), 320 (letter to Benjamin Rush, September 23, 1800).

31. Jefferson's acknowledgment from his letter to Judge John Tyler, March 29, 1805, in Jefferson, *The Writings of Thomas Jefferson*, 11:69. Jefferson's biographers— who typically devote just a few pages to the First Inaugural—are universally robust in their praise of this speech. Ellis considers it "an eloquent" expression of "panoramic wisdom," a "seminal statement in American history," and something that "can be read with profit on several levels" (*American Sphinx*, 192, see also 181). Malone writes of its "enduring appeal" because of its "verbal felicity" and "timelessness" of thought (*Jefferson the President*, 17). And Peterson recommends it as "an address to be studied and pondered in the cool reflection of the written word," for never was Jefferson's "happy faculty of condensing whole chapters into aphorisms more brilliantly displayed" (*Thomas Jefferson*, 655). Only relatively recently, though, have political theorists and intellectual historians turned to this document for extensive review. The First Inaugural proves an important text in Peter Onuf's argument in *Jefferson's Empire, the Language of American Nationhood*, 106–7—the speech here is also described as an affirmation of and call to American "bonds of affection." More sustained treatments of the text can be found in Stephen Browne, *Jefferson's Call for Nationhood*, and Noble Cunningham Jr., *The Inaugural Addresses of President Thomas Jefferson, 1801 and 1805*.

32. Letter to Francis Hopkinson, March 13, 1789, in Jefferson, *Writings*, 941; Ellis, *Founding Brothers*, 210; Ellis, *American Sphinx*, 218–19; McCullough, *John Adams*, 536–37; Aldrich and Grant, "The Antifederalists," 295–326; Lerche "Jefferson and the Election," 468–69; Weisberger, *America Afire*; Ferling, *Adams v. Jefferson*, esp. chapter 10.

33. Lerche, "Jefferson and the Election," 470n4; Jefferson, *Extracts from the Gospels*, 10; Luebke, "Jefferson's Anti-Clericalism," 344–47; Ellis, *American Sphinx*, 130.

34. For a reference on New England women burying their Bibles, see Driesbach, *Wall of Separation*, 18; for Jefferson's thoughts on clerics, see Luebke, "Jefferson's Anti-Clericalism"; Jefferson, *Extracts from the Gospels*, 387.

35. See D'Elia, "Limits of Philosophical Friendship," and Sheridan's introduction to *Jefferson's Extracts from the Gospel*, especially pages 12–17.

36. Jefferson, *Writings*, 1089, emphasis added.

37. These and all subsequent references to Jefferson's First Inaugural are taken from "Jefferson's Inauguration Address, March 4, 1801" as found in *Papers of Thomas Jefferson*, 33:148–52, for convenience included as appendix C. Jefferson strikes a similar note in the middle of the speech when he refers to America as "a chosen country" and "the world's best hope" (biblical imagery Lincoln later picks up on).

38. Ellis, *American Sphinx*, 301; the comment on the young and politically ambitious Jefferson can be found in *American Sphinx* (119) as can the quotes on Jefferson's rhetoric (301, 119). As Dreisbach, *Wall of Separation*, 57, explains, the famous Danbury Letter, where Jefferson introduces the "wall of separation" metaphor, was specifically written to explain why Jefferson would not continue such a tradition. See also Driesbach, "Sowing Useful Truths," 462–66.

39. Malone, *Jefferson the President*, 18.

40. Ibid., 18; besides his famous flurry of "midnight" appointments of Federalist judges to the federal judiciary, most of which were made during the weeks prior to the inaugural but *after* it became clear Jefferson had won the election, John Adams publicly snubbed Jefferson by leaving town early on March 4, 1801, thus missing the inaugural activities. The midnight appointee most grating to Jefferson, John Marshall, a High Federalist, now chief justice of the Supreme Court and Jefferson's temporary secretary of state, had so made his displeasure of Jefferson's election known, and was so considered a figure of "perpetual mischief" for the Republicans, that Jefferson wrote Marshall a terse note, reminding him to be present at twelve o'clock sharp at the ceremonies, lest Marshall try to spoil the ceremony by showing up late to administer the oath of office (Ellis, *American Sphinx*, 176–77).

41. Ellis, *American Sphinx*, 182.

42. Besides working to retire the national debt (a welcome surprise to many Federalists), Jefferson allowed many Federalist officers to keep their government positions (Ellis, *American Sphinx*, 194–99). In detailing this, Ellis quotes a letter from Jefferson, who speaks of believing that by working to "conciliate the honest part of those who were called federalists, and do justice to those who have so long been excluded from it, I shall hope to be able to obliterate, or rather unite the names of federalists and republicans" (Ibid., 198). The letter's tone and lower-case spellings of the two parties further undermine Ellis's claim about the significance of the lower-case spellings of "republican" and "federalist" in the First Inaugural (Ibid., 183).

43. Peterson, *Thomas Jefferson*, 659.

44. As one firsthand witness wrote her sister-in-law, "The changes of administration, which in every government and in every age have most generally been epochs of confusion, villainy and bloodshed, in this our happy country take place without any species of distraction, or disorder. This day, has one of the most amiable and worthy men taken that seat to which he was called by the voice of his country" (as quoted in Malone, *Jefferson the President*, 17–18).

45. As recently as the contested 2000 election, George W. Bush turned, in his first news conference after securing victory, to the words of Jefferson's First Inaugural for language and ideas to help a highly divided America move forward (CNN, "Governor George W. Bush Delivers Remarks," December 19, 2000).

46. Even Jean Yarbrough, whose particularly thoughtful treatment of Jefferson comports with the argument of this chapter, suggests that "Jefferson never systematically explores what he means by happiness in general or the pursuit of happiness in particular. Nearly all of his comments about happiness occur in private correspondence addressed to a wide variety of family, friends, acquaintances, and even strangers, in which the meaning of happiness is often casually treated" (*American Virtues*, 14–15).

47. Contrast the point of the "let us" tone in Jefferson's Inaugural with the self-oriented and controlling tone of Andrew Jackson's First Inaugural, where the phrase "I shall" is employed six times in a speech half as long (U.S. Congress, *Inaugural Addresses of the Presidents*, 61–64). As previously noted, in Webster's 1828 dictionary "affection" prominently appears in the definitions of both "love" and "charity." Also, dreariness, or rather "dreary," is said to imply "both solitude and gloom," emphasizing in a second way that the lack of happiness appears connected to a lack of human connection.

48. Lane, *Loss of Happiness*, 273.

49. The first definition of "felicity" in Webster's 1828 dictionary is "Happiness, or rather great happiness."

50. In an "Opinion on the French Treaties" to Washington (1793), Jefferson argued that "the law of self-preservation overrules the laws of obligations to others." See Jefferson, *Writings*, 423. For quote, see McWilliams, *Fraternity in America*, 212.

51. Wilentz, "Details of Greatness," 31.

52. The other principles Jefferson recognizes are "support of state governments . . . as the most competent administrators of domestic concerns," "preservation of the general government . . . as the sheet anchor of our peace at home and safety abroad," "right of election by the people," "acquiescence in the decisions of the majority," "a well disciplined militia," "supremacy of the civil over the military authority," "economy in the public expense, that labor may be lightly burdened" (the third reference to keeping government collection and spending of monies at a minimum), "honest payment of our debts," "encouragement of agriculture, and of commerce as its handmaid," "diffusion of information," the "protection of habeas corpus," and "trial by juries." Combined with the "freedom of religion" and the "freedom of the press," these are what Jefferson believes "form the bright constellation" that guided America through its "revolution" from English rule and now must guide

it through its "reformation" of Federalist rule. The sole exception in this list of minimalist ideals is Jefferson's commitment to the "encouragement of agriculture, and
of commerce as its handmaid." This highlights a heretofore underemphasized point.
Jefferson's post–Priestley/Rush moral world was never exclusively liberal/rational–
Christian. Always in the mix was a significant current of classical republican attention to the virtues found in laboring the land and enjoying the pastoral life. By
privileging agriculture over commerce—yet not to the exclusion of the latter—
Jefferson simultaneously honors his conviction that people should be free in the
choice of their pursuits as he acknowledges that a nation of farmers was more likely
to preserve the freedoms and ideals of the Declaration than a nation of merchants.
As Jefferson once wrote to John Jay in 1785, "Cultivators of the earth are the most
valuable citizens. They are the most vigorous, the most independent, the most virtuous, & they are tied to their country, & wedded to its liberty & interests, by the most
lasting bonds" (Jefferson, *Writings*, 818).

53. Ibid., 1110, emphasis added.

54. Writing well into his retirement, in an 1816 letter to Joseph C. Cabell, Jefferson says, "Let the national government be entrusted with the defence of the nation,
and its foreign and federal relations; the State governments with the civil rights,
laws, police, and administration of what concerns the State generally; the counties
with the local concerns of the counties, and each ward direct the interests within
itself" (Ibid., 1380).

55. Jefferson, *Papers of Thomas Jefferson*, 2:420.

56. Jefferson, *Selected Writings of Jefferson*, 361–62, emphasis added.

57. The first quote is found in Jefferson, *Writings*, 1087–1088; the second quote is
found in Jefferson, *Extracts from the Gospels*, 360, emphasis added. The use here of
"moral agents" is again a reminder that Jefferson's later concept of Christian love
builds on an earlier "moral sense" understanding of love Jefferson developed in college, *prior to* the Declaration (Yarbrough, *American Virtues*, 17–18). This suggests
that Jefferson saw "social love" and philosophical liberalism as compatible at the
time of the Declaration, the difference being that later this social love took on more
distinct Christian hues and political importance than Jefferson saw in 1776.

58. See Butterfield, "The Dream of Benjamin Rush," 297–319; Cappon, *The
Adams-Jefferson Letters*, 284–86; Peterson, *Thomas Jefferson*, 953; and Ellis, *Founding Brothers*, 206–48.

59. Letter to Miles King, Sept. 26, 1814 in Jefferson, *Extracts from the Gospels*,
360.

60. In the *Great Instauration*, Francis Bacon—whom Jefferson considered one of
the "greatest men the world has ever produced"—immodestly argued for an intellectual master plan to reconstruct *all* human knowledge upon "proper foundations"
(Jefferson, *Selected Writings of Jefferson*, 558; Bacon, *New Atlantis*, 2). Bacon's use
of the word "instauration" employs the term mostly according to only one of its
meanings: the "institution, founding, or establishment" of something—in Bacon's
case, the worldwide founding of an entirely new scientific epistemology of inductive
reasoning. But "instauration" may also mean "the action of restoring or repairing"
something (*Oxford English Dictionary* VII, 1043). Starting with his First Inaugural,
Jefferson appears to be trying to effect an American "instauration" of Christianity in

a way that reflects *both* meanings of this archaic term. At one level, Jefferson wants to *restore* Christianity to its original and pure principles, stripping from it what he believes are the garblings of the early Apostles, church fathers, and sectarian ministers of his day. But on another level, because he believed Christianity became corrupted almost as soon as it left the lips of Jesus, Jefferson hopes to restore original Christianity so as to "lay the *foundation* of a genuine christianity" that never took root (Jefferson, *Extracts from the Gospel*, 383, emphasis added).

61. See Jefferson, *Extracts from the Gospel*, 352, 369, 388; Jefferson titles this second work, "The Life and Morals of Jesus," which he put together sometime between 1819 and 1820. The work still exists and is similar to the *Philosophy* though it focuses more on the details of Jesus's career and offers, in parallel columns, corresponding passages from Greek, Latin, and French versions of the New Testament.

62. In 1816, Van der Kemp, alerted to Jefferson's views by John Adams, contacted Jefferson for a copy of the "Syllabus" to assist him in his writing of a biography of Christ. Jefferson's hopes were again piqued that he might have a qualified colleague to help him anonymously advance his ideas of a rational Christianity, and Jefferson gladly sent Van der Kemp the "Syllabus" as well as the "Philosophy of Jesus" (discussed above) but on the strict condition that he not reveal the real author. Unbeknownst to Jefferson, Van der Kemp had a long history of planning great scholarly projects but bringing very few of them to realization, and this proved to be the case on his intended project with Jefferson. Over time, Jefferson sadly but accurately came to the conclusion that Van der Kemp would not produce anything of use (Jefferson, *Extracts from the Gospel*, 383).

63. See Noll, *America's God*, 174.

PART THREE

Lincoln and the
Refounding of America

*[Lincoln] was bigger than his country—bigger than all the
Presidents together. Why? Because he loved his enemies
as himself . . . he was a Christ in miniature, a saint of
humanity, whose name will live thousands of years.*

Leo Tolstoy, Feb 8, 1909

*Whoever would understand in his heart the meaning of
America will find it in the life of Abraham Lincoln.*

Ronald Reagan, first inaugural

From Tom to Abe

I n the election of 1860, Harriet Beecher Stowe's support for Lincoln was tepid. His first inaugural left her cold. She found it godless. And his first eighteen months in office only brought her more disappointment—at times even fury—as she observed what appeared to be his general passivism and occasional retrograde conservatism on the issue of slavery. In the fall of 1862, however, she was heartened to hear talk of an Emancipation Proclamation and paid a visit to the White House in November to plead with the president to act. According to family tradition, Lincoln greeted her by remarking, "So you're the little woman who wrote the book that made this great war!"

Even if Lincoln did not actually say it, there is more than a little truth in this fabled exaggeration. Prompted by a visceral reaction against the Fugitive Slave of Law of 1850, Stowe, a New England housewife (daughter of Lyman Beecher and sister of Edward, Henry Ward, and Catharine Beecher, an already famous collection of ministers and reformers), began writing an attack on slavery in novel form. Published in March of 1852, Stowe's work, *Uncle Tom's Cabin*, enjoyed instant and stratospheric success. Within a year, an unprecedented three hundred thousand copies had sold (this in a population of roughly twenty-four million people), a feat only outdistanced that year by the Bible. It was also the first American novel to sell more than a million copies and, consistent with nineteenth-century culture, the book was further circulated by lending libraries, shared widely by networks of families and friends, and oftentimes read aloud to whole households. Additional evidence for how *Uncle Tom's Cabin* absolutely saturated Northern life is found in the well-documented proliferation of paintings, china, plays, needlework, and other artistic media inspired by the book. In the first year of publication, more than three hundred babies in Boston were named "Eva," many of them in honor of the novel's heroine. Because of its popularity and the monumental nature of the issue it addressed, *Uncle Tom's Cabin* still stands as the most politically influential novel in American history.[1]

If this point is lost on most contemporary audiences, it is because the book now rarely makes it onto any teacher's required reading list, thanks among other things to its sometimes honey-sweet sentimentality and the racially demeaning images that have come to be associated with the moniker of the novel's beloved hero, "Uncle Tom." But the novel is a better, more sophisticated piece of literature than is often assumed, and the prevailing image of "Uncle Tom" as a black sycophant seeking white approval has more to do with the wildly popular minstrel shows that were inspired by the novel than by the novel itself. For those few still willing to read the book, Stowe's original Uncle Tom emerges as a powerful Christ figure whose understanding and dignified practice of *agape* was a critical component of the book's immediate appeal and its broad success in making the injustice of slavery all the more ugly and unacceptable to the Bible-drenched culture of antebellum America.[2]

Charity, it turns out, is central to the entirety of Stowe's story, not just Tom's character, a point recognized by Leo Tolstoy, whose own admiration for the book rested significantly on his sense that it was one of the highest examples of a work of art "flowing from the love of God and man"[3] As early as the Preface, Stowe signals that her aim is to "awaken sympathy and feeling for the African race, as they exist among us," hoping that her work is part of "another and better day" dawning wherein the "great master chord of Christianity, 'good-will to man'" will eliminate the utterly cruel institution of southern slavery.[4] Said another way, Stowe's controlling aim is to reform white America's sense of Christian love to include an entire race of people previously subhuman and nearly invisible.[5]

One of Stowe's several strategies to achieve this is to provide the reader with a string of compelling characters who model great human sympathy regardless of race. This sense of color-blind compassion is practiced best by those most genuinely religious, and it challenges, in a rich difference of degrees and ways, the worst prejudices and practices of southern slavery.[6] Stowe's most effective strategy, though, is to bring the novel to a close by juxtaposing the wretched, soul-destroying malice of Simon Legree, white plantation owner, with the Christic, awe-inspiring love of Uncle Tom, black slave.

Simon Legree remains one of the most malevolent figures in all of American fiction.[7] His depravity is so foul and pronounced as to poison even his slaves. At Legree's plantation—unlike other plantations in the novel where a vibrant sense of human community prevails among slave populations—the slaves live together in but a barbaric semblance of society almost entirely devoid of love, trust, or mutual aid. When Tom arrives, he

> looked in vain among the gang . . . for companionable faces. He saw only sullen, scowling, imbruted men, and feeble, discouraged women, or women that were not women,—the strong pushing away the weak,—the gross, unrestricted animal selfishness of human beings, of whom nothing good was expected and desired; and who, treated in every way like brutes, had sunk as nearly to their level as it was possible for human beings to do.[8]

Symbolically situated as the southernmost plantation in the novel, Legree's is truly a living Hell, something the reader recognizes Tom has been steadily descending toward since the opening of the story, when his more humane master, Mr. Shelby, was forced to sell Tom.

The full poignancy of this final destination for Tom is not just that conditions are so despicably mean as to warrant outrage, it is the double offense that someone as selfless and kind as Tom is forced to suffer such cruelty and ignominy. As the novel opens, Tom is revealed as a character who not only refuses several prime opportunities to escape his enslaved condition but who allows himself to be sold "down river" to preserve his master's estate.[9] As Lionel Trilling first pointed out years ago, such actions and the dispositions that produced them got grossly distorted in the "Uncle Tom" character—a stooped figure of shuffling, grinning, and fawning subservience—of the widely attended stage productions which followed in the novel's wake.[10] But such a caricature is clearly at odds with Stowe's vision of Tom as

> a large, broad-chested, powerfully made man, of a full glossy black, and a face whose truly African features were characterized by an expression of grave and steady good sense, united with much kindness and benevolence. There was something about his whole air self-respecting and dignified, yet united with a confiding and humble simplicity."[11]

Tom's own explanation for his willingness to comply with Shelby's decision to sell him off involves a principle that reveals more strength and large-heartedness than could be supplied by some narrowly utilitarian and self-loathing desire to please his master. To his distraught wife Tom explains that "It's better for me alone to go, than to break up the place and sell all" which would have undoubtedly meant the breaking up of many of the slave families, whatever it may have meant for Mr. Shelby.[12] Here, in this generous spirit of self-sacrifice, the shadow of Christ first falls on Tom and grows as the story unfolds.

As Tom readies to leave his family, he wakes his sleeping children for the "last time," not unlike Christ with his apostles in the Garden of Gethsemane (Matt. 26:40). Tom then "raise[s] up his heavy box on his shoulder," like a cross, and "meekly" follows his new master (John 19:17). Once in the transport wagon, Tom's legs are shackled, causing an audible murmur among the gathered slaves and his former owners, the Shelbys. With Jesus-like reserve, however, Tom accepts the treatment silently (Mark 15:1–5; Isaiah 53:7).[13] When it is finally revealed that this whole episode, initiated because Mr. Shelby's pecuniary interest trumped his affection and admiration for Tom, starts a chain reaction of events that culminates in Tom's mortal flogging at Legree's plantation, these early scenes and descriptions become nothing less than a modern recreation of Christ's betrayal by Judas into ruthless Roman hands.[14]

Tom's character of Christlike strength and love comes through most vividly in the final crucible of Legree's plantation. His first day in the fields, Tom helps Lucy, a near-spent slave, by putting into her bag cotton he has picked, ignoring her objections that he will be punished for doing so. Unfortunately Legree was looking to fashion Tom into an unfeeling overseer, so when Lucy and Tom weigh their bags, Legree still declares Lucy's underweight and commands Tom to flog her. Tom, to the surprise of Legree and the rest of the plantation, refuses. Respectfully but resolutely, he informs Legree,

> I'm willin' to work night and day, and work while there's life and breath in me; but this yer thing I can't feel it right to do; and, Mas'r, I *never* shall do it,—*never*! . . . Mas'r, if you mean to kill me, kill me; but, as to my raising my hand agin any one here, I never shall,—I'll die first!" (italics in original)[15]

Legree, barely able to control his "beast"-like rage, yells at Tom that he has bought him "body and soul" and that Tom's Bible demands that Tom obey his rightful master. Tom once again stands firm and does so specifically on biblical grounds. In words clearly reminiscent of the Pauline formulation "ye are bought with a price; be not ye servants of men" (1 Cor. 7:23), Tom cries out, "No! no! no! my soul an't yours, Mas'r! You have n't bought it,—ye can't buy it! It's been bought and paid for by one that is able to keep it." With this, Legree unleashes the "fiendish" Sambo and Quimbo—slaves and hardened overseers who hate each other and soon come to hate Tom—to give Tom a "breakin' in."[16]

But Tom never breaks. In fact, the harder and more violent Legree's treatment becomes, the greater becomes Tom's love of man and God until finally, it is reported, his own will "entirely merged in the Divine."[17] Not long thereafter, when Cassy—one of Legree's slave concubines— provides Tom with the means and encouragement to kill Legree, Tom refuses. And when Cassy counters she will do it, he forbids her with the same intensity and language with which he resisted Legree's commands to flog Lucy.

> No, no, no! . . . No, ye poor, lost soul, that ye must n't do. The dear, blessed Lord never shed no blood but his own, and that he poured out for us when we was enemies. Lord, help us to follow his steps, and love our enemies.[18]

Tom's commitment to this ideal no doubt faces its greatest test when Cassy decides to escape and Tom is once again beaten, this time for refusing to tell Legree where Cassy is hiding, which Tom knows.[19] Legree instructs Sambo to thrash out "every drop" of Tom's blood if necessary to get him to divulge what he knows, a command standing in dramatic contrast with Tom's earlier uttered promise to Legree that

> if you was sick, or in trouble, or dying, and I could save ye, I'd give ye my heart's blood; and if taking every droop of blood in this poor old body would save your precious soul, I'd give 'em freely (see Luke 22:44).[20]

In one of the most moving scenes in a book, Tom opens his swollen eyes as the relentless beating progresses to the point where even Tom recognizes he will soon die. He then looks up at Legree and says, "Ye poor miserable crittur! . . . there an't no more ye can do! I forgive ye, with all my soul!'" (see Luke 23:34).[21]

The power of this scene and the whole conclusion of the book points simultaneously in two different directions. Sambo and Quimbo, "the two savage men" responsible for carrying out the worst of Tom's physical punishments, are finally moved to a tearful repentance for their "wicked" deeds and care for Tom tenderly in his dying moments.[22] By Tom's "stripes [they] were healed" of the "malice" that had come to so corrupt their every human relationship—another clear Christological pattern (1 Peter 2:1, 16, 21, 24). George Shelby, son of Mr. Shelby, who had from his youth adored Tom and did all he could to protect and help Tom and his family, arrives on the scene just soon enough to hear Tom's final testimony and feels overcome by a different impulse.

> Oh, Mas'r George! *Heaven has come!* I've got the victory!—The Lord Jesus has given it to me! Glory be to his name! . . . I loves every creatur' everywhar!—it's nothing *but* love! Oh, Mas'r George, what a thing't is to be a Christian! (italics in original).[23]

As Tom slips from life to death, George is filled with anger toward the "loathsome" Simon Legree, yet he found that "something in that dying scene had checked the natural fierceness of youthful passion," and he slipped away with as few words as possible.[24] Tom's influence, even in death, was to inspire restraint, gentleness, mercy, and forgiveness, all distinct fruits of the Christian love for others he always preached and so supremely practiced right up through his very last breath.

Yet the few words George Shelby did offer before departing included a direct threat to Legree, uttered in "forced composure," that "this innocent blood shall have justice." George further swears on Tom's resting site, "Oh, witness that, from this hour, I will do *what one man can* to drive out this curse of slavery from my land!" (italics in original).[25] Even as the story closes with a clear tribute to Uncle Tom as an idealized man of charity, a believing, long-suffering soul whose patience, mercy, and forgiveness reach Christic dimensions, the pathos of the scene unavoidably bubbles over into a clear demand for active justice. In that spirit, Stowe's very last lines are an unmistakably stern warning to all of America.

> Both North and South have been guilty before God. . . . Not by combining together, to protect injustice and cruelty . . . is this Union to be saved,—but by repentance, justice and mercy; for, not surer is the eternal law by which the millstone sinks in the ocean, than that stronger law by which injustice and cruelty shall bring on nations the wrath of Almighty God![26]

Stowe's book clearly struck a chord, and at an absolutely pivotal moment. In the decade leading up to the Civil War, *Uncle Tom's Cabin* revealed the inhumanity of slavery by showing its profound cruelties exercised upon a population portrayed in a truly human character typically denied in the prevailing culture. Stowe also effectively heightened the revulsion of this pointed contrast by focusing slavery's inhumanity upon an African American who was a near-superhuman practitioner of the Christian charity that so much of white, Protestant America espoused but did not live. Ironically, then, the fictional forgiveness and mercy of Uncle Tom, grounded in his biblically guided love of God and man, made for many Northerners a better case for real black justice than justice argued theoretically ever did.

This returns us to that early insight from Winthrop's "Model" speech that Christian charity, as the form of the virtues, cannot simply be reduced to compassion, or mercy, or forgiveness, or even all those things combined, for charity also cries out for justice. Said another way, Tom's deep wellspring of pure love for God and others inspires in him a malice-free, suffering patience in the face of Southern injustice, yet by having their own Christian sentiments of human compassion broadened and deepened by Tom's example, many readers of Stowe's book were moved to find the unjust sufferings of Southern slavery absolutely unacceptable. The great and tragic aporia here is that this newly triggered charitable impulse to eliminate the gross injustice of slavery resulted in the spilling of oceans of blood—numberless acts of violence that Tom himself would not perform. A path to greater insight into this tragic puzzle can be seen in the way that *Uncle Tom's Cabin* culminates in scenes and language that eerily foreshadow the sermonic voice of Lincoln's Second Inaugural uttered on the eve of Northern victory in the Civil War and Lincoln's own Christic demise. That the charity of Stowe's influential novel closely prefigures that of Lincoln's best speech and final moments suggests that a potent and complex sense of Christian love was vital in leading America into and then out of its bloodiest conflict, the national survival of which capped the creation of American democracy.

Notes

1. Stowe's attitude toward Lincoln is discussed in more detail in White, *Lincoln's Greatest Speech*, 92–94. For Lincoln's comment, see Stowe, *Harriet Beecher Stowe*, 203. The best examination of the novel's popularity and impact is found in Gossett,

American Culture; also see the discussion in Pinckney, introduction to *Uncle Tom's Cabin*, by Harriet Stowe, ix, xiii, xvi. For additional discussion of the novel's unrivaled political influence, see Tompkins, *Sensational Designs*, xi, 122; Donovan , *Evil, Affliction*, 3; Valiunas, "The Great American Novel," 31.

2. See Andrew Delbanco, *Required Reading*, 49–66, for a treatment of the literary qualities of the book and as a prominent exception to the rule that *Uncle Tom's Cabin* no longer makes it onto anyone's required reading list.

3. Tolstoy, *What Is Art?* 242.

4. Stowe, *Uncle Tom's Cabin*, v.

5. See also Donovan, *Evil, Affliction*, 47; and Delbanco, *Required Reading*, 59.

6. Some of the more memorable characters who demonstrate this kind of humane concern for others are George and Mrs. Shelby, who help their own slave Eliza escape and persistently work to rescue Tom from other mean-spirited owners (*Uncle Tom's Cabin*, 44–60, 115–17, 442–48); the Ohio Quakers who help Eliza unite with her husband George and escape to Canada (*Uncle Tom's Cabin*, 148–57, 204–21); and little Eva, whose pure love of Topsy transforms the young slave girl into a religious believer and transforms Miss Ophelia's uncharitable paternalism of Topsy into genuine affection (*Uncle Tom's Cabin*, 304–5, 310–19, 321, 330).

7. For the character of Simon Legree, see Donovan, *Evil, Affliction*, 13; and Tompkins, *Sensational Designs*, 138.

8. Stowe, *Uncle Tom's Cabin*, 372.

9. Ibid., 12–13, 49–50.

10. As discussed in Pinckney, introduction to *Uncle Tom's Cabin*, by Harriet Stowe, vii.

11. Stowe, *Uncle Tom's Cabin*, 32.

12. Ibid., 50.

13. Ibid., 107, 111–12.

14. See also Delbanco, *Required Reading*, 59; and Tompkins, *Sensational Designs*, 134.

15. Stowe, *Uncle Tom's Cabin*, 381–82.

16. Ibid., 382–83, 438.

17. Ibid., 419–20.

18. Ibid., 423.

19. Ibid., 438–39.

20. Ibid., 440–41.

21. Ibid., 441.

22. Ibid., 441–42.

23. Ibid., 445–46.

24. Ibid., 446.

25. Ibid., 448.

26. Ibid., 476–77.

CHAPTER 5

"Hail Fall of Fury! Reign of Reason, All Hail!"

Abraham Lincoln remains the best wordsmith who ever occupied the White House. Among the most quoted and lyrical presidential lines he ever composed are the last of his First Inaugural. Speaking to those who still "love the Union" even if wary of the direction they think he will take the country on the charged issue of slavery, he pleads,

> We are not enemies, but friends. We must not be enemies. Though passion may have strained, it must not break our *bonds of affection*. The mystic chords of memory, stretching from every battlefield, and patriot grave, to every living heart and hearthstone, all over this broad land, will yet swell the chorus of the Union, when again touched, as surely they will be, by the better angels of our nature.[1]

It has rarely been observed, but this is a distinct echo of Jefferson's First Inaugural call for the "affection" he, too, felt was critical to preserving a well-ordered union. In fact, the outline of Lincoln's closing paragraph, including the precise phrase "bonds of affection," was supplied by William Seward, incoming secretary of state, who advised Lincoln in a lengthy pre-inaugural memo that his first address should include a few "words of affection"; Seward explicitly pointed to Jefferson's First Inaugural as a model.[2]

This was not hard advice for Lincoln to follow. As early as his first prominent exchanges with Stephen Douglas—those of 1854 not 1858—Lincoln argued that the Constitution was "conceived" in a "spirit of fraternal affection," cemented a "social bond of Union," and is dependent upon a "national feeling of brotherhood."[3] Even before this, in the two best speeches of his early political career, the famous Lyceum and Temperance Addresses, Lincoln offered a deeply theoretical account of how affectionate, caring attachment between citizens and their representative government is constituent of long-term success and health for any democratic society—a point too often passed over by Lincoln scholars who fail to see how such notions form a consistent core to Lincoln's political philosophy.[4] So he not only accepted and improved the language of Seward's suggested closing passage, he worked in an additional reference noting his fervent desire for a "restoration" of America's "fraternal sympathies and affections."[5]

From the start of his political career, Lincoln demonstrated a considerable and thoughtful worry about the hazards to democracy of human hatred. He also showed a modest degree of appreciation for Christian ideals of love and affection, though through much of his career this appreciation was filtered through a lens of religiously skeptical rationalism. Accordingly, in his two most notable early speeches, he employs several scriptural images and imperatives to combat the hatred and sustain the brotherly affection and love he believes is critical to preserving America's liberal democracy, but he does so primarily in light of a "political religion" of reverence for law and human reason to the virtual exclusion of biblical religion's reverence for God and divine revelation. Just how this is so is the focus of this chapter. Subsequent chapters will reveal that while combating hatred, sustaining bonds of affection, and holding to the rule of law remain essential components of Lincoln's political philosophy, the highly rationalistic sense of *caritas* and "political religion" that underpins these efforts in his early career finally gives way to a profoundly theistic sense. Lincoln's Second Inaugural is the crowning statement of this shift.

The Lyceum Address

On January 27, 1838, Lincoln—just weeks shy of his twenty-ninth birthday—delivered an address to the Young Men's Lyceum of Springfield, Illinois, titled "The Perpetuation of Our Political Institutions."[6] Lincoln begins this address with a spoken song of praise for America's "fundamental blessings," including her "peaceful possession, of the fairest portion of the earth" and political institutions more conducive to "civil and religious liberty" than any in recorded history. While there is a kind of hymnal quality to Lincoln's opening, the speech's prevailing secularity is evidenced in that nowhere does it suggest that thanks for the noted national "blessings" are owed to God. Rather, appreciation is directed only to a "hardy, brave, and patriotic" band of departed ancestors. Quite different from Winthrop, who saw his fellow colonists as covenant makers in a godly land provided by a Heavenly Father, Lincoln sees his fellow citizens as "legal inheritors" of a "goodly land" provided by earthly "fathers," meaning all those who valiantly fought for and thoughtfully created the American republic.[7]

Here, Lincoln vividly contrasts the "legacy" of great deeds "performed" by these earthly fathers with the non-efforts of his audience (four times in this first paragraph Lincoln says that the current generations simply "find(s)" itself in such a blessed state). This is to prepare his listeners for what is coming: a call—a quasi-religious call—for a more active, devoted commitment to the rule of law. Such a call is necessary, as he sees it, because the great tasks of the founding generation, "nobly" rearing up an unparalleled "political edifice of liberty and equal rights," stand in enviable contrast with the more limited, less glorious and therefore less inspiring tasks of the current generation, which are "*only,* to transmit" these blessings down "to the latest generation" (emphasis added). Whatever inclination to lethargy may be embedded in these more mundane tasks, here it must be noted that the performance of such tasks remains an ethical imperative driven by "gratitude to our fathers, justice to ourselves, duty to posterity, and *love* for our species in general" (emphasis added).

For Lincoln, perpetuating American institutions of liberty appears, at root, a work of love transcending the immediate boundaries of time and space—a work of love for the human species everywhere, born and yet to be born. There is a Winthropian ring to all this. Lincoln never specifically spoke, as far as we know, of America as a "City upon a Hill," but he did believe that America's constitutional union was "the world's best hope," even the "last best, hope of earth."[8] On the other hand, Lincoln's primary aim was not the spread and preservation of love or charity, but individual liberty, a mission decidedly more Jeffersonian than Winthropian. And whatever principle of love Lincoln has in mind that obligates this aim of protecting and perpetuating liberty, it was likely influenced by, but in the end stops well short of, any kind of robust notion of Christian charity that situates the love of man in the love of God—a point hinted at in God's conspicuous (for Lincoln's day) absence from this first paragraph.

As Lincoln proceeds with the speech, he identifies what he sees is the major threat to the preservation of liberty. It is not foreign invasion. America's natural advantages in wealth, geography, manpower, and patriotism make such a threat negligible.[9] The greater threat, he argues, is internal. More specifically, the chief culprit seems to be an "increasing disregard for law" which betokens an "ill-omen" of possible death "by suicide." But as Lincoln continues, it becomes clear that the lack of commitment to the rule of law itself has a deeper cause, as well as a more pernicious effect than the specific injustices that happen when law is disregarded. Lincoln points at the deeper cause in his very next breath when he condemns "the growing disposition to substitute the wild and furious passions, in lieu of the sober judgment of the Courts." Before plumbing the depths of this thought, Lincoln pursues the more pernicious effect of mobocracy, incidents of which appear "common to the whole country," North and South.

He begins in the South, discussing recent events in Mississippi where vigilante hangings of some gamblers, and some supposedly insurrecting slaves and their white accomplices, got so out of control that the bodies seen hanging from trees rivaled the "native Spanish moss of the country, as a drapery of the forest." Moving north, he notes the "horror-striking scene" in St. Louis, where a "mulatto" who was accused of murdering a prominent citizen "was seized in the street, dragged to the suburbs of the city, chained to a tree, and actually burned to death." Lincoln does not mention here, though he does allude to it later, a third incident that loomed over his audience more than all others.[10] In November 1837, just two months before the Lyceum Address, a mob in nearby Alton, Illinois, just north of St. Louis, murdered the rabid abolitionist and anti-Catholic editor Elijah P. Lovejoy and threw his press into the Mississippi River. Later in the address Lincoln refers to these events, though he mentions neither Alton nor Lovejoy by name, only making a passing reference to "throwing printing presses into rivers [and] shooting editors."

Lincoln asserts that these vigilante crimes, "abstractly considered," are "but a small evil." The loss of a few gamblers ("worse than useless in any community") or a likely murderer (whom Lincoln now, playing off the prejudices of his audience, calls a "negro" instead of a "mulatto") is of "little consequence." But the lawlessness behind their deaths he does consider a weighty evil. Where the rule of law fails to prevail, those who are *not* gamblers or murderers are just as "likely to hang or burn" as those who *are*. In the name of correcting a specific injustice, vigilantism is likely to commit other acts equal to or greater than the original injustice. But even these things are not the "full extent of the evil." The worst evil, the most pernicious effect, of "mob law" is that it strikes at the "strongest bulwark of any Government," namely the "attachment of the people."

The terms Lincoln uses to describe this attachment are illuminating. When the "vicious portion of the population" is allowed to institute its own justice, it is also certain to "ravage and rob" as it pleases. When this happens, "Government cannot last." Why? The *feelings* of the best citizens will become more or less alienated from it" (emphasis added). In such a case, the government is "without friends." And the few remaining friends it may have are too few to "make their friendship effectual." When a mobocratic spirit rules the land, the American people will find that "the alienation of their *affections* from the Government is the natural consequence" (emphasis added). For Lincoln, this is the one true point of "danger" for American liberty. Later in the address he will, again, emphasize and clarify that only when the people fail to be "united with each other, [and] attached to the government" will tyranny have any chance to prevail in America. One thinks here of Tocqueville's line that "a despot will likely forgive his subjects for not loving him, provided they do not love each other."[11] In sum, for Lincoln, the worst effect of mob law is how it ruptures a unity of the citizenry, breaking down affectionate attachments between them and for the government that represents them as a whole. And again, the deepest cause of this rupture is not mob law per se, but the "furious passions" that drive vigilante justice. If, as Lincoln indicates in his first paragraph, love for humanity obligates the living generation to perpetuate liberty to all future generations, human hatred poses the living generation's greatest threat to doing so.

To protect against this one point of danger, to curb such violent passions and maintain such fraternal connections, Lincoln calls for "political religion." A careful analysis of what this political religion is and why, precisely, Lincoln sees this is as such a necessary protection for America shows, yet again, just how deep and fundamental was his concern—from his earliest political stirrings—over an angry and malicious thirst for revenge as the single greatest threat to sound democratic rule. Lincoln's own summary of what he means by "political religion" is best.

Let every American, every lover of liberty, every well wisher to his posterity, swear by the blood of the Revolution, never to violate in the least particular, the laws of the country; and never to tolerate their violation by others. As the patriots of seventy-six did to the support of the Declaration of Independence, so to the support of the Constitution and Laws, let every American pledge his life, his property, and his sacred honor;—let every man remember that to violate the law, is to trample on the blood of his father, and to tear the character of his own, and his children's liberty. Let reverence for the laws, be breathed by every American mother, to the lisping babe, that prattles on her lap—let it be taught in schools, in seminaries, and in colleges;—let it be written in Primmers, spelling books, and Almanacs;—let it be preached from the pulpit, proclaimed in legislative halls, and enforced in courts of justice. And, in short, let it become the *political religion* of the nation; and let the old and the young, the rich and the poor, the grave and the gay, of all sexes and tongues, and colors and conditions, sacrifice unceasingly upon its altars.

The first question this passage naturally raises is to what extent is Lincoln's political religion genuinely grounded in the Judeo-Christian tradition. Some see a strong connection in that Lincoln's plea for a political religion clearly adopts many of the forms of biblical religion.[12] The problem with this reading, though, is that Lincoln's position retains almost nothing of the transcendent substance of biblical religion. His political religion has its own earthly "altars" and icons. The patriarchs of Israel are fully replaced by the "patriots of seventy-six." The "blood of the revolution" replaces the blood of Christ as the sacramental medium. And even at the "pulpit" of traditional religion, Lincoln recommends preaching a "reverence for the laws" made by man with nary a word about the worship of God or the laws of the prophets.

Only in Lincoln's last two paragraphs does one encounter anything approaching religious otherworldliness. But such images are subsumed by the American founding. Israel's temple of the "Most High God" is replaced with America's "temple of liberty." The anticipation of Christ's resurrection and second coming yields to the anticipation of America remaining "free to the last . . . [till] the last trump shall awaken our Washington."[13] Lincoln's very last line is his most biblical line: "Upon these let the proud fabric of freedom rest, as the rock of its basis; and as truly as has been said of the only greater institution, 'the gates of hell shall not prevail against it.'" The reference to "the only other greater institution" would seem to place Christianity over American democracy in Lincoln's own value system.[14] But even this line, when considered in full context, fundamentally cuts against any argument that Lincoln's political religion is based on the divine direction and final authority of the Judeo-Christian God. To begin with, the speech does not make a single reference to God. Furthermore, the scriptural basis for the last line (Matthew 16:18: "thou art Peter, and upon this rock I will build my church; and the gates of hell shall not prevail against it.") is loaded with meaning quite at odds with how Lincoln is using it.

Within commonplace understandings of traditional Christianity—Protestant and Catholic—there are a number of different interpretations concerning "this rock" mentioned in Matthew 16. These include notions that the rock refers to Christ himself, a confession of faith in Christ as the Messiah (as Peter utters in verse 16), Christ's earthly teachings, and Peter himself as inspired and authoritative leader of the other apostles after Christ's crucifixion.[15] The key thing here is that each of these interpretations is imbued with a concept of revelation. Whether the foundation is Christ revealing himself or his teachings to his church, or whether that foundation is Peter's divine witness ("flesh and blood hath not revealed it unto thee, but my Father which is in heaven," Matt. 16:17) of the Messianic Christ, or his spiritual leadership of the other apostles (it is Peter, on the day of Pentecost, who explains to the others the miraculous outpouring of the Holy Spirit—see Acts 2), "this rock" stands as a kind of fundamental symbol for *revealed* religion.

Yet consider how Lincoln uses the image: "upon these let the proud fabric of freedom rest, as the rock of its basis." To know, in this case, what "the rock" is that supports freedom, one must identify the noun antecedents of "these." For this we must look back to the previous paragraph, which offers up things like "general intelligence, sound morality and, in particular, a reverence for the constitution and laws." And where do these things come from? Lincoln says they are formed from "materials" that are "hewn from the solid quarry of sober reason." Were there a serious fusion in this address between the temporal politics of the founders and the biblical religion of the prophets and apostles, then there should be at least a modest space for mortal reasoning *and* divine revelation to work together. But Lincoln is emphatic: "reason, cold, calculating, unimpassioned reason, *must* furnish *all* the materials for [the] support and defence" of free government (emphasis added). Said another way, the political religion of the Lyceum Address is a credo built on a rock hewn exclusively from unaided human reason.[16]

Such a reading is consistent with the great consensus of Lincoln scholars concerning his religious perspective at this time in his life. Lincoln was well-acquainted with Christianity and occasionally acknowledged a higher power that he sometimes called Providence or God, but more often called Fate or Necessity. However, he was a conspicuous nonchurchgoer who never professed a particular creed, was openly critical of the Bible as an unimpeachable source of moral truth, and was heavily inclined toward a rationalist skepticism.[17] The only substantial and concrete statement we have from Lincoln himself on the matter comes eight years *after* the Lyceum speech, during his 1846 bid for a seat in Congress. Responding to a withering attack from his opponent, popular Methodist circuit rider Peter Cartwright, who was painting Lincoln as a nonbelieving "infidel" and "open scoffer at Christianity" (thus giving Lincoln every political incentive in the world to assert a firm Christian faith), Lincoln published a "Handbill Replying to Charges of Infidelity."[18] In part, this reads,

> That I am not a member of any Christian Church, is true; but I have never denied the truth of the Scriptures; and I have never spoken with intentional disrespect of religion in general, or of any denomination of Christians in particular. It is true that in early life I was inclined to believe in what I understand is called the "Doctrine of Necessity"— that is, that human mind is impelled to action, or held in rest by some power, over which the mind itself has not control; and I have sometimes (with one, two or three, but never publicly) tried to maintain this opinion in argument. The habit of arguing thus however, I have, entirely left off for more than five years. And I add here, I have always understood this same opinion to be held by several of the Christian denominations. The foregoing, is the whole truth, briefly stated, in relation to myself, upon this subject.[19]

What is striking about this "whole truth" of the matter is that while Lincoln never denies the truth of the scriptures, he never affirms them as true either. He claims to have never spoken in a derogatory way toward religion in general, but he does not here take the opportunity to speak approvingly of religion in general. And while he rejects "open" enemies of religion, he is mum about quiet nonbelievers. Nothing here really challenges, and much of it supports, the notion that the young Lincoln was much more of a friendly skeptic than a devout believer in Christianity.

A more plausible explanation, therefore, of Lincoln's political religion is that it is the effective republican response of a civic humanist battling against the problems of time and citizen lethargy.[20] That Lincoln is concerned about the passivity of the current generation has already been noted in the discussion of his first paragraph, where Lincoln also throws down the specific challenge to pass on American liberty *"undecayed* by the lapse of time" (emphasis added). But these themes and their relationship to one another are addressed most directly in the back half of the speech, just after his call for and explanation of political religion, where Lincoln makes two subtle critiques of the American founding.

Lincoln introduces his first critique by suggesting that it is little to "wonder at" that America's constitutional democracy has worked thus far. Up until the time of the current generation, the founding of America occupied and channeled the energies of "men of ambition and talents" who "thirst and burn for distinction" because of the "celebrity and fame, and distinction" almost sure to follow those who proved central to the "success of that experiment." But now, Lincoln argues, *time* has taken America "through that period" and there is "nothing left to be done in the way of building up" this historic project. Consequently, men of "towering genius"—who history tells us will always arise and who by definition "disdain a beaten path"—now have no other recourse to satisfy their ambitions than to "set boldly to the task of pulling down" America's great democratic success.[21] Because time has allowed for a full harvesting in the "field of glory" associated with establishing freedom, political religion is needed to inspire less ambitious, more lethargic citizens to stand together and for their free government against those whose "ruling passion" for glory would lead them to destroy American liberty. While the founding was an effective channel for the ambition that can make men tyrants, this channel is now closed.

Lincoln also speaks of "another reason" why the American founding, the War for Independence in particular, has only limited power against the forces of time. Here he begins by noting that during the Revolution and shortly thereafter, the war and remembrances of the war had a "powerful influence" and politically salutary effect on "the passions of the people." These passions of the people we might call the popular passions to distinguish them from the passion for glory of those belonging to the "family of the lion, or the tribe of the eagle." The popular passions are different, and they break down into two sets. The first set includes, according to Lincoln, "jealousy, envy, and avarice," which he argues are

"incidental" to human nature. They are inherent yet of more minor consequence, thus they remain "common" in times of peace, prosperity, and
strength. This first set of the popular passions, Lincoln argues, were "in
a great measure smothered and rendered inactive" by the "scenes of the
revolution."

The second set of popular passions includes "hate . . . and revenge,"
which he considers more "deep rooted" in our nature.[22] These were
therefore not simply smothered over, but directed outwards "exclusively
against the British nation" instead of against fellow Americans. By Lincoln's reasoning, the Revolutionary War took the most common and
"basest principles of our nature" and either suppressed them (as with
jealousy, envy, and avarice), or turned them into "active agents" (as with
hatred and revenge) engaged in "the noblest of causes—that of establishing civil and religious liberty." In doing so, Lincoln imputes to the
Revolution both a noble aim—securing liberty—and a noble effect—
steering a popularly shared tendency to malicious conflict away from fellow Americans. But he also argues that this noble effect cannot outlive
time and by inevitably fading puts at risk the accomplishments of the
war's noble aim.

The effect fades because time erases the most vivid reminders of the
war. After the Revolution, the "scars of wounds" received in battle by a
"husband, a father, a son or a brother" created a "living history" of the
Revolution that could be "found in every family" and "read and understood alike by all, the wise and the ignorant." As long as these vivid
marks of passion directed in the noble aim of liberty were paraded constantly before the eyes of the citizenry, they were a "fortress of strength"
against threats to liberty because they served as effective visual vehicles
for steering our deepest passions of hatred and revenge toward a foreign
foe. This is key. As noted in the analysis of the first part of the speech,
America's increasing disregard for law is itself driven by the deeper problem of the "wild and furious passions" which forms the single most via-
ble threat to America's liberal democracy. By steering such natural,
furious, popular passions outward, Revolutionary War wounds and scars
militate against a malicious lawlessness within. But this presents a
problem.

As per the speech's opening, America has become too strong against
foreign invasion, which basically blocks any effective channel for this
basest set of popular passions to be nobly directed. Yet not only is threat
of invasion nil, the Revolution is over and even the memory of it "must

fade, is fading, has faded." In particular, the living history of war wounds can be "read no more forever" because those histories have gone the way of all the earth.[23] Thus, "the silent artillery of time has done" what an "invading foeman could never do." It destroyed a critical pillar of America's fortress of liberty, namely the myriad of powerful physical symbols that so effectively directed hatred and revenge away from fellow citizens.

To all this, Lincoln concludes that "passion has helped us; but can do so no more. It will in the future be our enemy." Lincoln would seem to be referring here to both the ruling passion for greatness (now unable to be channeled into the glory of setting up free government because that field of glory is filled) and the deepest of the two popular passions, namely hatred and revenge (now unable to be channeled outward against an international enemy). The lesser popular passions of jealousy, envy, and avarice are not considered here as they were never "of help" in the first place, only smothered over. Between the ruling passion for greatness and the popular passion of hate, though, the main enemy for Lincoln is the latter. The ruling passion of intense ambition is by definition rarer than the popular passion of malice and revenge. And, as the first half of the speech made clear, it is only when the popular passions of hatred and revenge, "the wild and furious passions," get out of hand and break up attachments between the people and their government that a way is even made possible for the ruling passion of ambition to slake its thirst.

In the face, then, of this worry about passion—hatred and revenge in particular—Lincoln concludes by preaching his political religion of "sober reason," of "cold, calculating, unimpassioned reason" that would empower and enshrine a "reverence for the constitution and laws." In many respects, this reading comports well with the notion of Lincoln as a civic humanist directly battling against time with an ageless political religion of reason, a religion that corrects the deficiencies of the American founding trapped in a process of losing its power to sustain itself. Undoubtedly Lincoln is more concerned here with the political difficulties attendant to the inexorable passage of time and broad citizen lethargy in the face of tyranny than he is about any kind of national failure to recognize and embrace divine wisdom, something he seems worried about not at all.

The problem, however, with a strict civic humanist reading of Lincoln here is that it misses that the chief and deepest problem for Lincoln is neither time nor lawlessness, nor is it the natural human impulses of envy or avarice at odds with the common good (Lincoln, unlike many in the civic republican tradition, appears to comfortably accept this latter problem as "common" to human politics and something more easily suppressed in times of crisis or necessity). Rather, the chief culprit is human malice, the "wild and furious passions," the "deep rooted principles of hate, and the powerful motive of revenge." Such an error does not make a significant difference in reading Lincoln's Lyceum Address. At most it fails to illuminate Lincoln's earlier-noted and perplexing reticence to mention the details of the famous acts of mobocracy in nearby Alton that happened a few months before the Lyceum Address. Though Lincoln abhorred the Alton riot, he was also no fan of Lovejoy's aggressive anti-Catholic and abolitionist agitation. What the Alton riot and Lovejoy's provocations had in common is that both were highly emotional responses of malice injurious to the reasonable rule of law. Thus Lincoln had to find a way to repudiate both Alton and Lovejoy. By mentioning the riot but not much of its details, Lincoln's artful rhetoric explicitly condemns events at Alton even as it implicitly censures—by manifestly refusing to defend or honor—Lovejoy and his movement.[24]

The real problem, though, with the civic humanist reading of Lincoln is that it establishes a lens that produces an increasingly distorted picture of Lincoln's political philosophy as it matures. By reducing Lincoln's political religion to championing a reverence for purely man-made law, put in a form solely if ingeniously designed to overcome time, it closes off the Lincoln student to the more genuinely and traditionally religious spirit that he developed in later life and which had more than a modest influence on his politics. It also closes off the student to how early, how often, and how consistently his political philosophy was grounded in a singular concern about the problem of human hatred—a topic he tackles in a slightly different way in the other great speech of his early career.[25]

Temperance Address

In February of 1842, Lincoln spoke to the Springfield chapter of the Washingtonian Temperance Society, a national reform organization started by a handful of recovered alcoholics.[26] Lincoln begins the speech by noting that while the Temperance movement has been in existence for more than two decades, it has only "just now" become effective. The stated goal of his speech, therefore, is to elucidate the "rational causes" behind this new success. Such a goal is consistent with Lincoln's faith in the powers of "cold, calculating, unimpassioned reason," as expressed in his Lyceum Address just four years earlier. Yet, given this reasserted faith in cold reason, it is interesting that in the speech's third sentence Lincoln applauds the Temperance movement for no longer being a "cold abstract theory" but a "living, breathing, active" agent for positive change. In doing so, he suggests, somewhat ironically, that while cold reason must be used to identify the source of this successful change, the source itself appears to be something warmer and livelier than cold, theoretical reasoning.

Lincoln chalks up the Temperance movement's frigid and ineffective past mainly to its former "champions" and "tactics." The critical deficiency of the old champions—mainly preachers, lawyers, or hired agents—was that they had "no sympathy of feeling or interest" in those whom they would change. Rather they acted in highly self-oriented ways, pursuing a religious fanaticism, vanity, and avarice that left them suffering from a clear "want of approachability" with the "mass of mankind." By contrast, the new champions—largely those who had once themselves struggled with a destructive addiction to alcohol—stand ready to "convince and persuade" without compensation of personal advantage. The new champions therefore have a power the old champions did not because their "sincerity" and "sympathy" could not be denied. For Lincoln, "there is a logic, and an eloquence" in this that "few, with human feelings, can resist." The full *logic* for how honest feelings of concern serve as the rational cause of the Washingtonians' success is delineated in greater detail as Lincoln moves his analysis from the character of the old champions to their "system of tactics."

Lincoln explains that the approach of the old champions was suffused with far too much "denunciation." This is both "impolitic and unjust." Lincoln finds aggressive denunciation an *impolitic* tactic because it ignores the realities of human nature, a nature which is "God's decree, and can never be reversed." This nature is such that it always prefers the friendly "accents of entreaty and persuasion" to being "driven." *Driven* here does not necessarily mean coerced, but it does indicate a rhetorical strategy of sharp verbal accusation and denigration. But even this is a bad strategy as far as Lincoln is considered because it just does not work. Because of human hardwiring, denunciation is typically met with "denunciation, crimination with crimination, and anathema with anathema." Thus, when a "lordly Judge" rages against the intemperate as the source of "all vice and misery and crime in the land," the very best that can be hoped for is that those in error will come to "acknowledge the truth of such denunciations" very slowly, if ever.

The logic of the Washingtonians' success is that their character and tactics reveal a genuinely warm human sympathy and kindness that— reason informs us—reaches people as they generally are and ever will be, and in a way that the cold character and vilifying tactics of the old reformers never could. Stressing the argument to the point of hyperbole, Lincoln declares that even if "your cause be naked truth itself," turned into the heaviest lance of sharpest steel and thrown with "Herculean force," rarely will it "pierce" the heart and mind of an offender when handled without "sincere friend[ship]." As Lincoln sees it, "when the conduct of men is designed to be influenced, persuasion, kind unassuming persuasion, should ever be adopted." Amplifying the point yet again just a few lines later, Lincoln concludes, "Such is man, and so *must* he be understood by those who would lead him, even to his own best interest" (italics in original).

The language throughout these lines is clearly generic enough (e.g., "when the conduct of men") to indicate that Lincoln's remarks here pertain to more than just the Temperance movement in particular. The same can be said of Lincoln's comments in the very next paragraph where he praises the new champions because they are "practical philanthropists" rather than "mere theorizers" who are "incapable of feeling." Lincoln continues,

> Benevolence and *charity* possess their hearts entirely; and out of the abundance of their hearts, their tongues give utterance. 'Love through all their actions runs, and all their words are mild.' In this spirit they speak and act, and in the same, they are heard and regarded. And when such is the temper of the advocate, and such of the audience, no good cause can be unsuccessful (emphasis added).

Not just the Temperance movement, but any good cause, including the cause of American democracy, advances best with leaders whose character and tactics are rooted in a genuine love and concern for others.

Douglas Wilson persuasively shows that in Lincoln's pre-Springfield days he demonstrated a well-documented "power to hurt"—both verbally and physically—when provoked in the rough and tumble world of frontier America. But by the time Lincoln comes to New Salem (where he lived just before moving to Springfield), he had "virtually given up fighting and had become something of a peacemaker."[27] David Donald confirms that by the time Lincoln delivered his Temperance Address he clearly "wanted to be regarded as a generous opponent" and from that point on was almost always "unwilling to hurt the feelings of a colleague." Among other things, this helps to explain Lincoln's heavy reliance on humor. Often Lincoln's humor allowed him to say difficult things, or gain political advantage, in the kindest way. A reporter once described the way Lincoln "disposed" of a political opponent as "so genial and mirthful that the victim himself, had he been present, could not have taken umbrage at it." Even Stephen Douglas, the most likely person to be bitter about Lincoln's success, was forced to admit in the heat of debate with Lincoln that he was "a kind, amiable . . . and honorable opponent."[28]

Besides revealing something about Lincoln's own political leadership style and philosophy and indicating that the kind and sympathetic approach of the Washingtonians is to be recommended to democratic leaders more generally, the passages just examined also emphasize that a genuinely caring leadership is not simply to be equated with a nonjudgmental facilitation of a people's self-chosen wants. As the very nature of the Temperance movement presupposes, there may be moments when people—be they a local group of alcoholics or the democratic masses—will not see or be able to independently pursue what is in their "own best interest." At those times, such people must be kindly shown and persuaded to pursue their true self-interest by someone wiser and more self-disciplined than themselves. The lesson here, one which has been building from the start of the speech and will carry through to the end, is that those who would reform society, including political reformers, must combine warm human sympathy and cold calculated reason. Lincoln's "practical philanthropist" must also be a practical philosopher. Truth, no matter how sharp and fast, in the hands of the uncaring (the "mere theorizer") is a useless instrument. But on the face of it, caring absent truth (a reasoned understanding of what is truly and rationally good for another person) is no solution either.

A classic illustration of how Lincoln believed careful reason must temper the impulse to simply give people what they say they need, even as charity demands of the giver, is found in Lincoln's 1848 written response to a request from his stepbrother, John D. Johnston, for some money.

> Dear Johnston: Your request for eighty dollars, I do not think it best, to comply with now. At the various times when I have helped you a little, you have said to me "We can get along very well now" but in a very short time I find you in the same difficulty again. Now this can only happen by some defect in your *conduct*. What that defect is I think I know. You are not *lazy*, and still you *are* an *idler*. I doubt whether since I saw you, you have done a good whole day's work, in any one day. You do not very much dislike to work; and still you do not work much, merely because it does not seem to you that you could get much for it. This habit of uselessly wasting time is the whole difficulty; and it is vastly important to you, and still more so to your children that you should break this habit. It is more important to them, because they have longer to live, and can keep out of an idle habit before they are in it; easier than they can get out after they are in. You are now in need of some ready money; and what I propose is, that you shall go to work, "tooth and nails" for some body who will give you money [for] it. Let father and your boys take charge of things at home—prepare for a crop, and make the crop; and you go to work for the best money wages, or in discharge of any debt you owe, that you can get. And to secure you a fair reward for your labor, I now promise you, that for every dollar you will, between this and the first of next May, get for your own labor, either in money, or in your own indebtedness, I will then give you one other dollar.[29]

Kind but not uncritical, Lincoln's charity makes a generous offer but one that takes into account candid observations of Johnson's nature as well as a certain view of human flourishing which entails principles of hard work and individual responsibility.

As previously noted, Lincoln felt that an unkind spirit of denunciation was not only "impolitic," but also "unjust." Here the problem rests not so much with denunciation in the face of basic human nature, but denunciation in the face of an environment generally supportive of the action in question. Lincoln finds the tactics of the old champions unjust because they ran counter to the "universal sense of mankind," which has historically tolerated and even promoted the use of alcohol. Because the universal sense on "any subject, is an argument, or at least an influence not easily overcome," people should be excused—to a certain extent—in acting according to that sense. Note that the universal sense need not be right or true in order to be a justification. The fact that it exists, rightly or wrongly, justifies so acting to some degree. It also restrains what leaders might legitimately do to condemn such action even when they have some rare insight that the universal sense of the matter is wrong.

Interestingly, in the case at hand, Lincoln takes exception to the universal sense of the matter, suggested by the fact that he was himself a nondrinker and, as the end of the address will show, saw and abhorred the consequences of heavy drinking.[30] When the overwhelming message of one's environment is telling one something is okay, moral culpability is reduced, and leaders who fail to recognize this are unjust. Thus, consistent with his view that even justice demands some degree of accommodation to actions with unjust consequences (Lincoln will detail the injustices he sees stemming from intemperance at the end of the address), if society significantly accepts or supports such actions, Lincoln the teetotaler refrains from what the old reformers would not: open and aggressive condemnation of those who drink.

At the end of this argument, Lincoln offers an obiter dictum indicating that the success of arguments for the "existence of an over-ruling Providence" heavily depends upon a universal sense. Said another way, Lincoln makes the issue of God's existence "mainly" a matter of "argument," an argument whose success depends on a "universal sense" that may or may not be true. That Lincoln makes this particular point about God's existence—seemingly unnecessary to the rest of his argument—in the same breath that he defends a universal sense on the subject of alcohol with which he disagrees strongly suggests that the religious skepticism of the Lyceum Address is still at work in the Temperance Address. Of course, the universal sense of eighteenth-century America tended to accept the existence of a biblical God. Yet in recognition of a widely prevailing sense that the God of the Bible did exist, Lincoln, here and elsewhere, practices what he preaches and refuses to denounce, and could even be said to accommodate, orthodox Christian believers in their basic belief in God.

Lincoln does, however, offer a slightly less subtle attack on a particular strain of orthodox Christianity itself. Proceeding with his remarks, Lincoln notes that the other great "error" of the old reformers is seen in their treatment of the "habitual drunkards." These, Lincoln says, the old reformers wrote off as "utterly incorrigible," "damned without remedy," cut off from any saving "grace." These were therefore to be cast out and neglected now that temperance in the future might prevail. Here Lincoln clearly equates the stance of the old reformers with certain and prominent strains of Calvinism—courtesy of the legacy of Winthrop and others—that accepted the utter depravity of man and only held out hope for those redeemed in God's selective grace. Here Lincoln issues some of the most stinging rhetoric of his early political career and suggests some limits to his own principles of generally reforming the wayward with great patience and love.

> There is something so repugnant to humanity, so uncharitable, so cold-blooded and feelingless . . . we could not love the man who taught it—we could not hear him with patience. The heart could not throw open its portals to it. The generous man could not adopt it. . . . It looked so fiendishly selfish . . . that the noble minded shrank from the manifest meanness of the thing.

In pleasing contrast, for Lincoln, the new reformers labor for "all" now living and "all hereafter to live" and give hope to "all" and despair to "none." This attitude is inspired not by something radically different from Christianity but, as Lincoln sees it, some better form of Christianity than he finds in the more hard-core strain of Reformed/Calvinist theology and (as he puts it) the "doctrine of unpardonable sin," which he here repudiates. Rather, Lincoln ties the new champions to traditions of Christianity that stress (as he puts it) "While the lamp holds out to burn, the vilest sinner may return," borrowing here from the famous English hymnody of Isaac Watts, whose eighteenth-century nonconformist Calvinism took a more gentle and widely sympathetic turn than most.

The ambiguous relationship between the concept of charity in this speech and notions of biblical charity is further underscored in the next section of the speech where Lincoln again turns to Christianity as a yardstick and promoter for the love he sees in the character and deeds of the new reformers. Here Lincoln calls upon everyone to sign the Washingtonians' temperance pledge to give every "moral support and influence" possible to the undisciplined drinker. This, by the way, reaffirms the earlier point that broadly sympathetic leadership need not refrain from taking the rhetorical or practical steps for making morally right or socially useful behavior more fashionable and morally wrong or socially damaging behavior more "unfashionable." Lincoln calls upon everyone to sign the temperance pledge so that the drinker will see all around him "kindly and anxiously pointing him onward; and none beck-oning him back, to his former miserable 'wallowing in the mire.'" Here there is a view about what is good or not good for humans, which Lincoln does not refrain from putting in stark moral terms: "onward" to sobriety, or downward to a "wallowing in the mire" for drunkenness—a direct quote from 2 Peter 2:22, where past sinners returning to sin are described as dogs returning to vomit and washed pigs returning to mud. Yet rather than place heaviest emphasis on stigmatizing drinking, as the old reformers did, Lincoln skips the dog-to-vomit image and moves on to place greater emphasis on popularizing temperance by asking for universal support in signing the movement's pledge.

Lincoln could not understand, and says as much, how those unwilling to sign such a pledge lest it appear they once had an alcohol problem could truly consider themselves Christians. As he puts it,

> surely no Christian will adhere to this objection. If they believe, as they profess, that Omnipotence condescended to take on himself the form of sinful man, and, as such to die an ignominious death for their sakes.

Note how Lincoln's use of the impersonal pronoun "they" distances himself from the ranks of Orthodox Christians. Yet even if Lincoln himself does not believe in the notion of Christ's condescension and atonement, his comments here reveal a certain admiration for the concept, an admiration that strengthens his view that democratic reform must resist moral sanctimoniousness and charitably engage in the work of reform, even at the risk of besmirched reputation and worldly taint. This reveals in Lincoln an unusual departure from what has otherwise been, thus far, a quite Jeffersonian stance. Even in his later more "Christian" phase, Jefferson found the whole idea of Christ's atonement morally repugnant.

Lincoln concludes this section of his speech by making a statement that goes far to explain his patient and generous spirit. Speaking of alcoholism, he says,

> In my judgment, such of us as have never fallen victims, have been spared more from the absence of appetite, than from any mental or moral superiority over those who have.

Lincoln's unwillingness to grant the regularly sober an inherent "moral superiority" over the habitual drinker goes far to explain Lincoln's

own "enlarged philanthropy" toward the drinker. Weaknesses due to
inherited conditions are to be mostly pitied, not endlessly condemned.
Nevertheless, while such appetites are to be greatly pitied, the inappro-
priate behavior in question is not to be mindlessly tolerated. Thus the
earlier call to have everyone "kindly [but] anxiously point" the errant
soul "onward" in the correct direction, and thus, in this same paragraph,
intemperance is clearly labeled a "vice" and even made out to be a blood-
sucking, rapacious "demon," akin to the "Egyptian angel of death" who
would slay the first or the fairest of each family.

Lincoln's determination to designate intemperance as a manifest evil
reveals the depths of his abhorrence of such a condition and, again, his
willingness to condemn the sin even as he models and pleads for more
kindness and sympathy for the sinner. Of course, the sin here is hardly
one against the God of the Bible since that God's existence is, for Lincoln, still an open question at best. Yet the battle against intemperance
is one Lincoln clearly raises to a religious level. The biblical imagery of
this latter passage is but a reverberation of Lincoln's second paragraph,
where intemperance was made out to be a "great adversary," one with its
own "temples" and "altars," and "human sacrifices" and "rites of idola-
trous worship."

In the face of intemperance as nothing less than bloodthirsty paganism, Lincoln would marshal a strong counterforce. This force is not
Christianity per se, though by now it should be clear that this counterforce has a distinctly biblical air about it, taking a number of explicit
cues from Christian teachings of redemption and love. The word that
Lincoln actually uses to describe this force is that of "revolution." And,
in further describing this revolution, Lincoln layers it with yet more of
an *agapic* quality.

Supposing revolutions were judged by the amount of misery they
afflict or alleviate, Lincoln hazards that the Temperance movement—if
successfully conducted—would go down as the "grandest the world shall
ever have seen." By explicit comparison, this means grander than that
of 1776. Unlike almost all ambitious politicians, then and now, Lincoln
unflinchingly discusses the American Revolution's significant "evils."
The question of whether going to war, under any condition, is consistent
with a full spirit of Christian charity is a long and current debate in
Christian theological circles. Generally, though, the ideal of charity is
acknowledged to dissuade from war, and if it ever does excuse it, it does

so along exacting moral grounds with certain limitations on its execution.[31] Lincoln tilts in this general direction. His compassionate awareness of the high human cost and collateral damage always associated
with war made him extremely reticent concerning national conflict. For
instance, he was profoundly opposed to the start of the war with Mex-
ico.[32] He was no pacifist, though. He greatly admired the American Revolution, calling it, as he does here, something of which "all are justly
proud" and praising it for its "glorious results," which include a matchless "political freedom" for America, a solution to history's toughest
problem (self-government), and the world's best germinating seed for the
"universal liberty of mankind." But his politically unique and morally
acute sense for the "inevitable price" of such "blessings"—one might say,
his intense compassion for those innocents whose lives are torn asunder
by even a just war—cause him to speak up here, without varnish, concerning how the American Revolution brought "famine, swam in blood
and rode on fire; and long, long after, the orphan's cry, and the widow's
wail, continued to break the sad silence that ensued." By contrast, in the
Temperance revolution he finds

> a stronger bondage broken; a viler slavery, manumitted; a greater
> tyrant deposed. In it, more of want supplied, more disease healed,
> more sorrow assuaged. By it no orphans starving, no widows weeping.
> By it, none wounded in feeling, none injured in interest. Even the
> dram-maker, and dram seller, will have glided into other occupations
> so gradually, as never to have felt the shock of change.

Painfully cognizant of the inhumane consequences of war, among the
worst evils he sees—marring the other many "glorious" consequences of
liberty this war fostered—are the ugly sounds of the "orphan's cry, and
the widow's wail," whereas the Temperance movement stops the
"orphans starving" and "widows weeping." Lincoln struck this same
theme at the outset of his address where he notes that by reforming
once-drunken husbands and fathers, the Temperance movement rescues
these men themselves and consequently provides for "once naked and
starving children" as well as "wives long weighed down with woe, weeping, and a broken heart." Such thoughts all stand in distinct affinity with
Christianity's "royal law of love," or charity, as described in the opening
chapters of the epistle of James, where the active and compassionate
love of neighbor—especially attending to the "fatherless and widows in

their afflictions"—is made out to be the very definition of "pure religion and undefiled" (James 1:27, 2:8).

Evidence that Lincoln's thoughts here are more than just talk can be seen in the now well-documented fact that even during his more caustic and pugilistic youth, Lincoln exhibited an "inability to ignore the helpless," a trait which only increased over time and was sometimes pursued at the risk of losing social standing or botching important business.[33] During his early political career, Lincoln argued that "providing for the helpless young and afflicted" (through "orphanages" and "charities" among other things), while not the leading object of government, is certainly a *legitimate* object of government" (emphasis added).[34] He also publicly challenged Stephen Douglas's view that virtually any program of government "beneficence" is "unjust, inexpedient, and unconstitutional."[35] Lincoln's "beau ideal of a statesman" was Henry Clay, whose "American System" was committed to a wide range of beneficial public works.[36] In one of the last speeches he gave before becoming president, he spoke to a group of German immigrant workers, saying, "I hold that while man exists, it is his duty to improve not only his own condition, but to assist in the ameliorating mankind."[37] In that same speech, he indicated he was in favor of parceling out government-owned wilderness lands so that "every poor man may have a home."

This description must be qualified, though, by the notion that Lincoln's attitudes about a more active, ameliorative role for government were considerably tempered by his belief in the "tendency to undue expansion" in such matters. His fundamental commitment to the Jeffersonian doctrine of human liberty in the Declaration left him cautious about the size and scope of government. Consequently, his philosophy appears to be one of trying to do "something, and still not do too much."[38] He believed that what "the people can individually do as well for themselves, government ought not to interfere"[39] and was accordingly a staunch defender of capitalism, declaring in 1859

> That men who are industrious, and sober, and honest in the pursuit of their own interests should after a while accumulate capital, and after that should be allowed to enjoy it in peace, and also if they should choose when they have accumulated it to use it to save themselves from actual labor and hire other people to labor for them is right.[40]

A compassionate spirit of public help to those in need and a firm defense of individual freedom and the "right to rise" according to one's abilities remain dueling touchstones throughout his entire career.[41] By the time he becomes president, these two impulses unite in what he concisely declares *is* the "leading object" of government. In a message to Congress in special session on July 4, 1861, he asserts,

> to elevate the condition of men—to lift artificial weights from all shoulders—to clear the paths of laudable pursuit for all—to afford all, an unfettered start, and a fair chance, in the race of life.

Where charity and liberty most naturally meet is in the eradication of artificial handicaps, like slavery, and the amelioration of seriously disadvantaged starts in life, like orphanage, which threaten a system of fair, meritocratic reward of freely pursued endeavor. Ever the principled pragmatist, he adds that "partial, and temporary departures" from this ideal may come about from "necessity," but otherwise, he reiterates, "this is the leading object of government."[42]

Lincoln also appears moved that the Temperance revolution's sense of compassion reached even beyond the intemperate themselves and their affected family members, but to those conceivably considered the enemy. He praises the revolution for the way it would have "none wounded in feeling, none injured in interest." Not only do the tactics of the Washingtonians show great sympathy to those suffering from addiction, they show great sympathy to the "dram-maker" and "dram-seller" whose livelihood and self-interest are pitted against the aims of the Washingtonians. The new reformers' gradualist approach—changing lives one at a time and steadily shaping public opinion (making it "unfashionable" not to be part of the Temperance movement)—makes overall changes to the system "so gradually" that the makers and sellers of spirits will have adequate time to relocate to different professions. Their lives and happiness matter too, and the universal sense which has given them license to peddle drink makes a more aggressive attempt to destroy their livelihood an act of injustice—despite the array of evils and injustices Lincoln has now revealed in intemperance supported by the alcohol trade.

Here again the basic tenets of Lincoln's Temperance Address find active expression in his larger and later political thought. This is most notably observed in the clear commonalities between Lincoln's sentiments concerning the best way to deal with intemperance and his tactics

vis-à-vis the problem of slavery. Lincoln's first and always favored solution to the problem of slavery was to eradicate it *gradually*. The metaphor
he liked to use was that of treating slavery like a "cancer," stopping it
from spreading into the territories, thus putting it in remission or slow
death, rather than trying to aggressively remove it.[43] Not only was this
the "peaceful way" of doing things, it would make change for the South
less shocking and disruptive.[44] Their lives and happiness mattered too.
And Lincoln's concern for Southern slaveholders stems from the same
kind of equalitarianism at work in the Temperance Address that made
Lincoln so generous toward both alcoholics and purveyors of alcohol. "I
have no prejudice against the Southern people," he said in 1854.

> They are just what we would be in their situation. If slavery did not
> now exist among them, they would not introduce it. If it did now exist
> among us, we should not instantly give it up.[45]

Or as he said in 1860, "Human nature is the same—people at the South
are the same as those at the North, barring the difference in circumstances."[46] If the intemperate more often than not inherited a genetic
disposition to such behavior, slaveholders inherited a regional geography
where the broad ("universal") sense of the issue not only allowed but
encouraged slaveholding practices. Lincoln denounced *slavery* itself just
as he denounced intemperance itself, but he rarely if ever denounced
slaveholders, thus acting more like the new rather than old champions
in their approach to the intemperate and sellers of drink. Furthermore,
Lincoln was singularly annoyed by rabid abolitionists, who, like the old
champions of intemperance, often sanctimoniously appropriated the
themes and language of the Bible to justify the "furious passions" of
their hard, condescending, impolitic, and sometimes violently uncharitable stance.

While Lincoln's general condemnation of war, patient willingness to
see many of the ugly actions of others explained by forces out of their
control, and his keen sense of compassion for orphans and widows and
even enemies—all neatly on display in the Temperance Address—
suggest a proximity between his thoughts and biblical teachings of love,
the close of his address is a stark reminder that Lincoln is no full-
blooded Christian. In the end, the religious force Lincoln would marshal
against the national evil of intemperance looks more like an expansion

of the secular "political religion" of his Lyceum Address than a firm move toward the "pure religion" of New Testament Christianity.[47]

As Lincoln begins the peroration of this address, he reveals that the Temperance revolution's true greatness rests in the critical role it can play in guiding America to an idealized state of freedom. As Lincoln has just explained, the Temperance revolution helps break a different and "stronger bondage," meaning the tyranny of alcohol addiction he considers both a "viler slavery" and "greater tyrant" than America suffered under King George. For Lincoln, alcohol addiction deprives one of a "moral freedom" no less significant than the "political freedom" established by the Revolution. This is not to suggest Lincoln would sacrifice political liberty for moral liberty alone. Both are essential; the one is ever a "noble ally" to the other. For Lincoln, "victory shall be complete" only when *both* the "moral freedom" of the Temperance revolution and the "political freedom" of the American Revolution are "nurtured to maturity." Only then will Americans drink the "draughts of perfect liberty." Of such a moment, Lincoln declaims, "Happy day, when all appetites controlled, all passions subdued, all matters subjected, mind, all conquering mind, shall live and move the monarch of the world. Glorious consummation! Hail fall of fury! Reign of Reason, all hail!"

Certain Christian doctrines proclaim that true liberty is found in freedom from sin, or over immorality—the freedom to be good. Recall, this was Winthrop's position in the "Little Speech" on liberty. But for Winthrop, such freedom was completely shaped and colored by a wide range of biblically revealed prohibitions and obligations. Lincoln's position is different. First, his moral freedom is to work in tandem with a "civil liberty" Winthrop would have found anathema in its nineteenth-century manifestation of broad democratic practice largely shorn of ecclesiastical direction. Plus, Lincoln's own sense of moral freedom appears to be limited to a conquering of certain physical inclinations that are not wrong per se, but wrong so far as they overwhelm one thing, human rationality. In particular, he sees out-of-control "appetites" (like that for alcohol as discussed in the Temperance Address) and the unmanageable "passions" of "Fury" (as also mentioned here but discussed in more detail in the Lyceum Address) as conditions fundamentally at odds with the true "monarch of the world," which is not the God of the Bible, but "mind, all conquering mind" and the "Reign of Reason." Where human reason reigns and is worshipped ("all hail"), appetites will come under control, fury will fall, and a rich and complete fusion of moral and political freedom will prevail.

Toward this grand end, Lincoln marshals a cultural force of religious dimensions. Though hardly a handmaiden to salvation and a life of righteousness before God, this force does employ biblical language, imagery, and ideals—especially ideals connected to love of neighbor: compassion over malice, communal attachment over individual isolation and apathy, justice tempered by mercy. But such language, imagery, and ideals are always in the service of human reason and to ends entirely earthly and civil. Just as in the Lyceum Address, Lincoln brings all this to a fine point in the Temperance Address by practically deifying America's great earthly, civil hero of political freedom, constitutional order, and moral self-restraint: George Washington. Speaking on Washington's birthday to a group bearing his name, Lincoln closes his address by saying:

> We are met to celebrate this day. Washington is the mightiest name of earth—long since the mightiest in the cause of civil liberty; still mightiest in moral reformation. On that name, a eulogy is expected. It cannot be. To add brightness to the sun, or glory to the name of Washington, is alike impossible. Let none attempt it. In solemn awe pronounce the name, and in its naked deathless splendor, leave it shining on.

It does not appear that anytime after the Lyceum Address Lincoln actually ever again uttered the phrase "political religion." But the Temperance Address clearly indicates that four years later, Lincoln is still practicing the concept, even if he has now expanded it to something not only aimed at political freedom but also a greater moral freedom without which political freedom cannot succeed. It is perhaps more accurate to say that what dominates Lincoln's best early speeches is some notion of political or civil religion in the direction suggested by Rousseau, even if Lincoln stops short of Rousseau's open hostility to and explicit break with Christianity as providing a shell for this civil religion. Believing that Christianity triggered an insuperable divide between the kingdoms of God and man that made "good polity impossible in Christian states" and empowered an only seemingly meek people to rise up "into the most violent of earthly despotisms," Rousseau looked to virtually everything but the forms and ideals of Christianity to carry civil religion. What Lincoln and Rousseau both seem to feel, though, is that a republic requires a "civil profession of faith" involving a few simple "social sentiments," which, while necessarily cloaked in the language and aesthetics of the divine, remain devised and articulated by earthly, political sovereigns for the sole purpose of engendering those virtues necessary to unify and sustain the state.[48] In this early stage of his career, Lincoln's political religion aimed at curtailing a few basic impulses that overwhelm sober reason, self-control, active resistance to tyranny, and citizen unity—all virtues he thought essential to sound and happy self-rule. If Lincoln's early political religion draws, contra Rousseau, some symbolic and substantive inspiration from Christianity, especially charity's horizontal dimension, or love of neighbor, it culls little or nothing from Christianity's vertical dimension, or love of God. Nowhere does God appear to lovingly initiate moral regeneration or to be lovingly obeyed. Divine adoration, to the extent it can be called divine, is exclusively directed to mortal men made gods, namely the Founding Fathers, Washington in particular. Rousseau would have approved of this.

The striking continuities and differences between Lincoln's overall position here and his presidential rhetoric must now be considered.

Notes

1. Lincoln, *Collected Works*, 4:271 (emphasis added).

2. For the full, original "bonds of affection" passage suggested by Seward and masterfully edited by Lincoln, see Lincoln, *Selected Speeches and Writings*, 489. Seward's comments to Lincoln are quoted and discussed in White, *Lincoln's Greatest Speech*, 74–75.

3. Lincoln, *Collected Works*, 2:252, 272.

4. In a number of important works otherwise filled with sympathy and great insight for how Lincoln's ethical and political views connect and develop over time, there remains surprisingly little attention given to these early speeches. And when it is given, little theoretical weight is placed on the way that affectionate human ties between citizens forms a consistent core to Lincoln's political philosophy throughout his career. Richard Carwardine's prize-winning treatment of Lincoln as moral political leader mentions both speeches several times, but mostly in passing (*Lincoln*, 11, 17, 28, 46, 54–55). Douglas L. Wilson's specific examination of the early Lincoln also gives but brief treatment to the speeches, quickly exploring (then mostly dismissing) the thesis that the Lyceum Address reveals in Lincoln a Napoleonic complex, and praising, in the Temperance Address, Lincoln's growing sense of empathy and commitment to self-control (*Honor's Voice*, 195–97, 260–62). William Lee Miller's "ethical biography" of Lincoln profitably reads both addresses together and in more detail (*Lincoln's Virtues*, 130–53). For the Lyceum Address, though, his argument focuses on how Lincoln handles the specific incident of mobocracy (the

Lovejoy incident), which he separates from the second half of the speech on the potential rise of a tyrant, neither of which he ties to Lincoln's concern over the lack of affectionate ties between citizens. And his treatment of the Temperance Address is primarily devoted to revealing Lincoln's attack on Christian self-righteousness. Two of the most sustained treatments of these speeches come from political theorists Glen Thurow (who offers the key Straussian reading, seeing in Lincoln "a guide who stands between God and man") and William Corlett (who offers a postmodern reading of Lincoln as godless civic republican). See Thurow, *Abraham Lincoln*, 19, 117; and Corlett, "Lincoln's Political Religion," 520–40, and *Community without Unity*, 91–118. My differences with these scholars will be developed in more detail throughout this chapter and part of chapter seven. In doing so, my argument will echo in some places the work of Lucas Morel, another political theorist whose book *Lincoln's Sacred Effort* carefully examines these speeches but, again, without extended attention to notions of affection/love/charity that serve as both undercurrents and surface themes to Lincoln's early and late rhetoric.

5. Lincoln, *Collected Works*, 4:266.

6. Ibid., 1:108–15.

7. A careful exegesis of these remarks and surrounding statements gives credence to Corlett's argument, contra Thurow's, that Lincoln's political religion was grounded in a secular civic humanism rather than a revealed religious theology.

8. Lincoln, *Collected Works*, 2:126, 5:537.

9. As Lincoln notes in an unusual flight of verbal fancy, "Shall we expect some transatlantic military giant, to step the Ocean, and crush us at a blow? Never! All the armies of Europe, Asia, and Africa combined, with all the treasure of the earth (our own excepted) in their military chest; with a Buonaparte for a commander, could not by force, take a drink for the Ohio, or make a track on the Blue Ridge, in a trial of a thousand years" (Lincoln, *Collected Works*, 1:109).

10. Oates, *With Malice toward None*, 47; Donald, *Lincoln*, 82; Thomas, *Abraham Lincoln*, 72.

11. Tocqueville, *Democracy in America*, 484–85. This is not to suggest that Lincoln was explicitly familiar with this line from Tocqueville.

12. Thurow, *Abraham Lincoln*, 35.

13. See the good discussion of this in Morel, *Lincoln's Sacred Effort*, 38.

14. Thurow, *Abraham Lincoln*, 36.

15. Barker, *NIV Study Bible*, 1463; May and Metzger, *New Oxford Annotated Bible*, 1192–93.

16. That even Thurow senses something of the thinness of interpretive ice on which he stands is revealed in his confession that the tying of the founding to biblical religion is, in the Lyceum, a "suggestion" and something that can only be viewed in "full flower in the Gettysburg Address and the Second Inaugural" (*Abraham Lincoln*, 36).

17. See, Wilson, *Patriotic Gore*, 99; Oates, *With Malice toward None*, 28–29; Temple, *Abraham Lincoln*, 24; Donald, *Lincoln*, 48–49; Wilson, *Honor's Voice*, 308–9; and Guelzo, *Abraham Lincoln*, 34–39. Even William Wolf's *Lincoln's Religion*— originally published as *The Almost Chosen People* (1959)—a text Thurow relies on heavily and which portrays Lincoln as much more believing and religious in his early

career than most other scholars will grant, admits that in the New Salem years, those immediately preceding his Springfield Lyceum speech, Lincoln, influenced by his reading of Paine and Volney, suffered his greatest "doubts and questionings" about things religious and considered himself a "Doubting Thomas" (Wolf, *Lincoln's Religion*, 51). Also, the text which Wolf relies on to show that this more intense period of doubt was soon replaced with his "former implicit faith in the Bible" has been classified by Fehrenbacher and Fehrenbacher (who have painstakingly investigated the reliability of the most important second-hand reports of Lincoln's utterances) as a "quotation about whose authenticity there is more than average doubt" (Fehrenbacher and Fehrenbacher, *Recollected Works*, liii, 372).

18. Donald, *Lincoln*, 114; Lincoln, *Selected Speeches and Writings*, 54–55.

19. Lincoln, *Selected Speeches and Writings*, 54–55.

20. Corlett, "Lincoln's Political Religion," 521.

21. Lincoln does suggest that "emancipating slaves" may be the one positive contribution by which someone could rival the fame of the Founders—an argument that has led many commentators to suggest an early self-revelation that Lincoln's later effort as the Great Emancipator was driven mostly if not entirely by a Machiavellian resolve for glory. See Richard Carwardine's dismissal of such a reading (*Lincoln*, 11).

22. Most interpreters, including Morel, conflate these two sets of popular passions, thus missing the degree to which Lincoln's strategy is specifically directed at hatred and revenge (*Lincoln's Sacred Effort*, 36–37).

23. Of course, the war will never be forgotten entirely, but it cannot help but grow "more and more dim by the lapse of time."

24. Thomas, *Abraham Lincoln*, 72; Donald, *Lincoln*, 82. This tack also had the advantage of playing to the pro-slavery leanings of southern-situated Springfield.

25. To be fair, both Corlett and Thurow acknowledge human passion as a serious concern of Lincoln's address (Thurow, *Abraham Lincoln*, 31–32, 36–37; Corlett, *Community without Unity*, 106–8). Thurow devotes a section, though the shortest one, in his chapter on the Lyceum Address to the subject of "The Passions of the People." But his analysis leads him to see political religion less as a solution to human hatred and more as a solution to the limits of reason in rule. Corlett devotes more attention to Lincoln's "Taming the Wild and Furious Passions," the title of one of the longer sections in his book. However, he never distinguishes between the different kinds of passions, as Lincoln does and as has been done here, thus missing the singular importance of the issues of human hatred and revenge. Furthermore, Corlett praises the innovation of Lincoln's statesmanship for "creating" a "tradition"—by definition a cultural inheritance that lives well beyond the generation that created it—in the form of a political religion that "opposed the flow of time" by "forc[ing] citizens to worship collective laws." The defect here is that Corlett is so enamored with the genius behind the form of Lincoln's solution (i.e., a strong tradition impervious to time) that he fails to examine adequately the merits of the "substance" of Lincoln's solution (i.e., a secular worship of law). The combination of these things—failure to acknowledge Lincoln's specific and singular concern about the problem of human hatred and an almost blind celebration of Lincoln's political religion as a form set only *against* time and a substance set only *for* a humanistic reverence of law—keep Corlett mostly on track in his analysis of Lincoln's Lyceum

Address and other early writings. But they put him off track just enough that by the time Corlett reaches Lincoln's later work on the war—the Second Inaugural in particular—he will miss the mark entirely.

26. Lincoln, *Collected Works*, 1:271–79.

27. As quoted in Wilson, *Honor's Voice*, 296, 304, 306–7.

28. Lincoln, *Collected Works*, 2:377, 2:512. Donald, *Lincoln*, 83; for further information on Lincoln's heavy reliance on humor, ibid., 149; for the comment made by Stephen Douglas, ibid., 210.

29. Lincoln, *Collected Works*, 2:15–16.

30. Donald, *Lincoln*, 82.

31. For an especially rich, literary treatment of how religious sentiments in America just before the Civil War could push toward both pacifism on one hand and violent abolitionism on the other, see Marilynne Robinson's Pulitzer Prize–winning novel *Gilead*—though most Christian Americans at the time were somewhere between these two extremes. Even for those who justify war on Christian grounds, there remains much debate about what rises to a justifiable cause and serves as an unjustifiable means of military execution (Elshtain, *Just War Theory*).

32. When serving in Congress a few years later, Lincoln was vigorously opposed to the Mexican War. In one rarely noted piece of private correspondence to Herndon during this time, Lincoln mentions a speech by a fellow antiwar Whig which Lincoln regarded as "the very best speech, of an hour's length, I have ever heard" (Lincoln, *Collected Works*, 1:448). Penning the note to Herndon after having just heard the address, the typically unemotional Lincoln wrote, "My old, withered, dry eyes, are full of tears yet" (ibid.).

33. Wilson, *Honor's Voice*, 296, 304, 306–7.

34. Lincoln, *Collected Works*, 2:220–21.

35. Ibid., 2:152.

36. Ibid., 3:29.

37. Ibid., 4:202.

38. Ibid., 1.489.

39. Ibid., 2:220.

40. Ibid., 3:459.

41. Gabor Boritt details how important the chance to succeed economically was to Lincoln throughout his career (*Lincoln and Economics*). From the beginning, many of Lincoln's arguments against slavery were made in terms of the damage such an institution does to the general right even of free whites to keep what they earn and to the ability to prosper in a market of free labor. From his earliest days, he suggested that the notion of "you toil and I will enjoy the fruits of your labor" to be the original sin (Lincoln, *Collected Works*, 1:457). Here I differ somewhat with Deneen, stressing that Lincoln's sense that slavery is truly "another form" of the original sin in that it is a direct act of disobedience against "divine will" only comes toward the end of his career. Early on, Lincoln thought slavery genuinely wrong and used widely recognized biblical imagery to convey the seriousness of its wrongness, but at least at this stage of his career he appears more a capitalistic humanist with a poetic streak than a devout theist with genuine scriptural convictions about man's

fallen nature. See Deneen, *Democratic Faith*, 277–78. While the scriptural convictions come and the compassion for others only intensifies, the capitalism never departs.

42. Lincoln, *Collected Works*, 4:438.

43. Ibid., 2:274.

44. Ibid., 3:313.

45. Ibid., 2:255.

46. Ibid., 4:9.

47. This is a reference, again, to James 1:27 in the King James Version, the version of the Bible Lincoln knew. "Pure religion and undefiled before God and the Father is this, to visit the fatherless and widows in their affliction, and to keep himself unspotted from the world." The more modern New International Version uses language closer to that of Lincoln's. "Religion that God our Father accepts as pure and faultless is this: to look after orphans and widows in their distress and to keep oneself from being spotted by the world."

48. Rousseau, *Social Contract*, 298–309.

CHAPTER 6

"This Nation, Under God"

The closing passage of Lincoln's First Inaugural—"though passion may have strained, it must not break our bonds of affection"— affirms that as Lincoln begins his presidency, roughly two decades after delivering the Lyceum and Temperance Addresses, he remains as concerned as ever over the threat that "passion" poses to America's constitutional order. In extolling the country's "bonds of affection," he also appears to be as concerned as ever about the unity and attachments between citizens this passion threatens. And, in appealing to the nation's "better angels" and "mystic chords of memory," he seems to again be engaged in a priestly act of political religion. The question here is how, if at all, this is different from Lincoln's earlier position.

To begin with, it is clear that Lincoln's carefully argued commitment to and plea for a scrupulous honoring of the Constitution, which dominates his First Inaugural, very much reflects the main aim of his political religion as originally formulated in the Lyceum Address—that aim being to thwart a disregard for law. Lincoln opens his address by reassuring the South that he had no intention for—had formally bound himself against—a "lawless invasion" of the South to eradicate slavery, an institution he would not interfere with anywhere it was legally allowed. And even though the "moral sense of the people imperfectly supports" something like the Constitution's fugitive slave law, his administration would continue to enforce it. Nor would he "construe the Constitution or laws, by any hypercritical rules," acknowledging that it will be "safer for all" to abide by all those "acts which stand unrepealed." On the basis of this same reasoning, though, he denies Southern states a right to revolt. They would have such a right, "in a moral point of view," if they were being deprived of any "vital" natural or constitutional right. But since all such rights were "plainly assured," grounds for Southern revolution break down, standing alone on the principle of "anarchy"—or, as he put it to uproarious laughter along his whistle-stop tour to Washington, a principle of "free-love" instead of "regular marriage."[1]

Besides highlighting Lincoln's lifelong commitment to reason and the rule of law, this evidence of Lincoln's unending devotion to the Constitution emphasizes a point that has thus far gone underemphasized. From beginning to end, Lincoln's larger political philosophy always presumed a kind of dualistic view of human nature.

To those who would secede from the constitutional Union—making secession a generally feasible right—Lincoln asks if ever there would be a social condition with "harmony only" and a "perfect identity of interests." His own answer is that "unanimity is impossible." His precise argument about how this relates to secession is less important than its overall implication—that he sees man's natural condition as one of breaking down into faction. This requires the banking and cooling influence of the Constitution, where

> a majority, held in restraint by constitutional checks, and limitations
> . . . is the only true sovereign of a free people. Whoever rejects it, does,
> of necessity, fly to anarchy or despotism.

The reasoning here is classically Madisonian, and the corresponding picture of human nature is therefore somewhat dark. But, again, the whole speech's view of human nature is not purely dark. The rule of law and constitutional counterpoise must cool and channel the impulses of America's darker angels, those passionate, selfish, and tyrannous desires that constantly push humans toward either anarchy or despotism. But Lincoln holds this in the very same speech that he repeatedly extols America's "fraternal sympathies and affections," "virtue," "bonds of affection," "better angels," and spirit of friendship ("can aliens make treaties easier than friends makes laws?" "we are not enemies, but friends"). And, again, these are simply echoes of earlier statements of his where he publicly argued that the Constitution itself was "conceived" in a "spirit of fraternal affection" and the Union was built upon a "national feeling of brotherhood."[2]

For Lincoln, the creation of America's constitutional Union and its ongoing survival depend upon qualities of human sympathy and affection that cannot be presumed to play a front-and-center role in its constitutional architecture. The same kind of dualism is clearly at work in Lincoln's early speeches, where he reveals that human passions—from avarice and greed to hatred and revenge—well up in the very same people he calls to live by reason and the rule of law and who critically sustain that rule of law by an affection for one another and for their government, and by a charitable concern for all whose passions threaten freedom.

The one novel element on March 4, 1861, is that the few truly sacral aspects of Lincoln's recommendations are supplied by revealed religion. No sacred praise here for Washington. No call for public worship of reason, mind, or legal order. Lincoln does, however (three sentences before his closing) specifically indicate that "Intelligence, patriotism, Christianity, and a firm reliance on Him, who has never yet forsaken this favored land, are still competent to adjust, in the best way, all our present difficulty."

Such talk of God and specific praise of Christianity can hardly be found in Lincoln's early rhetoric anywhere. This seems to have come only as Lincoln moved into his role as president.

On February 11, 1861, roughly one month before his inaugural, Lincoln offered a brief farewell from the back of his train departing Springfield, Illinois, for Washington, D.C. That same day, in Montgomery, Alabama, representatives of the eight recently seceded states were holding a constitutional convention and would soon inaugurate Jefferson Davis as the first president of the Confederacy. In this context, Lincoln says,

> My friends—No one, not in my situation, can appreciate my feeling of sadness at this parting. To this place, and the kindness of these people, I owe everything. Here I have lived a quarter of a century, and passed from a young man to an old man. Here my children have been born, and one is buried. I now leave, not knowing when, or whether ever, I may return, with a task before me greater than that which rested upon Washington. Without the assistance of that Divine Being, who ever attended him, I cannot succeed. With that assistance I cannot fail. Trusting in Him, who can go with me, and remain with you and be everywhere for good, let us confidently hope that all will yet be well. To His care commending you, as I hope in your prayers you will commend me, I bid you an affectionate farewell.[3]

Of Lincoln's stated trust in a "Divine Being" here, some see little difference between this and Lincoln's early doctrine of necessity, or possibly deistic sense of fate. Even Allen Guelzo, who thoughtfully

appreciates in Lincoln some kind of later move in the direction of biblical faith, has suggested that immediately following the Springfield Farewell there is little to indicate that Lincoln felt "any personal interest in
the Almighty," and that the only religious vocabulary in his first inaugural is limited to references to his oath "registered in Heaven" and to the
closing image of the "better angels of our nature"—a construct more
human than divine.[4]

But this is to ignore the First Inaugural line just quoted ("Intelligence,
patriotism, Christianity, and a firm reliance on Him, who has never yet
forsaken this favored land, are still competent to adjust, in the best way,
all our present difficulty."). Furthermore, along his whistle-stop journey
to Washington from Springfield, Lincoln makes numerous statements
similar to those of his farewell and first inaugural. Later in the day of
departing from Springfield he tells a group of folks in Lafayette, Indiana
"we are bound together, I trust in Christianity, civilization, and patriotism, and are attached to our country and our whole country." The next
day in Cincinnati he speaks of America "under the Providence of God,
who has never deserted us." The day after this he addresses the Ohio
legislature in Columbus and promises to "turn, then, and look to the
American people and to that God who has never forsaken them" and
reassures that "all we want is time, patience, and a reliance on that God
who has never forsaken this people." The next day in Steubenville, Ohio,
he offers a distinct echo of the Springfield farewell, acknowledging that
his ability will prove fruitless "unless sustained by the great body of the
people, and by the Divine Power, without whose aid we can do nothing."
Over the remaining two weeks of his journey, he continues to make
statements expressing either America's, or his own, reliance on God: "I
must trust in that Supreme Being who has never forsaken this favored
land"; "I shall be most happy indeed [to] be an humble instrument in the
hands of the Almighty." This includes remarks in Newark, New Jersey,
that are a near carbon copy to those made in Springfield. "With my own
ability I cannot succeed, without the sustenance of Divine Providence,
and of this great, free, happy, and intelligent people. Without these I
cannot hope to succeed; with them I cannot fail."[5]

These observations support the conclusion of Lincoln biographers
David Donald and Richard Carwardine, who argue that by the time of
his election, he was undergoing some kind of religious transformation—
likely facilitated by the grief over the death of a son, an increasingly challenging marriage, and the burdens he felt as a relatively inexperienced

political figure facing the task of reaffirming and extending America's founding ideals and holding the Union together in the face of sectionalism turned secession.[6] That said, though, it must be kept in mind that Lincoln never became what one might call an "orthodox" believer, and the precise nature of his private faith remains a bit of a mystery. He never publicly confessed Christ as his savior, got baptized, took communion, or officially joined a church. As Mary Lincoln put it, he "was a religious man by nature . . . but it was a kind of poetry in his nature, and he was never a technical Christian."[7] This, in conjunction with Lincoln's earlier and well-documented preference for reason over revelation, may help to explain why not all scholars are inclined to give serious attention to the later development and authenticity of his religious character.[8] But to deny that a bright and distinctly biblical faith and morality of some sort develop in Lincoln's last years—starting in 1860 and growing in intensity each year as the war proceeds—is to ignore more than just the reports of those closest to him during his life and some of his best chroniclers today. It is also to deny Lincoln's own words, especially as put forth in and around some of his most important presidential speeches and proclamations, culminating in his Second Inaugural, which Lincoln himself regarded as his best speech. What becomes increasingly clear in these works is that during this all-important administration, Lincoln increasingly took moral and political cues that have more to do with the "pure religion" of the Bible than the "political religion" of his skeptical early years. In particular, a recognition of God and a desire to please and follow him—*agape*'s vertical dimension—breaks onto the scene for Lincoln, increases over time, and further shapes and strengthens what was already a long-standing sense of human compassion—*agape*'s horizontal dimension—even as Lincoln tragically leads America through its most violent civil conflict.[9] Three episodes in particular are revealing.

Thanksgiving

One of the more significant political–cultural legacies of Lincoln's biblical turn in the context of the Civil War was the establishment of Thanksgiving, a tradition not completely unique to America though perhaps celebrated here with a particularly religious air and intensity. During his presidency, Lincoln called for a national day of thanksgiving or prayer ten different times (nine formal, one informal), the first coming just six months into his presidency.[10] And he began his very last public address, offered on April 11, 1865, two days after Lee surrendered to Grant, by acknowledging that "a call for a national thanksgiving is being prepared."[11] Consider this sampling from his earliest proclamations.

that they then and there implore spiritual consolations in behalf of all who have been brought into affliction by the casualties and calamities of sedition and civil war, and that they reverently invoke the Divine Guidance for our national counsels. (April 10, 1862)

it is the duty of nation as well as of men, to own their dependence upon the overruling power of God, to confess their sins and transgressions . . . by His divine law, nations like individuals are subjected to punishments and chastisements in this world . . . . We have grown in numbers, wealth and power, as no other nation has ever grown. But we have forgotten God. . . . I do hereby request all the People to abstain, on that day, from their ordinary secular pursuits, and to unite, at their several places of public worship and their respective homes, in keeping the day holy to the Lord, and devoted to the humble discharge of the religious duties proper to that solemn occasion. (March 30, 1863)

and invoke the influence of His Holy Spirit to subdue the anger, which has produced, and so long sustained a needless and cruel rebellion, to change the hearts of the insurgents, to guide the counsels of the Government with wisdom adequate to so great a national emergency, and to visit with tender care and consolation throughout the length and breadth of our land all those who, through the vicissitudes of marches, voyages, battles and sieges, have been brought to suffer in mind, body or estate, and finally to lead the whole nation, through the paths of repentance and submission to the Divine Will, back to the perfect enjoyment of Union and fraternal peace. (July 15, 1863)

For those eager to make Lincoln out to be a consistently devout and relatively orthodox Christian of his day, the importance of these proclamations has often been exaggerated. But for most modern scholarship, just the opposite appears to be the case. Passing references to these proclamations occur only occasionally in contemporary academic literature on Lincoln, and the proclamations themselves are quoted even more rarely. Currently, in the three most prominent anthologies of Lincoln's thought there are exactly zero selections from these pronouncements.[12]

On October 3, 1863, responding to the several requests of Sarah Josepha Hale (editor of a prominent ladies' magazine) for "a National and fixed Union Festival," Lincoln issued a call for a day of "Thanksgiving and Praise to our beneficent Father who dwelleth in the Heavens" on the last Thursday of November—the establishment of America's regular November Thanksgiving holiday.[13] A portion of Lincoln's statement reads:

> No human counsel hath devised nor hath any mortal hand worked out these great things. They are the gracious gifts of the Most High God, who, while dealing with us in anger for our sins, hath nevertheless remembered mercy. It has seemed to me fit and proper that they should be solemnly, reverently and gratefully acknowledged as with one heart and one voice by the whole American People. . . . And I recommend to them that while offering up the ascriptions justly due to Him for such singular deliverances and blessings, they do also, with humble penitence for our national perverseness and disobedience, commend to His tender care all those who have become widows, orphans, mourners or sufferers in the lamentable civil strife in which we are unavoidably engaged, and fervently implore the interposition of the Almighty Hand to heal the wounds of the nation and to restore it as soon as may be consistent with the Divine purposes to the full enjoyment of peace, harmony, tranquility of the Union.[14]

Given its role in establishing such an important American tradition, this is the most famous of Lincoln's proclamations. It also stands as an interesting link between Lincoln's earlier and later outlooks. While the statement's continuing concern for widows and orphans reveals an important continuity with at least his Temperance Address, the discussion of a political order operating beyond "human counsel" and under the "Almighty Hand" of God instead of the "mortal hand" of man is altogether a new wrinkle in Lincoln's rhetoric.

Lincoln was obviously not the first to proclaim an American Thanksgiving. It was a practice that predated even John Winthrop, starting famously under Governor Bradford at the Plymouth colony in 1621. George Washington initiated the first formal Thanksgiving under the Constitution—specifically to give thanks for the Constitution—and called for a second after the successful resolution of the Whiskey Rebellion. But between Washington and Lincoln, only John Adams and James Madison called for days of prayer and thanksgiving, and Madison later regretted doing so. Not only does this suggest that Lincoln revived a lost tradition, but that he revived and enshrined a tradition largely aborted by Thomas Jefferson. In a letter dated January 1, 1802, sent to his attorney general, Levi Lincoln, Jefferson wrote that as an "advocate of religious freedom," he "long wished to find" an appropriate time and place to explain "why I do not proclaim fastings and thanksgivings, as my predecessors did." In so doing, Jefferson's stated hope was to plant "useful truths and principles among the people, which might germinate and become rooted among their political tenets."[15]

Lincoln also considered himself a staunch champion of religious liberty—recall the particular mention of "civil *and* religious liberty" found in the Lyceum Address, not to mention that he praises America's "civil *and* religious liberty" in his very first proclamation for a day of fasting. It may be that in a certain sense Lincoln saw the proclamations as an act of religious liberty. The son of Secretary Seward, who had jokingly encouraged Lincoln to "steal" from the governors the right to name Thanksgiving Day, reported that Lincoln responded by saying a president "had as good a right to thank God as a Governor."[16] One of the ways Lincoln squared his desire to lead America in national acts of repentance and thanksgiving with his commitment to honor religious freedom was to resist the request of Sarah Hale to issue an executive order applicable to those under the president's direct control (the District of Columbia, the territories, and the armed forces) and to pressure the governors of the individual states to follow suit. Instead, Lincoln simply requested without mandate that his "fellow citizens" join in the observance, thereby skirting the issues of legal authority and right.[17]

But even more significant than how Lincoln instituted the Thanksgiving practice is that he did it. Here his difference with Jefferson can only be understood as a manifestation that Lincoln had at that point developed quite a different view from Jefferson's about the role of God in American politics. For Jefferson, even in his latter Unitarian phase, God remained a distant, inactive, nonpunishing force in politics. Lincoln, at least by the years of his wartime administration, increasingly came to endorse the Winthropian notion that America's political health and very survival were contingent on some humble recognition of and determination to follow a more active God of intervening punishment and reward. If Lincoln was already moving in this direction when elected in 1860, a chain of events starting in 1862 greatly expedited this religious makeover.

The Emancipation Proclamation

For the Lincolns, 1862 began in tragedy. In February, their son Willie died, likely from typhoid fever caused by the White House's polluted water system. While Mary Lincoln developed an even more erratic emotionalism, she and many others noticed that her husband became even more religious. Thereafter, observations of Lincoln's religiosity became more frequent and reliable, including firsthand accounts of people who heard the president speak of being "driven many times upon knees" in prayer, or who stumbled across him in the act of praying—something never credibly claimed about the prepresidential Lincoln. Joshua Speed, Lincoln's best friend and fellow doubter from the Illinois days, distinctly remembers encountering Lincoln in the White House during this phase reading the Bible intently. Speed announced himself by saying, "Well, if you have recovered from your skepticism, I am sorry to say that I have not." Lincoln soberly replied, "You are wrong, Speed, take all of this book upon reason that you can, and the balance on faith, and you will live and die a happier and better man." As David Donald describes it, Lincoln's Bible "customarily" lay on his desk, and "when he could spare the time from his duties, he sought an answer to his questions in [its] well-thumbed pages."[18]

During this same time, Lincoln increasingly brooded over slavery, especially over the idea of emancipation. As Lincoln saw it, a precipitous move on emancipation would destroy the Union by alienating conservative Republicans, war Democrats, and key border state representatives, all of whom were key to maintaining a ruling coalition and most of whom vehemently opposed emancipation. However, by the summer of 1862, the dismal performance of Union forces and the spreading sense in the North that the war was now as much about slavery as it was about preserving the Union convinced Lincoln that it was finally time to reverse his position. On July 21, 1862, Lincoln announced to a surprised and instantly divided cabinet that he was ready to free all slaves in the rebel states as a "fit and necessary military measure," the *only* constitutionally legal means he thought possible.[19]

On the advice of Secretary of State Seward, Lincoln waited to announce this to the nation until after a great Union victory, lest it look to foreign powers like a move of weakness and desperation. On August 30, it appeared such a moment had finally arrived. General Pope reported that he had fought a desperate battle at Manassas—just twenty-five miles southwest of Washington, D.C.—and driven General Lee's forces from the field of action. Unfortunately, Lee's army left the field of battle only to turn back on Pope's troops, catching them by surprise and driving them back to the outskirts of Washington. This bitterly disappointing and alarming second report threw Lincoln into a near catatonic state of despair. Two days later, when several of his own cabinet officials signed a petition against his decision to replace General Pope with George McClellan, it was observed that Lincoln seemed "wrung by the bitterest anguish," and he openly announced to his cabinet officers that he "felt almost ready to hang himself."[20]

On the same day, Lincoln wrote himself a memo, titling it "Meditation on the Divine Will." Here is the full text of the memo, which vividly foreshadows the thinking and syntax of his Second Inaugural.

> The will of God prevails. In great contests each party claims to act in accordance with the will of God. Both *may* be, and one *must* be wrong. God can not be *for*, and *against* the same thing at the same time. In the present civil war it is quite possible that God's purpose is something different from the purpose of either party—and yet the human instrumentalities, working just as they do, are of the best adaptation to effect His purpose. I am almost ready to say this is probably true— that God wills this contest, and wills that it shall not end yet. By his mere quiet power, on the minds of the now contestants, He could have either *saved* or *destroyed* the Union without a human contest. Yet the contest began. And having begun He could give the final victory to either side any day. Yet the contest proceeds.[21]

Lincoln's secretaries, Nicolay and Hay, who were more intimately acquainted with Lincoln and his deepest thoughts during his presidency than anyone else, and not regarded for religious faith themselves, noted that this fragment was "not written to be seen of men. It was penned in the awful sincerity of a perfectly honest soul trying to bring itself into closer communion with its Maker."[22]

Just days after Lincoln wrote out his "Meditation," Lee unnerved the entire North by invading Maryland. With this as a backdrop, Lincoln was visited by a group of Chicago Christians who urged him to emancipate the slaves right away. In a rare moment of angry impatience, Lincoln decried, "It is my earnest desire to know the will of Providence in this matter, And if I can learn what it is I will do it!" Allen Guelzo has crisply captured how, on September 17, the day of the battle of Antietam—the bloodiest single day of the war but a battle that forced Lee to end his invasion of the North—Lincoln felt he had finally heard the miraculous voice of Providence on this matter. Lincoln met with his cabinet on September 22 to propose language for the emancipation proclamation. According to several reliable reports, including this one from Secretary Welles, Lincoln said, among other things,

> he had made a vow, a covenant, that if God gave us the victory in the approaching battle, he would consider it an indication of the divine will and that it was his duty to move forward in the cause of emancipation. It might be thought strange that he had in this way submitted the disposal of matters when the way was not clear to his mind what he should do. God had decided this question in favor of the slaves. He was satisfied it was right, was confirmed and strengthened in his action by the vow and results.[23]

Against this rather devout backdrop, it is revealing that the actual Emancipation Proclamation Lincoln produced is a document that Richard Hofstadter famously characterized as having "all the moral grandeur of a bill of lading."[24]

The text does read as precisely what Lincoln thought it had to be—a strictly legalistic argument falling strictly within constitutional parameters, freeing slaves only in the rebel states and only as a matter of military necessity. A cynical reading of this is that Lincoln acted exclusively out of political calculation, simply walking a razor's edge between growing abolitionist voices and those in his coalition opposed to interfering with slavery. Lincoln's well-observed spiritual anguish over this move serves as an immediate counterweight to such a claim, but the claim does raise the important issue of the sometimes clashing sound of Lincoln's political ideals mixing with his actual practices. No doubt Lincoln was here bowing to political pressure from both sides. He was a man of plentiful ambition; his law partner Herndon said Lincoln's ambition was an engine that never rested. As Lincoln himself conceded to Stephen Douglas during their famous debates, "I claim no extraordinary exemption from personal ambition." But he did protest that his decision to challenge Douglas and marshal the support of old Whig–new Republican forces was not "solely, or even chiefly, for a mere personal object." His chief desire was to oppose the effort of Douglas and the Democrats to make human slavery, rather than human liberty, "universal and perpetual."[25] As Lincoln later claimed along the trail of his journey from Springfield to Washington in 1861, "I have never had a feeling politically that did not spring from the sentiments embodied in the Declaration of Independence."[26]

The record also clearly indicates that Lincoln's opposition to slavery was more than philosophical. Slavery was unjust from a theoretical ethical perspective *and* it was something offensive to genuine human compassion. Over his career, Lincoln declared that slavery and its defense were "plainly selfish," and fundamentally out of sync with the "chords of [human] hearts," "a sense of justice, and human sympathy," "all tendencies in the human heart to justice and mercy," and, significantly, "the Christian rule of charity." Often fond of looking to and quoting Henry Clay throughout his career, Lincoln held that to perpetuate slavery, one would have to "repress all sympathy, and all humane, and benevolent efforts among free men."[27]

The challenge for Lincoln was that unlike more extreme social reformers like Senator Charles Sumner, who always wanted Lincoln to move faster and farther against slavery, Lincoln found it patently irresponsible and dangerously counterproductive to strike forward on freeing the slaves without care for the consequences. Consequences mattered, especially when it came to preserving the fragile good of democratic freedom. Lincoln knew he could not let his sense of liberal justice and heartfelt concern for the slaves get the best of his need to coldly calculate an emancipation that would comply with the rule of law and comport with the public opinion necessary to maintain effective democratic rule.

There is again one well-marked difference in all of this with Lincoln's earlier attitudes expressed in the Lyceum and Temperance Addresses. In preparing the Emancipation Proclamation, Lincoln combines his firm belief in natural rights liberty, his warm sense of human sympathy, and his cool reasoning about legal and political necessities with an urgent desire to seek and follow Divine instruction. The actual words of the Emancipation Proclamation may indeed be considered morally vapid, but the process that produced those words was governed by *agapic* ideals, running from heartfelt compassion for human slaves to a devout desire to follow the will of God. The document is, for Lincoln, a clear civic expression of his love for man and God articulated in the most careful way given the political and constitutional constraints he honored. It is an early political expression of Lincoln's new charity—one that sutures a soulful desire to act in concert with divine direction to an already acute care for his fellow human beings, all of whom (free and slave, North and South) he regarded as naturally entitled to liberty and all of whom, including himself, were obligated to follow the laws of the land—especially constitutional law.

A key point in all this is that whatever religious reorientation Lincoln experienced during the first years of his presidency, he remained ever committed to the Declaration of Independence and America's constitutional Union. Nowhere is this better expressed than at Gettysburg, Pennsylvania, on November 19, 1863.

The Gettysburg Address

In his First Inaugural, Lincoln argued that the looming conflict with the South was about one thing—preserving the Union. As late as August 1862, during his intense wrestle with the subject of emancipation, Lincoln publicly explained to Horace Greeley (editor of the influential *New York Tribune*) that "my paramount object in this struggle is to save the Union, and is not either to save or to destroy slavery." This hardly contravenes the point just made about Lincoln's commitment to the Declaration. His view, held at least as early as his eulogy of Henry Clay in 1852, was that the "cause" and "advancement" of human liberty critically "depended on the continued Union of these United States."[28] But this does indicate that by the fall of 1863, Lincoln publicly amended his position in laying bare the war's deepest purposes in response to the request to offer "a few appropriate remarks" at the dedication of the Gettysburg battleground as the final resting place for eight thousand men killed in action.[29]

Considered by many an unmatched expression of political wisdom and literary grace, the intellectual thrust of the Gettysburg Address ironically rests on the inability of words (their "poor power") to achieve what was asked of the moment.[30] Halfway into this compressed classic of 266 words, Lincoln acknowledges that a ceremony to "dedicate a portion" of the Gettysburg battlefield as a sacred resting spot for the dead is "altogether fitting and proper." In his very next breath, though, he says this is impossible. The problem is that words, even those expressing the most elegant or sacred ideas, cannot possibly hallow the ground of the Gettysburg battlefield any more than it already has been hallowed by the "brave men, living and dead, who struggled" upon it.

Lincoln does see, however, a way for "the living" to appropriately honor "these dead." Fitting words will not do, but fitting deeds will. Warriors and civilians alike must "highly resolve" that the dead "shall not have died in vain." They, the living, must "be dedicated here to the unfinished work which they who fought here have thus far so nobly advanced." They, the living, must be "dedicated to the great task remaining before" the nation. The "unfinished work" and "great task" before them is the successful prosecution of a war, though now the war is about something more than just preserving the Union. That something is what America was originally "dedicated" to "four score and seven years ago"— meaning 1776, the year the country was "conceived in liberty" as a "new nation." This is all to say that Lincoln *re*dedicates the Union and its preservation to the Jeffersonian principle and fundamental truth that "all men are created equal," the ground of inherent human rights to "life, liberty, and the pursuit of happiness."[31] Thus, the newly consecrated purpose of the war is to practically extend the original yet partial birth of "Liberty" in 1776 to a "new birth of freedom" for "all men."

When Lincoln spoke of a new birth of freedom, he may have meant something more than a broader extension of the old freedom of 1776 to a regional class of people heretofore denied their natural rights, though he surely meant at least that. Something that points us in the direction of seeing something more in the newness of the "new birth" is the multiplicity of intertwined images of life and death found in the speech. In Lincoln's opening sentence America is "conceived in liberty" and "brought forth" by "fathers." In its last sentence America seeks a "new birth of freedom," one that "shall not perish" (the controlling aim of his Lyceum speech). In between are numerous alternating images of life and death ("brave men, living and dead," "us the living . . . these honored dead" etc.), and of giving life by sacrificing life ("who here gave their lives that that nation might live," "they gave the last full measure of devotion"). The apologue of birth/death/rebirth is one marbled throughout Western culture, though it does not find expression in most versions of philosophical liberalism that raise the rights of individuals to a social-intellectual position of unchallenged predominance. Rather, such imagery finds its most repeated and vivid expressions in the Bible, where there reigns a recurring metaphysic of new and eternal life replacing old and mortal life, and where charity's highest call ("greater love hath no man") asks one to lay down one's life for one's friends, notably modeled in the atoning sacrifice of Jesus Christ (John 15:13; 1 John 3:16).

The point here can easily be overmade. This imagery in the Gettysburg Address, much like that in the political religion of Lincoln's earliest speeches, is marshaled mostly in the service of civil rather than heavenly aims. Nevertheless, this imagery would seem to accentuate that the prominent foreground of the Gettysburg Address—the notion that America must be unfailingly rededicated to protecting and expanding the implementation of the truth that "all men are created equal"—is ensconced in a soft biblical background, something conveyed in the speech's first six words. "Four score and seven years ago" takes Lincoln's listeners back to 1776. It also takes them back to the Bible, reflecting an Old Testament system of counting. This would appear a conscious move on Lincoln's part, for such a system of counting was archaic even in Lincoln's day yet would have been recognized as a biblical construction by the highly churched and scripturally versed audiences of his day. Additionally, if the speech opens with an *implicit* biblical brushstroke, it concludes with an *explicit* one. In Lincoln's last line, America's "new birth of freedom" is recognized straightforwardly as something coming forth in a "nation, under God."

Such analysis would have to remain purely speculative were it not for the way Jerusalem and Philadelphia meet again, and get transposed, in Lincoln's Second Inaugural. In this later speech, the Gettysburg Address's primary theme that "all men are created equal" recedes to the background in a speech that more than any other by a sitting president declares that America is a "nation, under God" with *agapic* obligations. Only after digesting what Lincoln says in his Second Inaugural can one more clearly make out what Lincoln is only vaguely pointing at in the Gettysburg Address. That is, America's new birth of freedom is in part made new and can only be made possible and perpetuated by a complimentary new birth of charity.

Notes

1. Lincoln, *Collected Works*, 4:195.
2. Ibid., 2:252, 272.
3. Ibid., 4.190–91.
4. Guelzo, *Abraham Lincoln*, 318–19. Guelzo sees change coming later.
5. Lincoln, *Collected Works*, 4:192, 199, 204, 207, 220–21, 236, 234. Also see 4:226, 241, and 246 where Lincoln expresses "above all . . . faith in the Supreme Ruler of nations."
6. Carwardine, *Lincoln*, 220, and Donald, *Lincoln*, 337. An electronic search of all eight volumes of the *Collected Works of Abraham Lincoln* (available at the Abraham Lincoln Association website) reveals that Lincoln made 331 recorded references to "God," and more than two-thirds of those (230) were made in the last four years

of his life (roughly corresponding to four-and-a-half volumes of the eight-volume set of his writings) *after* he was elected president.

7. For an account of Lincoln never officially becoming an "orthodox Christian," see Peterson, *Lincoln in American Memory*, 218; for Mary Lincoln's quote, see Herndon and Weik, *Life of Lincoln*, 359–60.

8. Corlett has already been noted. Michael Lind, in his 2004 book on Lincoln, *What Lincoln Believed: The Values and Convictions of America's Greatest President*, goes to some length to argue that Lincoln's God was purely the "God of the philosophers," meaning Enlightenment figures like Paine and Volney, and that his noted use of the Bible was purely instrumental, given that Lincoln entirely embraced secular reason over scriptural revelation, 21–22, 48–56. Oates, *With Malice toward None*, and Thomas, *Abraham Lincoln*, barely touch on Lincoln's religion in their standard biographies, and never in terms of how it affected his presidential years. Political scientist J. David Greenstone, author of *The Lincoln Persuasion*, sees Lincoln as a great humanitarian as well as political leader but concludes that Lincoln draws upon religion upon religion more as a "resources of his culture" than a possibly legitimate "substantive belief," 9, 34, 218, 283. In *Honor's Voice*, see 309, Wilson shows how Lincoln's more youthful and open scoffing of religion is replaced in his middle years with a more politic presentation of friendliness toward religion without offering much reason to believe that Lincoln's earlier disbelief ever changed. Though, to his credit, in Wilson's more recent treatment of Lincoln's presidential rhetoric, Wilson takes seriously the Carwardine thesis of a "new religious position" in Lincoln. See *Lincoln's Sword*, 261.

9. Even older scholars like Randall and Current, who held that "since Lincoln's death, more words have been wasted on the question of his religion than on any other aspect of his life," conclude that during the Illinois years Lincoln demonstrated very little religious inclination, but that during the White House years, "Lincoln was a man of more intense religiosity than any other President the United States has ever had" (as quoted in Randall and Current, *Lincoln the President*, 372, 375). Randall is still considered by some contemporary historians to be the "greatest Lincoln scholar of all time." See Neely, *Abraham Lincoln Encyclopedia*, 255. William Lee Miller, who hopes to avoid the question of Lincoln's religion in his look at "Lincoln's ethics in theory and practice," also acknowledges that Lincoln changed in some fashion from the aggressive skepticism of his youth, and he nicely catalogues the many ways it could be said that Lincoln's life increasingly manifested and expressed the ideals and practices of the Christian virtue of charity, namely his spirit of "forgiveness," "mercy," "sympathy, and "generosity" (*Lincoln's Virtues*, 85, 90).

10. Lincoln, *Collected Works*, 4:482. Over the next two years, Lincoln signed off on three more proclamations for Thanksgiving for Northern victories and another day of "national humiliation, fasting and prayer": November 27, 1861 (5:32), April 10, 1862 (5:185–86), March 30, 1863 (6:155–56), and July 15, 1863 (6:332–33).

11. Lincoln, *Collected Works*, 8:399–400.

12. A good example of exaggerating Lincoln's orthodox Christian views is Hill's chapter "The Proclamations of a Christian President," as found in *Abraham Lincoln: Man of God*. For the three most prominent anthologies of Lincoln thought, see Lincoln, *Selected Speeches and Writings*; Lincoln, *Lincoln on Democracy*; and Lincoln,

Political Thought. Writing of these pronouncements, Neely asserts that often "their significance is exaggerated" (Neely, *Abraham Lincoln Encyclopedia*, 308). It is true that in more than half the cases Lincoln was acting in response to the requests—Neely says "demands"—of others. Yet, contrary to Neely's suggestive language, there is no evidence that Lincoln ever felt forced to make such statements. In at least one of the cases when Lincoln notes that he is acting in compliance with a congressional request, he is also quick to note, though he did not need to, that he did so "cordially concurring with" and "heartily approving of" their "devotional design" (Lincoln, *Collected Works*, 7:432). It is also true, as Neely points out, that several of these pronouncements were ghostwritten for Lincoln, including the most famous one—the October 3, 1863, proclamation that formally establishes the tradition of the modern Thanksgiving holiday. However, all these statements prominently went out under Lincoln's own signature. Even Neely is ultimately forced to confess that they "cannot be dismissed as unrelated to him" (*Abraham Lincoln Encyclopedia*, 308).

13. For documentation of the requests made by Sarah Hale, see Neely, *Abraham Lincoln Encyclopedia*, 307. This message, written for Lincoln by William Seward, establishes the tradition of making, by presidential proclamation, the last Thursday of November a national day of Thanksgiving. This tradition lasted until December 26, 1941, when Franklin D. Roosevelt signed a congressional resolution making "the fourth Thursday of November in each year" a legal "national holiday" (Randall, "Lincoln and Thanksgiving," 12). Apparently the move to enshrine the "fourth" Thursday (instead of the last) was to cater to business interests desiring to extend the window of Christmas shopping between Thanksgiving and December 25th.

14. Lincoln, *Collected Works*, 6:496–97. Over the course of his presidency, Lincoln issued three more formal proclamations for days of prayer or Thanksgiving.

15. Concerning America's Thanksgiving traditions, see J. G. Randall's article "Lincoln and Thanksgiving" as printed in the *Lincoln Herald*. For information about the resolution of the Whiskey Rebellion, see Hough, *Proclamations for Thanksgiving*, 30–35. For the letter to attorney general Levi Lincoln, see Jefferson, *The Writings of Thomas Jefferson*, 10:305.

16. As quoted in Goodwin, *Team of Rivals*, 577.

17. Emphasis added both times. One of Lincoln's more powerful statements on the topic of rights can be found in the platform he drafted for the Whigs, mapping out their position on the anti-Catholic riots of 1844. Lincoln wrote, "The guarantee of the rights of conscience, as found in our Constitution, is most sacred and inviolable," and anyone who attempts to "abridge or interfere with these rights . . . directly or indirectly, [shall] have our decided disapprobation, and shall ever have our most effective opposition" (Lincoln, *Collected Works*, 1:337–38). See ibid., 6:497; and Randall, "Lincoln and Thanksgiving," 12–13, for discussion of the constitutional issues.

18. Mary puts the time of Lincoln's religious awakening in 1862, just after the death of their son Willie (Herndon and Weik, *Life of Lincoln*, 359). Donald suggests the fact that Mary sees the transformation coming later better reflects the noted lack of intellectual intimacy between the Lincolns than it does the president's actual state of faith. She was simply slow to recognize something that was well under way two years earlier (Donald, *Lincoln*, 337). On observations on Lincoln's prayer life, see

Peterson, *Lincoln in American Memory*, 225. For the Speed quotations and description of Lincoln's Bible, see Donald, *Lincoln*, 514 and 503, as well as Fehrenbacher and Fehrenbacher, *Recollected Works*, 414. On another occasion, Speed recalls Lincoln saying to him "Speed, you had better be without money than without religion" (Fehrenbacher and Fehrenbacher, *Recollected Works*, 414).

19. The notion of emancipating Southern slaves through military fiat as commander-in-chief was not new to Lincoln in 1862. The same day that news of the firing on Ft. Sumter reached Washington, D.C., Charles Sumner, the powerful and respected Senate Republican from Massachusetts, marched to Lincoln's office to remind him that emancipation was a military option well within his war powers (Donald, *Lincoln*, 363); also see Oates, *With Malice toward None*, 307. For more on Lincoln's early views, see Donald, *Lincoln*, 363–64; Guelzo, *Emancipation Proclamation*, 13–111, and Oates, *With Malice toward None*, 252–53. As quoted in Donald, *Lincoln*, 365.

20. Lincoln, *Collected Works*, 5:486. See also Oates, *With Malice toward None*, 315.

21. Lincoln, *Collected Works*, 5:403–04.

22. As quoted in Nicolay and Hay, *Abraham Lincoln*, 6:342. As Neely notes, Hay liked to assert that "Republicanism," not Christianity, was "the sole hope of a sick world" and that Lincoln was "Republicanism incarnate" (Neely, *Abraham Lincoln Encyclopedia*, 142). Elsewhere, though, Nicolay and Hay explain that some people, judging mostly by utterances from his "callow youth," have found in Lincoln an "atheist," whereas others with "laudable intentions" recall "improbable conversations" to prove his "orthodoxy." Nicolay and Hay, however, "have only to look at his authentic public and private utterances to see how deep and strong *in all the latter part of his life* was the current of his religious thought and emotion" (emphasis added). In fact, they conclude, it was the forces at play in his presidential years in particular that "all contributed to produce, in a temperament naturally serious and predisposed to a spiritual view of life and conduct, a sense of reverent acceptance of the guidance of a Superior Power" (6:340).

23. The encounter with the Chicago Christians is recorded in Donald, *Lincoln*, 374. Welles's diary is generally acknowledged as "one of the best sources of inside information on the Lincoln administration" (Ibid., 468). Another highly reliable and compatible recollection of this event comes from the notes of Salmon Chase, Lincoln's often troublesome secretary of the treasury, taken down shortly after the meeting. He reports that Lincoln announced, "I determined, as soon as [the rebel army] should be driven out of Maryland, to issue a proclamation of emancipation as I thought most likely to be useful. I said nothing to anyone; but I made the promise to myself and (hesitating a little) to my Maker. The rebel army is now driven out, and I am going to fulfill that promise" (Fehrenbacher and Fehrenbacher, *Recollected Works*, 96). For the quotation by Welles, see ibid., 474. Breaking with historians who have long and widely neglected this aspect of this episode, Richard Carwardine shows in even greater detail that there is "every sign" that a "providential intervention both shaped the thinking by which [Lincoln] reached the most profound of his decisions, for emancipation, and—even more powerfully—steeled his nerve to stand

by the implications of that decision once made" (*Lincoln*, 193–220). Guelzo highlights the surprise of Lincoln's cabinet, which seemed flabbergasted that Lincoln decided, let alone announced, that he was taking such a monumental state action based on "the strength of a sign from God." This in turn causes Lincoln to half apologize that this might "seem strange" but reaffirm that "God has decided this question in favor of the slaves. He was satisfied it was right" (as quoted in Guelzo, *Emancipation Proclamation*, 153).

24. Hofstadter, *American Political Tradition*, 169.

25. Lincoln, *Collected Works*, 2:548.

26. Ibid., 4:240.

27. Ibid., 2:222, 2:247, 2:265, 3:80, 3:204, 2:131.

28. Ibid., 5:388, 2:126.

29. Wills, *Lincoln at Gettysburg*, 20, 25.

30. Lincoln, *Collected Works*, 7:23.

31. Thurow spends considerable time discussing Lincoln's shift here from "truth" to "proposition," suggesting that Lincoln is indicating a change in the epistemic nature of the statement "all men are created equal" (Thurow, *Abraham Lincoln*, 72–78). For a convincing counterargument that Lincoln consistently regards the notion that "all men are created equal" as a fundamental "truth," see Morel's *Lincoln's Sacred Effort*, 16–17.

CHAPTER 7

A Model of Civic Charity

O riginal in length, style, and content, Lincoln's Second Inaugural is without peer in presidential rhetoric—a point well-acknowledged on the left (Alfred Kazin: "the most remarkable inaugural address in our history—the only one that has ever reflected literary genius") and the right (George Will: the "only" presidential inaugural that "merits a place in the nation's literature"). Especially when read in tandem with the Gettysburg Address, the speech stands as a singularly profound embodiment of America's deepest moral impulses. A powerful force for forging national bonds of affection then and now, these remarks are the culminating statement of Lincoln's unique political and, ultimately, religious discernment that preserved this country through the Civil War and refounded the nation by fashioning a broader and deeper civic commitment to both natural rights liberalism and ideals of Christian charity.

Admirers of Lincoln who continue to insist the speech is basically "irrelevant" to his political philosophy and who disparage those who admire the speech have an erroneously narrow view of what that philosophy was, and they belittle Lincoln himself. When filing away his personal copy of his Second Inaugural, Lincoln, who was not much given to self-praise, was heard to say, "Lots of wisdom in that document, I suspect." A week after delivering the address, Lincoln wrote to Thurlow Weed, saying of the speech, "I expect the latter to wear as well as—perhaps even better than—any thing I have produced."[1]

Odd Beginning/Unprecedented Ending

On March 4, 1865, Lincoln delivered his Second Inaugural from the eastern portico of the U.S. Capitol. To those inclined to see such things, signs of a "new birth of freedom" seemed everywhere. With Grant's Army of the Potomac safely dug in around Petersburg, Virginia—the last line of defense and chief supply center for the Confederate capital of Richmond, which was being defended by Lee's largest and most important fighting unit—and Sherman's unstoppable force of destruction moving up from the South, the end of the Civil War was imminent. Roughly one month earlier, the Thirteenth Amendment, which would finally abolish slavery everywhere in America, was passed by the House and sent to the states. Roughly three months earlier, a gleaming new statue of liberty had been placed on the newly finished iron dome of the Capitol building—thus marking the physical completion of the central structural symbol of American self-rule. To many, the new statue appeared to be looking down on Lincoln's audience "blessing the moment with her outstretched arms."[2] Even nature seemed to mark the moment.

Dark clouds that had brought buckets of rain down on the District of Columbia for days, including early on the day of the inaugural, were still hovering and threatening to make things a muddier mess than they were already. Yet when Lincoln stepped forward to speak, a burst of sunshine split through the morning's gloomy miasma, showering "the spectacle with glory and with light." Chief Justice Chase—recently appointed to his position by Lincoln despite his painfully disloyal behavior as secretary of the treasury—saw it as a most auspicious sign indicating "the dispersion of the clouds of war and the restoration of the clear sun light of prosperous peace." Eyewitness Noah Brooks noted that "every heart beat quicker at the unexpected omen."[3]

Against such a propitious backdrop, Lincoln's opening is shockingly spare. His first two sentences simply indicate that "there is less occasion for an extended address than there was" for his First Inaugural, where it was more "fitting and proper" to detail a "course to be pursued." This presages that Lincoln is about to deliver what remains the shortest inaugural address in presidential history—only four paragraphs totaling 703 words. This dismissive air concerning how little the situation called for barely masks what Garry Wills calls the great "daring" if not "effrontery" of Lincoln's minimalist approach.[4]

At one level it is true that with Lee's army pinned at Richmond, "little that is new could be presented" concerning the war at that moment. However, concluding as Lincoln does that the immediate military context justifies such a placid opening and overall brevity seems to ignore that America in 1865 was facing a web of sticky issues even more complex and far-reaching than those facing America in 1861, when Lincoln delivered a lengthy speech filled with precisely drawn constitutional and political arguments.[5] It may be that Lincoln just did not know what to say. Lincoln believed that deciding on the proper terms for restoring the Southern states to the Union was "the greatest question ever presented to practical statesmanship." By all accounts, Lincoln's mind moved methodically and slowly on such intricate matters of significance—and did so as much out of philosophy as aptitude. "My policy is to have no policy" was something of a personal credo for Lincoln. Stated in hyperbolic terms, this reflected his career-long view that despite holding fast to certain core convictions—which Lincoln did—the right policy could only be determined by a complex array of forces feeding into the policy-formation process of the moment, an instinct Lincoln shared with someone like Winthrop, as we saw. To do this effectively meant, for Lincoln, assiduously gathering facts, contemplating history, anticipating implications, working out an argument against its best counterattack, and allowing time, circumstance, public promotion, and private negotiation to settle things into a workable solution. His self-chosen metaphor was pilots on western rivers (he had been one himself) who knew they wanted to get downstream but only steered from "point to point" as they could see—which was often not far.[6] Lincoln also insisted on carefully testing and preparing public opinion at the most foundational level. "No policy that does not rest upon some philosophical public opinion can be permanently maintained," Lincoln argued the year he campaigned for president.[7] Unlike the First Inaugural, where Lincoln could build on ideas he had been honing for a decade or more, the Second Inaugural called for addressing an entirely new set of issues. Even if Lincoln had worked out a basic new vision for the future of the Union, he had not had much time to prepare public opinion for receiving it.

Whatever merits this supposition has, it does not go far enough to explain a related anomaly in Lincoln's opening paragraph. While Lincoln expresses a "high hope for the future" with respect to the war, strikingly, "no prediction in regard to it is ventured." Where almost any other elected leader, then or now, would have grabbed this moment to revel in a mixture of national self-congratulation and political self-promotion, Lincoln refuses to forecast victory and mentions no specific accomplishments during the last four years of his presidency. This is true from the moment he opens his mouth and says "at this second appearing," an understated summation of the fact that he had been reelected as president, which had not happened in the past thirty-two years of peaceful American presidential history. The most energy he musters about anything in this first paragraph is the obvious but hardly reassuring notion that "all else chiefly depends" on the "progress of our arms."[8]

If Lincoln's opening paragraph and overall approach are perplexing, his concluding paragraph reaches a generosity so grand and unexpected as to nearly defy human comprehension. By nature, Lincoln hated war, recognizing from the days of his Temperance Address the painful and gross evils of war even in such noble fights as the American Revolution. How much it must have pained him then to have to preside over the bloodiest of all American conflicts. Union and Confederate deaths, including those after the war from disease and wounds, approach the one million mark. And the Civil War's massive physical wreckage of farms, buildings, roads, and rail systems, as great as it was, cannot even begin to compare with the lasting and incalculable emotional and psychological wreckage left behind—whether from memories of hand-to-hand combat, live amputations in field hospitals, face-grinding poverty for those bereft of a husband or father, or the inconsolable loss of a son or sons. The personal abuse Lincoln took as president during this war is also unparalleled. Perhaps no president has ever been treated so disrespectfully by so many of his fellow executive officers and so pitilessly caricatured throughout the national culture, North and South. By word and sketch he was made out to be everything from an awkward and incompetent baboon to evil incarnate,[9] and the frothing hatred of him by much of the South would soon trigger his assassination. All of this eventually drove his refined and intelligent wife insane. Yet, remarkably, at this moment when that "deep rooted principle of hate, and the powerful motive of revenge" he had preached against as early as the Lyceum Address were clearly surging throughout America and likely pressing in upon Lincoln's own breast, he concludes his Second Inaugural

> With malice toward none; with charity for all; with firmness in the right, as God gives us to see the right, let us strive on to finish the work we are in; to bind up the nation's wounds; to care for him who shall have borne the battle, and for his widow, and his orphan—to do all which may achieve and cherish a just, and a lasting peace, among ourselves, and with all nations.[10]

That Lincoln could arrive at such a profound and active love for "all"—reducing many listeners to tears—in the teeth of such hostility and accumulated pain remains a breathtaking example of human benevolence and moral discipline. It was a moment of "sublime excessiveness," like Christ's pronouncements at the Sermon on the Mount. Such an act by an official head of state in such a situation appears without precedent in the civil history of the world.[11]

Critical keys to how and why Lincoln ends as he does are found in his two middle paragraphs, which also explain his most unusual opening.

"With Malice toward None"

The first theme to emerge in Lincoln's second paragraph is the theme of "all." With his First Inaugural as a point of reference, Lincoln begins this paragraph by noting that "four years ago, *all* thoughts were anxiously directed to an impending civil-war" (emphasis added). Lincoln then unleashes a torrent of fifteen more uses of the term "all" or synonymous pronouns (italicized here for emphasis): In the second paragraph's second sentence, "*All* dreaded it—*all* sought to avert it." One line later, "*both* parties deprecated war." In paragraph three, "*All* knew" that slavery was somehow the cause of the war, "*Neither* party" foresaw the length and magnitude of the war, "*neither* anticipated" that slavery would be abolished (in the form of the Thirteenth Amendment) before the war was over, "*Each* looked" for an easier and less fundamental triumph, "*Both* read the same Bible and prayed to the same God, and *each* invokes His aid against the other," "the prayers of *both* could not be answered, that of *neither* has been answered," God gives to "*both* North and South this terrible war." This culminates in paragraph four's opening, "With malice toward *none;* with charity for *all.*"

Lincoln, like Winthrop and Jefferson before him, understood that human difference—perceived or real—is often a considerable source of friction and hate. That Lincoln could himself resist such hatred had much to do with his unceasing ability to see a great sameness between citizens, North and South, regardless of their respective attitudes and practices. The considerable lengths he goes to in this brief speech to hammer away early and often at the similarities between the two sides showcase Lincoln's determination to restore national bonds of affection by effectively diminishing the perceived differences between the two regions.

As shown in chapter five, much of Lincoln's ability to see broad similarities across diverse populations stemmed from a view of human nature that was fairly constant and universal—Northerners, being human, would likely be doing what Southerners were doing had they been born into preexisting Southern environments and regional interests. But here in the Second Inaugural, Lincoln deepens this point about the natural sameness of American humanity, North and South, by placing both regions on a similar footing before a providential God. The key passage reads

> The Almighty has his own purposes. "Woe unto the world because of offences! For it must needs be that offences come; but woe to that man by whom the offence cometh!" If we shall suppose that American Slavery is one of those offences which, in the providence of God, must needs come, but which, having continued through His appointed time, He now wills to remove, and that He gives to both North and South this terrible war, as the woe due to those by whom the offence came, shall we discern therein any departure from those divine attributes which the believers in a Living God always ascribe to Him? Fondly do we hope—fervently do we pray—that this mighty scourge of war may speedily pass away. Yet, if God wills that it continue, until all the wealth piled by the bond-man's two hundred and fifty years of unrequited toil shall be sunk, and until every drop of blood drawn with the lash, shall be paid by another drawn with the sword, as was said three thousand years ago, so still it must be said "the judgments of the Lord, are true and righteous altogether."[12]

Here, Lincoln emphatically declares publicly what he was slowly coming to believe during those dismal days of September in 1862 when he was wrestling with the issue of emancipation. This is that whatever American citizens may do or want, "God wills this contest, and wills that it shall not end yet."[13] At Gettysburg, Lincoln closed his speech by softly playing the note, just once, that America was a nation "under God." Now Lincoln blasts out that note, repeatedly, in *forte*. Neither some distant god (small case "g") of nature nor an impersonal fixed force of fate or necessity, the God of Lincoln's Second Inaugural is the "Living God" of the Bible—a work explicitly mentioned once then quoted from, or distinctly alluded to, four more times. This God of the Bible is mentioned fewer than fourteen times, and four of these references are followed by active, controlling verbs, indicating that God "wills" (twice) and "gives" (twice) the conditions in which Americans live. Before detailing how this more prominent notion of a nation under God advances Lincoln's notion of human sameness, and how together these two notions help root out the poison of malice and clear the way for the awe-inspiring charity of Lincoln's last paragraph, it should first be noted how it explains Lincoln's perplexingly brief and understated opening.

The chief reason Lincoln cannot say much about the war, especially its end and aftermath, is that even though he is commander-in-chief of the dominant army perfectly positioned to force the surrender of a trapped and weakened opponent, he recognizes that neither he nor anyone else has any real control over the war, or anything approaching a certain prediction of its future. In his First Inaugural, he pointed to the South, saying directly to his "dissatisfied fellow countrymen" that the "momentous issue of civil war" was in *their* "hands," not his. Four years later, he now asserts that the Civil War, from the beginning, has rested outside the control of human hands of any kind. No one started the war, "the war came." The real force behind the war, including its start and continuation, is God, and the "Almighty has his own purposes," which neither the North nor South nor Lincoln himself can fully comprehend or anticipate. Just as everyone—including Lincoln—misread the future length and horror of the war at his inaugural "four years ago," so everyone might be misreading the end of the war now. This is far more than a practical worry that the ever resourceful and wily Southern forces will find a way to escape the noose again, as some have suggested. Rather, it is a sweeping and radical sense of contingency, one predicated on the notion that God's full and infinite providential purposes are finally unknowable to finite human beings. Thus, despite every sign to the contrary, Lincoln cannot count out the prospect that the war may "yet . . . continue."

Besides explaining Lincoln's enigmatic refusal to anticipate, let alone celebrate, the war's end, this third paragraph also fosters the theme of human sameness between the North and South. A full vision of God and his intentions and will is beyond the ken of both sides and any single individual, including Lincoln himself. Roughly the same in basic human nature, the North and the South are also equal in their inability to fathom the entirety of God's designs and "purposes." At best there is, to use Reinhold Niebuhr's apt formulation, a "partiality" to each side in their views and commitments.[14] The degree to which Lincoln holds this position is regularly missed. In his Meditation on the Divine Will penned during the anguished days before deciding on emancipation, Lincoln wrote, speaking of God's willing the continuation of the war, "I am almost ready to say this is probably true." Lincoln is now no longer *almost* ready to say it, he says it. The question is, does he say it is true, or *probably* true? Upon close examination, nowhere does Lincoln categorically assert that his interpretation of the war as a divine punishment to America for the sin of slavery is the whole, firm truth of the matter. Lincoln only says "If we shall suppose" it is the case. That he *thinks* this is the case is patently clear. That he *knows* it is the case is another matter. A fully just retribution for all of the "unrequited toil . . . and every drop of blood drawn with the lash" due to two and a half centuries of American slavery—"one hour of which is worse," claimed Frederick Douglass, than the years of bondage the Founding Fathers rose up to oppose in the American Revolution—would surely seem to be, but may not be, or may not be the only thing, behind God's willing the start and continuation of "this terrible war."[15] "The Almighty has His own purposes." Lincoln himself is on the same level with his listeners, unable to comprehend the full will of God. This is all critical to the spirit of Lincoln's conclusion. Recognition that all humans are inescapably biased and unenlightened concerning the whole truth of humanity's God-ordered existence fosters a humble self-conception and patience with others that greatly tempers human hostility.

What Lincoln strongly supposes concerning the war and God's will reinforces the human sameness of North and South at yet another level which contributes yet again—and most powerfully yet—to Lincoln's close. In addition to sharing similar human natures and certain epistemic limits, citizens of the North and South share the blame for the war. By supposing that God "gives to both North and South this terrible war, as the woe due to those by whom the offence [of slavery] came," Lincoln shifts attention away from those who physically instigated and sustained the war to those who physically instigated and sustained slavery. Lincoln did not need to spell out that even if the South was now the only side fighting for slavery, the North was complicit in establishing and commercially supporting the original "offense," which had existed in America for more than "two hundred and fifty years"—long before any real abolition movement got under way in the North. Rooting the long and continuing woes of the Civil War in a divine judgment against the *historical* practice of slavery effectively makes both sides responsible for the start, magnitude, and duration of the war. Paradoxically, this also makes the North and the South blameless before each other. By revealing God as pouring out nationwide justice for centuries of nationwide injustice, Lincoln takes from the near-victorious North the moral high ground for severe sanctions against the South for hostilities pursued under the clever military leadership of Lee and Jackson, and he takes from the near-vanquished South the resentful low ground for retribution against Grant's bulldog tactics and Sherman's "total war" marches. These things have more to do with God's will and purposes than the decisions of any one mortal actor or group of actors. Thus, with plenty of guilt and innocence resting on both sides in this divine drama, neither side can justly bear ire toward the other.

These converging streams of thought that emphasize the common humanity of North and South under the rule of a providential God go far to prepare Lincoln's audience for that first clause of his extraordinary fourth paragraph, "with malice toward none." But such thoughts—as intellectually robust and rhetorically powerful as they may be—do not go quite far enough to finally excise the vengeful bile undoubtedly building up in the land. Furthermore, Lincoln intends to lead his audience beyond a passive absence of malice to an active "charity for all." Both the why and how of Lincoln's determination to foster love where hate currently prevails come through a careful consideration of Lincoln's final paragraph examined against sentiments that ran throughout his career.

"With Charity for All"

The last line of Lincoln's last paragraph is a challenge to the country "to do all" that is necessary "to achieve and cherish a just, and a lasting peace, among ourselves, and with all nations." The tasks Lincoln has in mind are specifically laid out in the immediately prior clauses: "to bind up the nation's wounds" and "to care for him who shall have borne the battle, and for his widow, and his orphan." Two things are striking here. First, the pronouns are manifestly generic. It is the "nation's" wounds that must be healed, and care must be rendered to "him"—presumably meaning all soldiers, clad blue or gray—and "his" widow and "his" orphan. The rhetorical sweep of Lincoln's charity is national rather than regional, implicitly closing the speech on a theme running throughout the entire address, the theme of "all." Second, references to war wounds, widows, and orphans conjure up critical constructs of Lincoln's earliest, best speeches, and several statements in between. From the Temperance Address to private musings to his Thanksgiving proclamations to this crowning speech of his presidency, Lincoln worries about and pleads for the care of the helpless, especially those bereft of a father or husband.

Lincoln's call to help widows and orphans was never mere rhetoric. In the previous year, Lincoln worked closely with Charles Sumner (an ardent abolitionist often impatient with Lincoln) to make sure that the widows and orphans of a contingent of black federal soldiers—recently liberated slaves who had never been able to marry officially under Southern law—received government aid. There appears to be larger lessons in all this. Lincoln's lifelong and specific singling out of widows and orphans as appropriate objects of governmental aid emphasizes that all of us come into the world utterly helpless and dependent—orphans are a stark reminder of this universal fact. Besides subtly reaffirming the theme of human sameness that pervades his address and is so critical to his final call for charity, this notion highlights the mistaken ontology behind so much philosophical liberalism that so often stands ill-equipped to recognize the political importance of love. Humans do not just spring into existence as fully formed, rational, and independent adults choosing for themselves political principles and social arrangements from a state of nature (Locke) or an original position behind a veil of ignorance (Rawls). An affectionate and self-denying care for others must first attend to us all and raise us from utter dependency to the point where we can begin to function more independently before it even makes sense to discuss the justice and the nature of protecting and preserving the free life of an adult. Liberty for all is not even possible without a prevenient charity for all.[16]

Patrick Deneen makes yet another extended point about Lincoln's prominent concern for widows and orphans. By virtue of his view of humanity's inescapable fallibility and weakness even as adults, Lincoln sees everyone as a kind of nineteenth-century widow or orphan in the sense of lacking true independence and self-sufficiency. Thus, Lincoln's final passage works in harmony with the rest of the address to take the reader beyond a simple physical concern for actual widows and orphans to a recognition that all Americans stand with individual shortcomings that make communal society necessary and possible only if that society is in some sense charitable. This, of course, harks back in a certain sense to the opening lines of Winthrop's "Model" speech, which grounded the need for a community of charity in the ineradicable fact that no human being is beyond needing the help of others in some important form or another.[17]

While caring for widows and orphans is treated with prominence and considerable consistency in Lincoln's early and late writings, there is a highly illuminating difference between the way Lincoln treats war wounds here in the Second Inaugural and in his earlier Lyceum Address. Understanding this difference enriches our understanding of the Second Inaugural's call for active charity and reveals both weighty departures from and similarities with the political religion of his younger days. It could be argued that in the Lyceum Address, Lincoln demonstrates a slightly perverse wish that the wounds of the Revolutionary War could last forever. It must be granted at least that Lincoln's position was that as long as those wounds lasted, they would stand as "pillars of strength," turning man's natural passions of hate outward, thus helping to secure America's temple of liberty.[18] As was argued in chapter five, this means that time qua time is not really the enemy in the Lyceum Address. Time is the enemy only as it erases the hatred-channeling wounds of war. It was precisely because the wounds of the Revolution could not last forever that Lincoln felt forced to advance a timeless political religion as a necessary defense against the real enemy, the lurking sense of malice and revenge that rests deep in human nature.

By contrast, in the Second Inaugural, Lincoln's explicit wish is that the wounds of war will be actively healed as quickly as possible. From this it ineluctably follows that as time can ultimately erase the physical wounds of any war, time is now, for Lincoln, not an enemy but an ally that cannot come quickly enough. Why are wounds—and by implication the passage of time—treated so differently in the Second Inaugural? Lincoln does not fully explain this in the last paragraph, but by suggesting that the binding up of wounds incurred in a civil war is essential to a "lasting" civil peace, his reasoning seems transparent. Wounds delivered and still visible within the house of friends will have a completely different effect than wounds delivered from a distant enemy in a noble cause. In the aftermath of civil war, the wounds of a father, brother, husband, or son, instead of channeling hatred outward against a foreign foe, will constantly ignite the passions against the neighbor-enemy who inflicted the injury. The power to forgive, that is, the power to live peaceably without malice, will be made more difficult—perhaps impossible—by the inability to forget fostered by the "living history" of hatred embodied in the surviving wounds of the Civil War.

This presents a real conundrum. If malice cannot be finally eradicated nor long-lasting peace established without active charity—tenderly dressing and healing and erasing the wounds of those who shall have "borne the battle"—how can active charity go to work in the presence of a particularly virulent strain of malice? Strong malice must be cleared away first so that vigorous charity can do its work. But strong malice cannot be cleared away until vigorous charity does it work.

The political religion of Lincoln's earlier days hardly seems the solution to this problem. It may once have been a satisfactory strategy, but the venomous anger trailing in the wake of the Civil War was of a different and deeper quality—its grip was wider and stronger than the natural state of human hatred in post-Revolutionary America. And, even as romantically characterized in the Lyceum Address, Lincoln's early political religion was at best meant to *suppress* this milder strain of hate. Nothing about the rationalized worship of law purported to actively remove, or even significantly reduce, the exceptional malice of internecine strife. What is needed here, then, is not Lincoln's manifestly secular "political religion," but the "pure religion" of *agapic* love. For many, only a divine command to care for a neighbor and love an enemy as oneself, even in the face of glaring injustice, can rupture the vengeful and malicious impulses that block reconciliation with and active care for a formerly violent other.[19]

By suggesting that both North and South share in the guilt and innocence of the war and its excesses, and proceed under the guiding hand of God who punishes justly and commands his children to love even their enemies as themselves, Lincoln's Second Inaugural forestalls revenge on, and encourages compassion for, both sides. The biblically grounded charity of Lincoln's speech strikes a quick blow at the passions, rebuking hatred as a sin. This blow is immediately followed by charity's call to active care. These things then work back and forth on each other in a positive cycle of full human healing. The more that wounds are bound up and healed on both sides, the more likely both sides will live in amicable peace; the more amity prevails, the more easily will the dedicated work of healing take place. The *caritas* of Lincoln's Second Inaugural can break the Civil War's cycle of hatred and revenge in ways far more effective than can the political religion of the Lyceum Address.[20]

As potent as Lincoln's speech is, thus far described, its full political genius is yet to be laid bare. Lincoln's thematic tapestry of human sameness, the limitations of knowledge, and God's just and providential rule of the earth converge at the speech's end in a sublime sense of charity for all. But these themes alone produce a serious political problem. While it is able to create the conditions necessary for mercy, forgiveness, care, and reconciliation in a situation otherwise seething with malice, such a tapestry fails to create the conditions necessary for practical political rule in a fallen world. The charity of Lincoln's last paragraph is made possible, in part, by taking judgment out of the hands of man and placing it in the hands of God ("it may seem strange that any men should dare to ask a just God's assistance in wringing their bread from the sweat of other men's faces; but let us judge not that we be not judged"). Practical political rule, though, depends on the daily making of human judgments. The final genius of Lincoln's speech is that it culminates in what is arguably the most theologically rich and humanly compassionate lines ever written by a successful political/military leader, yet it does so without sacrificing a real-world commitment to social order and a transcendent sense of political justice.

"With Firmness in the Right"

In making his primary argument for human sameness, Lincoln is careful to suggest repeatedly that it is not a perfect sameness. The North was committed to "saving the Union without war," while the South was committed to "destroy it without war." The South "would make war rather than let the nation survive," whereas the North "would accept war rather than let it perish." The South sought to "perpetuate, and extend" slavery, but the North sought only to "restrict the territorial enlargement of it." And though the North is not to consider ("judge") the South as moral inferiors because they hold slaves and plead for a just God's help to do so, he does confess that the South's doing so seems "strange." There is a war being fought; there are two sides to the war; the two sides are not exactly the same.

Along with this, Lincoln also modulates his theme of human inability to fathom the will of God. Even if there is an inherent bias in any political-historic commitment due to the inability of humans to comprehend and faithfully abide by the whole truth of the situation, Lincoln's position hardly descends into Nietzschean nihilism or the radical contingency of a Richard Rorty.[21] There are some things people know. Lincoln indicates that both sides "knew" (rather than, say, *thought*) the "peculiar and powerful interest" of slavery was the "cause of the war." Lincoln fortifies this three sentences later where he refers again to the interest of slavery as the "the *cause* of the conflict," this time underlining the word "cause" in the original handwritten text.[22] Apropos to arguments above, neither side may know precisely how slavery is the cause. They only know that "somehow" it is the "cause," or at least *a* cause of the war, but they know it to be a cause. To know precisely how it is the cause would require a wider grasp of the whole than Lincoln indicates is humanly possible. Nevertheless, they all apparently know slavery is causally connected to the war, and they can and should know that the institution of Southern slavery is a moral wrong before God and man. The North now essentially accepts this. The South does not. And this stands at the heart of the differences that exist between both sides.

Immediately following Lincoln's stirring call to proceed "with charity for all," he adds, "with firmness in the right, as God gives us to see the right, let us strive on to finish the work we are in." Such counsel qualifies Lincoln's earlier instruction to "judge not that we be not judged." On some things man will be given by God the light to "see the right" and in defense of that right man is expected, though not forced ("let us"), to be "firm." And not just passively firm, citizens are also to be active, to "strive" and "finish" the "work" of what heaven-blessed vision of "right" they are given.

The use of the term "right" in this context is particularly rich in meaning. At one level it conveys a sense of general, moral correctness—that which is morally right over that which is morally wrong. But at a more specific level, it conveys the idea of man's universal, natural right to individual liberty, to choose for oneself how one will live and be ruled. That this second meaning of right can also be read into the text and is the main thrust of his point is underscored by Lincoln's explicit request to "finish the work we are in." This strikes a clear connection with a sentiment in the opening lines of the speech where Lincoln indicates that "on the progress of our arms . . . all else chiefly depends." That which was in "progress," namely the war, *had* to be finished, everything ("all") else depended on it. And Lincoln's closing request to "finish the work" also strikes a clear connection with the "unfinished work" to which Lincoln rededicated America at Gettysburg. That is, again, the work of a war being fought for the principle that "all men are created equal"—the foundation of the basic right of human freedom everywhere. Such a commitment, of course, suggests that whatever Lincoln's sense of charity calls for in terms of generosity and care toward others, it is incompatible with pure pacificism.

After Lincoln took his second oath of office with his hand on a Bible, he bent over and kissed the page to which the book had been randomly opened. Again taken by the symbolism of it all, Chief Justice Chase noted that his lips rested on Isaiah 5:27–28:

> None shall be weary nor stumble among them; none shall slumber nor sleep; neither shall the girdle of their loins be loosed, nor the latchet of the shoes be broken; Whose arrows are sharp, and all their bows are bent, their horses' hoofs shall be counted like flint, their wheels like a whirlwind.

Of this well-documented incident, popular Civil War historian Bruce Catton notes, "The text was apt; Mr. Lincoln was most alert this spring to guard against weariness and stumbling, and he wanted his armies to keep driving."[23] Despite Lincoln's early sense of fatalism turned providentialism ("I have found all my life as Hamlet says: 'There is a divinity that shapes our ends, Rough-hew them how we will'"), he remained fiercely committed to human action. Nowhere is this better stated than in a letter to Eliza P. Gurney, a Quaker minister from Philadelphia, written six months before his Second Inaugural, right around the time he also wrote his Meditation on the Divine Will. Foreshadowings of Lincoln's Second Inaugural in this letter are numerous.

> The purposes of the Almighty are perfect, and must prevail, though we erring mortals may fail to accurately perceive them in advance. We hoped for a happy termination of this terrible war long before this; but God knows best, and has ruled otherwise. We shall yet acknowledge His wisdom and our own error therein. Meanwhile we must work earnestly in the best light He gives us, trusting that so working still conduces to the great ends He ordains.[24]

For Lincoln, godly orchestration of the world and limited human vision never excused a shoulder-shrugging surrender to circumstances. Lincoln nowhere tackles, theoretically at least, the millennium-long debate about how a world ruled by Providence can be squared with mortal agency and human striving. He nevertheless seems committed to both. Energy, initiative, and work were ever the obligation of mortal agents. And the key piece of "work" facing the nation, a work Lincoln was leading "in the best light" he felt God was giving him, was the work of war dedicated to a "new birth" of human freedom.[25]

What must never be forgotten about Lincoln's awesomely charitable last paragraph is that as he spoke, Grant's long-range guns were pounding away at the Confederacy's one last fixed point, and, with Lincoln's reluctant blessing, Sherman was slashing and burning his way up through the South. Lest the significance—even horror—of this be missed, between Lincoln's Second Inaugural (March 4) and Lee's surrender to Grant (April 9), approximately twenty-five thousand American soldiers were killed or wounded in the continuing skirmishes of civil conflict. Contrast this with the ten thousand American soldiers that were killed or wounded in the *entire* eight-year period of the American Revolution.[26] However profound the moral humility and human benevolence of Lincoln's closing call for charity, it stands marshaled with a determined, vigorous, even violent defense of America's constitutional Union and the natural rights of individual liberty to which it is dedicated.

Civic Charity

The pervasive influence of Christian charity on this sermonic speech is both distinct and, the historical record overwhelming suggests, genuine. A profound reverence for God, an earnest desire to be in harmony with him—sacral expressions of *agape*'s command to love God—abound in this address more than any other presidential inaugural, maybe any other presidential speech of any kind. A willingness to forgive an enemy, an active and heartfelt sense of compassion for human suffering— moving expressions of *agape*'s command to love neighbor as self— similarly stand out here above all other presidential rhetoric. Yet even as it is recognized that Lincoln's text deeply imbibes from the "pure religion" of New Testament inspiration rather than Lincoln's earlier "political religion" of purely human making, the speech itself should not be mistaken as an explicitly Christian revelation.

Nowhere does Lincoln mention Christ, or even Christianity—which at least got a nod in his First Inaugural. And though a very real, national temporal salvation appears at stake in the speech's teaching, any sense of individual spiritual salvation through God's redeeming grace, or any promise of a pleasant and heavenly afterlife, is entirely absent. Furthermore, if Lincoln believes that man can only truly love others and God if God first loves man, he does not ever say so, publicly or privately. The address remains, at its core, a civic document with a civic aim. What the speech could then be said to hold up is a model of *civic* charity—a blend of politically practical, philosophically liberal, and genuinely held Christian insights that shore up, even as they gently revise, the American founding Lincoln adored.

With a just God to satisfy and a national community renewed in liberty to protect, but without each other to blame, the *caritas* of Lincoln's Second Inaugural interdicts a spirit of hatred and revenge on both sides and elicits a miraculous response of forgiveness and benevolence, undoubtedly helping to rekindle the "bonds of affection" he pleaded for in his First Inaugural. Yet it does this even as it rallies the North to prosecute the war to a successful end, no matter how bloody. Lincoln's model of civic charity, shadowing its purely theological analogue of Christian charity, is a "form of the virtues," simultaneously insisting on the practice of mercy and of justice in the political context of America, a point neatly reflected in the symmetry of the speech's final paragraph.

When roughly broken out by clause, the last paragraph—which is actually one long sentence strung together with a punctuation more appropriate to poetry than prose—looks like this.

> *With* malice toward none;
> *with* charity for all;
> *with* firmness in the right, as God gives us to see the right,
> let us strive on to finish the work we are in;
> *to* bind up the nation's wounds;
> *to* care for him who shall have borne the battle, and for his widow and
>   his orphan—
> *to* do all which may achieve and cherish a just, and a lasting peace among
>   ourselves. . . .

Note how the plea to strive on to "finish the work" unifies the whole paragraph, sitting perfectly balanced between a set of three "with" commands and a set of three "to" commands, which commands sit in chiastic relationship to one another. The finishing of this work is to be done "with" (1) an absence of malice, (2) charity, and (3) firmness in the right. The connotation of commands (1) and (2) tilt toward attitudes of mercy (eliminating anger and fostering a forgiving love toward ones' foes).

Command (3), on the other hand, tilts back in the direction of justice (calling for firmness in pursuit of the right). The finishing of the work also beckons Lincoln's audience "to" (1) bind up wounds, (2) actively care for the wounded and helpless, and (3) do whatever is necessary to achieve a peace that is lasting and "just." Once again, commands (1) and (2) connote acts of mercy, whereas command (3) is an explicit commitment to ensuring that liberal justice prevails.

At the time of Lincoln's speech, the primary symbol of political justice was near completion. The Thirteenth Amendment was successfully working its way through the states. This was a great source of satisfaction to Lincoln and a kind of double reminder that Lincoln's civic charity does not lead to an overreliance on the generous, merciful, forgiving side of *agape*. Besides the content of the amendment itself, the fact that Lincoln was still working so carefully within the parameters of constitutional law—seeking to change that law to come into greater harmony with natural human equality—shows a continuing strict adherence to this document which affirms that man's natural character needs to be reined in by an elaborate system of checks and balances between separated powers so that the selfish and even tyrannous ambitions of all can cancel each other out.[27] Civic charity indeed pleads that the better angels of our nature—our affectionate attachments and concern for others—play a modest public role much of the time and a significant role in times of crisis when forming and reforming (reunifying) a union. Yet civic charity also recognizes some variant of man's fallen nature, predicating that union on the assumption that man will generally act in his own self-interest and has the potential to follow a passionate rage, both of which threaten the fundamental rights of others.

At the time of Lincoln's speech, the main, practical work of mercy had only just begun. For all intents and purposes, it began with the very words Lincoln was speaking. Immediately after delivering his remarks, Frederick Douglass, whose famous July 4 oration of years earlier had excoriated all American celebrations of freedom, called the speech "a sacred effort." The work of mercy would continue on April 9 at Appomattox Court House, where Grant, acting in the general spirit and instruction of Lincoln, greatly relieved Lee by offering him, in the friendliest possible atmosphere, the most generous possible terms. Confederate soldiers would have to lay down their arms but would get to keep their horses. They would not be taken prisoner or tried for treason. When Lee informed Grant that he could not feed his more than a thousand federal prisoners and then added "I have nothing for my own men," Grant unhesitatingly proposed giving Lee federal rations for twenty-five thousand men. Asked if that was enough, Lee said, "Plenty, an abundance I assure you." Later in the month, after Lincoln's assassination, General William "War Is All Hell" Sherman, eager to follow Lincoln's lead, proposed terms of peace to General Joseph Johnston so generous that they went beyond anything Lincoln would have approved and were in fact countermanded by Washington, D.C.[28]

The work of mercy in Lincoln's model of civic charity was cut short and utterly overwhelmed almost immediately after John Wilkes Booth fired a single, well-placed bullet into the back of Lincoln's head a little more than a month after Lincoln's Second Inaugural. On the day Lincoln died, the Republican senatorial caucus met to map out a "line of policy less conciliatory than that of Mr. Lincoln." A day later, the *Chicago Tribune*, one of Lincoln's most consistent and influential champions, editorialized,

> Yesterday we were with the late President, for lenity; he had been so often right and wise; he had so won our confidence that we were preparing to follow and support him in a policy of conciliatory kindness; today we are with the people for justice.[29]

The harsh focus on justice the country then took under the leadership of the radical Republicans and inflexible incompetence of Andrew Johnson is a matter of historical record. The language and logic of Lincoln's Second Inaugural were commanding, but for fully successful application they required his active leadership. Lincoln not only articulated a model of civic charity for America to follow, he was himself a model of civic charity who inspired others by his own deeply held and carefully thought-out commitments to *agape* and its simultaneous call for both mercy and justice. It may be that Lincoln would have been too kind and lenient to the South in his postwar policies. The best of the radical Republicans were admirably committed to preventing old southern ways—practices inimical to the dignity and freedom of black Americans—from continuing in some barely disguised form.[30] But, lacking Lincoln's sense of charity for all—a charity that fought to end slavery even as it looked to forgive Southern Confederates and help them back into the Union—too many of the radical Republicans marched forward with a sense of justice untempered by mercy, or, even worse, marched forward with an open spirit of revenge—the kind of spirit Lincoln had condemned from the start of his political career. As a result, whatever victories for black justice they achieved, radical Republicans left a long wake of sectional hatred that has abated only in quite recent memory, to say nothing of the racial hatred that has not yet abated. It is speculation to suggest how Reconstruction would have gone had Lincoln lived. But even if Lincoln's initial instincts concerning Reconstruction bordered on the too generous (as they did so often when Lincoln dealt with incompetent generals and insubordinate political leaders during the war), it seems most reasonable to assume that the warmth and calmness of his desire to see both justice and mercy served in love for all parties concerned would have provided a better path for securing social and political progress for former slaves *and* for resuscitating the dangerously broken bonds of affections between citizens North and South.

Notes

1. Kazin, *American Writer*, 120; Will, "Give It a Rest," 64; Corlett, "Lincoln's Political Religion," 521, and *Community without Unity*, 116. The move to dismiss the Second Inaugural got a prominent boost from Richard Hofstadter, *American Political Tradition*, 121, 124, 135, in the late 1940s. He begins his chapter on Lincoln by briefly misquoting the first few words of the last paragraph of the Second Inaugural, then ignoring the text as something out of character with Lincoln's reigning economic and political ambitions. Political theorist Steve Kautz, in his entry on Lincoln in the anthology *The History of American Political Thought*, alternatively sees in Lincoln a "remarkable humanity" but nowhere references the Second Inaugural and appears to accept Lincoln's early unbelieving "infidelity" as a lifelong condition (395–415; see 397, 414n6). Michael Lind, again in a book with a titular commitment to Lincoln's values and beliefs, quotes the last paragraph of the Second Inaugural in full but then says not one more word about it (*What Lincoln Believed*, 187). For Lincoln's own assessment, see Donald, *Lincoln*, 568; Lincoln, *Selected Speeches and Writings*, 450–51.

2. Nicolay and Hay, *Abraham Lincoln*, 10:143; Donald, *Lincoln*, 566; White, "Sermon on the Mount," 210.

3. White, "Sermon on the Mount," 211; Donald, *Lincoln*, 566; Brooks, *Washington in Lincoln's Time*, 239.

4. Technically, Washington's second inaugural is shorter, but his was a purely perfunctory two-paragraph statement of no note—offered without a sense of the ceremony that would later develop for second inaugurals (Wills, "Lincoln's Greatest Speech?" 63).

5. Wills nicely summarizes many of the pressing issues facing America in the spring of 1865 ("Lincoln's Greatest Speech?" 62). "Would the Confederacy be a conquered nation? Or would it be a continuing part of America, in which some had

committed crimes and others were innocent? How could the guilty be distinguished from the innocent, for assigning proper punishments or rewards? On what timetable? Under whose supervision? Using what instruments of discipline or reform (trials, oaths of allegiance, perpetual disqualification for office)? And what of the former slaves? Where they to be allowed the suffrage, indemnified for losses, given lands forfeited by the rebels, guaranteed work and workers' rights? The problems were endless, and the very norms for discussing them were still to be agreed on."

6. As quoted in Donald, *Lincoln*, 15, 467.

7. Lincoln, *Collected Works*, 4:17.

8. Donald stresses what a "remarkably impersonal address" this is, pointing out that after the opening paragraph, Lincoln never again used the first-person singular pronoun, "nor did he refer to anything he had said or done during the previous four years" (Donald, *Lincoln*, 566). See White, *Lincoln's Greatest Speech*, 43–47, for extended discussion of "at this second appearing."

9. For the toll of the war in the fullest human sense, see Philip S. Paludan, *"A People's Contest,"* 317. The best survey of Lincoln's popular imagery during his lifetime is found in Harold Holzer, Gabor S. Boritt, and Mark E. Neely Jr., *The Lincoln Image*.

10. Lincoln, *Collected Works*, 8:333–34, included for convenience as appendix D.

11. Emotional response of listeners as reported by Noah Brooks, White House correspondent and friend of Lincoln (*Washington in Lincoln's Time*, 239–40). Phrase of "sublime excessiveness" and comparison to the Sermon on the Mount from Timothy Jackson, *Priority of Love*, 69.

12. Speaking of the last sentence here, Donald has described this as "one of the most terrible statements ever made by an American public official" (Donald, *Lincoln*, 567).

13. Lincoln, *Collected Works*, 5:404.

14. Niebuhr, "Religion of Abraham Lincoln," 173.

15. Foner, *Life and Writings of Frederick Douglass*, 145.

16. The notion about charity always preceding liberty is one I take from Timothy Jackson, *Priority of Love*, 172. His statement is worth repeating in full here: "Relatively 'independent' persons do not just happen; they require cultivation and protection, especially when very young. Any society that cannot attend to this dependency will treat autonomous persons like 'manna from heaven' and thereby fail to support the necessary conditions for the emergence of its own citizenry."

17. Deneen, *Democratic Faith*, 285. For Lincoln's help to the widows and orphans of former slaves, see White, *Lincoln's Greatest Speech*, 176–77.

18. This should not be confused with a position that Lincoln was glad the wounds were incurred in the first place. The Temperance Address makes clear that he loathed the human maiming associated with war. However, now that the wounds were here, they served a useful purpose.

19. See chapter five, note 41.

20. Though he takes Lincoln's religious thought seriously, in a number of the same veins as this chapter, Stuart Winger ultimately sees moral and national humility as the lesson of the Second Inaugural, almost to the exclusion of charity, but this misses the fact that for Lincoln, national humility is key to charity and forgiveness.

The whole structure of the speech suggests that the former is in the service of the latter, not trumping the latter (Winger, *Lincoln, Religion*, 208).

21. Richard Rorty, *Contigency, Irony, and Solidarity*, especially chapter three.

22. Between these two sentences Lincoln continues to speak of the "interest" of slavery, thus leaving little room for anything else to be considered the cause. Also, by indicating that neither side anticipated this cause would cease with, or even before, the conflict ended, Lincoln is clearly alluding to the fact that slavery, by virtue of the Thirteenth Amendment's wending its way through the states, was on its way to extinction, which was not his original aim in sending troops to defend Fort Sumter. White makes the interesting observation that the first sentence, where Lincoln is explicit that slavery is the peculiar interest that is the cause of the war, stands at the "geographic and literary center" of the speech (*Lincoln's Greatest Speech*, 90).

23. As quoted in Catton, *Never Call Retreat*, 411; also see Randall and Current, *Lincoln the President*, 372.

24. Lincoln, *Collected Works*, 7:535.

25. Shortly before being elected president, Lincoln was asked in a letter by a young man about the "best mode of obtaining a thorough knowledge of the law." Lincoln's answer was, "The mode is very simple, though laborious, and tedious. It is only to get the books, and read, and study them carefully. . . . Work, work, work, is the main thing" (Lincoln, *Collected Works*, 4:121). Very early in his political career (1840) he wrote a memo to the Central Whig Committee urging "every Whig must not only know his duty, but must firmly resolve, whatever of time and labor it may cost, [to] boldly and faithfully do it" (1:201). On the vital differences between Lincoln's early sense of fatalism and later providentialism, see White, *Lincoln's Greatest Speech*, 133–38.

26. The first figure about the Civil War comes from Livermore, *Numbers and Losses*, culled from tables in 134–39; the second estimate about the Revolution comes from Washington Headquarters Services, "Principal Wars," Table 2–23.

27. Hamilton, Jay, and Madison, *The Federalist Papers 51*.

28. As quoted in Winik, *April 1865*, 184–90; for information about the terms given to Johnston, see Catton, *Never Call Retreat*, 440.

29. As quoted in Guelzo, *Abraham Lincoln*, 448–49.

30. The most recent and thorough treatment of how Lincoln's early plans for Reconstruction differed from those of the radical Republicans is found in William Harris's book titled, revealingly, *With Charity for All: Lincoln and the Restoration of the Union*.

Bonds of Freedom

The current identity of any political regime is tied to its founding. The notion that cultural recollection of such beginnings never fails to shape a contemporary society's moral vision, sense of purpose, and capacity to act is an insight as old as Plato. Thus, it still matters today that a number of key moments in the making of America were fashioned by the memorable words and deeds of political figures of uncommon intellect and skill who took New Testament teachings on love seriously, both personally and publicly.

We tend to remember the first of these figures, John Winthrop, only in caricature or barely at all. Both tendencies are unfair. The vices of Winthrop's model of Christian charity indeed made something like Jefferson's later model of natural liberty necessary, but its virtues provided a variety of enabling conditions for, and continuing correctives to, the rise of just such a republic. Here again we might listen carefully to Nathaniel Hawthorne, no Puritan apologist but one who always saw beyond simplistic moral dichotomies.

As *The Scarlet Letter* closes, after its searing indictment of Boston as a model of Puritan charity in actual practice, the reader catches a glimpse of Hester. She has returned to Boston of her own free will after self-exile to England and there remains to her last days with "sad eyes" looking forward to a future time when a "new truth" would be revealed to establish human relationships on a "surer ground of mutual happiness."[1] Of course, Hawthorne writes this with perfect knowledge that from Hester's perspective, a time will come when a self-evident "truth" will be declared, opening up the way for people to live together in the free "pursuit of happiness." That the Declaration of Independence establishes a polity while avoiding many of the sweeping moral judgments that could make Puritan life so grim and repressive is something few, starting with Hawthorne, would dispute. Yet it is often forgotten that *The Scarlet Letter* opens in a "Custom House" in nineteenth-century, democratic America, not on a scaffolding in seventeenth-century, Puritan New England. And Hawthorne's picture here—the passage being written primarily in his own autobiographical voice[2]—hardly reassures that Hester's sad hope finally finds full and happy expression in America's later constitutional republic. Over the entrance of the Custom House, a civil post of "Uncle Sam's government," sits that great symbol of free and democratic America itself, an ornamental eagle, of which Hawthorne remarks,

> With the customary infirmity of temper that characterizes this *unhappy* fowl, she appears, by the fierceness of her beak and eye and the general truculuncey of her attitude, to threaten mischief to the inoffensive community. . . . Nevertheless, vixenly as she looks, many people are seeking, at this very moment, to shelter themselves under the wing of the federal eagle; imagining, I presume, that her bosom has all the softness and snugness of an eider-down pillow. But she has no great tenderness, even in her best moods, and, sooner or later . . . is apt to fling off her nestlings, with a scratch of her claw, a dab of her beak, or a rankling wound from her barbed arrows.[3]

Coupled with Hawthorne's quiet suggestion that Winthrop held far more of the "good" than "evil" traits of this historic community, the opening and closing scenes of this text caution against excoriating Winthrop and his model of charity in favor of an unbracketed commitment to liberal democracy understood in exclusively secular and individualistic terms.[4] Hawthorne could view Winthrop not just with sympathy but with a degree of admiration because he established a national mythos that humans are social beings, dependent upon other social beings not just to survive but to flourish. Like so much of Hawthorne's own literature, Winthrop generally stood for a kindly recognition of the limitations, dependencies, and weaknesses that infect all human beings, an awareness which necessitates modesty in our political ambitions even as it further reminds us that we must actively and generously attend to the needs of all others, sometimes even beyond what reciprocal justice alone would demand.[5] The classically liberal core of American democracy often fails to teach us these things and seemingly lacks the rhetoric, symbols, ideals, and imagery necessary to inspire sensitivity to them. Thus, especially in times of crisis, even solid philosophical liberals like Jefferson look beyond this core to find materials to sustain national bonds of affection, believing that without such bonds free societies hold far less allure and ultimately cannot last. Nevertheless, liberal democracy as inspired by Jefferson and others appears an unmatched resource for mitigating the harsh intolerances and the unjust and undignified restrictions on freedom that always seem to follow in the wake of absolutist social doctrines like American Puritanism. It is thus fortunate that America has a figure like Lincoln in its past, a founder who provides an artful fusion of the sometimes diverging aims and assumptions of Winthropianism and Jeffersonianism. In the end, Lincoln's model of civic charity thankfully does what Jefferson's could not do, and just as thankfully does not do what Winthrop's did.

The scriptural linchpin of Lincoln's model of civic charity as laid out in his Second Inaugural is "Woe unto the world because of offences! For it must needs be that offences come; but woe to that man by whom the offence cometh." From this, Lincoln argues that it seems American slavery is one of those offenses, and since slavery was introduced and sustained by both North and South, "the war came" to both North and South. Formulating things this way, neither side can be angry with the other, nor with God, for his judgments are "true and righteous altogether" Lincoln argues, quoting Psalms 19:9. As Garry Wills puts it, Lincoln's "appeal to 'Gospel forgiveness' is preceded by a submission to 'Torah judgment.'" Put another way, Lincoln's New Testament "charity for all" works only in combination with the Old Testament's "Living God" of punishment. The basic thrust of Wills's point is correct, but the way he puts it obscures the fact that the first and most critical passages of scriptural judgment Lincoln cites ("Woe unto . . .") comes from the New Testament (Matt. 18:7), not the Old. Lincoln accepted and deeply understood the Old Testament foundations of New Testament theology better than many ministers of his day and many Christians now.[6] In this regard, Lincoln's theology trends toward a Puritan view.

Of course, by highlighting slavery as a gross offense before God, Lincoln's Second Inaugural also manifests the clearest of sympathies with doctrines of "natural right" that make the deprivation of any man's basic, inherent liberties a great act of injustice. The difference is that Lincoln's Jeffersonianism is situated in a political cosmos where God actively intervenes in the affairs of men, punishing them collectively for their sins, including violations of basic human agency, and commanding them

collectively to care for each other, including showing love to their enemies. This is just the kind of transcendent, personal, and providential
God of the Bible that Jefferson refused to insert into the Declaration
of Independence and consciously excised from his version of the New
Testament. Neither of the scriptural keys of Lincoln's Second Inaugural
discussed here (Psalms 19:9, Matt. 18:7) are found in the "bible" Jefferson made as president. In other words, Jefferson works to exclude from
his model of charity the two central scriptural verses upon which Lincoln hangs his. This is because Jefferson entirely rejected the Old Testament and carefully stripped from the New Testament anything that
contradicted modern rationalism or embodied the violent judgmentalism
of Calvinist Puritanism. As he wrote to John Adams very late in life, "I
can never join Calvin in addressing his god. . . . [Such] is not the God
whom you and I acknowledge and adore, the Creator and benevolent
governor of the world; but a daemon of malignant spirit."[7]

   Jefferson's liberalism helped move America away from the narrow
harshness that came to dominate Puritan New England, and his
watered-down form of Christianity helped heal the destabilizing incivili-
ties of 1800. Like Winthrop before him and Lincoln after him, he came
to see how vital bonds of affection between citizens were to any sound,
happy, and stable political order—including a political order fundamentally devoted to protecting individual freedom, as opposed to inculcating
virtue. However, absent an openness to the mystery of a living god of
mercy and justice—a mystery that unquestionably runs throughout both
Old and New Testaments—Jefferson's combination of modern democracy and diluted Christianity would have been far less potent in the face
of the overpowering spirit of mutual revenge lurking in 1865. Mollifying
the animosities between indignant Federalists and Republicans in 1800
can hardly be compared with neutralizing the acids boiling between the
North and South in 1865. Jefferson's particular model of liberty and
charity was able to inspire the social and political congeniality needed
for the moment in his day, but it could not match Lincoln's in its ability
to dissolve the bloody hatred of civil war. Such forgiveness and charitable reconciliation seems of necessity to depend upon an awesomely just
and merciful power beyond the full grasp of mortal reasoning alone—a
power Jefferson assiduously tried to minimize in civil society.

   To say all of this another way, the success of Lincoln's Second Inaugural hinges on the acceptance of a God of love who exercises full and
sometimes punishing dominion over American politics. In seeing both

"the goodness and severity" of the Judeo-Christian God (Rom. 11:22), Lincoln's deity looks far different even from the one Jefferson appears to embrace later in life, and more like the one found in "A Model of Christian Charity." However, Lincoln's political theology differs from John Winthrop's in that Lincoln's sense of God's unfathomability and of man's limitations before that God is far more sweeping than Winthrop's. On this particular point, it might be said that Lincoln was more Puritan than the Puritans themselves, for whom Calvin's teaching that God was beyond comprehension was a central tenet of faith. Lincoln's is an intense cautiousness concerning the full meaning of the evidence that the visible, rational world provides about the moral, spiritual world. Such prevailing uncertainty leaves him unwilling to predict imminent human events (like the end of the war) and unable to let the North blame the South for the unjust start of the war (despite the South's firing on Fort Sumter) or let the South blame the North for the devastating end of the war (despite Sherman's march to the sea). Building off a life-long skepticism of meeting any present political problem with doctrinaire solutions, Lincoln's later theological position brought him near to a Christian existentialism. One can almost as easily hear Lincoln, as Kierkegaard, assert that "life can only be understood backwards, but must be lived forwards."

Lincoln's sense for humanity's inescapable finitude and frailty comports in many respects with Winthrop's "Model" speech, especially the opening where a call to charity is grounded in the providential inequalities and insufficiencies of human beings everywhere. But in the end, the closing rhetoric of Winthrop's "Model" speech cuts back against this position shared with Lincoln. Though Winthrop himself typically embraced a more cautious, Lincoln-like reserve of judgment which was similarly grounded in a consciousness of human fallibility and the complexity of human existence, he also laid out a covenantal formula of national survival at the end of his "Model" speech that prompted in others, and sometimes in himself, a necessarily confident, at times even desperate, sense of what constituted God's will concerning the most minute details of life in the Massachusetts Bay Colony. The certitude, sweep, and critical significance of Winthrop's civil covenant made way for the prompt identification and harsh punishment of violations, large and small. With Lincoln, however, there was far less certitude about the mind and will of God. Concomitantly, there was far less certitude about anyone's standing before God. To those tempted to severely condemn

Southern slaveowners, Lincoln counsels his listeners, "let us judge not that we be not judged" (closely paraphrasing Matt. 7:1). His entire address is a powerful condemnation of the practice of slavery itself but not of the current slaveholders. That Lincoln can share in Winthrop's God but escape the wide-ranging oppression and accusation of "Iron" John Endicott in favor of a human generosity that approaches that of Uncle Tom has much to do with his conviction of the general inscrutability of God's intentions and human guilt.

That said, Lincoln's broad epistemic doubts do not produce in him an utter moral relativism. He is not, in the end, fully postmodern or fully existential in the way those terms are now often understood. Lincoln's mature political thought firmly rested on two solid truth claims about humanity. The first is that all humans are free to determine the direction of their individual lives because they are natural equals with one another. Lincoln attested to the truth of this throughout his career and fought to ensure that the country became ever more dedicated to it. The second truth—something Lincoln embraced later—is that all humans are "under God," specifically the God of the Bible, who directs the affairs of men and who commands love for himself and for other human beings. Besides the Second Inaugural itself, Lincoln's clearest testimonial of this second truth comes in a letter to Thurlow Weed written just after he gave that speech, in which he noted it would be unpopular in the near term because people would not like hearing that their will was at odds with God's. Continuing, this lifelong politician whose public role and success always required broad popularity and who, as early as the Temperance Address, carefully theorized about and strongly counseled against too much moral scolding, explained to Weed that "to deny it, however, in this case, is to deny that there is a God governing the world. It is a *truth* which I thought needed to be told."[8]

In the concrete realities of civic life, these two truths often seem to stand in conflict with one another. Where classical liberal thought separates religion and political power and minimizes the role of government, *agape* infuses every aspect of one's life—including the political—with a drive to acknowledge and lovingly obey God and to show forth active and heartfelt concern for all. And yet there also seems to be a deep harmony and positively reinforcing relationship between these truths, especially when blended together by Lincoln's deft touch into civic charity. Charity grounded in a certain biblical view of the nature of man—one that recognizes man's dignity but also his fallen tendencies toward selfishness and

faction—underscores the practical wisdom of looking to a limited constitutional government of checks and balances for securing a social order
that is both ethical and stable. At the same time, charity reminds us that
an overcharged ethic of individualism and self-sufficiency denies important aspects of our humanity and endangers the political and economic
institutions most inclined to honor the natural rights of the individual.
It is only some form of charity throughout the community that makes
the existence of a free people possible, starting with the deep care and
generosity required to raise young and vulnerable life to a life capable of
responsible democratic citizenship. It also appears that affectionate ties
between citizens critically help a liberal polity stave off tyrannical and
anarchic forces that threaten the rule of law and help it enjoy its freedom
in a condition of national satisfaction and happiness. And while these
bonds of affection may spring from many sources, it seems there are distinct times and places where the power of *agape*—with its transcendent,
commanding call to love as well as its recognition of the neediness of all
humans before God and each other—is singularly suited to overcoming
the callousness, passions, and hatred so able to rupture such bonds.

Civic charity also attunes a nation to the human needs and democratic aspirations of those beyond its borders, even as it tempers against
a universalizing imperialism. In his second annual message to Congress,
Lincoln declared that the eyes and ears of the "world" and all future
humanity down to the "latest generation" would take in and never forget
how the country handled the challenge before them. This sounds much
like Winthrop's stirring call to New England to become a "City upon a
Hill." Lincoln was not challenging America to adopt wide-ranging practices of Christian love. Rather, he was calling on the country to survive
the crucible of civil war and maintain the integrity of a union increasingly dedicated to that great truth of natural human right, thus standing
as the "last, best hope of Earth" for the spread of liberty.[9] If that was
America's potential before the war ended, then could Lincoln have seen
it as anything less after the war ended with the Union intact and slavery
successfully abolished? Certainly that is how many Christians of his day
regarded the country. Yet, unlike the views of many believers of his day,
the second of Lincoln's great truths reasserts a moral chasm between
God and all American citizens. In this way, America as the grand hope
of human freedom everywhere moves forward under Lincoln but with a
chastened sense of judgment, ability, and goodness, a sense that cuts
against the kind of national overoptimism, self-righteousness, and desire

to control that can so easily infect any sense of world leadership. For Lincoln, America's commitment to liberty made it a "great promise to all the people of the world to all time to come," but it was his deep reading of biblical charity that taught him that America could do so, at best, as God's "*almost* chosen people" (emphasis added).[10]

An unimpeachable recommendation of Lincoln's unique synthesis of Christian charity and natural liberty would require convincing proof of the truths of the Declaration and the Bible. While no such proofs can be offered here or anywhere anytime soon, neither can proofs of the falseness of these claims. So what if, as Lincoln came to believe, they are both true? What if it is true that man is by nature entitled to be free *and* there is a God in heaven who rules the earth and demands that humans love him and love each other? If these things are true, what should our politics look like? Since Machiavelli, ascendant voices in political philosophy have simply assumed that *caritas* is either ethically nonbinding or should play little or no role in our civic life. But we might consider the loss to this country had Lincoln offered his Second Inaugural by the strictures of so much modern political theory. Lincoln and his thought still matter today because virtually all Americans act and speak as if his first truth claim concerning natural liberty is true, and vast numbers of Americans still accept on faith some version of the second claim concerning Christian charity. These two truth claims supply different instincts that have become permanent elements in our politics. When blended they defy strict party label, which does much to explain Lincoln's continuing broad appeal and cultural influence.[11] Singularly committed to robust versions of both claims, Lincoln developed a political vision and rhetoric well-suited to steer America toward a model of civic charity. Such a model combines Winthropian and Jeffersonian ideals into a dynamic equilibrium supported by an intellectual framework that recognizes the inherent partiality of any political-historic commitment.

Where some will insist that Lincoln's political philosophy is an illogical mix of contradictory notions, others will recognize in it the manifestation of a gifted intellectual and moral iridescence, a Tocquevillian knack for uniting the spirit of religion and the spirit of liberty so that each supports the other instead of destroying it.[12] It is perhaps a conceit purely of the modern mind post-Descartes that only a perfectly tidy and consistent system of thought can serve as the basis for effective human direction. Lincoln, like Aristotle, saw things differently. Even if there

exists a theoretical tidiness to the true and best solution for social organization, Lincoln—especially the later, more religious Lincoln—never
thought it was within the full grasp of mere mortals. Nor, though, did he
consider that this indetermination left him staring into the abyss. Rather
than be undone—left in the grip of inaction—by the apparent incom-
mensurability of moral goods (justice and mercy, liberty and love), Lincoln pressed ahead like an exquisite painter who finds a way to
harmonize the "acid green of the grass with the ravishing red of the
skirt." While the task was often melancholic for him—recognizing as he
did the costly tradeoffs involved in honoring these competing
demands—he nevertheless flourished as a leader, becoming by many
accounts the most admired president of all time.[13]

Unlike Jefferson's attempt at an instauration of Christianity by striking out the divine and original core of that tradition's theology, Lincoln's
instauration of America itself sought a careful preservation of this country's liberal core. But he could do so only by explicitly ensconcing it in
the Christian *caritas* of its earliest Puritan traditions, a *caritas* which this
study has shown gave significant birth and sustaining influence to that
liberal core. Lincoln remade America entirely out of old cloth but produced a garment with the luster and strength of something brand-new.
With its compassion and wisdom, Lincoln's sacred effort got us through
the union's most desperate hour. Where it was rejected after that hour,
America incurred some of its longest and bitterest scars. Even today, it
draws America together in a vigorous devotion to liberty and a reverent
spirit of mutual concern. With sagacious and moving art, it refuses to let
us forget that temporal and eternal bonds of affection may just be the
bonds that make us free.

A POSTSCRIPT ON THE LINCOLN MYTH

The myth of Lincoln as a second Christ began almost the instant he died. Some might say the argument of this book trends in that direction. A closing word, then, about that.

Arguably, the myth of Lincoln as second Christ began with Frederick Douglass. The day Lincoln passed away, Douglass, who had been sitting in but not asked to speak at a hastily formed public memorial service in Rochester, New York, was called out by the audience at the end to make some remarks. Extemporaneously, he stood and said

> Though Abraham Lincoln dies, the Republic lives. . . . It may be in the inscrutable wisdom of Him who controls the destinies of Nations, that the drawing of the Nation's most precious heart's blood was necessary to bring us back to that equilibrium which we must maintain if the Republic was to be permanently redeemed.

Two months later, Harvard scholar and poet Oliver Wendell Holmes would pen a memorial verse for Lincoln reading

> Oh let the blood by murder spilt
> Wash out the stricken children's guilt
> And sanctify our nation![14]

Given the state of antebellum faith in America and an unusual number of likenesses between the life of Lincoln and Christ, it is no surprise that a concept of "Lincoln as Second Christ" developed shortly after he was shot. Both Christ and Lincoln were born of obscure parentage, in crude, outdoor structures, and were plagued with rumors of illegitimacy. Both rose to great prominence despite their impoverished beginnings. Both experienced lives of great suffering and eventual martyrdom due to their successful efforts to reform the moral world around them. Lincoln's last photo reveals a face that is a sunken-eyed reservoir of pain, carved up by deep, subcutaneous lines of worry and discouragement.[15]

Yet through all of this suffering—perhaps in part because of it—they both demonstrated a remarkable compassion. In 1909, Leo Tolstoy said in a widely published interview that he saw Lincoln as "a Christ in minia-ture, a saint of humanity," someone who was "bigger than his country—bigger than all the Presidents together. Why? Because he loved his enemies as himself." Even Lincoln's old law partner, Herndon, who was

never able to appreciate Lincoln's religious transformation and spent a
fair amount of time trying to disprove it, found that the presidency intensified Lincoln's inherent love into a religious virtue. As Herndon put it,
"Do you not see Lincoln's Christ like charity—liberality—toleration
loom up and blossom above all?"[16] In terms of modern scholarship, even
in *The Inner World of Abraham Lincoln*, where Michael Burlingame
devotes a whole chapter to "Lincoln's Anger and Cruelty"—which proves
what is granted here, that Lincoln was not perfect—Burlingame
concludes:

> The remarkable thing about Lincoln's temper is not how often it
> erupted, but how seldom it did, considering how frequently he
> encountered the insolence of epaulets, the abuse of friends and oppo-
> nents alike, and the egomaniacal selfishness of editors, senators, rep-
> resentatives, governors, cabinet members, generals, and flocks of
> others who pestered him unmercifully about their own petty concerns.
> It is no wonder that John Hay marveled in 1863, "While the rest are
> grinding their little private organs for their own glorification[,] the old
> man is working with the strength of a giant and the purity of an angel
> to do this great work." Hay might well have added, "with the forbear-
> ance of a saint."[17]

Most uncanny are those parallels associated with the deaths of Lincoln and Christ. First, there is the distinct similarity between Jesus' triumphant entry into Jerusalem (Matthew 21:1–10) just days before his
crucifixion, and Lincoln's triumphant entry into defeated Richmond just
days before his assassination. Donald describes the latter:

> Landing without notice or fanfare, the President was first recognized
> by some black workmen. Their leader, a man about sixty, dropped his
> spade and rushed forward, exclaiming, "Bless the Lord, there is the
> great Messiah! . . . Glory, Hallelujah!" . . . Quickly word of the Presi-
> dent's arrival spread, and he was soon surrounded by throngs of blacks,
> who shouted, "Bless the Lord, Father Abrahams Come."[18]

With respect to the actual day Lincoln was shot, Friday, April 14, 1865,
even the president's more secularly oriented biographers cannot help but
note that it was "Good Friday," the day much of the Christian world
mournfully celebrates the anniversary of the death of Christ on the
cross. And at least one historian attuned to the importance religion held

for Lincoln recently noted and gives good reason to believe in Mary Lincoln's recollection that moments before Lincoln was shot while watching a play at Ford's Theater, he leaned over to her and told her that he wanted to "visit the Holy Land and see those places hallowed by the footsteps of the Savior."[19] And then there is the lamentable matter of how both came to a torturous end. According to Thomas's account, immediately after being shot Lincoln—still alive—was taken from Ford's Theater to a modest home across the street where he was placed

> upon a bed, diagonally because of his great height. His breath came in long gasps. Examination showed that the bullet had entered the back of the head toward the left side and lodged near his right eye. . . . Throughout the night the watchers at the bedside maintained their hopeless vigil. . . . Mrs. Lincoln sobbed in the front room. Stanton hurried in and out as he signed and dispatched orders. And always from the bedroom came the moan of that labored breathing. . . . From time to time the doctors gave the President stimulants and removed blood clots to relieve the pressure on the brain. Beyond that there was nothing they could do. . . . The President seemed to cling tenaciously to life. At last, however, the tortured breathing slowed. It became faint. At 7.22 in the morning of April 15, 1865 Abraham Lincoln gained peace—and immortality.[20]

For nine hours, Lincoln labored under the agonizing pain of his mortal wound.

In the late 1940s, intellectual historian Richard Hofstadter wrote a famous essay challenging the view of Lincoln as a leader who suffers for the "moral burdens of a blundering and sinful people" and then "redeems them with hallowed Christian virtues—'malice toward none and charity for all.'" As Hofstadter sees it, Lincoln's "atonement and redemption" for the country's sin of slavery was a political myth that held an incomparable grip on the American political tradition but was one ultimately irreconcilable with the real Lincoln, who was "thoroughly and completely" a politician whose lodestar was economic prosperity rather than national righteousness. Even Lincoln's fabled opposition to slavery was, for Hofstadter, primarily guided by economic considerations and fueled by political ambition.[21]

Following Hofstadter, numerous twentieth-century rationalist historians and social scientists have argued that the Lincoln myth must be disregarded by any thinking person because it just is not true. In their efforts, many of them have tried to do to the memory of Lincoln what Jefferson did to the New Testament; they have tried to neuter it of any connection to the divine.[22] To the extent that Lincoln is regarded as an actual Christ, some character of deified perfection that died to expatiate the sins of the American people for their collective sin of slavery, these scholars are undoubtedly correct. Modern scholarship does well to remind us of Lincoln's mortal flaws. Furthermore, *agape*'s first commandment makes the worship of any man a grave sin (Matt. 22:36–38, Exod. 20:1–5). For any who take biblical faith seriously, to remake Lincoln a second Christ is both intellectually unjustified and spiritually blasphemous. Yet to fail to recover Lincoln as a human but nevertheless a mythopoetic model of civic charity would be to deprive ourselves of a uniquely authentic embodiment of all the key aspirations critical to the making and preserving of America—an America perhaps more dependent than it knows upon the supernal bonds of affection.

To many contemporary minds, only the tangible and the literal can express the full and clear truth of our human experience. For such minds, myths can only be considered falsehoods unworthy of being embraced by anyone with any degree of intellectual integrity. But in some cases, to be left with only the tangible and literal actually empties our world of certain truths—truths that find their best and most accurate expression in more mythical and symbolic images.[23] Lincoln, no doubt a man of sober reason, considered himself importantly shaped in his political and personal morality by just such powerful images.[24]

Lincoln grew up reading much, but in very few books. One of these was Parson Mason Weems's *Life of George Washington*. Honest Abe, whose life of cool reason resisted genuine and open religious belief until quite late in life, said on several occasions how much this book affected him. He even spoke of the book at a stop on his way to Washington, D.C., for his first inaugural, saying that "I recollect thinking then, boy even though I was, that there must have been something more than common that those men struggled for."[25] The heroic if hagiographic exploits Lincoln read about left an indelible impression on him, taught him then in a powerful way what he still believed was true later, that there were certain things worth sacrificing for, including freedom for oneself and others. More than some kind of spiritless, encyclopedic reporting of all knowable details, it was the mythical quality of these stories—the symbolic and moving glimpses of something unordinary—that captured an instructive moral reality for Lincoln. And surely something about this also helps to explain why, as Lincoln left his legal practice and immersed himself in the political and ethical quandaries facing Civil War America, he read less and less of history, law, and political science (such as it was in the nineteenth century) but consumed Shakespeare.[26] The point here is not to advocate the study of classic fiction over the social sciences, and it is certainly not to make an anti-intellectual argument for the return of hagiography. It is simply to strike a note of caution about the possible loss of insight for a society that reflexively dismisses anything beyond the purely prosaic.

In this light, consider the civic power and benefit of the Lincoln Memorial. Immediately after it was completed, the Lincoln Memorial became, and remains, the single most visited national monument in the country. Its outer shell is that of a classical Greek temple. Inside sits an enormous marble Lincoln who kindly looks down on the humble and comparatively tiny admirer, or worshiper. On the walls are carved in their entirety two of America's most sacred political texts, the Gettysburg Address and the Second Inaugural—a speech that Felix Frankfurter once observed is "cemented with blood, a moral heritage which, when drawn upon in times of stress and strife, is sure to find specific ways and means to surmount difficulties that may appear to be insurmountable."[27]

There is something here that goes to the heart of Lincoln's lifelong statesmanship. From his very first speeches to his very last, Lincoln consistently held that while America's admirable and constitutionally erected political structure of rights, laws, and checks and balances was essential to combating unjust infringements of human freedom, it was not enough. The human malice that poses the single greatest threat to American freedom is such that it must further be smothered by inspiring symbols and rhetoric enshrined in the larger culture with a kind of religious awe or reverence. If true, then surely America is a better place, surely its bonds of affection have been strengthened by the numerous pilgrimages to this quasi-religious shrine where mythic and emotive renditions of Lincoln and his *agape* warmly instruct and inspire the visitor well beyond the power of the cold, flat facts.[28]

There is, though, a danger in the Lincoln shrine in how close it comes to slipping back into the most extreme and profane manifestations of the Lincoln myth—where Lincoln is actually made a god. Lincoln himself utterly repudiated such a move. At his famous landing at Richmond where he was welcomed as a messiah, people fell upon their knees and tried to kiss his feet. "Don't kneel to me," Lincoln rebuked them with embarrassment. "That is not right. You must kneel to God only, and thank him for the liberty you will hereafter enjoy."[29] Not only did Lincoln emphatically deny a deific status, he presumed the very opposite of divine, revelatory gifts by confessing a general inability to fathom the mind and will of God on almost all specific matters of national importance. Even on the gravest political and moral issues of his day, Lincoln proceeded with immense flexibility, rarely presupposing a clearly—let alone divinely—right or wrong answer. On the few issues where he thought he recognized God's will, such as when to emancipate the slaves in rebel territory, he saw only "through a glass darkly," *after* a prodigious reasoning of the facts with an especially careful consideration of public opinion and positive law. Lincoln's politics were moored by what he considered certain verities, namely his lifelong recognition of the truths of the Declaration of Independence and an acknowledgment later in life that a biblical God who commands his children to believe in gratitude and to love one another rules the earth and thereby exerts an important providential influence over earthly politics. However, holding these general truths did not produce in him a repository of some special, detailed godly knowledge that translated into a rigid, wide-ranging set of policy prescriptions.

The lesson here is a careful one. To replace the now exploded and profane myth of Lincoln as a second Christ with a revitalized tradition that grandly honors Lincoln *as a man*, though a highly unique man who maintained the union and extended human freedom with heroic resolve and extraordinary Jesus-like qualities and instincts, is to set an inspirational cultural ideal against dangerous, democracy-wrecking impulses of malice lurking in the human heart. We would forget this to our loss. Yet Lincoln's Second Inaugural suggests there are times when the frame of mind necessary for sustaining the social harmony and rule of law essential to liberty in America cannot be exclusively anthropocentric. Human reason and human heroes had their fundamental place in Lincoln's life and political thought, and they should in ours too. But, as Lincoln came to see, at certain moments exclusively mortal sources of inspiration—unaided reason, philosophical liberalism, the law, proud and memorable accomplishments of earlier heroes and generations—ultimately prove incapable of rallying the human compassion and meekness necessary to mollify those darker angels of human nature that can tear a republic apart or leave it vulnerable to tyranny. Lincoln made a monumental contribution—sacred texts, iconic images, inspirational memories—to the country's stock of civil religion. However, to the degree that civil religion takes its cues from Lincoln and his Second Inaugural, it cannot be civil religion in the Rousseauian sense, meaning a man-made vessel for the purposes of the state alone, as was the "political religion" of Lincoln's Lyceum Address. Rather, it is a manifestation of a religion purportedly not of Lincoln's or any mortal man's making even if it is necessarily expressed in broad civic terms and without sectarian distinction, as befitting a large democratic polity of various faith perspectives. Religion in some form was always politically useful to Lincoln. But at the very apex of his career, his attraction to biblical teachings of love for God and man appear more grounded in his sense of their veracity than in their utility. In fact it was only a strong sense of the transcendent truth of these teachings that gave them the unique political force they had for both Lincoln and his listeners. All this suggests that to let even the most inspiring mortal relics of a civil religion—however biblically grounded— overshadow its divine source would be to choose the lesser part, religiously and politically. And if that source is indeed divine, we would forget this to our loss too.

Notes

1. Hawthorne, *The Scarlet Letter*, 177–78.
2. Ibid., 4, 5.
3. Ibid., 6 (emphasis added).
4. In the "Custom House" essay, Hawthorne makes reference to "all the Puritanic traits, both good and evil" of even the most persecuting of his own Puritan ancestors (Hawthorne, *The Scarlet Letter*, 9). Also see his "Main-street" story, where he speaks of the lasting "unfavorable influences" of American Puritanism standing "among many good ones" (*Tales and Sketches*, 1039).
5. From Georgiania's tiny but ineradicable natural flaw in "The Birth-Mark" to the picture of the natural depravity of the human heart that closes "Earth's Holocaust," Hawthorne's fiction persistently comes down on the side of accepting that human nature—flawed as it might be—is the tragic and immovable fact of human community. In the *Blithedale Romance*—the story of a group of people striving for an idealized life shorn of all market inequalities and the judgmentalism of American religion and conventional norms—Zenobia fares worse than her Puritanical doppelganger, Hester Prynne. In the end, Zenobia commits suicide. To fully and caustically condemn everything about Winthrop because of some demonstrable imperfections of thought and action would seem, by the light of Hawthorne's works, to replace one form of Puritanism—with its ungenerous and uncompromising enforcement of an ideal moral order—with another (Hawthorne, *Blithedale Romance*, 229–234). Also

see Catherine Zuckert, *Natural Rights*, 71–83, and Flannery O'Connor's "Introduction to a Memoir of Mary Ann," a fascinating tribute to the legacy of Hawthorne's
reserved but very real and influential sense of charity as grounded in an embrace of
human imperfection, found in O'Connor, *Collected Works*, 822–31.

6. Wills, "Lincoln's Greatest Speech?" 66. Many Christian intellectuals, from
Reinhold Niebuhr to Mark Noll, argue that Lincoln's model of *biblical* charity in the
Second Inaugural is far more profound in its *Christian* understandings and conclusions than anything offered by the best-trained and most prominent ministers of Lincoln's day (Niebuhr, "Religion of Abraham Lincoln," 172; Noll, "Pray to the Same
God," 1–2). On the dust jacket of William Wolf's *Lincoln's Religion*, Niebuhr goes so
far as to say that "Lincoln has always been my hero in religion and statecraft."

7. Evidence that he consciously excises it is found in the fact that he does
include Matthew 18:1–6, skips verse 7 as well as verses 8–18, then resumes with 19–
31. It must be noted, however, in his second compilation pulled together in retirement, he does include Matthew 18:7. See Jefferson, *Extracts from the Gospel*, 89,
94–95. For the letter he wrote to John Adams, see ibid., 410.

8. Lincoln, *Collected Works*, 8:356 (emphasis added).

9. Ibid., 5:537.

10. Though he stresses how much Lincoln's Second Inaugural was at odds with
most theologians of the day who continued to see America in a kind of special, covenant relationship with God, Mark Noll also concludes that "Lincoln nonetheless
never entirely gave up the myth of the chosen nation" (*America's God*, 431–35). Lincoln refers to America as God's "almost chosen people" in an address in Trenton,
New Jersey, on his way to assume the presidency (Lincoln, *Collected Works*, 4:236).

11. Such a claim is worthy of a book-length treatment itself. Simply consider that
Jane Addams, whose early Progressivism "aroused the social conscience of America"
and alleviated an immense amount of national suffering, devoted an entire chapter
in her autobiography, *Twenty Years at Hull-House*, to the "Influence of Lincoln"
(Addams, *Social Thought*, viii; Addams, *Twenty Years at Hull-House*, 23); Theodore
Roosevelt and Martin Luther King Jr., who both prominently turned to Lincoln to
help heal the racial divide, the latter standing literally in the shadow of the Lincoln
Memorial offering an exceptionally Lincolnesque address combining ideals of natural liberty and *agape* (Roosevelt, *American Problems*, 3–4; King, *Essential Writings*,
217); and Ronald Reagan, who in his first inaugural directed the gaze of his audience
across the National Mall and beyond the Reflecting Pool to the "dignified columns
of the Lincoln Memorial" and praised Lincoln as the embodiment of America while
crisply asserting the twin truths of Lincoln's mature political philosophy, namely that
"We are a nation under God, and I believe God intended us to be free," and who in
his second inaugural dubbed his effort to rein in the size and role of government,
out of respect for that freedom, a "new emancipation" (U.S. Congress, Senate, *Inaugural Addresses*, 333–34, 336, 341).

12. Tocqueville, *Democracy in America*, 43.

13. Pierre Manent, *City of Man*, 166. One also thinks here of the F. Scott Fitzgerald line, "The test of a first-rate intelligence is the ability to hold two opposed ideas
in mind at the same time and still retain the ability to function" (Fitzgerald, "The
Crack-Up," 1007). This thought shaped an important conclusion in one of the most

influential books of modern business management (a field more relevant to political science than is generally thought), *In Search of Excellence*, by Thomas Peters and Robert Waterman. The conclusion is that the world's very best leaders inevitably prove adept at "managing ambiguity and paradox" because the world's largest and most successful organizations are typically founded on paradox, or a collection of principles seemingly at odds with each other (Peters and Waterman, *In Search of Excellence*, 89–118).

14. Douglass, *Frederick Douglass Papers*, 4:76; Holmes, *Poetical Works*, 208.

15. Merrill Peterson neatly documents a variety of cultural manifestations indicating how far and deep "the conception of Lincoln as second Christ" has run in America and around the world (*Lincoln in American Memory*, 217–226). For similarities between Christ and Lincoln, see Oates, *With Malice toward None*, 4; and Donald, *Lincoln*, 605. For the physical toll and intense grief, see Wolf, *Lincoln's Religion*, 115. For Lincoln's last photo, see Mellon, *The Face of Lincoln*, 88, 186.

16. Peterson, *Lincoln in American Memory*, 185–86; Tolstoy, *The World*, Feb. 8, 1909; Randall and Current, *Lincoln the President*, 376.

17. Burlingame, *The Inner World*, 208.

18. Donald, *Lincoln*, 576.

19. For the first quote, see Oates, *With Malice toward None*, 426; and Thomas, *Abraham Lincoln*, 518. Fehrenbacher does not firmly dispute the authenticity of this statement, but he does suggest there is more than "average doubt" about it. However, Guelzo, who is by no means out to make Lincoln a devout Christian, counters Fehrenbacher's primary reservation effectively. See Fehrenbacher and Fehrenbacher, *Recollected Works*, 297; Guelzo, *Abraham Lincoln*, 434.

20. Thomas, *Abraham Lincoln*, 521.

21. Hofstadter, *American Political Tradition*, 121, 124, 135. By Hofstadter's estimation, Lincoln stood above all else for providing "opportunities for social ascent to those born in its lower ranks" through establishing a free-wheeling capitalism, shorn of unfair (because uncompetitive not because immoral) slave labor and supported by government-sponsored internal improvements which would aid local enterprise (135). Hofstadter does cede to Lincoln a certain "private religious intensity" (123). Considering Lincoln's "Christian virtues" grossly "incompatible" with the pride and aggressive individualism and acquisitiveness attendant to his burning political appetites and economic aspirations, Hofstadter sees Lincoln as destined from the start for "high tragedy" (123), and, in the end, one who discovers utter "heartache in his triumph" (173).

22. Doris Kearns Goodwin's otherwise impressive treatment of Lincoln's management of the rivalrous aims of those leaders around him—which took political genius but also remarkable moral discipline—is a prime example of how Lincoln's Christic qualities often get excised. Her *Team of Rivals*, over nine hundred pages, offers just a couple of paragraphs on Lincoln's religious outlook (481–82, 699) that barely suggest such might help explain his great magnanimity. With respect to the famous Tolstoy interview, which supplied an epigraph for the introduction to section three of this book, Goodwin also draws an epigraph and then in the text itself describes in detail the story and setting for Tolstoy's interview (ix, 747–48). In both cases, though, she carefully edits out the claim that the chief reason Tolstoy thought Lincoln was

bigger than all other presidents was because he was "a Christ in miniature, a saint of humanity" someone who "loved his enemies [read rivals] as himself."

23. Cassirer, *Language and Myth*, 6. Also see Brent Gilchrist's work on myth as a vital piece of the American political tradition in his *Cultus Americanus*.

24. Donald, *Lincoln*, 30–31.

25. Lincoln, *Collected Works*, 4:236; Wilson, *Lincoln before Washington*, 7.

26. Wilson, *Lincoln before Washington*, 8–9.

27. For an account of the most visited national monument, see Peterson, *Lincoln in American Memory*, 216; as quoted in ibid., 354.

28. This challenges that school of thought that characterizes America's tradition of civil religion as primarily a sacralizing of America's liberal individualistic ethos. See Huntington, *American Politics*, 18, 72–73; and Boorstin, *Lost World*, 28, 136, 140, 147. The Lincoln shrine glorifies human liberty to be sure, but connects that liberty to a sacrificial charity at odds with a Union devoted solely to a crass, reductivist market liberalism. In other words, the reading here takes us back in the direction of Robert Bellah's foundational essay on civil religion wherein he cites Lincoln in particular for introducing themes of personal sacrifice and spiritual redemption into America's civil religion (Bellah, "Civil Religion in America," 9–11). This view also comports to a certain degree with Conrad Cherry's more recent emphasis on the power and danger of the sense of national chosenness that abounds in so much of American civil religion (Cherry, *God's New Israel*, 18–19). Again, the divine censure of the Second Inaugural carved into the stone walls of the Lincoln Memorial conjures up the image of America as God's "*almost* chosen people" (the phrase Lincoln coined on his way to assume the presidency in 1861), a reminder that far from some perfectly saintly, even deified, City upon the Hill, this nation was significantly marked by moral imperfection and a limited understanding of God's true purposes concerning its role in the world.

29. Donald, *Lincoln*, 576.

APPENDIX A

John Winthrop's "A Model of Christian Charity" Speech[1]

(Cover Note)[2]

A MODEL OF CHRISTIAN CHARITY.

Written
On Board the Arbella,
On the Atlantic Ocean.
By the Honorable John Winthrop Esquire.

In His passage, (with the great Company of Religious people, of which Christian Tribes he was the Brave Leader and famous Governor;) from the Island of Great Britain, to New-England in the North America. Anno 1630.

(Contemporaneous Transcription)

CHRISTIAN CHARITY.

A MODEL HEREOF.

[1]   God Almighty in his most holy and wise providence hath so disposed of the condition of mankind, as in all times some must be rich some poor, some high and eminent in power and dignity, others mean and in subjection.[3]

THE REASON HEREOF.

[2] 1. Reason: First, to hold conformity with the rest of His works, being delighted to show forth the glory of his wisdom in the variety and difference of the Creatures and the glory of his power, in ordering all these differences for the preservation and good of the whole, and the glory of his greatness that as it is the glory of princes to have many officers, so this great King will have many Stewards counting himself more honored in dispensing his gifts to man by man, than if he did it by his own immediate hand.

[3] 2. Reason: Secondly, That He might have the more occasion to manifest the work of his Spirit: first, upon the wicked in moderating and restraining them: so that the rich and mighty should not eat up the poor, nor the poor, and despised rise up against their superiors, and shake off their yoke; 2ly in the regenerate in exercising his graces in them, as in the great ones, their love mercy, gentleness, temperance etc., in the poor and inferior sort, their faith patience, obedience, etc:

[4] 3. Reason: Thirdly, That every man might have need of other, and from hence they might be all knit more nearly together in the Bond of brotherly affection: from hence it appears plainly that no man is made more honorable than another or more wealthy etc., out of any particular and singular respect to himself but for the glory of his Creator and the Common good of the Creature, Man; Therefore God still reserves the property of these gifts to himself as Ezek. 16:17. he there calls wealth his gold and his silver etc. Prov. 3:9. he claims their service as his due honor the Lord with thy riches etc. All men being thus (by divine providence) ranked into two sorts, rich and poor; Under the first, are comprehended all such as are able to live comfortably by their own means duly improved; and all others are poor according to the former distribution. There are two rules whereby we are to walk one towards another: JUSTICE and MERCY. These are always distinguished in their Act and in their object, yet may they both concur in the same Subject in each respect; as sometimes there may be an occasion of showing mercy to a rich man, in some sudden danger of distress, and also doing of mere Justice to a poor man in regard of some particular contract etc. There is likewise a double Law by which we are regulated in our conversation one towards another: in both the former respects, the law of nature and the

law of grace, or the moral law or the law of the gospel, to omit the rule of Justice as not properly belonging to this purpose otherwise then it may fall into consideration in some particular Cases: By the first of these laws man as he was enabled so withal [is] commanded to love his neighbor as himself upon this ground stands all the precepts of the moral law, which concerns our dealings with men. To apply this to the works of mercy this law requires two things first that every man afford his help to another in every want or distress. Secondly, that he perform this out of the same affection, which makes him careful of his own good according to that of our Savior Matt 7:12 Whatsoever ye would that men should do to you. This was practiced by Abraham and Lot in entertaining the Angels and the old man of Gibea.[4]

[5]   The Law of Grace or the Gospel hath some difference from the former in these respects first the law of nature was given to man in the estate of innocency; this of the gospel in the estate of regeneracy: 2ly, the former propounds one man to another, as the same flesh and Image of god, this as a brother in Christ also, and in the Communion of the same spirit and so teacheth us to put a difference between Christians and others. Do good to all especially to the household of faith;[5] upon this ground the Israelites were to put a difference between the brethren of such as were strangers though not of the Cannanites. 3ly: The Law of nature could give no rules for dealing with enemies for all are to be considered as friends in the state of innocency, but the gospel commands love to an enemy. proof. If thine Enemy hunger feed him; Love your enemies do good to them that hate you Matt 5:44.

[6]   This Law of the gospel propounds likewise a difference of seasons and occasions there is a time also when a christian must sell all and give to the poor as they did in the Apostles' times. There is a time also when a christian (though they give not all yet) must give beyond their ability, as they of Macedonia. Cor. 2:6. likewise community of perils calls for extraordinary liberality and so doth Community in some special service for the Church.[6] Lastly, when there is no other means whereby our Christian brother may be relieved in this distress, we must help him beyond our ability, rather than tempt God, in putting him upon help by miraculous or extraordinary means.

[7]   This duty of mercy is exercised in the kinds, Giving, lending, and forgiving.

[8] Question. What rule shall a man observe in giving in respect of the measure?

[9] Answer. If the time and occasion be ordinary he is to give out of his abundance – let him lay aside, as God hath blessed him. If the time and occasion be extraordinary he must be ruled by them; taking this withal, that then a man cannot likely do too much especially, if he may leave himself and his family under probably means of comfortable subsistence.

[10] Objection. A man must lay up for posterity, the fathers lay up for posterity and children and he is worse than an Infidel that provideth not for his own.[7]

[11] Answer: For the first, it is plain, that it being spoken by way of comparison it must be meant of the ordinary and usual course of fathers and cannot extend to times and occasions extraordinary; for the other place the Apostle speaks against such as walked inordinately, and it is without question, that he is worse than an Infidel who through his own Sloth and voluptuousness shall neglect to provide for his family.

[12] Objection. The wise man's Eyes are in his head (saith Solomon)[8] and forseeth the plague, therefore we must forecast and lay up against evil times when he or his may stand in need of all he can gather.

[13] Answer: This very Argument Solomon useth to persuade to liberality. Eccl: 2:1. cast thy bread upon the waters etc.: for thou knowest not what evil may come upon the land Luke 16. make you friends of the riches of Iniquity; you will ask how will this be? very well. for first he that gives to the poor lends to the lord, and he will repay him even in this life an hundred fold to him or his. The righteous is ever merciful and lendeth and his seed enjoyeth the blessing; and besides we know what advantage it will be to us in the day of account, when many such Witnesses shall stand forth for us to witness the improvement of our Talent. And I would know of those who plead so much for laying up for time to come, whether they hold that to be Gospel Matt 16:19. Lay not up for yourselves treasures upon earth etc. if they acknowledge it what extent will they allow it; if only to those primitive times let them consider the reason whereupon our Savior grounds it, the first is that they are subject

to the moth, the rust the Thief. Secondly, They will steal away the heart, where the treasure is there will the heart be also. The reasons are of like force at all times therefore the exhortation must be general and perpetual which [applies] always in respect of the love and affection to riches and in regard of the things themselves when any special service for the church or particular distress of our brother do call for the use of them; otherwise it is not only lawful but necessary to lay up as Joseph did to have ready upon such occasions, as the Lord (whose stewards we are of them) shall call for them from us: Christ gives us an Instance of the first, when he sent his disciples for the Ass, and bids them answer the owner thus, the Lord hath need of him;[9] so when the Tabernacle was to be built his [servant][10] sends to his people to call for their silver and gold etc.; and yields them no other reason but that it was for his work, when Elisha comes to the widow of Sareptah[11] and finds her preparing to make ready her pittance for herself and her family, he bids her first provide for him, he challengeth first god's part which she must first give before she must serve her own family, all these teach us that the lord looks that when he is pleased to call for his right in anything we have, our own Interest we have must stand aside, till his turn be secured, for the other we need look no further than to that of John 1. he who hath this world's goods and seeth his brother be in want and thou canst help him, thou needest not make doubt, what thou shouldst do, if thou lovest god thou must help him.

[14]   Question: What rule must we observe in lending?

[15]   Answer: Thou must observe whether thy brother hath present or probable, or possible means of repaying thee, if there be none of these, thou must give him according to his necessity, rather than lend him his as he requires; if he hath present means of repaying thee, thou art to look at him, not as an Act of mercy, but by way of Commerce, wherein thou art to walk by the rule of Justice, but, if his means of repaying thee be only probably or possible then is he an object of thy mercy thou must lend him, though there be danger of losing it Deut. 15:7. If any of thy brethren be poor etc. thou shalt lend him sufficient that men might not shift off this duty by the apparent hazard, he tells them that though the Year of the Jubilee were at hand (when he must remit it, if he were not able to repay it before) yet he must lend him and that cheerfully:[12] it may not grieve thee to give him (saith he) and because some might object,

why so I should soon impoverish myself and my family, he adds with all thy Work etc. for our Savior Matt 5:42. From him that would borrow of thee turn not away.

[16] Question: What rule must we observe in forgiving?

[17] Answer: Whether thou didst lend by way of Commerce or in mercy, if he have nothing to pay thee [thou] must forgive him (except in case where thou hast a surety of a lawful pledge) Deut. 15:2. Every seventh year the Creditor was to quit that which he lent to his brother if he were poor as appears verse: 8[4]: save when there shall be no poor with thee. In all these and like Cases Christ was a general rule Matt 7:22. Whatsoever ye would that men should do to you do ye the same to them also.[13]

[18] Question: What rule must we observe and walk by in cause of Community of peril?

[19] Answer: The same as before, but with more enlargement towards others and less respect towards ourselves, and our own right hence it was that in the primitive Church they sold all had all things in Common, neither did any man say that that which he possessed was his own[14] likewise in their return out of Captivity, because the work was great for the restoring of the Church and the danger of the enemies was Common to all Nehemiah exhorts the Jews to liberality and readiness in remitting their debts to their brethren, and disposeth liberally of his own to such as wanted and stand not upon his own due, which he might have demanded of them,[15] thus did some of our forefathers in times of persecution here in England,[16] and so did many of the faithful in other Churches whereof we keep an honorable remembrance of them, and it is to be remembered that both in the Scriptures and latter stories of the Churches that such as have been most bountiful to the poor Saints especially in these extraordinary times and occasions god hath left them highly Commended to posterity, as Zacheus, Cornelius, Dorcas,[17] Bishop Hooper,[18] the Cuttler of Brussells and divers others observe again that scripture give no caution to restrain any from being over liberal this way; but all men to the liberal and cheerful practice hereof by the sweetest promises as to instance one for many, Isaiah 58:6. Is not this the fast that I have chosen to loose the bonds of wickedness, to take

off the heavy burdens to let the oppressed go free and to break every Yoke, to deal thy bread to the hungry and to bring the poor that wander into thy house, when thou seest the naked to cover them etc. then shall thy light break forth as the morning, and thy health shall grow speedily, thy righteousness shall go before thee, and the glory of the Lord shall embrace thee, then thou shalt call and the lord shall Answer thee etc. 2:10:[19] If thou power out thy soul to the hungry, then shall thy light spring out in darkness, and the lord shall guide thee continually, and satisfy thy Soul in drought, and make fat thy bones, thou shalt be like a watered Garden, and they shall be of thee that shall build the old waste places etc. on the contrary most heavy curses are laid upon such as are straightened towards the Lord and his people Judges 5:[23]. Curse ye Meroz because the[y] came not to help the Lord etc. Pro. [21:13] He who shutteth his ears from hearing the cry of the poor, he shall cry and shall not be heard: Matt 25:[41] Go ye[20] cursed into everlasting fire etc. [42.] I was hungry and ye fed me not. 2 Cor. 9:[6]. He that soweth sparingly shall reap sparingly.

[20]   Having already set forth the practice of mercy according to the rule of god's law, it will be useful to lay open the grounds of it also being the other part of the Commandment and that is the affection from which this exercise of mercy must arise, the Apostle tells us that this love is the fulfilling of the law,[21] not that it is enough to love our brother and so no further but in regard of the excellency of his parts giving any motion to the other as the Soul to the body and the power it hath to set all the faculties on work in the outward exercise of this duty as when we bid one make the clock strike he doth not lay hand on hammer which is the immediate instrument of the sound but sets on work the first mover or main wheel, knowing that will certainly produce the sound which he intends; so the way to draw men to the works of mercy is not by force of Argument from the goodness or necessity of the work, for though this course may enforce a rational mind to some present Act of mercy as is frequent in experience, yet it cannot work such a habit in a Soul as shall make it prompt upon all occasions to produce the same effect but by framing these affections of love in the heart which will as natively bring forth the other, as any cause doth produce the effect.

[21]   The definition which the Scripture gives us of love is this Love is the bond of perfection.[22] First, it is a bond, or ligament. 2ly, it makes the

work perfect. There is no body but consists of parts and that which knits these parts together gives the body its perfection, because it makes each part so contiguous to other as thereby they do mutually participate with each other, both in strength and infirmity in pleasure and pain, to instance in the most perfect of all bodies, Christ and his church make one body: the several parts of this body considered apart before they were united were as disproportionate and as much disordering as so many contrary qualities or elements but when Christ comes and by his spirit and love knits all these parts to himself and each other, it is become the most perfect and best proportioned body in the world Eph. 4:16. Christ by whom all the body being knit together by every joint for the furniture thereof according to the effectual power which is in the measure of every perfection of parts a glorious body without spot or wrinkle the ligaments hereof being Christ or his love for Christ is love 1 John 4:8. So this definition is right Love is the bond of perfection.

[22]   From hence we may frame these Conclusions.

[23]   1 first all true Christians are of one body in Christ 1 Cor. 12: 12–13, 17, 27 Ye are the body of Christ and members of [your?] part.

[24]   2ly. The ligaments of this body which knit together are love.

[25]   3ly. No body can be perfect which wants its proper ligaments.

[26]   4ly. All the parts of this body being thus united are made so contiguous in a special relation as they must needs partake of each others strength and infirmity, joy, and sorrow, weal and woe. 1 Cor. 12:26. If one member suffers all suffer with it, if one be in honor, all rejoice with it.

[27]   5ly. This sensibleness and Sympathy of each others Conditions will necessarily infuse into each part a native desire and endeavor, to strengthen defend preserve and comfort the other.

[28]   To insist a little on this Conclusion being the product of all the former truth hereof will appear both by precept and pattern 1 John 3.10. ye ought to lay down your lives for the brethren[23] Gal. 6:2. bear ye one another's burdens and so fulfill the law of Christ.

[29]   For patterns we have that first of our Savior, who out of his good will in obedience to his father, becoming a part of this body, and being knit with it in the bond of love, found such a native sensibleness of our infirmities and sorrows as he willingly yielded himself to the death to ease the infirmities of the rest of his body and so heal their sorrows: from the like Sympathy of parts did the Apostles and many thousands of the Saints lay down their lives for Christ again, the like we may see in the members of this body among themselves. 1 Rom. 9. Paul could have been content to have been separated from Christ that the Jews might not be cut off from the body:[24] It is very observable which he professeth of his affectionate partaking with every member: who is weak (saith he) and I am not weak? who is offended and I burn not; and again. 2 Cor. 7:13. therefore we are comforted because ye were comforted. of Epaphroditus he speaketh Phil. 2:30. that he regarded not his own life to do him service so Phebe. and others are called the servants of the Church,[25] now it is apparent that they served not for wages or by Constraint but out of love, the like we shall find in the histories of the church in all ages the sweet Sympathy of affections which was in the members of this body one towards another, their cheerfulness in serving and suffering together how liberal they were without repining harborers without grudging and helpful without reproaching and all from hence they had fervent love amongst them which only makes the practice of mercy constant and easy.

[30]   The next consideration is how this love comes to be wrought; Adam in his first estate was a perfect model of mankind in all their generations, and in him this love was perfected in regard of the habit, but Adam Rent in himself from his Creator, rent all his posterity also one from another, whence it comes that every man is borne with this principle in him, to love and seek himself only and thus a man continueth till Christ comes and takes possession of the soul, and infuseth another principle love to God and our brother: And this latter having continual supply from Christ, as the head and root by which he is united get the predominencey in the soul, so by little and little expels the former 1 John 4:7. love cometh of god and everyone that loveth is born of god, so that this love is the fruit of the new birth, and none can have it but the new Creature, now when this quality is thus formed in the souls of men it works like the Spirit upon the dry bones Ezek. 37. bone came to bone, it gathers together the scattered bones of perfect old man Adam and knits them into one body again in Christ whereby a man is become again a living soul.

[31]   The third Consideration is concerning the exercise of this love, which is twofold, inward or outward, the outward hath been handled in the former preface of this discourse, for unfolding the other we must take in our way the maxim of philosophy, simile simli gaudet or like will to like; for as it is things which are carved[26] with disaffection to each other, the ground of it is from a dissimilitude or [blank] arising from the contrary or different nature of things themselves, so the ground of love is an apprehension of some resemblance in the things loved to that which affects it, this is the cause why the Lord loves the Creature, so far as it hath any of his Image in it, he loves his elect because they are like himself, he beholds them in his beloved son: so a mother loves her child, because she thoroughly conceives a resemblance of herself in it. Thus it is between the members of Christ, each discerns by the work of the spirit his own image and resemblance in another, and therefore cannot but love him as he loves himself: Now when the soul which is of sociable nature finds any thing like to itself, it is like Adam when Eve was brought to him, she must have it one with herself this is flesh of my flesh (saith she) and bone of my bone she conceives a great delight in it, therefore she desires nearness and familiarity with it: she hath a greater propensity to do it good and receives such content in it, as fearing in the miscarriage of her beloved she bestows it in the inmost closet of her heart, she will not endure that it shall want any good which she can give it, if by occasion she be withdrawn from the Company of it, she is still looking towards the place where she left her beloved, if she hear it groan she is with it presently, if she find it sad and disconsolate she sighs and mourns with it, she hath no joy, as to see her beloved merry and thriving, if she see it wronged, she cannot bear it without passion, she sets not bounds of her affections, nor hath any thought of reward, she finds recompense enough in the exercise of her love towards it, we may see this Acted to life in Jonathan and David. Jonathan a valiant man endued with the spirit of Christ, so soon as he Discovers the same spirit in David had presently his heart knit to him by this ligament of love, so that it is said he loved him as his own soul, he takes so great pleasure in him that he strips himself to adorn his beloved, his father's kingdom was not so precious to him as his beloved David, David shall have it with all his heart, himself desires no more but that he may be near him to rejoice in his good he chooseth to converse with him in the wilderness even to the hazard of his own life, rather than with the great Courtiers in his father's Palace; when he sees danger towards him, he spares neither care pains,

nor peril to divert it, when Injury was offered his beloved David, he could not bear it, though from his own father, and when they must part for a Season only, they thought their hearts would have broke for sorrow, had not their affections found vent by abundance of Tears: other instances might be brought to show the nature of this affection as of Ruth and Naomi and many others, but this truth is clear enough. If any shall object that it is not possible that love should be bred or upheld without help of requital, it is granted but that is not our cause, for this love is always under reward it never gives, but it always receives with advantage: first, in regard that among members of the same body, love and affection are reciprocal in a most equal and sweet kind of Commerce. 2ly [3ly], in regard of the pleasure and content that the exercise of love carries with it as we may see in the natural body the mouth is all the pains to receive, and mince the food which serves for the nourishment of all the other parts of the body, yet it hath no cause to complain; for first, the other parts send back by secret passages a due proportion of the same nourishment in a better form for the strengthening and comforting the mouth. 2ly the labor of the mouth is accompanied with such pleasure and content as far exceeds the pains it takes: so it is in all the labor of love, among christians, the party loving, reaps love again as was showed before, which the soul covets more than all the wealth of the world. 2ly [4ly]. nothing yields more pleasure and content to the soul than when it finds that which it may love fervently, for to love and live beloved is the soul's paradise, both here and in heaven: In the State of Wedlock there may be many comforts to bear out the troubles of that Condition; but let such as have tried the most, say if there be any sweetness in that Condition comparable to the exercise of mutual love.

[32]   From the former Considerations ariseth these Conclusions.

[33]   1 First, This love among Christians is a real thing not Imaginary.

[34]   2ly. This love is as absolutely necessary to the being of the body of Christ, as the sinews and other ligaments of a natural body are to the being of that body.

[35]   3ly, This love is a divine spiritual nature free, active strong Courageous permanent under valuing all things beneath its proper object, and

of all the graces this makes us nearer to resemble the virtues of our heavenly father.

[36]   4ly, It rests in the love and welfare of its beloved, for the full and certain knowledge of these truths concerning the nature use [and] excellency of this grace, that which the holy ghost hath left recorded 1 Cor. 13.[27] may give full satisfaction which is needful for every true member of this lovely body of the Lord Jesus, to work upon their hearts, by prayer meditation continual exercise at least of the special [power] of this grace till Christ be formed in them and they in him all in each other knit together by this bond of love.

[37]   It rests now to make some application of this discourse by the present design which gave the occasion of writing of it. Herein are 4 things to be propounded: first the persons, 2ly, the work, 3ly, the end, 4ly the means.

[38]   1. For the persons, we are a Company professing ourselves fellow members of Christ, In which respect only though we were absent from each other many miles; and had our employments as far distant, yet we ought to account ourselves knit together by this bond of love, and live in the exercise of it, if we would have comfort of our being in Christ, this was notorious in the practice of the Christians in former times, as is testified of the Waldenses[28] from the mouth of one of the adversaries Aeneas Sylvius,[29] mutuo [solent amare] penè antequam norint they used to love any of their own religion even before they were acquainted with them.

[39]   2ly. for the work we have in hand, it is by a mutual consent through a special overruling providence, and a more than ordinary approbation of the Churches of Christ to seek out a place of Cohabitation and Consortship under a due form of Government both civil and ecclesiastical. In such cases as this the care of the public must oversway all private respects, by which not only conscience,[30] but mere Civil policy doth bind us; for it is a true rule that particular estates cannot subsist in the ruin of the public.

[40]   3ly. The end is to improve our lives to do more service to the Lord the comfort and increase of the body of christ whereof we are members

that ourselves and our posterity may be the better preserved from the Common corruptions of this evil world to serve the Lord and work out our Salvation under the power and purity of his holy Ordinances.

[41]   4ly for the means whereby this must be effected, they are two fold, a Conformity with the work and end we aim at, these we see are extraordinary, therefore we must not content ourselves with usual ordinary means whatsoever we did or ought to have done when we lived in England, the same must we do and more also where we go: That which the most in their Churches maintain as a truth in profession only, we must bring into familiar and constant practice, as in the duty of love we must love brotherly without dissimulation,[31] we must love one another with a pure heart fervently[32] we must bear one another's burdens,[33] we must not look only on our own things, but also on the things of our brethren, neither must we think that the lord will bear with such failings at our hands as he doth from those among whom we have lived, and that for three Reasons.

[42]   1. In regard of the more near bond of marriage, between him and us, wherein he hath taken us to be his after a most strict and peculiar manner which will make him the more Jealous of our love and obedience so he tells the people of Israel, you only have I known of all the families of the earth therefore I will punish you for your Transgressions.[34]

[43]   2ly, because the lord will be sanctified in them that come near him. We know that there were many that corrupted the service of the Lord some setting up Altars before his own, others offering both strange fire and strange Sacrifices also; yet there came no fire from heaven, or other sudden Judgment upon them as did upon Nadab and Abihu[35] who yet we may think did not sin presumptuously.

[44]   3ly, When God gives a special Commission he looks to have it strictly observed in every Article, when he gave Saul a Commission to destroy Amaleck he indented with him upon certain Articles and because he failed in one of the least, and that upon a fair pretence, it lost him the kingdom, which should have been his reward, if he had observed his Commission:[36] Thus stands the cause between God and us we are entered into covenant with him for this work, we have taken out a Commission, the Lord hath given us leave to draw our own Articles we

have professed to enterprise these Actions upon these and these ends, we have hereupon besought him of favor and blessing: now if the Lord shall please to hear us, and bring us in peace to the place we desire, then he hath ratified this Covenant and sealed our Commission, [and] will expect a strict performance of the Articles contained in it, but if we shall neglect the observation of these Articles which are the ends we have propounded, and dissembling with our God, shall fall to embrace this present world and prosecute our carnal intentions, seeking great things for ourselves and our posterity, the Lord will surely break out in wrath against us be revenged of such a perjured people and make us know the price of the breach of such a Covenant.

[45]   Now the only way to avoid the shipwreck and to provide for our posterity is to follow the Counsel of Micah, to do Justly, to love mercy, to walk humbly with our God,[37] for this end, we must be knit together in this work as one man, we must entertain each other in brotherly Affection, we must be willing to abridge ourselves of our superfluities, for the supply of other necessities, we must uphold a familiar Commerce together in all meekness, gentleness, patience and liberality, we must delight in each other, make each others' Conditions our own rejoice together, mourn together, labor, and suffer together, always having before our eyes our Commission and Community in the work, our Community as members of the same body, so shall we keep the unity of the spirit in the bond of peace,[38] the Lord will be our God and delight to dwell among us, as his own people and will command a blessing upon us in all our ways, so that we shall see much more of his wisdom power goodness and truth than formerly we have been acquainted with, we shall find that the God of Israel is among us, when ten of us shall be able to resist a thousand of our enemies, when he shall make us a praise and glory, that men shall say of succeeding plantations: the Lord make it like that of New England: for we must consider that we shall be as a City Upon a Hill,[39] the eyes of all people are upon us; so that if we should deal falsely with our god in the work we have undertaken and so cause him to withdraw his present help from us, we shall be made a story and a by-word through the world, we shall open the mouths of enemies to speak evil of the ways of god and all professors for god's sake; we shall shame the faces of many of god's worthy servants, and cause their prayers to be turned into Curses upon us till we be consumed out of the good land where we are going: And to shut up this discourse with that

exhortation of Moses that faithful servant of the Lord in his last farewell to Israel Deut. 30. Beloved, there is now set before us life, and good, and death and evil in that we are Commanded this day to love the Lord our God, and to love one another to walk in his ways and to keep his Commandments and his Ordinances, and his laws, and the Articles of our Covenant with him that we may live and be multiplied, and that the Lord our God may bless us in the land where we go to possess it: But if our hearts shall turn away so that we will not obey, but shall be seduced and worship [serve] other Gods our pleasure, and profits, and serve them; it is propounded unto us this day, we shall surely perish out of the good Land whither we pass over this vast Sea to possess it;

> Therefore let us choose life,
> that we, and our Seed,
> may live; by obeying his
> voice, and cleaving to him,
> for he is our life, and
> our prosperity.

Notes

1. As explained in chapter one, this is the text as found in the *Winthrop Papers* (II: 282–95), but I have modernized all archaic spellings and numbered each paragraph (treating all of Winthrop's stand-alone sentences as a paragraph) to help the reader follow my interpretation in chapters one and two.

2. This introductory passage comes from a cover note found on the only known seventeenth-century manuscript of the "Model" speech (owned by the New-York Historical Society). It is clear that the cover note was written by someone other than Winthrop and that it was added later. For the various views of when, exactly, the address may have been delivered and the company departed, see Dawson, "John Winthrop's Rite of Passage."

3. The editors of the *Winthrop Papers* (hereafter WP) note that this might be compared with the "difference between principalitie and popularie" phrase found in Vol. I: 37.

4. WP notes that the scriptural references here are Genesis 18–19 and Judges 19:16–21. There is also a suggestion that for the Genesis passages, there is relevant marginalia in the Geneva version of the Bible—the version Winthrop is quoting in this sermon.

5. WP notes scriptural reference Gal. 6:10

6. This reference is unclear; neither 1 Cor. 2:6, nor 2 Cor. 2:6 seems to link to this passage.

7. WP notes scriptural reference 1 Tim. 5:8.

8. WP notes scriptural reference Eccl. 2:14.

9. *WP* notes Matt. 21:2–3.

10. *WP* notes the servant is Zerubbabel as found in Ezra 3 and Haggai 2—see marginalia in Geneva text.

11. *WP* notes 1 Kings 17:8–24 and Luke 5:26.

12. *WP* notes Deut. 15:7–11 and Lev. 25:35–42.

13. This is the reference that appears in the *WP* text, but certainly Winthrop meant Matt. 7:12.

14. *WP* notes Acts 2:44–45 and 4:32–35.

15. *WP* notes Nehemiah 5 and specifically quotes the from the pithy Geneva marginalia: "By nature the rich is not better than the poor."

16. The use of the phrase "here in England" suggests to Dawson that when Winthrop delivered the address, he may have been on board the *Arbella*, but that the ship had not yet left the shores of England (Dawson, "John Winthrop's Rite of Passage," 227).

17. *WP* notes Luke 19:8–10 and Acts 9:36–42; 10.

18. *WP* explains that Bishop John Hooper was a famous Protestant martyr who regularly fed the poor of Worcester.

19. *WP* simply prints 2:10; however, the scripture quoted is not Isaiah 2:10 but rather Isaiah 58:10.

20. Speaking of those who failed to attend to the hungry, thirsty, naked, and imprisoned.

21. *WP* notes Romans 13:10.

22. *WP* notes Col. 3:14, which reads in the Geneva version: "love, which is the bond of perfectness."

23. Winthrop, *[Unabridged] Journal of John Winthrop*, 6, notes that clearly the reference should be 1 John 3:16.

24. See verses 3–4.

25. *WP* notes Romans 16:1.

26. *WP* notes that the text is "corrupted" here (the word printed in *WP* is "carued").

27. Perhaps the definitive New Testament statement on charity.

28. A twelfth-century Protestant sect founded by Peter Waldo in the French and Italian Alps, later massacred in 1545 by Francis I.

29. One of the Roman popes, Pius II, who opposed the group.

30. *WP* notes that above the copyist's "consequence" a later hand-interlined "conscience."

31. *WP* notes Romans 12:9–10.

32. *WP* notes I Peter 1:22.

33. *WP* notes Galatians 6:2.

34. *WP* notes Amos 3:2.

35. *WP* notes Leviticus 10:1–2.

36. *WP* notes 1 Samuel 15, 28:16–18.

37. *WP* notes Micah 6:8.

38. *WP* notes Ephesians 4:3.

39. *WP* notes Matt. 5:14.

APPENDIX B

Thomas Jefferson's "original Rough draught" of the Declaration of Independence[1]

A Declaration of the Representatives of the UNITED STATES OF AMERICA, in General Congress assembled.

When in the course of human events it becomes necessary for a people to advance from that subordination in which they have hitherto remained, & to assume among the powers of the earth the equal & independant station to which the laws of nature & of nature's god entitle them, a decent respect to the opinions of mankind requires that they should declare the causes which impel them to the change.

We hold these truths to be sacred & undeniable; that all men are created equal & independant, that from that equal creation they derive rights inherent & inalienable, among which are the preservation of life, & liberty, & the pursuit of happiness; that to secure these ends, governments are instituted among men, deriving their just powers from the consent of the governed; that whenever any form of government shall become destructive of these ends, it is the right of the people to alter or to abolish it, & to institute new government, laying it's foundation on such principles & organising it's powers in such form, as to them shall seem most likely to effect their safety & happiness. prudence indeed will dictate that governments long established should not be changed for light & transient causes: and accordingly all experience hath shewn that mankind are more disposed to suffer while evils are sufferable, than to right themselves by abolishing the forms to which they are accustomed. but when a long train of abuses & usurpations, begun at a distinguished period, & pursuing invariably the same object, evinces a design to subject them to arbitrary power, it is their right, it is their duty, to throw off such government & to provide new guards for their future security. such has been the patient sufferance of these colonies; & such is now the necessity which constrains them to expunge their former systems of government. the history of his present majesty, is a history of unremitting

injuries and usurpations, among which no one fact stands single or solitary to contradict the uniform tenor of the rest, all of which have in
direct object the establishment of an absolute tyranny over these states.
to prove this, let facts be submitted to a candid world, for the truth of
which we pledge a faith yet unsullied by falsehood.

he has refused his assent to laws the most wholesome and necessary
for the public good:

he has forbidden his governors to pass laws of immediate & pressing
importance, unless suspended in their operation till his assent should be
obtained; and when so suspended, he has neglected utterly to attend to
them.

he has refused to pass other laws for the accomodation of large dis-
tricts of people unless those people would relinquish the right of representation, a right inestimable to them, formidable to tyrants alone:

he has dissolved Representative houses repeatedly & continually, for
opposing with manly firmness his invasions on the rights of the people:

he has refused for a long space of time to cause others to be elected,
whereby the legislative powers, incapable of annihilation, have returned
to the people at large for their exercise, the state remaining in the mean
time exposed to all the dangers of invasion from without, & convulsions
within:

he has endeavored to prevent the population of these states; for that
purpose obstructing the laws for naturalization of foreigners; refusing to
pass others to encourage their migrations hither; & raising the conditions of new appropriations of lands:

he has suffered the administration of justice totally to cease in some
of these colonies, refusing his assent to laws for establishing judiciary
powers:

he has made our judges dependant on his will alone, for the tenure of
their offices, and amount of their salaries:

he has erected a multitude of new offices by a self-assumed power, &
sent hither swarms of officers to harrass our people & eat out their
substance:

he has kept among us in times of peace standing armies & ships of
war:

he has affected to render the military, independant of & superior to
the civil power:

he has combined with others to subject us to a jurisdiction foreign to
our constitutions and unacknoleged by our laws; giving his assent to

their pretended acts of legislation, for quartering large bodies of armed troops among us;

for protecting them by a mock-trial from punishment for any murders they should commit on the inhabitants of these states;

for cutting off our trade with all parts of the world;

for imposing taxes on us without our consent;

for depriving us of the benefits of trial by jury;

for transporting us beyond seas to be tried for pretended offences: for taking away our charters, & altering fundamentally the forms of our governments;

for suspending our own legislatures & declaring themselves invested with power to legislate for us in all cases whatsoever:

he has abdicated government here, withdrawing his governors, & declaring us out of his allegiance & protection:

he has plundered our seas, ravaged our coasts, burnt our towns & destroyed the lives of our people:

he is at this time transporting large armies of foreign mercenaries to compleat the works of death, desolation & tyranny, already begun with circumstances of cruelty & perfidy unworthy the head of a civilized nation:

he has endeavored to bring on the inhabitants of our frontiers the merciless Indian savages, whose known rule of warfare is an undistinguished destruction of all ages, sexes, & conditions of existence:

he has incited treasonable insurrections in our fellow-subjects, with the allurements of forfeiture & confiscation of our property:

he has waged cruel war against human nature itself, violating it's most sacred rights of life & liberty in the persons of a distant people who never offended him, captivating & carrying them into slavery in another hemisphere, or to incur miserable death in their transportation thither. this piratical warfare, the opprobrium of *infidel* powers, is the warfare of the CHRISTIAN king of Great Britain. determined to keep open a market where MEN should be bought & sold, he has prostituted his negative for suppressing every legislative attempt to prohibit or to restrain this execrable commerce: and that this assemblage of horrors might want no fact of distinguished die, he is now exciting those very people to rise in arms among us, and to purchase that liberty of which *he* has deprived them by murdering the people upon whom *he* also obtruded them; thus paying off former crimes committed against the *liberties* of one people, with crimes which he urges them to commit against the *lives* of another.

in every stage of these oppressions we have petitioned for redress in the most humble terms; our repeated petitions have been answered by repeated injury. a prince whose character is thus marked by every act which may define a tyrant, is unfit to be the ruler of a people who mean to be free. future ages will scarce believe that the hardiness of one man, adventured within the short compass of 12 years only, on so many acts of tyranny without a mask, over a people fostered & fixed in principles of liberty.

Nor have we been wanting in attentions to our British brethren. we have warned them from time to time of attempts by their legislature to extend a jurisdiction over these our states. we have reminded them of the circumstances of our emigration & settlement here, no one of which could warrant so strange a pretension: that these were effected at the expence of our own blood & treasure, unassisted by the wealth or the strength of Great Britain: that in constituting indeed our several forms of government, we had adopted one common king, thereby laying a foundation for perpetual league & amity with them: but that submission to their parliament was no part of our constitution, nor ever in idea, if history may be credited: and we appealed to their native justice & magnanimity, as well as to the ties of our common kindred to disavow these usurpations which were likely to interrupt our correspondence & connection. they too have been deaf to the voice of justice & of consanguinity, & when occasions have been given them, by the regular course of their laws, of removing from their councils the disturbers of our harmony, they have by their free election re-established them in power. at this very time too they are permitting their chief magistrate to send over not only soldiers of our common blood, but Scotch & foreign mercenaries to invade & deluge us in blood. these facts have given the last stab to agonizing affection, and manly spirit bids us to renounce for ever these unfeeling brethren. we must endeavor to forget our former love for them, and to hold them as we hold the rest of mankind, enemies in war, in peace friends. we might have been a free & great people together; but a communication of grandeur & of freedom it seems is below their dignity. be it so, since they will have it: the road to glory & happiness is open to us too; we will climb it in a separate state, and acquiesce in the necessity which pronounces our everlasting Adieu!

We therefore the representatives of the United States of America in General Congress assembled do, in the name & by authority of the good people of these states, reject and renounce all allegiance & subjection to the kings of Great Britain & all others who may hereafter claim by, through, or under them; we utterly dissolve & break off all political connection which may have heretofore subsisted between us & the people or parliament of Great Britain; and finally we do assert and declare these colonies to be free and independant states, and that as free & independant states they shall hereafter have power to levy war, conclude peace, contract alliances, establish commerce, & to do all other acts and things which independent states may of right do. And for the support of this declaration we mutually pledge to each other our lives, our fortunes, & our sacred honour.

Note

1. As found in *The Papers of Thomas Jefferson*, 1:423–27.

APPENDIX C

Thomas Jefferson's First Inaugural[1]

March 4, 1801

Friends & Fellow Citizens,

Called upon to undertake the duties of the first Executive office of our country, I avail myself of the presence of that portion of my fellow citizens which is here assembled to express my grateful thanks for the favor with which they have been pleased to look towards me, to declare a sincere consciousness that the task is above my talents, and that I approach it with those anxious and awful presentiments which the greatness of the charge, and the weakness of my powers so justly inspire. A rising nation, spread over a wide and fruitful land, traversing all the seas with the rich productions of their industry, engaged in commerce with nations who feel power and forget right, advancing rapidly to destinies beyond the reach of mortal eye; when I contemplate these transcendent objects, and see the honour, the happiness, and the hopes of this beloved country committed to the issue and the auspices of this day, I shrink from the contemplation & humble myself before the magnitude of the undertaking. Utterly indeed should I despair, did not the presence of many, whom I here see, remind me, that, in the other high authorities provided by our constitution, I shall find resources of wisdom, of virtue, and of zeal, on which to rely under all difficulties. To you, then, gentlemen, who are charged with the sovereign functions of legislation, and to those associated with you, I look with encouragement for that guidance and support which may enable us to steer with safety the vessel in which we are all embarked, amidst the conflicting elements of a troubled world.

During the contest of opinion through which we have passed, the animation of discussions and of exertions has sometimes worn an aspect which might impose on strangers unused to think freely, and to speak and to write what they think; but this being now decided by the voice of the nation, announced according to the rules of the constitution all will of course arrange themselves under the will of the law, and unite in common efforts for the common good. All too will bear in mind this sacred principle, that though the will of the majority is in all cases to prevail, that will, to be rightful, must be reasonable; that the minority possess their equal rights, which equal laws must protect, and to violate would be oppression. Let us then, fellow citizens, unite with one heart and one mind, let us restore to social intercourse that harmony and affection without which liberty, and even life itself, are but dreary things. And let us reflect that having banished from our land that religious intolerance under which mankind so long bled and suffered, we have yet gained little if we countenance a political intolerance, as despotic, as wicked, and capable of as bitter and bloody persecutions. During the throes and convulsions of the ancient world, during the agonising spasms of infuriated man, seeking through blood and slaughter his long lost liberty, it was not wonderful that the agitation of the billows should reach even this distant and peaceful shore; that this should be more felt and feared by some and less by others; and should divide opinions as to measures of safety; but every difference of opinion is not a difference of principle. We have called by different names brethren of the same principle. We are all republicans: we are all federalists. If there be any among us who would wish to dissolve this Union, or to change its republican form, let them stand undisturbed as monuments of the safety with which error of opinion may be tolerated, where reason is left free to combat it. I know indeed that some honest men fear that a republican government cannot be strong; that this government is not strong enough. But would the honest patriot, in the full tide of successful experiment, abandon a government which has so far kept us free and firm, on the theoretic and visionary fear, that this government, the world's best hope, may, by possibility, want energy to preserve itself? I trust not. I believe this, on the contrary, the strongest government on earth. I believe it the only one, where every man, at the call of the law, would fly to the standard of the law, and would meet invasions of the public order as his own personal concern.—Sometimes it is said that man cannot be trusted with the government of himself. Can he then be trusted with the government of others? Or have we found angels, in the form of kings, to govern him? Let history answer this question.

Let us then, with courage and confidence, pursue our own federal and republican principles; our attachment to union and representative government. Kindly separated by nature and a wide ocean from the exterminating havoc of one quarter of the globe; too high minded to endure the degradations of the others, possessing a chosen country, with room enough for our descendants to the thousandth and thousandth generation, entertaining a due sense of our equal right to the use of our own faculties, to the acquisitions of our own industry, to honor and confidence from our fellow citizens, resulting not from birth, but from our actions and their sense of them, enlightened by a benign religion, professed indeed and practised in various forms, yet all of them inculcating honesty, truth, temperance, gratitude and the love of man, acknowledging and adoring an overruling providence, which by all its dispensations proves that it delights in the happiness of man here, and his greater happiness hereafter; with all these blessings, what more is necessary to make us a happy and a prosperous people? Still one thing more, fellow citizens, a wise and frugal government, which shall restrain men from injuring one another, shall leave them otherwise free to regulate their own pursuits of industry and improvement, and shall not take from the mouth of labor the bread it has earned. This is the sum of good government; and this is necessary to close the circle of our felicities.

About to enter, fellow citizens, on the exercise of duties which comprehend every thing dear and valuable to you, it is proper you should understand what I deem the essential principles of our government, and consequently those which ought to shape its administration. I will compress them within the narrowest compass they will bear, stating the general principle, but not all its limitations.—Equal and exact justice to all men, of whatever state or persuasion, religious or political:—peace, commerce, and honest friendship with all nations, entangling alliances with none:—the support of the state governments in all their rights, as the most competent administrations for our domestic concerns, and the surest bulwarks against anti-republican tendencies:—the preservation of the General government in its whole constitutional vigor, as the sheet anchor of our peace at home, and safety abroad: a jealous care of the right of election by the people, a mild and safe corrective of abuses which are lopped by the sword of revolution where peaceable remedies are unprovided:—absolute acquiescence in the decisions of the majority, the vital principle of republics, from which is no appeal but to force, the vital principle and immediate parent of the despotism:—a well disciplined militia, our best reliance in peace, and for the first moments of war, till regulars may relieve them:—the supremacy of the civil over the military authority:—economy in the public expence, that labor may be lightly burthened:—the honest payment of our debts and sacred preservation of the public faith:—encouragement of agriculture, and of commerce as its handmaid:—the diffusion of information, and arraignment of all abuses at the bar of the public reason:—freedom of religion; freedom of the press; and freedom of person, under the protection of the Habeas Corpus:—and trial by juries impartially selected. These principles form the bright constellation, which has gone before us and guided our steps through an age of revolution and reformation. The wisdom of our sages, and blood of our heroes have been devoted to their attainment:—they should be the creed of our political faith; the text of civic instruction, the touchstone by which to try the services of those we trust; and should we wander from them in moments of error or of alarm, let us hasten to retrace our steps, and to regain the road which alone leads to peace, liberty and safety.

I repair then, fellow citizens, to the post you have assigned me. With experience enough in subordinate offices to have seen the difficulties of this the greatest of all, I have learnt to expect that it will rarely fall to the lot of imperfect man to retire from this station with the reputation, and the favor, which bring him into it. Without pretensions to that high confidence you reposed in our first and greatest revolutionary character, whose pre-eminent services had entitled him to the first place in his country's love, and destined for him the fairest page in the volume of faithful history, I ask so much confidence only as may give firmness and effect to the legal administration of your affairs. I shall often go wrong through defect of judgment. When right, I shall often be thought wrong by those whose positions will not command a view of the whole ground. I ask your indulgence for my own errors, which will never be intentional; and your support against the errors of others, who may condemn what they would not if seen in all its parts. The approbation implied by your suffrage, is a great consolation to me for the past; and my future solicitude will be, to retain the good opinion of those who have bestowed it in advance, to conciliate that of others by doing them all the good in my power, and to be instrumental to the happiness and freedom of all.

Relying then on the patronage of your good will, I advance with obedience to the work, ready to retire from it whenever you become sensible how much better choices it is in your power to make. And may that infinite power, which rules the destinies of the universe, lead our councils to what is best, and give them a favorable issue for your peace and prosperity.

Note

1. As found in *The Papers of Thomas Jefferson*, Volume 33: 148–52.

APPENDIX D

Abraham Lincoln's Second Inaugural[1]

March 4, 1865

[Fellow Countrymen:]

At this second appearing to take the oath of the presidential office, there is less occasion for an extended address than there was at the first. Then a statement, somewhat in detail, of a course to be pursued, seemed fitting and proper. Now, at the expiration of four years, during which public declarations have been constantly called forth on every point and phase of the great contest which still absorbs the attention, and engrosses the enerergies [sic] of the nation, little that is new could be presented. The progress of our arms, upon which all else chiefly depends, is as well known to the public as to myself; and it is, I trust, reasonably satisfactory and encouraging to all. With high hope for the future, no prediction in regard to it is ventured.

On the occasion corresponding to this four years ago, all thoughts were anxiously directed to an impending civil-war. All dreaded it—all sought to avert it. While the inaugeral address was being delivered from this place, devoted altogether to *saving* the Union without war, insurgent agents were in the city seeking to *destroy* it without war—seeking to dissol[v]e the Union, and divide effects, by negotiation. Both parties deprecated war; but one of them would *make* war rather than let the nation survive; and the other would *accept* war rather than let it perish. And the war came.

One eighth of the whole population were colored slaves, not distributed generally over the Union, but localized in the Southern part of it. These slaves constituted a peculiar and powerful interest. All knew that this interest was, somehow, the cause of the war. To strengthen, perpetuate, and extend this interest was the object for which the insurgents would rend the Union, even by war; while the government claimed no right to do more than to restrict the territorial enlargement of it. Neither party expected for the war, the magnitude, or the duration, which it has already attained. Neither anticipated that the *cause* of the conflict might cease with, or even before, the conflict itself should cease. Each looked for an easier triumph, and a result less fundamental and astounding. Both read the same Bible, and pray to the same God; and each invokes His aid against the other. It may seem strange that any men should dare to ask a just God's assistance in wringing their bread from the sweat of other men's faces; but let us judge not that we be not judged. The prayers of both could not be answered; that of neither has been answered fully. The Almighty has His own purposes. "Woe unto the world because of offences! for it must needs be that offences come; but woe to that man by whom the offence cometh!" If we shall suppose that American Slavery is one of those offences which, in the providence of God, must needs come, but which, having continued through His appointed time, He now wills to remove, and that He gives to both North and South, this terrible war, as the woe due to those by whom the offence came, shall we discern therein any departure from those divine attributes which the believers in a Living God always ascribe to Him? Fondly do we hope—fervently do we pray—that this mighty scourge of war may speedily pass away. Yet, if God wills that it continue, until all the wealth piled by the bond-man's two hundred and fifty years of unrequited toil shall be sunk, and until every drop of blood drawn with the lash, shall be paid by another drawn with the sword, as was said three thousand years ago, so still it must be said "the judgments of the Lord, are true and righteous altogether."

With malice toward none; with charity for all; with firmness in the right, as God gives us to see the right, let us strive on to finish the work we are in; to bind up the nation's wounds; to care for him who shall have borne the battle, and for his widow, and his orphan—to do all which may achieve and cherish a just, and a lasting peace, among ourselves, and with all nations.

Note

1. As found in *The Collected Works of Abraham Lincoln*, 8:332–33.

BIBLIOGRAPHY

Achtemeier, Paul J., ed. *Harper's Bible Dictionary*. San Francisco: Harper and Row, 1985.

Adams, Brooks. *The Emancipation of Massachusetts: The Dream and the Reality*. Boston: Houghton, 1962.

Adams, Charles F. *Three Episodes of Massachusetts History*. Boston: Houghton Mifflin, 1892.

Adams, John, *Papers of John Adams*. Edited by Robert J. Taylor. Cambridge, MA: Harvard University Press, 1977.

———. *The Revolutionary Writings of John Adams*. Edited by C. Bradley Thompson. Indianapolis, IN: Liberty Fund, 2000.

Addams, Jane. *The Social Thought of Jane Addams*. Edited by Christopher Lasch. New York: Irvington, 1982.

———. *Twenty Years at Hull-House*. New York: Macmillan Company, 1912.

Aldrich, John H. *Why Parties? The Origin and Transformation of Political Parties in America*. Chicago: University of Chicago Press, 1995.

Aldrich, John H., and Ruth W Grant. "The Antifederalists, the First Congress, and the First Parties." *The Journal of Politics* 55 (May 1993): 295–326.

Amory, Hugh, and David D. Hall, ed. *The Colonial Book in the Atlantic World*. Cambridge: Cambridge University Press, 2000.

Anderson, Douglas. *A House Undivided: Domesticity and Community in American Literature*. Cambridge: Cambridge University Press, 1990.

Aquinas, Thomas. *Summa Theologica*. Translated by Fathers of the English Dominican Province. New York: Benzinger Brothers, Inc., 1947.

Auchincloss, Louis. *The Winthrop Covenant*. Boston: Houghton Mifflin, 1976.

Augustine. *On Christian Doctrine*. Translated by D. W. Robertson Jr. New York: Liberal Arts Press, 1958.

Bacon, Francis. *New Atlantis and the Great Instauration*. Arlington Heights, IL: Harlan Davidson, 1989.

Banks, Charles Edward. *The New Organon and Related Writings*. New York: Macmillan Publishing Company, 1960.

―――. *The Winthrop Fleet of 1630: An Account of the Vessels, the Voyage, the Passengers and Their English Homes from Original Authorities.* Baltimore: Genealogical Publishing Co., 1961.

Banning, Lance. *Jefferson and Madison: Three Conversations from the Founding.* Madison, WI: Madison House Publishers, Inc, 1995.

―――. *The Jefferson Persuasion: Evolution of a Party Ideology.* Ithaca, NY: Cornell University Press, 1978.

Baritz, Loren. *City on a Hill: A History of Ideas and Myths in America.* New York: Wiley, 1964.

Barker, Kenneth, ed. *The NIV Study Bible.* Grand Rapids, MI: Zondervan Publishing House, 1995.

Becker, Carl L. *The Declaration of Independence: A Study in the History of Political Ideas.* New York: A. A. Knopf, 1942.

Bellah, Robert N. "Civil Religion in America." *Daedalus* (2005): 40–56.

Bercovitch, Sacvan. *The American Jeremiad.* Madison: University of Wisconsin Press, 1978.

―――. *The Puritan Origins of the American Self.* New Haven, CT: Yale University Press, 1975.

Berlant, Lauren. *The Anatomy of a National Fantasy: Hawthorne, Utopia, and Everyday Life.* Chicago: University of Chicago Press, 1991.

Berlin, Isaiah. *Four Essays on Liberty.* New York: Oxford University Press, 1969.

―――. *The Proper Study of Mankind: An Anthology of Essays.* Edited by Henry Hardy and Roger Hausheer. New York: Farrar, Straus and Giroux, 1998.

Bloom, Allan, ed. *Confronting the Constitution: The Challenge to Locke, Montesquieu, Jefferson, and the Federalists from Utilitarianism, Historicism, Marxism, Freudianism, Pragmatism, Existentialism.* Washington: AEI Press, 1990.

Boorstin, Daniel J. *The Lost World of Thomas Jefferson.* New York: H. Holt, 1948.

Boritt, Gabor. *Lincoln and the Economics of the American Dream.* Memphis, TN: Memphis State University Press, 1978.

Boyd, Julian P., and Gerard W. Gawalt. *The Declaration of Independence: The Evolution of the Text.* Washington, DC: Library of Congress, 1999.

Bozeman, Theodore Dwight. *To Live Ancient Lives: The Primitivist Dimension in Puritanism.* Chapel Hill: University of North Carolina Press, 1988.

Bremer, Francis J. *John Winthrop: America's Forgotten Founding Father.* Oxford: Oxford University Press, 2003.

―――. *The Puritan Experiment.* New York: St. Martin's Press, 1976.

―――. "Remembering—and Forgetting—John Winthrop and the Puritan Founders," *The Massachusetts Historical Review* http://www.historycoop erative.org/journals/mhr/6/bremer.html (March 1, 2006).

———. "To Live Exemplary Lives: Puritans and Puritan Communities as Lofty Lights." *Seventeenth Century* 7 (Spring 1992): 27–39.

Brooks, Noah. *Washington in Lincoln's Time*. New York: The Century Co., 1895.

Brooks, Van Wyck. *Van Wyck Brooks: The Early Years*. Edited by Claire Sprague. Boston: Northeastern University Press, 1993.

Brown, Katherine. "Freemanship in Puritan Massachusetts." *The American Historical Review* 59, no. 4 (1954): 865–83.

———. "A Note on the Puritan Concept of Aristocracy." *The Mississippi Valley Historical Review* 41, no. 1 (1954): 105–12.

Browne, Stephen H. *Jefferson's Call for Nationhood: The First Inaugural Address*. College Station: Texas A&M University Press, 2003.

Burlingame, Michael. *The Inner World of Abraham Lincoln*. Chicago: University of Illinois Press, 1994.

Burstein, Andrew. *The Inner Jefferson: Portrait of a Grieving Artist*. Charlottesville: University Press of Virginia, 1995.

Bush, George. Excerpts from President Bush's Thanksgiving Day Proclamation. *Washington Post*, November 26, 1992, sec A, p. 27.

Butterfield, Lyman H. "The Dream of Benjamin Rush: The Reconciliation of John Adams and Thomas Jefferson." *The Yale Review* 40, no. 2 (1950): 297–319.

Cappon, Lester J. *The Adams–Jefferson Letters: The Complete Correspondence between Thomas Jefferson and Abigail and John Adams*. Chapel Hill: University of North Carolina Press, 1959.

Carroll, James. *Mortal Friends*. Boston: Morrissey Street LTD, 1978.

Carwardine, Richard. *Lincoln*. Harlow, U.K.: Pearson Longman, 2003.

Cassirer, Ernst. *Language and Myth*. New York, Dover Publications, 1946.

Catton, Bruce. *Never Call Retreat*. New York: Simon and Schuster, 1965.

Cherry, Conrad, ed. *God's New Israel: Religious Interpretations of American Destiny*. Chapel Hill: University of North Carolina Press, 1998.

Chesterton, G. K. *The Wisdom of Father Brown*. London: Cassell, 1928.

Clinton, William J. "Commencement Address at Portland State University in Portland Oregon, 13 June 1988." *Weekly Compilation of Presidential Documents*, June 19, 1998.

———. "Commencement Address at the United States Coast Guard Academy in New London Connecticut, 17 May 2000." *Weekly Compilation of Presidential Documents*, May 19, 2000.

CNN. "Governor George W. Bush Delivers Remarks," December 13, 2000. *Election 2000*. At http://www.cnn.com/ELECTION/2000/transcripts/121300/bush.html. Accessed June 21, 2005.

Cobb, William W., Jr. *The American Foundation Myth in Vietnam*. Lanham, MD: University Press of America, 1998.

294   BIBLIOGRAPHY

Colacurcio, Michael J. *Doctrine and the Difference: Essays in the Literature of New England.* New York: Routledge, 1997.
————. *The Province of Piety: Moral History in Hawthorne's Early Tales.* Durham, NC: Duke University Press, 1995.
————. "The Woman's Own Choice": Sex Metaphor, and the Puritan "Sources" of *The Scarlet Letter.*" In *New Essays on "The Scarlet Letter,"* edited by Michael Colacurcio. Cambridge: Cambridge University Press, 1985.
Coles, Romand. *Rethinking Generosity: Critical Theory and the Politics of Caritas.* Ithaca, NY: Cornell University Press, 1997.
Corlett, William S., Jr. "The Availability of Lincoln's Political Religion." *Political Theory* (November 1982): 520–40.
————. *Community without Unity.* Durham, NC: Duke University Press, 1989.
Cunningham, Noble E., Jr. *The Inaugural Addresses of President Thomas Jefferson 1801 and 1805.* Columbia: University of Missouri Press, 2003.
Cuomo, Mario. "A Tale of Two Cities." Speech delivered July 16, 1984, at the Democratic National Convention, San Francisco. *Associated Press,* n.d.
Dawson, Hugh J. "'Christian Charitie' as Colonial Discourse: Rereading Winthrop's Sermon in Its English Context." *Early American Literature* 33, no. 2 (1998): 117–48.
————. "John Winthrop's Rite of Passage: The Origins of the 'Christian Charitie' Discourse." *Early American Literature* 26, no. 3 (1991): 219–231.
Delbanco, Andrew. *The Puritan Ordeal.* Cambridge, MA: Harvard University Press, 1989.
————. *The Real American Dream: A Meditation on Hope.* Cambridge, MA: Harvard University Press, 2000.
————. *Required Reading: Why Our American Classics Matter Now.* New York, The Noonday Press, 1997.
D'Elia, Donald. "Jefferson, Rush, and the Limits of Philosophical Friendship." In *Proceedings of the American Philosophical Society.* Vol. 117. No. 5. Philadelphia: The American Philosophical Society, 1973.
Deneen, Patrick J. *Democratic Faith.* Princeton, NJ: Princeton University Press, 2005.
Diggins, John Patrick. *On Hallowed Ground: Abraham Lincoln and the Foundations of American History.* New Haven, CT: Yale University Press, 2000.
————. *The Lost Soul of American Politics.* Chicago: University of Chicago Press, 1984.
Donald, David Herbert. *Lincoln.* New York: Simon & Schuster, 1995.
Donovan, Josephine. *Uncle Tom's Cabin: Evil, Affliction, and Redemptive Love.* Boston: Twayne Publishers, 1991.

Douglass, Frederick. *The Frederick Douglass Papers*. New Haven, CT: Yale University Press, 1991.

Dreisbach, Daniel. "'Sowing Useful Truths and Principles': The Danbury Baptists, Thomas Jefferson, and the 'Wall of Separation.'" *Journal of Church and State* 39 (Summer 1997): 455–502.

———. *Thomas Jefferson and the Wall of Separation between Church and State*. New York: New York University Press, 2002.

Dukakis, Michael S. "The Democrats in Atlanta." *New York Times*, Friday, July 22, 1988, sec. A, p. 10.

Dworkin, Ronald. *A Matter of Principle*. Cambridge, MA: Harvard University Press, 1985.

Elazar, Daniel J. *Covenant and Constitutionalism: The Great Frontier and the Matrix of Federal Democracy*. Vol. 3, *The Covenant Tradition in Politics*. New Brunswick, NJ: Transaction Publishers, 1998.

Ellis, Joseph J. *American Sphinx: The Character of Thomas Jefferson*. New York: Alfred A. Knopf, 1997.

———. *Founding Brothers*. New York: Alfred A. Knopf, 2000.

Elshtain, Jean Bethke. *Just War Theory*. New York: New York University Press, 1992,

Fehrenbacher, Don E., and Virginia Fehrenbacher, eds. *Recollected Works of Abraham Lincoln*. Stanford, CA: Stanford University Press, 1996.

Ferling, John. *Adams vs. Jefferson: The Tumultuous Election of 1800*. Oxford: Oxford University Press, 2004.

Fischer, David Hackett. *Albion's Seed: Four British Folkways in America*. New York: Oxford University Press, 1989.

Fitzgerald, F. Scott. "The Crack-Up." In *American Literary Masters*, vol. 2. Edited by Charles R. Anderson. New York: Holt, Rinehart and Winston, 1965.

Foner, Philip S., ed. *The Life and Writings of Frederick Douglass: Early Years 1817–1849*. New York: International Publishers, 1975.

Foster, Stephen. *The Long Argument: English Puritanism and the Shaping of New England Culture, 1570–1700*. Chapel Hill: University of North Carolina Press, 1991.

———. *Their Solitary Way: The Puritan Social Ethic in the First Century of Settlement in New England*. New Haven, CT: Yale University Press, 1971.

Freeman, Douglass Southall. *Lee: An Abridgement in One Volume of the Four-Volume R. E. Lee*. New York: Simon and Schuster, 1997.

Freud, Sigmund. *Civilization and Its Discontents*. Translated and edited by James Strachey. New York: W. W. Norton and Company, 1989.

Frisch, Morton J., and Richard G. Stevens, ed. *American Political Thought*. Itasca, IL: F. E. Peacock, 1983.

Gaustad, Edwin S. *Sworn on the Altar of God*. Grand Rapids, MI: Eerdmans, 1996.

Gilchrist, Brent. *Cultus Americanus: Varieties of the Liberal Tradition in American Political Culture, 1600–1865*. Lanham, MD: Lexington Books, 2007.

Gomes, Peter, "A Pilgrims Progress: The Bible as Civic Blueprint," *New York Times Magazine*, April 18, 1999, 102–103.

Goodwin, Doris Kearns. *Team of Rivals: The Political Genius of Abraham Lincoln*. New York: Simon and Schuster, 2005.

Gossett, Thomas F. *Uncle Tom's Cabin and American Culture*. Dallas, TX: Southern Methodist University Press, 1985.

Grayzel, Solomon. *A History of the Jews, from the Babylonian Exile to the End of World War II*. Philadelphia: Jewish Publication Society of America, 1947.

Green, Ian. *Print and Protestantism in Early Modern England*. Oxford: Oxford University Press, 2000.

Greenstone, J. David. *The Lincoln Persuasion: Remaking American Liberalism*. Princeton, NJ.: Princeton University Press, 1993.

Guelzo, Allen C. *Abraham Lincoln: Redeemer President*. Grand Rapids, MI: Eerdmans Publishing Company, 1999.

———. *Lincoln's Emancipation Proclamation: The End of Slavery in America*. New York: Simon and Schuster, 2004.

Hall, David D., ed. *Antinomian History: A Documentary History 1636–38*. Middletown, CT: Wesleyan University Press, 1968.

———. "The Experience of Authority in Early New England." *The Journal of American and Canadian Studies* 23 (2005): 3–32.

———. *The Faithful Shepherd: A History of the New England Ministry in the Seventeenth Century*. Chapel Hill: University of North Carolina Press, 1972.

———, ed. *Puritans in the New World: A Critical Theory*. Princeton, NJ: Princeton University Press, 2004.

Hallett, Garth L. *Christian Neighbor Love: An Assessment of Six Rival Versions*. Washington, DC: Georgetown University Press, 1989.

Hamilton, Alexander, John Jay, and James Madison. *The Federalist Papers*. Introduction by Charles R. Kesler. Edited by Clinton Rossiter. New York: Mentor, 1999.

Hamowy, Ronald. "Declaration of Independence." In *Encyclopedia of American Political History: Studies of the Principal Movements and Ideas*, edited by Jack P. Greene. New York: Charles Scribners' Sons, 1984.

———. "Jefferson and the Scottish Enlightenment: A Critique of Gary Wills's *Inventing America: Jefferson's Declaration of Independence*." *The William and Mary Quarterly* 36 (October 1979): 503–24.

Harris, William C. *With Charity for All: Lincoln and the Restoration of the Union*. Lexington: University Press of Kentucky, 1997.

Hauerwas, Stanley. "The Politics of Charity." *Interpretation* 31 (July 1977): 251–62.

Hawthorne, Nathaniel. *The Blithedale Romance*. New York: Penguin Books, 1983.

———. *The House of the Seven Gables*. New York: Tom Doherty Associates, 1988.

———. *The Scarlet Letter: An Authoritative Text, Essays in Criticism and Scholarship*. Edited by Seymour Lee Gross. New York: Norton, 1988.

———. *Tales and Sketches*. New York: Library Classics of the United States, 1996.

Helo, Ari, and Peter Onuf. "Jefferson, Morality, and the Problem of Slavery." *The William and Mary Quarterly* 60 (July 2003): 583–614.

Herndon, William H., and Jesse W. Weik. *Life of Lincoln*. Cleveland, OH: World Publishing Company, 1943.

Heyrman, Christine Leigh. "A Model of Christian Charity: The Rich and the Poor in New England, 1630–1730." Ph.D. dissertation, Yale University, 1997.

Hill, John Wesley. *Abraham Lincoln: Man of God*. New York: G. P. Putnam's Sons, 1920.

Hirschman, Nancy J., and Christine Di Stefano, eds. *Revisioning the Political: Feminist Reconstructions of Traditional Concepts in Western Political Theory*. Boulder, CO: Westview Press, 1996.

Hofstadter, Richard. *The American Political Tradition: And the Men Who Made It*. New York: Vintage Books, 1989.

Holland, Matthew. "Christian Love and the Foundations of American Politics: Winthrop, Jefferson, and Lincoln." In *Democracy and Its Friendly Foes: Tocqueville and Political Life Today*, edited by Peter Lawler, 137–54. Lanham, MD: Lexington Books, 2004.

———. "Remembering John Winthrop—Hawthorne's Suggestion." Heldref Publications, *Perspectives on Political Science* 36 (Winter 2007): 4–14.

———. "'To Close the Circle of Our Felicities': *Caritas* and Jefferson's First Inaugural." *Review of Politics* 66 (Spring 2004): 181–206.

Holmes, Oliver Wendell. *The Poetical Works of Oliver Wendell Holmes*. Boston: Houghton Mifflin Company, 1975.

Holzer, Harold, Gabor S. Boritt, and Mark E. Neely Jr. *The Lincoln Image: Abraham Lincoln and the Popular Print*. New York: Scribner, 1984.

Hooker, Thomas. "Abstracts of Two Sermons by Rev. Thomas Hooker, from the Shorthand Notes of Mr. Henry Wolcott." Transcribed by J. Hammond Trumbull. In Collections of the Connecticut Historical Society, vol. 1. Hartford, CT, 1860.

Hough, Franklin, ed. *Proclamations for Thanksgiving*. Brigham Young University Library. Albany, NY: Munsell and Rowland, 1995. Text-fiche.

Huntington, Samuel P. *American Politics: The Promise of Disharmony*. Cambridge, MA: Belknap Press, 1981.

Innes, David C. "Bacon's New Atlantis: The Christian Hope and the Modern Hope." *Interpretation* 22 (Fall 1994): 3–38.

Jackson, Timothy P. *Love Disconsoled: Meditations on Christian Charity*. Cambridge: Cambridge University Press, 1999.

———. *The Priority of Love: Christian Charity and Social Justice*. Princeton, NJ: Princeton University Press, 2003.

Jaffa, Harry. *Crisis of the House Divided: An Interpretation of the Issues in the Lincoln-Douglas Debates*. Chicago: University of Chicago Press, 1982.

———. *How to Think about the American Revolution*. Durham, NC: Carolina Academic Press, 1978.

Jayne, Allen. *Jefferson's Declaration of Independence: Origins, Philosophy, and Theology*. Lexington: University Press of Kentucky, 1998.

Jefferson, Thomas. *Jefferson's Extracts from the Gospels: "The Philosophy of Jesus" And "The Life and Morals of Jesus."* Edited by Dickinson W. Adams and Ruth W. Lester. Princeton, NJ: Princeton University Press, 1983.

———. *Jefferson's Literary Commonplace Book*. Edited by Douglas L. Wilson. Princeton, NJ: Princeton University Press, 1989.

———. *The Life and Selected Writings of Thomas Jefferson*. Edited by Adrienne Koch and William Harwood Peden. New York: The Modern Library, 1993.

———. *The Literary Bible of Thomas Jefferson: His Commonplace Book of Philosophers and Poets*. Edited by Gilbert Chinard. Baltimore, MD: Johns Hopkins Press.

———. *The Papers of Thomas Jefferson*. Edited by Julian P. Boyd et al., 27 vols. to date. Princeton, NJ: Princeton University Press, 1950.

———. *Writings*. Edited by Merrill D. Peterson. New York: Library of America, 1984.

———. *The Writings of Thomas Jefferson*. Edited by Albert Ellery Bergh. Washington, DC: Thomas Jefferson Memorial Association of the United States, 1907. Vol. 1–20.

Johnson, Paul. *A History of the American People*. New York: Harper Collins, 1998.

Kane, Joseph Nathan. *Presidential Fact Book*. New York: Random House, 1998.

Kasindorf, Martin. "Governor Schwarzenegger Takes Office: 'I Feel a Great Responsibility Not to Let the People Down.'" *USA Today*, November 18, 2003, sec. A, p. 3.

Kautz, Steven. "Abraham Lincoln: The Moderation of a Democratic States-man." In *History of American Political Thought*, edited by Bryan-Paul Frost and Jeffrey Sikkenga. Lanham, MD: Lexington Books, 2003.

Kazin, Alfred. *God and the American Writer*. New York: Vintage Books, 1997.

Kennedy, John F. *Let The Word Go Forth: The Speeches, Statements, and Writings of John F. Kennedy*. Edited by Theodore C. Sorensen. New York: Delacorte Press, 1998.

Ketcham, Ralph. *James Madison*. Charlottesville: University Press of Virginia, 1996.

Kierkegaard, Søren. *Works of Love: Some Christian Reflections in the Form of Discourses*. Translated by Howard and Edna Hong. New York: Harper and Row Publishers, 1962.

King, Martin Luther, Jr. *A Testament of Hope: The Essential Writings of Martin Luther King, Jr.* Edited by Washington James Melvin. San Francisco: Harper and Row Publishers, 1986.

Kloppenburg, James T. *The Virtues of Liberalism*. New York: Oxford University Press, 1998.

Koch, Adrienne. "Power and Morals and the Founding Fathers." *The Review of Politics* 15, no. 4 (1953): 470–90.

Lane, Robert E. *The Loss of Happiness in the Market Democracies*. New Haven, CT: Yale University Press, 2000.

Lerche, Charles O., Jr. "Jefferson and the Election of 1800: A Case Study in the Political Smear." *The William and Mary Quarterly* 5 (October 1948): 467–91.

Levack, Brian P. *The Witch-Hunt in Early Modern Europe*. 2d ed. New York: Longman Group Limited, 1995.

Lewis, C. S. *The Four Loves*. San Diego, CA: A Harvest Book/Harcourt Brace and Company, 1991.

Lincoln, Abraham. *The Collected Works of Abraham Lincoln*. Edited by Roy P. Basler. New Brunswick NJ: Rutgers University Press, 1953. Volumes 1–8.

———. *Lincoln on Democracy*. Edited by Mario M. Cuomo and Harold Holzer. New York: Harper Collins Publishers, 1990.

———. *The Political Thought of Abraham Lincoln*. Edited by Richard N. Current. New York: Macmillan Publishing Company, 1967.

———. *Selected Speeches and Writings*. Edited by Don E. Fehrenbacher. New York: Vintage Books, 1992.

Lind, Michael. *What Lincoln Believed: The Values and Convictions of America's Greatest President*. New York: Doubleday, 2004.

Livermore, Thomas L. *Numbers and Losses in the Civil War in America: 1861–65*. New York: Kraus Reprint Co., 1969.

Locke, John. *John Locke's Two Treatises on Government*. Edited by Peter
Laslett. New York: Mentor Book, 1965.
———. *A Letter Concerning Toleration*. Edited by James H. Tully. Indianap-
olis, IN: Hackett Publishing Company, 1983.
———. *Second Treatise of Government*. Edited by Crawford Brough Mac-
pherson. Indianapolis, IN: Hackett Publishing Company, 1980.
Lott, Trent. *US, Senator Trent Lott (R-MS) Delivers Republican Response to
the President's Radio Address*. January 6, 2001. FDCH Political
Transcripts.
Lucas, Stephen E. "Justifying America: The Declaration of Independence as
a Rhetorical Document." In *American Rhetoric: Context and Criticism*,
edited by Thomas W. Benson: Carbondale: Southern Illinois University
Press, 1989.
Luebke, Fred. "The Origins of Thomas Jefferson's Anti-Clericalism."
Church History 32 (September 1963): 344–56.
Lutz, Donald S. "From Covenant to Constitution in American Political
Thought." *Publius* 10 (Fall 1980): 101–33.
Macfarlane, Alan. *Witchcraft in Tudor and Stuart England: A Regional and
Comparative Study*. London: Routledge and Kegan Paul, 1970.
Machiavelli, Niccolò. *The Prince*. Translated by Harvey C. Mansfield Jr.
Chicago: University of Chicago Press, 1985.
Maier, Pauline. *American Scripture: Making the Declaration of Indepen-
dence*. New York: Vintage, 1998.
Malone, Dumas. *Jefferson the President: First Term*. Boston: Little, Brown
and Company, 1970.
Manent, Pierre. *The City of Man*, trans. by Marc A. LePain. Princeton:
Princeton University Press, 1998.
Mansfield, Harvey. Introduction to *The Prince*, by Niccolò Machiavelli.
Translated by Harvey C. Mansfield Jr. Chicago: University of Chicago
Press, 1998.
Mason, George. *The Papers of George Mason, 1725–1792*. Edited by Robert
Allen Rutland. Chapel Hill: University of North Carolina Press, 1970.
Massachusetts Department of Education. "MFLC Community Profiles,"
Boston, 2002. http://mflc.doe.mass.edu/needs.asp?municipality=035
(May 4, 2005).
Mather, Cotton. *Magnalia Christi Americana, Books I and II*. Edited by Ken-
neth Ballard Murdock and Elizabeth W. Miller. Cambridge, MA: Belk-
nap Press, 1977.
Matthews, Richard K. *The Radical Politics of Thomas Jefferson: A Revisionist
View*. Lawrence. University Press of Kansas, 1984.
May, Herbert, and Bruce Metzger, eds. *The New Oxford Annotated Bible
with Apocrypha*, New York: Oxford University Press, 1973.

McCullough, David. *1776*. New York: Simon and Schuster, 2005.

———. *John Adams*. New York: Simon and Schuster, 2001.

McManus, Edgar J. *Law and Liberty in Early New England: Criminal Justice and Due Process, 1620–1692*. Amherst: University of Massachusetts Press, 1993.

McNeills, John T., ed. "John Calvin." In *Institutes of the Christian Religion*. Ford Lewis Battles, trans. Philadelphia: Westminster Press, 1960.

McWilliams, Wilson C. *The Idea of Fraternity in America*. Berkeley: University of California Press, 1973.

Mellon, James, ed. *The Face of Lincoln*. New York: Viking Press, 1979.

Mencken, Henry Louis. *A Little Book in C Major*. New York: John Lane, 1916.

———. *A Mencken Chrestomathy*. New York: Alfred A. Knopf, 1953.

Michaelsen, Scott. "John Winthrop's 'Modell' Covenant and the Company Way." *Early American Literature* 27, no. 2 (1992): 85–100.

Miller, Joshua. *The Rise and Fall of Democracy in Early America, 1630–1789: The Legacy for Contemporary Politics*. University Park: Pennsylvania State University Press, 1991.

Miller, Perry. *Errand into the Wilderness*. Cambridge, MA: Harvard University Press, 1978.

———. *Nature's Nation*. Cambridge, MA: Belknap Press of Harvard University Press, 1967.

———. *The New England Mind: The Seventeenth Century*. New York: The Macmillan Company, 1939.

———. *The Puritans*. New York: Harper and Row, 1963.

Miller, William L. *Lincoln's Virtues: An Ethical Biography*. New York: Knopf, 2002.

Morel, Lucas E. *Lincoln's Sacred Effort: Defining Religion's Role in American Self-Government*. New York: Lexington Books, 2000.

Morgan, Edmund S. *The Genuine Article: A Historian Looks at Early America*. New York: W. W. Norton & Co., 2004.

———. "John Winthrop's 'Model of Christian Charity' in a Wider Context." *The Huntington Library Quarterly* 50, no. 2 (1987): 145–51.

———. *The Puritan Dilemma: The Story of John Winthrop*. Boston: Little Brown, 1958.

———. *Roger Williams: The Church and the State*. New York: W. W. Norton and Company, 1967.

———. *Visible Saints: The History of a Puritan Idea*. Ithaca, NY: Cornell University Press, 1963.

Morison, Samuel E. *The Intellectual Life of Colonial New England*. New York: New York University Press, 1956.

Morone, James A. *Hellfire Nation: The Politics of Sin in American History.* New Haven, CT: Yale University Press, 2003.

Moseley, James G. *John Winthrop's World: History as a Story, the Story as History.* Madison: University of Wisconsin Press, 1992.

Neely, Mark E., Jr. *The Abraham Lincoln Encyclopedia.* New York: Da Capo Press, 1982.

Nicolay, John G., and John Hay. *Abraham Lincoln: A History.* New York: The Century Co., 1990.

Niebuhr, Reinhold. "The Religion of Abraham Lincoln." *The Christian Century* 10 (February 1965) 172–75.

Niebuhr, Richard. "The Idea of Covenant and American Democracy." *Church History* 23 (June 1954): 126–35.

Nietzsche, Friedrich. *Basic Writings of Nietzsche.* Translated and edited by Walter Kaufmann. New York: Modern Library, 2000.

Niles, H. *Principles and Acts of the Revolution in America.* Facsimile Republication, Maywood, CA: Kunkin-Turner Publications, 1961.

Noll, Mark A. *America's God: From Jonathan Edwards to Abraham Lincoln,* Oxford: Oxford University Press, 2002.

———. "'Both . . . Pray to the Same God': The Singularity of Lincoln's Faith in the Era of the Civil War." *Journal of the Abraham Lincoln Association* (Winter 1997): ed.1, 1–26.

Nygren, Anders. *Agape and Eros.* Translated by Philip S. Watson. Philadelphia: Westminster, 1953.

Oates, Stephen B. *With Malice toward None: A Life of Abraham Lincoln.* New York: Harper Collins, 1977.

O'Connor, Flannery. *O'Connor: Collected Works.* New York: Library of America, 1988.

Onuf, Peter S. *Jefferson's Empire: The Language of American Nationhood.* Charlottesville: University Press of Virginia, 2000.

Outka, Gene. *Agape: An Ethical Analysis.* New Haven, CT: Yale University Press, 1972.

Paludan, Philip S. *"A People's Contest": The Union and the Civil War, 1861–1865.* New York: Harper & Row, 1988.

Parrington, Vernon L. *Main Currents in American Thought.* Vol. 1, *The Colonial Mind.* New York: Harcourt, Brace and World, 1927.

Paulick, Michael. "The Mayflower Pilgrims and Thomas Wilson's Christian Dictionarie." http://www.newenglandancestors.org/publications/NEA//71_012_Mayflower.asp.

Perry, Ralph Barton. *Puritanism and Democracy.* New York: Vanguard Press, 1944.

Peters, Thomas J., and Robert H. Waterman Jr. *In Search of Excellence: Lessons from America's Best Run Companies.* New York: Harper and Row, 1982.

Peterson, Merrill D. *Lincoln in American Memory*. New York: Oxford University Press, 1994.

———. *Thomas Jefferson and the New Nation: A Biography*. New York: Oxford University Press, 1970.

Pinckney, Darryl. Introduction to *Uncle Tom's Cabin*, by Harriet Beecher Stowe. New York: Penguin Group, 1998.

Plato. *The Republic of Plato*. Translated by Allan Bloom. New York: Basic Books, 1968.

Pulsipher, Jenny Hale. *Subjects unto the Same King*. Philadelphia: University of Pennsylvania Press, 2005.

Raimo, John. *Biographical Directory of American Colonial and Revolutionary Governors, 1607–1789*. Westport, CT: Meckler Books, 1980.

Randall, J. G. "Lincoln and Thanksgiving." *Lincoln Herald*. Harrogate, TN: Lincoln Memorial University Press, 1947, 10–13.

Randall, J. G., and Richard N. Current. *Lincoln the President: Last Full Measure*. New York: Dodd, Mead & Company, 1955.

Rawls, John. *A Theory of Justice*. Oxford: Clarendon Press, 1972.

Richardson, Henry S. *Democratic Autonomy: Public Reasoning about the Ends of Policy*. New York: Oxford University Press, 2002.

Robinson, Marilynne. *Gilead*. New York: Farrar, Straus and Giroux, 2004.

Rogers, John. *A Treatise of Love*. London. 1629. Available at Early English Books Online. http://eebo.chadwyck.com/home.

Roosevelt, Theodore. *American Problems*. New York: Scribners, 1926.

Rorty, Richard. *Contingency, Irony, and Solidarity*. Cambridge: Cambridge University Press, 1989.

Rousseau, Jean-Jacques. *The Social Contract and Discourses*. London: David Campbell Publishers, 1993.

Rossiter, Clinton L. *The Political Thought of the American Revolution*. New York: Harcourt Brace and World, 1963.

Rush, Benjamin. *The Autobiography of Benjamin Rush: His "Travels through Life" Together with his Commonplace Book for 1789–1813*. Vol. 25, *Memoirs of the American Philosophical Society*. Princeton, NJ: Princeton University Press, 1948.

Rutland, Robert Allen. *George Mason: Reluctant Statesman*. Baton Rouge: Louisiana State University Press, 1961.

Rutman, Darrett Bruce. *John Winthrop's Decision for America, 1629*. Philadelphia: Lippincott, 1975.

———. "My Beloved and Good Husband." *American Heritage* (August 1962): 24–27, 94–96.

———. *Winthrop's Boston: Portrait of a Puritan Town, 1630–1649*. Chapel Hill: University of North Carolina Press, 1965.

Ryskamp, Charles. "The New England Sources of 'The Scarlet Letter.'" American Literature 31 (November 1959): 257–72.

Safire, William. "On Language: Rack up That City on a Hill." New York Times, April 24, 1988, sec. 6 page 18.

Schaar, John H. "Liberty/Authority/Community in the Political Thought of John Winthrop." Political Theory 19 (November 1991): 493–518.

Schatz, Morris. Ethics of the Fathers in the Light of Jewish History. New York: Bloch, 1971.

Schlesinger, Arthur M. "The Lost Meaning of the 'Pursuit of Happiness.'" The William and Mary Quarterly 21 (July 1964): 325–28.

Schweninger, Lee. John Winthrop. Boston: Twayne, 1990.

Seay, James L. Open Field, Understory: New and Selected Poems. Baton Rouge: Louisiana State University Press, 1997.

Seton, Anya. The Winthrop Woman. Boston: Houghton Mifflin, 1958.

Steele, Tomas J. "Tom and Eva: Mrs. Stowe's Two Dying Christs." Negro American Literature Forum 6 (Autumn 1972): 85–90.

Stephanopoulos, George. All Too Human: A Political Education. Boston: Little Brown, 1999.

Stern, Chaim. Pirké Avot. Hoboken, NJ: Ktav Publishing, 1997.

Sterne, Laurence. A Sentimental Journey through France and Italy. London: Oxford University Press, 1968.

Stowe, Charles Edward, and Lyman Beecher Stowe. Harriet Beecher Stowe: The Story of Her Life. Boston and New York: Houghton Mifflin Company, 1911.

Stowe, Harriet Beecher. Uncle Tom's Cabin. With an afterword by John William Ward. New York: Penguin Books USA Inc, 1966.

Sumner, William Graham. What Social Classes Owe to Each Other. Caldwell, ID: Caxton Printers, 1989.

Szczesiul, Anthony E. "The Canonization of Tom and Eva: Catholic Hagiography and Uncle Tom's Cabin." American Transcendental Quarterly 10 (March 1996): 59–72.

Taylor, Paul. "Mondale Rises to Peak Form; Candidate Eloquent in Fight for 'Caring' Government." Washington Post, October 26, 1984. First section, A1.

Temple, Wayne C. Abraham Lincoln: From Skeptic to Prophet. Mahomet, IL: Mayhaven Publishing, 1995.

Thomas, Benjamin P. Abraham Lincoln: A Biography. New York: Modern Library, 1968.

Thompkins, Jane. Sensational Designs: The Cultural Work of American Fiction 1790–1860. New York: Oxford University Press, 1985.

Thurow, Glen E. Abraham Lincoln and American Political Religion. New York: State University of New York Press, 1976.

Tocqueville, Alexis de. *Democracy in America.* Translated and edited by Harvey Mansfield and Delba Winthrop. Chicago: University of Chicago Press, 2000.

Tolstoy, Leo. *What Is Art? and Essays on Art.* Oxford: Oxford University Press, 1929.

UN General Assembly. *September 11, 2001: Attack on America, Mayor Rudolph W. Giuliani, Opening Remarks to the United Nation General Assembly Special Session on Terrorism.* October 1, 2001.

U.S. Congress. Senate. *Inaugural Addresses of the Presidents of the United States: From George Washington 1789 to George Bush 1989.* 101st Cong., 1st sess. S.101–10, 1989.

U.S. Presidents. *Public Papers of the Presidents of the United States.* Washington, D.C.: Office of the *Federal Register,* National Archives and Records Service. John F. Kennedy, 1961.

———. *Public Papers of the Presidents of the United States.* Washington, D.C.: Office of the *Federal Register,* National Archives and Records Service. Lyndon B. Johnson, 1964.

———. *Public Papers of the Presidents of the United States.* Washington, D.C.: Office of the *Federal Register,* National Archives and Records Service. Ronald Reagan, 1989.

Vale, Lawrence. *From the Puritans to the Projects: Public Housing and Public Neighbors.* Cambridge, MA: Harvard University Press, 1959.

Valiunas, Algis. "The Great American Novel? Uncle Tom's Cabin after a Century and a Half." *The Weekly Standard,* December 16, 2002, 31–32.

Vaughan, Alden T. *Roots of American Racism: Essays on the Colonial Experience.* New York: Oxford University Press, 1995.

———. "A Test of Puritan Justice." *The New England Quarterly* 38 (1965): 331–339.

Virgadamo, Peter Richard. "Colonial Charity and the American Character: Boston, 1630–1775." Ph.D. dissertation, University of Southern California, 1982.

Wall, Robert Emmet. *Massachusetts Bay: The Crucial Decade, 1640–1650.* New Haven, CT: Yale University Press, 1972.

Wallwork, Ernest. "Thou Shalt Love Thy Neighbor as Thyself: The Freudian Critique." *Journal of Religious Ethics* 10 (Fall 1982): 264–319.

Walzer, Michael. *The Revolution of the Saints: A Study in the Origins of Radical Politics.* Cambridge, MA: Harvard University Press, 1965.

Washington, George. *George Washington: A Collection.* Edited by W. B. Allen. Indianapolis, IN: Liberty Fund, 1998.

Washington Headquarters Services. "Principal Wars in Which The United States Participated: U.S. Military Personnel Serving and Casualties."

Department of Defense. Internet. At http://web1.whs.osd.mil/mmid/casualty/SMS223R.pdf (accessed March 29, 2001).

Weber, Max, C. *From Max Weber: Essays in Sociology.* Edited by Wright Mills and Hans Heinrich Gerth. New York: Oxford University Press, 1958.

———. *The Protestant Ethic and the Spirit of Capitalism.* Translated by Talcott Parsons. New York: Routledge, 1992.

Webster, Daniel. *The Papers of Daniel Webster.* Edited by Charles M. Wiltse. Vol. 1. Hanover, NH: University Press of New England, 1974.

Weil, Simone. *Gravity and Grace.* New York: Routledge, 2002.

Weisberger, Bernard A. *America Afire: Jefferson, Adams, and the Revolution of 1800.* New York: William Morrow, 2000.

White, Morton G. *The Philosophy of the American Revolution.* New York: Oxford University Press, 1978.

White, Ronald C., Jr. *Lincoln's Greatest Speech: The Second Inaugural.* New York: Simon and Schuster, 2002.

———. "Lincoln's Sermon on the Mount: The Second Inaugural." In *Religion and the American Civil War,* edited by Randall M. Miller, Harry S. Stout, and Charles Reagan Wilson. New York: Oxford University Press, 1998.

Whitmore, William Henry. *The Colonial Laws of Massachusetts: Reprinted from the Edition of 1660, with the Supplements to 1672: Containing also, The Body of Liberties of 1641.* Littleton, CO: Fred B. Rothman and Co., 1995.

Wilentz, Sean. "The Details of Greatness: American Historians versus American Founders." *New Republic,* March 29, 2004, 27–35.

Will, George. "Let Us . . . ? No, Give It a Rest." *Newsweek,* January 22, 2001, 64.

Williams, Roger. "The Letters of Roger Williams to Winthrop." In *Old South Leaflets.* Boston: Directors of the Old South Work, 1896.

Wills, Garry. *Inventing America: Jefferson's Declaration of Independence.* Garden City, NY: Doubleday, 1978.

———. *Lincoln at Gettysburg: The Words that Remade America.* New York: Simon and Schuster, 1992.

———. "Lincoln's Greatest Speech?" *The Atlantic Monthly,* September 1999, 60.

Wilson, Douglas, L. *Honor's Voice: The Transformation of Abraham Lincoln.* New York: Alfred A. Knopf, 1998.

———. *Lincoln before Washington: New Perspectives on the Illinois Years.* Champaign: University of Illinois Press, 1997.

———. *Lincoln's Sword: The Presidency and the Power of Words.* New York: Knopf, 2006.

Wilson, Edmund. *Patriotic Gore: Studies in the Literature of the American Civil War*. London: Hogarth Press, 1962.

Wilson, James Q. "Religion and Public Life." In *What's God Got to do with the American Experiment?* edited by E. J. Dionne Jr. and John J. DiIulio Jr. Washington DC: Brookings Institution Press, 2000.

Winger, Stuart. *Lincoln, Religion, and Romantic Cultural Politics*. Dekalb: Northern Illinois University Press, 2003.

Winik, Jay. *April 1865: The Month that Saved America*. New York: Perennial, 2002.

Winship, Michael P. *Making Heretics: Militant Protestantism and Free Grace in Massachusetts, 1636–1641*. Princeton, NJ: Princeton University Press, 2002.

Winthrop, John. *The [Abridged] Journal of John Winthrop, 1630–1649*. Edited by Richard S. Dunn and Laetitia Yeandle. Cambridge, MA: Belknap Press of Harvard University Press, 1996.

———. *The [Unabridged] Journal of John Winthrop, 1630–1649*. Edited by Richard S. Dunn, James Savage, and Laetitia Yeandle. Cambridge, MA: Belknap Press of Harvard University Press, 1996.

———. *Winthrop Papers*. Edited by Alley Forbes et al. Volumes 1–6. Boston: Massachusetts Historical Society, 1929.

Winthrop, Robert C. *Life and Letters of John Winthrop*. New York: Da Capo Press, 1971.

Wolf, William J. *Lincoln's Religion*. Philadelphia: Pilgrim Press, 1970.

Wood, Gordon S. *The Creation of the American Republic, 1776–1787*. Chapel Hill: University of North Carolina Press, 1969.

Wright, Thomas G. *Literary Culture in Early New England*. New Haven, CT: Yale University Press, 1920.

Yarbrough, Jean M. *American Virtues: Thomas Jefferson on the Character of a Free People*. Lawrence: University Press of Kansas, 1998.

Zuckert, Catherine H. *Natural Rights and the American Imagination: Political Philosophy in Novel Form*. Savage, MD: Rowman & Littlefield, 1990.

———. "On Reading Classic American Novelists as Political Thinkers." *Journal of Politics* 43 (August 1981): 683–706.

Zuckert, Michael P. *The Natural Rights Republic: Studies in the Foundation of the American Political Tradition*. Notre Dame, IN: University of Notre Dame Press, 1996.

INDEX

Bellah, Robert, 259n28
Bercovitch, Sacvan, 43
Berlant, Lauren, 85n13
Berlin, Isaiah, 16n7, 17n14
Bill of Rights, 93
"The Birth-Mark" (Hawthorne), 256n5
The Birth of Tragedy (Nietzsche), 11–12
The Blithedale Romance (Hawthorne),
  256n5
Bolingbroke, Lord, 101, 110, 132
Boritt, Gabor, 198n41
Boyd, Julian, 124n16
Bradford, William, 206
Bradshaw, William, 58
Bremer, Francis: on early Puritan views
  of Indians, 53n19; on Winthrop's ago-
  nies of conscience, 76; and Win-
  throp's goodness, 86n15, 88n41; and
  Winthrop's "Model" speech, 51n1;
  and Winthrop's sense of Puritan mis-
  sion, 87n36
Brooks, Noah, 220
Brooks, Van Wyck, 26n3, 74
Burlingame, Michael, 251
Bush, George W., 12, 74, 155n45

Callender, James, 137
Calvin, John: and charity, 37, 52n17; and
  Jefferson, 244
Calvinism: and Lincoln's Temperance
  Address, 186; and Puritans, 58; and
  Winthrop, 31, 36–37
Carr, Peter, 111, 126n44
Carroll, James, 88n38
Cartwright, Peter, 176
Carwardine, Richard, 195n4, 203–4,
  217n23
Catton, Bruce, 233
Charity and Its Fruits (Edwards), 35
charity/*caritas*, 7, 15n6, 16n11; and
  affection, 44–45; and *agape*, 7, 16n11;
  as always preceding liberty, 228,
  239n16; and Calvin, 37, 52n17; as
  Christian virtue, 6–9, 33–36; defin-
  ing, 7–9, 16n12; "democratic charity,"

15n6; Edwards on, 6–7, 35, 45; Jefferson on charity role of government,
145, 147, 155n50, 156n54; Lincoln on
careful reason and, 183–84; Lincoln's
early thoughts on government and,
190–91; and Lincoln's religious transformation, 204, 211–12; Lincoln's Second Inaugural and biblical charity,
243, 248, 257n6; Lincoln's Second
Inaugural and civic charity, 6, 13, 231,
234–38, 243–49; Lincoln's understanding of war and the spirit of,
188–90; as "metavalue," 35, 46, 52n12;
and modernity, 6–12; and the neighbor, 8; New Testament, 7, 8, 34, 49,
119–20; self-love/self-abnegation
challenge of, 55n35; Virginia Declaration of Rights and public duty of, 93–
95, 107; Washington's formal
statements on, 135. *See also agape*;
civic charity; Jefferson and Christian
charity; Winthrop's "A Model of
Christian Charity"
Chase, Salmon P., 4, 217n23, 220, 233
Cherry, Conrad, 259n28
Chicago Tribune, 237
Christian Dictionary (Wilson), 45, 54n30
church–state separation. *See* "wall of
separation" between church and
state (Jefferson's)
"City Upon a Hill." *See* Winthrop's
vision of a "City Upon a Hill"
civic charity, 5, 6, 13–14; and *agapic* love,
230, 234, 247; and biblical charity,
243, 248, 257n6; horizontal (compassionate) dimension, 13; and human
freedom (natural liberty), 246, 248;
and Lincoln's God, 244–45, 246; and
Lincoln's Second Inaugural, 6, 13,
231, 234–38, 243–49; modern barriers
to, 9–12; two truth claims of, 246–48;
vertical (pious) dimension, 13; and
view of all humans as under God,
246–48, 257n10; and Winthrop's discussion of *agape* in community,
49–50

natural liberty (*continued*)
Winthrop's "natural rights" doctrine, 86n25
Neely, Mark E., Jr., 215–16n12, 217n22
New Atlantis (Bacon), 10
New Testament: concept of forgiveness, 82; and Jefferson's "embrace" of Christianity, 133, 134–35, 151; Jefferson's selections of Jesus's teachings, 134–35, 151, 157nn61–62; John and *agape*, 8, 119–20; Last Supper and Jesus's teaching on charity, 119–20; Lincoln's Lyceum Address and Matthew's "this rock," 175; Matthew and *agape*, 7, 34, 49, 134; Sermon on the Mount, 8, 9–10, 72, 114, 134–35, 223
New York Times Magazine, 2
Nicolay, John G., 209, 217n22
Niebuhr, Reinhold, 225–26, 257n6
Nietzsche, Friedrich, 11–12, 231
Noll, Mark, 15n6, 257n10
Nygren, Anders, 16n11

Oates, Stephen B., 215n8
Old Testament, 16n13; *ahab*, 8; Jonathan's love for David, 75–76; Lincoln's New Testament "charity" and Old Testament God of punishment, 243, 248
Onuf, Peter, 125n33, 153n31

Parrington, Vernon, 26n3
Paulick, Michael, 54n30
Pequot War, 38–40, 53n21, 53n23
Perkins, William, 85n2
Perry, Ralph Barton, 71
Peterson, Merrill D., 153n31, 258n15
philia (fraternal love or friendship), 8
"The Philosophy of Jesus" (Jefferson), 134–35, 153n23, 157n62
Pirké Avot (Talmud), 16–17n13
Plato's *Republic*, 42
Plymouth Colony, 206
"Politics as Vocation" (Weber), 9–10
Pope, John, 208–9

Priestley, Joseph, 133, 134, 151
The Prince (Machiavelli), 9, 17n14
Pulsipher, Jenny, 53n21
Puritanism, American: and aristocratic rule, 66–67, 71; and civil liberty/natural liberty, 70; critics of/scholarly assault on, 2, 26n3, 74; and democracy, 67, 71; dual character and darker side of, 83–84, 90n49; Hawthorne's reaction to, 2, 13, 21–26, 63, 84, 241–42, 256n4; Indian–English relations, 38–40, 53n23, 53nn19–21; and Israelites, 37–38, 77; and Lincoln, 245; Massachusetts's treatment of black slaves, 37–38; Massachusetts's treatment of religious dissenters, 40, 59; and theocratic separation of church and state, 58; unsustainability over time, 83; Winthrop's defense of Puritan authority and liberty, 60–61; Winthrop's "Model" speech, 2, 37–40, 60–61, 73, 74, 77; and Winthrop's vision of a "City Upon a Hill," 73, 74

radical Republicans, 237–38
Randall, J. G., 215n9
Rawls, John, 31, 228
Reagan, Ronald, 74, 257n11
Reconstruction, 238
Republicans: and Jefferson's First Inaugural, 140–41, 154n42; and presidential election of 1800, 2–3, 138; radical Republicans, 237–38
Revolutionary War. *See* American Revolution and War for Independence
Robinson, Marilynne, 198n31
Robinson, Moses, 147
Rogers, "Roaring John," 45
Roosevelt, Franklin D., 216n13
Roosevelt, Theodore, 257n11
Rorty, Richard, 232
Rousseau, Jean-Jacques, 194–95
Rush, Benjamin: and Adams–Jefferson rift, 149; influence on Jefferson, 133–